A Dictionary of British History, 1815-1973

Books by the same author include:

Modern Belgium, Pall Mall/Praeger, New York, 1969
Farming, A. & C. Black, 2nd ed., 1970
A Short History of Farming, Macmillan, 1971
How it Happened, Basil Blackwell, 1971
Nineteenth-Century Reformers, Oxford University Press, 1971
Nineteenth-Century Statesmen, Oxford University Press, 1972
The Modern Netherlands, Pall Mall/Praeger, New York, 1972
A Day in the Life of a Victorian Farm Worker, Allen & Unwin, 1972
Travel and Communications, Harrap, 1972.
Newspapers, Heinemann, 2nd ed., 1972
A Day in the Life of a Victorian Factory Worker, Allen & Unwin, 1973
Factory Life and Work, Harrap, 1973
The Battle for Reform, Lutterworth, 1974

A Dictionary of British History, 1815–1973

FRANK E. HUGGETT

BASIL BLACKWELL · OXFORD

ISBN 0 631 15530 9

Printed in Great Britain by
Western Printing Services Ltd, Bristol and
bound by the Kemp Hall Bindery, Oxford

Introduction

This dictionary deals with the main personalities, events and trends in British political, social, economic, industrial and technological history from 1815 to the present day. People from earlier periods, major events in Empire, Commonwealth and foreign history, and foreign politicians, scientists and inventors have also been included, where they have had a big impact on British history. There are also some entries on cultural life in so far as it has affected social life and on some important economic terms.

Practically all of the entries are complete and self-contained, but there is a comprehensive system of cross references so that further information may easily be obtained if necessary. There are also time references at the end of many entries, which make it easy to trace the development of a particular subject backwards and forwards in time, and a large number of main topic entries. (See 'How to use this Dictionary'.)

The dictionary, which has been compiled with the needs of O-level and C.S.E. pupils in mind, is designed for constant reference, revision and research in the classroom, in the library, and at home. It is not intended to be a substitute for study, but a stimulus towards it. The dictionary is designed to be a handy, working tool, which allows a pupil to find information that he or she wants quickly and conveniently, instead of having to search, often fruitlessly and frustratingly, through many page references in an index. In this way, it frees the pupil for further research in other books, or allows him or her to build up further information about the person or event from the dictionary itself, by judicious use of the cross references and time references. It thus enables each pupil to work far more on his own, and at his own pace. The dictionary may also be found useful for initial investigations about the choice of projects and for line-of-development studies.

In a work of this kind, an author is dependent not only upon his own research, but also to a very great extent on the recent work of many other historians, and I would like to acknowledge my indebtedness to those historians who are too numerous to name. I have also had the advice of a number of teachers and lecturers in preparing this dictionary, and I should be most grateful to receive any suggestions for other topics and subjects, which might usefully be included in later editions.

Frank E. Huggett

How to use this Dictionary

People are entered under the surname, or title, by which they are most commonly known, e.g., Nuffield, Viscount, though a reference to him will also be found under his original name, William Richard Morris.

Other entries will be found under the initial letter of the first word of the phrase, excluding 'the'. For example, 'Boards of Guardians' will be found under the letter 'B' and 'jet planes' under the letter 'J'—all of them in alphabetical order.

Words in *italic type* indicate that there is an entry about this person, topic or event, which will provide further information if needed. (Not all other entries in the dictionary are indicated but only those which it is thought will provide really relevant information.)

At the end of many entries there are time references. For example, at the end of 'refrigeration' there is a time reference to:

←FOOD CANNING: FROZEN FOODS→

These lead back ← and onwards → to other developments, persons or events in the same field. By using these references it is easy to build up information about the development of a particular topic in time. (The references at the end of entries on prime ministers refer to the previous and succeeding prime minister of the same party. A full, chronological list will be found under 'Prime ministers'.)

In addition to hundreds of other topic entries, there are over 60 main topic entries. (For a list of them see below.) These are designed to act as general introductions to the subject. By using the numerous cross-references in *italic type* as topic starters, it is possible to build up a detailed knowledge of the subject from the dictionary itself or to expand or simplify individual points.

Topics

Agriculture
Air travel
Australia
Canada
Canals
Capitalism
Catholic emancipation
Chartism
Coal mining
Communications
Currency
Defence
Disarmament
Eastern Question
Education
Emigration
Empire and Commonwealth
Entertainment
Epidemics
Factory Acts
First World War
Food
Foreign policy
Free trade
Hospitals
Housing
Immigration
India
Industrial revolution
Ireland
Iron and steel industry
Law and order
Local government
Mass communications
Mechanical engineering
Medicine
Nationalization
New Zealand
Newspapers
Parliamentary reform
Political parties
Population
Prime ministers and monarchs
Public health
Railways
Reading
Religion
Roads
Science
Second World War
Ships
Social services
Socialism
Steam engines

Strikes
Taxation
Textile industry
Time
Trade unions
Unemployment
Women's emancipation

A

'Aaron Manby', the first iron steamboat, named after its builder Aaron Manby (1776–1850). It was built at his ironworks near Tipton, Staffordshire, and sent in sections by canal to Surrey Docks, Rotherhithe, where it was launched. Successful trials were held on the Thames in 1822 and shortly afterwards it sailed across the English Channel to be used in service on the River Seine in France. It was 120 feet long and had a speed of about 7 knots. It continued in service until the 1850s.

← ROB ROY: SIRIUS →

Abdication crisis, 1936, resulted from the decision of King Edward VIII (1894–1972) to marry Mrs Ernest Simpson, an American whose two previous marriages had been dissolved. But *divorce* was still considered shameful by the Church—particularly for the future wife of a king. Baldwin, the prime minister, gave Edward the choice of giving up the throne or Mrs Simpson. The King abdicated on 11 December 1936, when he was given the title of Duke of Windsor, and was succeeded by his brother, George VI (1895–1952). The Duke of Windsor married Mrs Simpson in the following year, when she became the Duchess of Windsor. Attitudes became exaggerated during the crisis. Some of the Establishment feared that Edward would be a radical king, because he had visited slums, sympathized with the unemployed, and wore modern clothes; but he was more moderate than they believed. Moreover, divorce was probably not so shocking to the mass of people as Baldwin and the Church thought it was.

Aberdeen, Earl of (1784–1860), peace-loving statesman who allowed himself to be pushed into the *Crimean War, 1854–1856*, by British public opinion, some of his Cabinet colleagues, and the French. He was educated at Harrow and Cambridge, and became Foreign Secretary under Wellington from 1828 to 1830 and again under Peel from 1841 to 1846. During his second term as Foreign Secretary he improved relations with the French and helped in 1846 to settle the *Oregon dispute* with the United States over its boundary with the British colony of Canada. After Peel's death in 1850, he became leader of the 'Peelites', Conservatives who supported *free trade*. In 1852 he formed a distinguished government of Whigs and 'Peelites', which included Gladstone, Palmerston, Russell and Edward Cardwell. But

Aberdeen was too weak to impose his will on such a mixture of powerful men with conflicting views and the country drifted into the avoidable Crimean War—the only major European war in which Britain was involved in the nineteenth century. He resigned as prime minister in 1855, after a vote of censure on the government's conduct of the war, and was succeeded by Palmerston.

← SIR ROBERT PEEL

Abortion. It was made legal to have an abortion in 1967, if two doctors thought that having a child would harm the physical or mental health of the woman. The number of abortions increased from 22,257 in the last nine months of 1968 to 83,851 in 1970. Previously, many women had gone to unlicensed 'back street' abortionists, who often used unhygienic, dangerous methods.

Act of Union, 1800, changed the course of Irish history by maintaining the power and ascendancy of the Protestant minority in the whole of Ireland without giving the Catholic majority its promised emancipation. As a result of the Act, Ireland became part of the United Kingdom, ruled directly from Westminster. Trade barriers between the two countries were abolished, though the Irish textile industry received some protection by tariffs or duties for twenty years. Ireland had to contribute two-seventeenths of the total budget of the United Kingdom. The Anglican churches of England and Ireland were united into a single church. The separate parliament in Dublin was abolished and the Irish were represented by 100 M.P.s at Westminster (later increased to 105); 28 Irish peers, elected for life by fellow Irish lords, and 4 bishops, in the House of Lords. Pitt, who passed the Act, had promised the Catholics some concessions, but these were not granted at the time. The Catholics still had to pay *tithes* to the Anglican church, and these were not replaced by a fixed rent charge until 1838. George III refused to grant the promised *Catholic emancipation.* Catholics could vote, but they were not allowed to become M.P.s and could not do so until the *Roman Catholic Relief Act* of 1829. The Act of Union, which came into effect in 1801, was passed following an unsuccessful uprising by the United Irishmen in 1798, aided by the French.

Acts of Parliament see **Bills**

Addington, Henry see **Viscount Sidmouth**

Adullamites. A name used by the radical John Bright to describe the

Whigs, led by *Robert Lowe* and E. Horsman, who opposed proposals by the Liberal government under Russell for further parliamentary reform in 1866. Russell's government fell and the Conservatives got into power, which allowed Derby and Disraeli to pass the Second Reform Bill (the *Representation of the People Act*) in 1867 'to dish the Whigs'. The cave of Adullam was where David took refuge in his flight from Saul and gathered together all the discontented.

Adulteration of Food, Drinks and Drugs Act, 1872. The first 'clean food' law making it illegal to add other ingredients to foodstuffs merely to increase the weight. Previously, dishonest traders often put plaster of Paris in confectionery, alum in bread, sand in pepper, water in beer and in milk, powdered clay in tea, horsemeat in sausages etc.
SALE OF FOOD AND DRUGS ACT, 1875 →

Afghanistan was important to Britain in the nineteenth century as a buffer state between Russia and British possessions on the north-west frontier of India, the gateway to the Indian empire. The British fought two wars against the Afghans through fears that they were coming under Russian influence. The first from 1839 to 1842 was fought in an attempt to replace the popular ruler, Dost Mohammed, by the exiled Shah Suja, who appeared to be more favourable to the British. But the attempt failed and the British lost 16,000 men. The second war was fought from 1878 to 1880 to make the Afghans accept a British Resident in the capital of Kabul, who could then influence, or control, their foreign policy. The Resident was murdered; there were anti-British demonstrations; and the British troops were finally withdrawn in 1880. Suspicions between Russia and Britain over their respective intentions in Afghanistan were lessened by the Anglo-Russian Entente of 1907.

Africa see **Scramble for Africa, South Africa, Rhodesia**

Agadir incident. A German attempt in 1911 to use 'gunboat diplomacy' to weaken the growing understanding between Britain and France under the *Anglo-French Entente, 1904*. Britain had agreed to French control of *Morocco* but the Germans claimed that this threatened their interests there and sent a gunboat to the Moroccan port of Agadir. Britain was alarmed that the Germans might try to turn Agadir into a naval base for themselves, and Lloyd George, then Chancellor of the Exchequer delivered a stern warning to Germany in a speech at the Mansion House, London. The Germans climbed down and recognized French rights in Morocco; in compensation, the French gave them a small area of the French Congo.

Agricultural Children's Act, 1873, banned all children under eight from working on farms.
← AGRICULTURAL GANGS' ACT, 1867

Agricultural depression. A disastrous slump in British farming which lasted from about 1875 to 1895. The main causes were the imports of cheap wheat from the United States and Canada; bad British harvests in 1879 and 1880; and serious outbreaks of disease among cattle. Many farmers went bankrupt; and more and more farm labourers left the land. Arable farmers were the worst affected: the total area of arable land was cut by a quarter and the acreage of wheat was halved. By the 1880s some livestock farmers had started to recover their prosperity.
← HIGH FARMING

Agricultural Gangs' Act, 1867, prevented children under eight from being employed in agricultural gangs which were hired out to the highest bidder for work on farms. Stone-picking and weeding were common tasks. The children often had a fourteen- or sixteen-hour day, including the walk to and from work.
AGRICULTURAL CHILDREN'S ACT →

Agricultural revolution. A rather vague term used to describe the changes in farming brought about by the *Enclosure Acts*, the growing of turnips for winter fodder, and the sowing of clover and other seed crops to create a temporary pasture for cattle. The main effects of these changes were to increase agricultural production and to provide fresh meat, instead of salted, in the winter. These changes started in the seventeenth century and the later achievements of *Jethro Tull*, *Robert Bakewell* and '*Turnip*' *Townshend* are now less highly regarded than they once were.

AGRICULTURE. The old *open field system*, which still prevailed over a broad band of central England at the beginning of the eighteenth century, prevented most improvements in farming methods. As all the farmers had to sow the same crops on their little strips of land in the open fields, it was usually impossible to secure agreement to sow the new crops of turnips and clover, introduced in the seventeenth century. Cattle mingled on the commons spreading disease, and much time was wasted in moving men and tools from one field to another. But perhaps the most serious drawback was that the system prevented richer men from investing money in agricultural improvement, as they could reap few benefits from doing so. Most of the open fields were gradually abolished as a result of about 3,500 separate *Enclosure Acts*, passed between 1730 and 1820. These Acts caused considerable hardship among those smallholders who became landless labourers. Their starvation wages had to be brought up to a living wage by the *Speenhamland system* introduced in 1795. Their plight became even worse in some parts of the country when the introduction of the *factory system* deprived their wives of the job of spinning wool at home and some of the men themselves of their part-time work as hand-loom weavers. But the Enclosure Acts enabled richer farmers to introduce improvements in agriculture and encouraged landowners to invest more money in their estates. One of the most persistent and vocal supporters of the enclosure movement was *Arthur Young* who became secretary of the *Board of Agriculture*, established in 1793. *Thomas Coke*, of Holkham, Norfolk, the first Earl of Leicester, showed how farming could be made to pay. The increase in food supplies produced by these improvements was a vital factor in making it possible for Britain to feed its fast-growing population in the second half of the eighteenth century and in providing a surplus to feed the factory workers in the new industrial towns at the end of the century.

During the Napoleonic wars there was a great increase in the demand for home-grown food: prices rose and more land was taken into cultivation. Farmers—and landowners—experienced a great prosperity and the Houses of Parliament, which were then dominated by the land-owning interests, tried to maintain this prosperity after the war by passing the *Corn Law* in 1815. This law was designed to keep the price of home-grown wheat as high as possible. It caused great opposition both among the new class of manufacturers who wanted cheap food for their workers so that they could keep their wages low, and among the farm workers who were too poor to buy enough bread—made from the wheat they themselves had grown. Unrest in the countryside led to the '*Swing*' *riots* of 1830; the *Tolpuddle Martyrs* were sentenced to *transportation* four years later for giving illegal oaths in forming a trade union. But pressure from the manufacturers, organized in the *Anti-Corn-Law League*, and the *Irish famine* resulted in the *Repeal of the Corn Law* in 1846. Although the landowners, led by *Derby* and *Disraeli*, foresaw their own ruin, the full effects of repeal were not felt until the 1870s. In fact, the succeeding period of *high farming*, which lasted from about 1850 to 1875, was one of great prosperity for farmers. Investment increased with big drainage programmes undertaken on clay soils. Greater use of farm machinery, including *Patrick Bell*'s reaper, was stimulated by the displays at the Great Exhibition of 1851. And there was a wider use of fertilizers, including guano (bird droppings imported from Peru) and artificial fertilizers developed by *Sir John Bennet Lawes.* The growth of *railways* enabled farmers to produce goods for more distant towns.

But the farm workers themselves did not share in this new prosperity. Some of them were little children of seven or eight years of age, who were commonly employed in many arduous tasks. Children under eight received some legal protection under the *Agricultural Gangs' Act, 1867*, and were banned from working on farms altogether by the *Agricultural Children's Act, 1873*, although there were cases of this law being evaded even in the 1890s. The adult farm workers conducted their own fight. In 1872 *Joseph Arch* formed the first successful national trade union for farm workers which succeeded in obtaining some increase in wages. But these small increases in pay were insufficient to halt the drift from the land, which had already started in the 1850s. In 1861 the proportion of the working population employed in agriculture was 18 per cent and by 1881 it was down to 12 per cent. This decline continued at an accelerating rate during the *agricultural depression.* Many landowners had to reduce or remit their rents, and they were further affected by the introduction of *estate duties* in 1894, which made it impossible for them to invest the large sums of money they had done in the past.

By 1900 there was some recovery in farming, with the growing demands for fresh milk, fruit and vegetables from the expanding towns; but it did not recover its prosperity until demand for all home-grown food soared again during the First World War. In 1917 farmers were given a guaranteed minimum price for the first time under the *Corn Production Act*, but this was repealed after the war. Farmers' prosperity did not last for long and there was a second slump between the two world wars. The industrial depression created large-scale unemployment among workers in the towns so that they could no longer afford to buy as much food. Other countries 'dumped' huge supplies of cheap food in Britain in an attempt to solve their own economic problems. The *Ottawa agreements* of 1932 allowed cheap food to be imported from the Commonwealth. In an attempt to save home agriculture, the *Wheat Act* was passed in the same year, which gave farmers a guaranteed price again. Marketing boards were also set up to regulate the price of other products such as milk and eggs. But the area of land under cultivation continued to decline and more workers left the land.

Farming prospered again during the Second World War, and the *Agriculture Act, 1947*, tried to maintain stability by giving guaranteed prices for a wide range of products. Since the end of the war, increasing mechanization through the use of more *tractors* and *combine harvesters* and the introduction of *factory farming* have caused a further decline in the number of farm workers, who now constitute about 3 per cent of the total working population. The entry of Britain into the *European Community* in 1973 means that it will have to adapt to the Community's common agricultural policy by 1978, unless it is changed meanwhile.

Agriculture Act, 1947, gave farmers guaranteed minimum prices for about three-quarters of their products. The prices were fixed at the annual price review made by the government. In recent years, these subsidies to farmers have cost about £200m. a year. Combined with the low-priced food imported from the Commonwealth, they provided cheap food in the shops. As a result of Britain entering the *European Community,* farmers' subsidies were due to end finally by 1978.

Air mail. The first, temporary air mail service was started between Hendon and Windsor in 1911 at the time of the coronation of King George V. Regular services were introduced by private air line companies after the First World War, first to Paris and then to other parts of the Continent. From 1936, *Imperial Airways* operated the Empire Air Mail Service, which allowed letters to be sent to any part of the Empire for the same charge as inland mail, then 1½d. Air mail is now carried by British Airways on behalf of the Post Office.

Air raids. The invention of airships and aeroplanes brought the home population into the front line for the first time in both world wars. The attacks were made only on a small scale in the First World War. About fifty air raids were made by German airships, developed by *Count von Zeppelin*, on many different parts of Britain, including Scotland. German planes also made about fifty attacks, mainly on London and the south-east. In all, about 1,000 civilians were killed. The devastating effects of raids by more modern planes were demonstrated during the Spanish Civil War (1936–9) by the Germans who were aiding General Franco. The German bombing of the defenceless market town of Guernica on 27 April 1937, shocked the conscience of the world, but within a few years much worse raids were being carried out by all the participants in the Second World War. About 30,000 British civilians were killed in the *Blitz* and a similar number in later attacks by *V1*s and *V2* rockets.

AIR TRAVEL. For many centuries man had been making attempts to fly by many different means, including large wings attached to the arms and body, but all of them had ended in failure. It was not until 1783 that the *Montgolfier brothers* succeeded in making a balloon in which man left the earth for the first time. The first flight in a balloon over England was made in the following year by an Italian Vincent Lunardi, and in 1785 two men crossed the Channel in a balloon. Balloons were at first used mainly as pleasure ground attractions, for military reconnaissance by Napoleon and other generals, and somewhat later for scientific experiments and observations in the atmosphere. Although flights of 1,000 miles or more had been made by the middle of the nineteenth century, the main drawback of balloons as a means of transport was that the direction of the flight could not be controlled. Oars were tried at first, and then in the 1850s, experiments were made with small engines. But the problem of producing a really useful lighter-than-air means of transport was not really solved until *Count von Zeppelin* built his first airship in 1900.

Meanwhile, other inventors had been making experiments with heavier-than-air-machines, gliders and model aeroplanes. They included *Sir George Cayley*, who is now generally accepted as the main discoverer of the principles of modern flight. In 1903 the *Wright brothers* made the first sustained controlled flights in an aeroplane and two years later they were making flights of over twenty miles. In 1909, a Frenchman, *Louis Blériot*, flew across the English Channel. The development of aircraft was stimulated by the First World War and *air raids* on Britain were made both by Zeppelins and planes. The first *Atlantic flights* were made in 1919 and in the same year the British firm, Handley Page Transport, started the first international scheduled air service to Paris and Brussels.

Airships continued to be built between the two world wars, but after the disastrous crash of the *R 101*, Britain abandoned them. Many new routes were pioneered by aviators, including *Amy Johnson.* In 1924 *Imperial Airways* was formed to carry passengers and *air mail* to most parts of the Empire and Commonwealth, and in 1939 it was taken over by *British Overseas Airways Corporation.*

The aviation industry was again stimulated by the Second World War, with the development of jet planes by *Sir Frank Whittle*, which gave Britain a short-lived lead in this field with the *Comet airliner* after the war. The wartime manufacture of *V2* rockets by the German von Braun opened the way to *space travel.*

Since the end of the last war, the growth of civil aviation services has been extremely rapid, with many competing airlines running services to all parts of the world. In 1920 just over 20,000 passengers were carried to and from Britain in British aircraft, while in 1970 British airlines alone carried over 20m. passengers. The growth of air traffic has brought to an end the era of the luxury passenger liner, like the *Queen Mary* and the *Queen Elizabeth*, though a new *Queen Elizabeth II* is in service as a luxury cruise ship. The rapidity of air travel has enabled many ordinary people to have *holidays* in foreign countries that they could only have dreamt about in previous times; and has brought businessmen, statesmen and relatives much closer together. With improvements in other *communications*, air travel has helped to make the world seem to be one place. But the blessings have not been entirely unmixed. Aircraft noise, particularly with supersonic planes like *Concorde*, has created intolerable living conditions for many thousands of people, and modern planes have made war even more deadly than it was before.

'Alabama' dispute. In 1862, during the American Civil War (1861–5), the cruiser Alabama, which had been ordered from Britain by the Confederate States of the south, was allowed to slip out of Birkenhead, where it had been built. The Confederates used it to capture many merchant ships of the Northern states. After the latter had triumphed in the war, the United States claimed damages from Britain. In 1871 Gladstone agreed to settle the claim by arbitration. Representatives of five countries (including Britain and the United States) awarded the U.S.A. £3½m. damages. This method of settling a dispute was a great step forward in international relations, but it was not popular with many of the Victorian public, who thought that Gladstone had acted weakly.
INTERNATIONAL COURT OF JUSTICE →

Alanbrooke, Viscount (1883–1963), field marshal and Chief of the Imperial General Staff, 1941–6, who played a great part in the direction of Allied strategy in Europe during the Second World War. His command of detail and his grasp of broad strategical concepts enabled him to express firm views to Churchill and later to United States' commanders and leaders.

Albert, Prince of Saxe-Coburg-Gotha (1819–61), German cousin of *Queen Victoria*, who became her husband in 1840. His stiff German manner made him unpopular with many members of the public and politicians and for that reason he was not given the title of Prince Consort until 1857. Although he avoided public involvement in politics, he had a very great influence on Victoria behind the scenes, for example, in her successful attempt to have *Palmerston* dismissed as Foreign Secretary in 1851. Albert's main aims were to increase the influence of the Queen in foreign affairs by insisting on her constitutional right to be informed and consulted, and by using the family network of related kings and princes in Europe. He also sought to maintain the status of the Crown at home. He was interested in social and industrial affairs and conceived the idea of the *Great Exhibition, 1851*.

Alcock and Brown. Sir John William Alcock (1892–1919) and Sir Arthur Whitten-Brown (1886–1948), British airmen who made the first direct flight across the Atlantic in a Vickers-Vimy plane in June, 1919. They flew from Newfoundland to Galway at an average speed of over 120 m.p.h. Shortly afterwards Alcock was killed on a flight to France. The British airship, *R 34*, also crossed the Atlantic in the same year.

← LOUIS BLERIOT: AMY JOHNSON →

Alexander of Tunis, Earl (1891–1969), field marshal, educated at Harrow and Sandhurst, a brilliant commander who served in many different theatres of operation in the Second World War. He fought with distinction in the First World War, being wounded three times, decorated with the D.S.O., M.C., and being awarded foreign decorations. Between the two world wars, he served on the north-west frontier in India. During the Second World War he commanded the rearguard at *Dunkirk*, and then as General Officer Commanding, Burma, successfully extricated many British and Indian soldiers after Japanese attacks in 1942. He was Commander-in-Chief in the Middle East from 1942 to 1943, when he co-ordinated the Allied advances from Egypt and Algeria, which resulted in the German surrender at Tunis in May 1943. He was then appointed Commander-in-Chief of the Allied Armies in Italy, 1943–4, and became Supreme Allied Commander in the Mediterranean, 1944–5. Under his command, the Allies drove the enemy out of Sicily and southern Italy. After *Anzio* they swept on and finally liberated the whole of Italy from German control. After the war he was Governor-General of Canada, 1946–52, and Minister of Defence, under Churchill, from 1952 to 1954. He was made an earl in 1952.

Amalgamated Society of Engineers, the first of the 'new model' unions, formed in 1851 out of a number of smaller unions for engineering workers. It had a high subscription for those days of 1*s.* a week, so that only skilled workers could afford to join and the union was able to build up large funds. After an initial struggle with the employers in 1852, the union followed a quiet, respectable course, avoiding strikes and settling disputes by talks with employers, restricting entry to the union to keep wages high, and providing big *friendly society* benefits for its members. The headquarters were in London, and William Allan was the secretary for over 20 years. In the 1880s, some younger members, including *Tom Mann*, tried to make the union adopt more radical policies. In 1921, the Society combined with other unions to form the Amalgamated Engineering Union.

American loan. With the abrupt ending of Lend–Lease after the end of the Second World War, Britain did not have enough dollars to buy the goods it needed from the United States. In 1947, the Labour government, under Attlee, negotiated a loan of £1,300m. from the United States and Canada.
← LEND-LEASE: MARSHALL AID →

Anglo-French Entente, 1904, ended a long period of friction between Britain and France over colonial territories, e.g., the *Fashoda incident.* Britain was given a free hand in Egypt in return for giving France a free hand in Morocco. German actions over *Morocco* brought the two countries closer together and military agreements, in case of war with Germany, were made in 1906, and naval agreements in 1912, but no formal alliance between the two countries was signed until the First World War had begun.
ANGLO-RUSSIAN ENTENTE →

Anglo-Japanese alliance, 1902, under which Britain and Japan agreed to aid each other if either were attacked by more than one other power. The treaty was of greater advantage to Japan than to Britain, as it left Japan free to attack Russia, which it did in 1904, gaining a surprising victory in the following year. Japan declared war on Germany on 23 August 1914, and captured the German colonies of the Caroline and Marshall islands in the Pacific, which it continued to occupy as *mandates* after the First World War. The alliance, which is sometimes said to mark the end of Britain's '*splendid isolation*' was allowed to lapse after the *Washington Conference* of 1921–2.

Anglo-Russian Entente, 1907, lessened outstanding differences between Britain and Russia over Afghanistan, Tibet and Persia. Although suspicions continued, particularly over Persia, it made it easier for the

three powers of Russia, France and Britain to collaborate before the First World War.
← ANGLO-FRENCH ENTENTE: TRIPLE ENTENTE →

Anti-Corn-Law League. An organization formed by seven manufacturers in Manchester in January 1839, to campaign for the *Repeal of the Corn Law.* The leaders were Richard Cobden and John Bright. The league published its own newspaper; used the penny post, which started in 1840, to send pamphlets to voters in all parts of the country; and brought pressure to bear on M.P.s. It was one of the first, and most successful, pressure group campaigns.
← CORN LAW, 1815: REPEAL OF THE CORN LAW, 1846 →

Anti-Slavery Society, formed in 1823, to campaign for the freeing of slaves in the British Empire, which was achieved in 1833. (See also *William Wilberforce.*)

Anzio beachhead, scene of fierce fighting in the Second World War when Allied troops landed behind the German flank at Anzio on the west coast of Italy and held out while other Allied forces attacked Monte Cassino and eventually linked up with them in May 1944. Allied armies, under the leadership of *General Alexander*, then went on to conquer all Italian and German forces in Italy.

Anzus Pact, a defence treaty between Australia, New Zealand and the United States made in 1951. In the event of an armed attack in the Pacific, each country agreed to 'act to meet the common danger in accordance with its constitutional processes'. The importance of the treaty from the British point of view was that it marked a sharp change of emphasis in the defence policy of Australia and New Zealand—away from the traditional links with Britain and towards the United States.

Apartheid. An official policy of rigid separation of white and black people which developed in *South Africa* after the Second World War. In theory, both races should have equal opportunities to develop in their own way, but in practice the white minority of about 4m. out of 23m. retains its wealth, power and supremacy. Non-white people's rights of residence, movement, choice of occupation and political freedom have been severely restricted. Bantustans, with limited powers of self-government, have been set up for blacks, but occupy only about 15 per cent of the total area of the country. The policy has been condemned by the United Nations and practically every other country in the world. There have been protests inside South Africa by the church, students, blacks and liberal whites and in Britain by anti-apartheid groups and some political and religious leaders. Apartheid was condemned by Harold Macmillan, then Conservative prime minister, on a visit to South Africa in 1960, when he said there was a 'wind of change' blowing through the African continent. South Africa left the Commonwealth in 1961, as a result of other members' increasing criticism of its policy of apartheid.

Appeasement. The policy, particularly associated with *Neville Chamberlain*, of trying to pacify *Hitler* by making concessions to his demands. Thus, Britain did not oppose the German reoccupation of the Rhineland in 1936; remained neutral in the Spanish Civil War, 1936–9, even though both the Germans and the Italians helped General Franco; took no action over the German takeover of Austria in 1938; and agreed to let Germany have part of Czechoslovakia under the *Munich agreement* of 1938. Critics of the policy say that Hitler could have been stopped by firm action at the start; but Britain was not prepared for war; wanted to avoid fighting Germany and Italy at the same time; and was not prepared to try to unite with Communist Russia against the German and Italian dictators, even if such an alliance had been possible. The policy was abandoned after the failure of the Munich agreement.
← COLLECTIVE SECURITY: CONTAINMENT →

Arch, Joseph (1826–1919), trade union leader and politician, born at Barford, Warwickshire. A farm labourer and Methodist preacher, he founded the National Agricultural Labourers' Union in 1872. It was the first effective national union for farm workers. In the first year, it gained 70,000 members and succeeded in raising wages by 1*s*.–3*s*. in most parts of the country by organizing a series of strikes. The farmers retaliated by locking out strikers and evicting them from their cottages, and the strikes ended by 1874. Support for the union declined and by 1889 there were less than 5,000 members. Arch was M.P. for north-west Norfolk from 1885–6 and 1892–1902.
← TOLPUDDLE MARTYRS: SIR GEORGE EDWARDS →

Arkwright, Sir Richard (1732–92), the 'father' of the *factory system*, born at Preston, Lancashire. He worked as a barber in Bolton and then started dealing in human hair which he sold to wig makers. In 1769 he patented a spinning frame, which produced a much stronger, but coarse, cotton thread by taking it through two pairs of rollers, one turning faster than the other, which stretched it and made the thread stronger. For the first time cotton could be used for the warp, or vertical threads, in weaving, as well as for the weft, so that an all-cotton cloth could be produced instead of one containing some wool or linen. The spinning frame had to be driven by a horse, or by water or steam power. This resulted in a revolutionary change in the textile industry. The employment of women and children as spinners in their own home eventually stopped; instead, they were employed in factories to operate machinery. Arkwright set up his first factory at Nottingham, where the spinning frame was driven by a horse. Two years later, in 1771, he opened his first cotton mill at Cromford, Derbyshire, where the machinery was worked by a water wheel. He opened many other cotton mills in Derbyshire and Lancashire and in 1784, in partnership with David Dale, opened the New Lanark Mills in Scotland, which were later taken over by *Robert Owen.* Arkwright was almost certainly not the inventor of the spinning frame (or water frame, as it was called, after water power was used to drive it), and his patent was cancelled in 1785. But he did more than any other man to develop it and, even more important, was responsible for the establishment of the factory system. He was knighted in 1786 and left a fortune of £500,000.

← JAMES HARGREAVES: SAMUEL CROMPTON →

Army reforms were carried out by *Edward Cardwell*, Liberal Secretary for War, 1868–74, and *Viscount Haldane*, Liberal Secretary for War, 1905–12.

Arnhem, a town in Holland, on the Rhine, where nearly 10,000 British parachutists of the First Airborne Division were besieged by the Germans for nine days in September 1944, during the Second World War. They had been dropped to seize bridges over the Rhine and thus speed up the Allied advance into Germany. Other Allied forces could not fight their way through to relieve them. Only just over 2,000 of the parachutists escaped to safety and the rest were killed, wounded, or reported missing.

Arnold, The Rev. Thomas (1795–1842), headmaster of Rugby, who was most closely associated with the reform of the inefficient *public schools* in the nineteenth century. After a distinguished career at Oxford, be became headmaster of Rugby in 1828. Dr Hawkins, Provost of Oriel College, Oxford, had predicted in his testimonial that Arnold 'would change the face of education all through the public schools of

England'. This he helped to do, by introducing the prefect system, choosing his masters with great care, and instiling the ideal of the Christian gentleman into his pupils. He published a number of books on history and religion and was appointed regius professor of history at Oxford in 1841.

← THE REV. GEORGE BUTLER

Artisans and Labourers Dwellings Act, 1868, the first Act giving local authorities powers to compel owners to pull down or repair insanitary houses, but very little was done. It is also known as the Torrens Act, after William Torrens (1813–94), a Liberal M.P., who introduced it as a private member's Bill in 1866. (See next entry.)

Artisans and Labourers Dwellings Improvement Act, 1875, gave local authorities powers of compulsory purchase for whole slum areas which were 'unfit for human habitation'; but few councils did so as they had to pay a high compensation to owners of the property. The Act was the work of *Viscount Cross* who was also responsible for the *Public Health Act, 1875*.

HOUSING OF THE WORKING CLASSES ACT, 1890 →

Arts Council of Great Britain was set up by the Labour government in 1946 to encourage music, drama, painting, sculpture and literature etc. It receives a government grant which is spent on subsidizing theatrical tours, art exhibitions etc. Much of the grant goes to the main opera and ballet companies in London.

Asquith, Herbert Henry (1852–1928) Liberal leader, whose feud with Lloyd George helped to wreck the party. He was born at Morley, Yorkshire and educated at the City of London School and Balliol College, Oxford. A barrister, he was Liberal M.P. for East Fife from 1886 to 1918 and Home Secretary from 1892 to 1895. He was one of those Liberals who supported the Boer War, 1899–1902, while Lloyd George was opposed to it. In 1905, he was appointed Chancellor of the Exchequer and succeeded Campbell-Bannerman as prime minister in 1908. Asquith appointed Lloyd George as Chancellor, and gave him full support in the radical reforms he carried out. In May 1915, during the First World War, Asquith formed a coalition government, but in the following year, Lloyd George combined with the Conservatives to get rid of Asquith for lack of vigour in prosecuting the war, and became prime minister himself in December 1916. Asquith opposed Lloyd George's coalition government, which was continued after the war

following the '*coupon' election,* and the feud between them continued until Lloyd George became leader of the Liberal party in 1926. By then the Liberal party had been gravely weakened. Asquith was made the first Earl of Oxford and Asquith in 1925.
← HENRY CAMPBELL-BANNERMAN: DAVID LLOYD GEORGE →

Association Football. Originally football was played in village streets between teams from neighbouring hamlets, but this form of the game died out in the eighteenth century. The modern game was introduced in public schools and at Cambridge University in the middle of the nineteenth century. The Football Association was formed in 1863. In 1885, the Association allowed clubs to employ professional players. The Football League, with 12 clubs, was formed in 1888. The first Cup Final, held at the Oval in 1872, was watched by only 2,000 spectators, but by the end of the century football had become a popular Saturday afternoon entertainment and the Cup Final was attracting crowds of 80,000.

Astor, Nancy (1879–1964), wife of the second Viscount Astor, born in Virginia, U.S.A. She was the first woman to take her seat as an M.P.—for Plymouth from 1919 to 1945.
← COUNTESS MARKIEVICZ: MARGARET BONDFIELD →

Atlantic cable for telegraph messages was successfully laid in 1866 by *Cyrus West Field.*

Atlantic Charter. An 8-point programme of post-war aims agreed by Churchill and Roosevelt, before the United States entered the Second World War. They included the rights of all peoples to choose their governments freely; economic co-operation and fewer restrictions on trade; freedom of the seas; a general security system; and freedom from want and fear. The meetings between the two leaders were held in warships off Newfoundland in August 1941.

Atlantic flights were first made by *Alcock and Brown* and the British airship *R 34* in 1919.

Atom bombs. British and American scientists collaborated in the development of the atom bomb during the Second World War. The first bomb was exploded over Hiroshima, Japan, on 6 August 1945, with casualties of about 240,000, including 60,000 from radio activity, and the second bomb was used against the port of Nagasaki on 9

August with a smaller number of casualties. (Estimates of casualties for both attacks vary greatly. The United States gave a figure of 79,400 for Hiroshima in 1960.) Japan surrendered shortly afterwards, though it had already made some overtures of peace through Russia before the bombs were dropped. The British government consented to the use of the bombs. Britain tested its first atomic bomb at Montebello Islands, Australia, in 1952.
HYDROGEN BOMB →

Atomic energy. The first nuclear power plant in the world to produce electricity on a commercial scale was opened at Calder Hall, Cumberland, in 1956. In 1970 almost one-tenth of Britain's electricity was produced by nuclear power.

Attlee, Clement Richard (1883–1967), Labour prime minister. Educated at a public school, Haileybury, and at University College, Oxford, he was converted to socialism by working in a social settlement in the East End of London as a young man. He was a lecturer at the London School of Economics from 1913 to 1923—apart from service in the First World War—and was elected Labour M.P. for Limehouse in 1922. During the second Labour minority government, from 1929 to 1931, he served under Ramsay MacDonald as Chancellor of the Duchy of Lancaster and then as Postmaster-General. He succeeded George Lansbury (1859–1940) as leader of the Labour party in 1935. In 1940 Attlee joined Churchill's wartime coalition government and was deputy prime minister from 1942 to 1945. He became prime minster in 1945, following the Labour party's landslide victory at the end of the war. He was the first Labour prime minister with a clear majority. During his first ministry from 1945 to 1950, many reforms were passed, some of which had been prepared by the coalition government during the war, for example the *Beveridge report* on social security. Using this report as a basis, the modern *welfare state* was created by the *National Insurance Act, 1946*, the *National Health Service Act, 1946*, and other measures. The *Trade Disputes and Trade Unions Act of 1927*, which had reduced the powers of the unions was repealed and the *Parliament Act, 1949*, further reduced the delaying powers of the House of Lords to a year. Subsidies were given to farmers by the *Agriculture Act, 1947*, and a programme of *nationalization* put many industries and institutions under State control, without arousing too much opposition, except in the case of iron and steel and road haulage. Demobilization of Servicemen and women was accompanied in an orderly way, on the general principle of 'first in, first out', except for key workers who were urgently wanted in civilian life. The arts were encouraged by the creation of the Arts Council of Great Britain in 1946.

But the government was troubled from the start by economic problems and the need to regain Britain's lost export markets. An *American loan* was negotiated in 1947 and a programme of *austerity* introduced. The situation was made worse by the *fuel crisis* of 1947, which put many workers out of a job for several months. In 1949 came the *devaluation* of the £.

India was at last given independence in 1947. After the start of the *cold war* in that year, Britain played a big part in the *Berlin airlift, 1948–9*, and also took part in the *Korean war, 1950–3*. In 1949, largely through the efforts of *Ernest Bevin*, Britain became a founding member of the North Atlantic Treaty Organization (NATO). General elections were held in 1950, when the Labour party got back into power with a greatly reduced majority of only six. It seemed that the government had run out of ideas and it was much weakened by the death of *Bevin*, and the resignations of *Cripps* because of ill health and of *Bevan* because of the introduction of Health Service charges for spectacles and dentures by the new Labour Chancellor, Hugh Gaitskell. Attlee called an election in October 1951, but was defeated and was succeeded by Churchill. He was created an earl in 1955.

← RAMSAY MACDONALD: HAROLD WILSON →

Attwood, Thomas (1783–1856), son of a Birmingham banker. His Birmingham Political Union, formed in 1830, played some part in securing parliamentary reform, and he also supported *Chartism*, and presented the first petition to the House of Commons in 1839. His main interest, however, was in *currency* reform. He wanted the government to abandon the *gold standard* as it had done during the Napoleonic wars, and let the Bank of England issue bank notes freely. He believed, in his own words, that it was 'plenty of money that makes prosperity' —a view that many economists would now question, believing that it creates *inflation*. He was M.P. for Birmingham from 1832 to 1840.

← FRANCIS PLACE: FEARGUS O'CONNOR →

Austerity. A policy introduced by *Sir Stafford Cripps*, who was Labour Chancellor of the Exchequer from 1947 to 1950. It involved higher taxation; the banning of travel abroad and the use of cars for pleasure; a reduction in imports; and an emphasis on exports under the slogan, 'export or die'. It was designed to overcome Britain's financial difficulties in the post-war period and to curb inflation.

← FUEL CRISIS

Austin, Lord (1886–1941), car manufacturer, born at Little Missenden, Buckinghamshire. He founded the Austin Motor Company in 1905 and it started making the Austin Seven or 'Baby' Austin in 1922. As it cost only £125, it made it possible for many of the lower middle classes to afford a car. His firm was merged with Morris Motors in 1952, to form the British Motor Corporation, which is now part of British Leyland. He was made a Lord in 1936.
← VISCOUNT NUFFIELD

AUSTRALIA. The colony of New South Wales was founded in 1788 as a settlement for British convicts who had been sentenced to *transportation*. Much of the rest of the country was explored or developed between 1820 and 1850 by free settlers. There was a *gold rush* following the discovery of gold in New South Wales and Victoria in the 1850s. Under the Australian Colonies Government Act, 1850, the four colonies of New South Wales, Victoria, South Australia and Tasmania were given the right to draft constitutions for responsible self-government. There was great rivalry, however, between the colonies, with different gauges on railways and tariff barriers between them. A federation of the original four colonies and two new ones—Queensland and Western Australia—was not set up until 1901 under the Commonwealth of Australia Act. Australia has long had a progressive social policy, except for the 'White Australia' policy which excludes Asian settlers, and the cruel treatment of native aborigines in the early days. Compulsory free education was introduced in some states before it was instituted in England, and some trade unions had gained shorter working hours than in Britain by the 1870s. Although farming is still important in Australia, industry has developed rapidly since the end of the Second World War and important finds of copper have been made. Even before Britain entered the European Community, Australia had started to turn to the United States for investment and defence, signing the *Anzus pact* with the United States and New Zealand in 1951. Japan is now one of its major trading partners. The population in 1968 was 12m. and immigration is still high, about 120,000 a year, though many of these immigrants now come from other European countries which has helped to weaken further the links with Britain.

Automation. A manufacturing or processing method in which virtually all of the work is done by machinery. A fully automatic flour mill was built at Wilmington, Delaware, by an American, Oliver Evans in 1785. Since the Second World War, automation, controlled by computers,

has been adopted in many British industries and has been partly responsible for increased unemployment.
← MASS PRODUCTION

Automobile Association was formed in 1905 to protect motorists following the growing number of prosecutions for speeding under the Motor-Car Act, 1903.

Avon, Earl of see **Anthony Eden**

'Axis', a term used by *Mussolini* in 1936 to describe the relationship of co-operation between Italy and Hitler's Germany. In May 1939, the two countries signed a formal alliance, the so-called 'Pact of Steel', but Mussolini, always the weaker partner, did not enter the Second World War, on Germany's side, until June 1940.

B

Baden-Powell, Lord (1857–1941), a soldier who won great popularity in Britain for his defence of the town of Mafeking during the Boer War, 1899–1902, which was besieged by the Boers for 217 days. He formed the *Boy Scouts* in 1908.

Baird, John Logie (1888–1946), inventor of television, born at Helensburgh, Scotland. As a young man he set up a small workshop in Hastings, Sussex, to develop television. In spite of poverty and bad health, by 1922 he had made his first television apparatus out of a wooden tea chest, a biscuit tin, bicycle lamp lenses, and other parts, held together by string, sealing wax and darning needles. On 26 January 1926, he gave the first demonstration of television in the world—in some rooms he had rented in Frith Street, Soho, London. The instrument, which used a revolving disc, not a cathode ray tube, was called a Televisor. Two years later he had given the first demonstration in the world of colour television and was making regular broadcasts of low-definition 30-line television on the medium waveband from a transmitter in London. His system was adopted by the B.B.C. in 1929, but was abandoned in 1937 in favour of the Marconi-E.M.I. 405-line system.
← SIR JOHN FLEMING

Bakewell, Robert (1725–95), stockbroker, born Dishley, Leicestershire,

who introduced a new breed of Leicester sheep and longhorn cattle. Both gave more meat, but of a poorer, fatter quality.
← VISCOUNT TOWNSHEND

Balance of payments. The difference between the total value of a country's imports and exports. (*Invisible exports* and imports are included.) In very simple terms, a plus value in the balance of payments for the year may indicate that a country has made more money than it has spent. (See also *Bank of England*.)

Balance of power. The nineteenth-century theory that peace could be preserved if the strength of one group of nations was in balance with that of another group. It had long been the aim of Britain to preserve a balance of power on the Continent of Europe, without becoming involved itself; but after the *Triple Alliance* was formed, Britain became a member of the *Triple Entente* in an attempt to keep the balance of power. The theory was discredited by the *First World War*, which was caused in part by the existence of these rival power blocs.
COLLECTIVE SECURITY →

Baldwin, Stanley (1867–1947), pipe-smoking, generally easy-going prime minister, who reflected the spirit of many of the middle classes in the years between the two world wars. He was born at Bewdley, Worcestershire, the son of a wealthy iron manufacturer, and educated at Harrow and Trinity College, Cambridge. He became Conservative M.P. for Bewdley in 1908 and held office from 1917 to 1922 in the coalition government of Lloyd George, and was partly responsible for the manoeuvres which caused the Conservatives to withdraw their support and bring the coalition government to an end in 1922. Bonar Law became prime minister and appointed Baldwin Chancellor of the Exchequer. When Law retired in 1923, Baldwin succeeded him as prime minister, but the Conservatives lost their majority at the general election in 1924. The minority Labour government fell before the end of the year and Baldwin got back into power. His second ministry, from 1924 to 1929, produced some reforms, including the Local Government Act, 1929, which abolished *Boards of Guardians*. The pension age was reduced from 70 to 65 in 1926 and the voting age for women was reduced from 30 to 21 in 1928. But little was done to tackle the country's basic economic problems or the growing unemployment. Baldwin was far more successful in dealing with the *General Strike* of 1926, which lasted just over a week.

When Ramsay MacDonald formed his *National Government* in 1931, he appointed Baldwin Lord President of the Council, and Baldwin succeeded him as prime minister in 1935. Much of his third ministry was taken up with the *abdication crisis* of 1936. Meanwhile, Germany was rearming and the international situation was becoming more tense with the Italian invasion of Abyssinia in October 1935, and the start of the Spanish Civil War in July 1936. But Baldwin, a master of inaction unless he was pushed, did very little to rearm, though in this he reflected the views of many Britons as the *Peace ballot* of 1935 had shown. He resigned in 1937 and was made an earl in the same year.

← BONAR LAW: NEVILLE CHAMBERLAIN →

Balfour, Arthur James (1848–1930), nephew of the Marquis of Salisbury, educated at Eton and Trinity College, Cambridge. He became a Conservative M.P. in 1874 and four years later private secretary to his uncle, whom he accompanied to the Congress of Berlin, 1878. He was appointed Chief Secretary for Ireland by his uncle in 1887, when he used a new Crimes Act, which allowed trial without a jury, with great vigour. He succeeded Salisbury as prime minister in 1902. During his ministry there were two important reforms: the *Education Act, 1902*, which started State secondary education, and the *Irish Land Purchase Act, 1903*, which allowed tenants to borrow money from the government to buy their smallholdings. But he was unable to hold the Conservatives together in the face of *Joseph Chamberlain*'s campaign for tariff reform and he resigned, at the end of 1905. In the elections held in January 1906, the Conservatives suffered a major defeat winning only 157 seats. Balfour was never prime minister again and resigned the party leadership in 1911 in favour of Bonar Law. But he continued to hold high office and to make declarations that had far-reaching consequences. During the First World War he was First Lord of the Admiralty from 1915 to 1916 and Foreign Secretary from 1916 to 1919 in the coalition governments. In November 1917, during the British victories against the Turks in the Middle East, Balfour made his famous declaration to Lord Rothschild, chairman of the British Zionist Federation, that Britain would support the idea of a national home for the Jews in Palestine, which resulted in Jews being admitted to Palestine on a quota system between the two world wars. He was the chief British delegate at the Washington conference of 1921 to 1922, which tried to limit the naval arms race. And as Lord President of the Council from 1925 to 1929, he attended the *Imperial Conference of 1926*, when he defined the new status of dominions. He was created an earl in 1922.

← MARQUIS OF SALISBURY: BONAR LAW →

Ballot Act, 1872, introduced secret voting at elections and thus made it far more difficult, if not impossible, for candidates to bribe or corrupt voters. Previously electors had had to call out the name of the candidate they had chosen in public.

← REPRESENTATION OF THE PEOPLE ACT, 1867: REPRESENTATION OF THE PEOPLE ACT, 1884 →

Bank Charter Act, 1844, passed by Peel, to help prevent bank failures. Many smaller banks had failed in the 1830s by issuing bank notes for which they did not have sufficient reserves of gold. (At that time many different banks could issue notes and as Britain was on the *gold standard* the banks were obliged to change banknotes for gold sovereigns on demand.) The Act fixed the amount of notes these banks could issue at the level each bank had in circulation at that time and they lost their right to issue notes entirely if they merged with another bank. At the same time, the Bank of England was prohibited from issuing banknotes in excess of £14m., unless it had sufficient gold to cover them. As a result of this measure, the Bank of England gradually became the main note-issuing body, though the last private bank to issue bank notes in England did not disappear until 1921.

Bank of England was established in 1694 and was nationalized in 1946. It exercises a great influence on the economy through Bank rate—the percentage charge it makes for lending money. This governs the general rate at which other banks will lend money to industry, so that if the rate is high there will be less tendency to invest. It also has an important influence on the *balance of payments*, as foreign speculators will tend to transfer their money to London if the rate is high, which shows up as a plus sign in the balance of payments.

Banting, Sir Frederick (1891–1941), Canadian doctor, who with *Charles Herbert Best*, discovered insulin in 1921, used in the treatment of diabetes, which has allowed many thousands of sufferers to live a much longer life. The discovery was made in the laboratory of J. J. R. Macleod at Toronto University and in 1923 Macleod and Banting were awarded the *Nobel prize* for medicine. Banting gave half of his share of the prize money to Best, who had worked with him in making the discovery. In the following year, Banting was knighted.

GERHARD DOMAGK →

Barnado, Dr Thomas John (1845–1905), opened his first home for destitute children in Stepney, London, in 1870 and shortly afterwards took over a nearby gin palace and turned it into a coffee palace, with a free medical service. There are now over 100 Dr Barnado's homes for children.

Bastille. A notorious prison in Paris—where many political prisoners were detained by the French king—which was captured and destroyed by workers at the start of the French revolution on 14 July 1789.

Battle of the Atlantic. The long-drawn-out fight by the British, and later American, ships and aircraft to keep the vital sea route to the New World free from attacks by German submarines during the Second World War. It was at its peak from June 1940 to August 1943, when bigger and better-protected convoys, improved depth charges and submarine detection devices, and long-range aircraft protection, caused increasing losses among German submarines. In May 1943, 37 submarines were sunk for the loss of 34 merchant ships—the first time the score was reversed.

Battle of Britain. An unsuccessful attempt by the German Luftwaffe (air force) to achieve mastery of the air over Britain between July and September 1940, as a prelude to an invasion by sea. Attacks were made on British fighter bases and there were many air battles between British and German fighter planes. The R.A.F. lost 915 planes and the Luftwaffe, 1,733. The British fighter pilots received the famous tribute from the prime minister, Churchill: 'Never in the field of human conflict was so much owed by so many to so few.'
THE BLITZ →

Battle of Jutland, 1916, the only major naval encounter between the British and German fleets in the North Sea off Denmark, during the First World War—and the first, and last, fight between battleships like *Dreadnoughts.* The British Grand Fleet under Admiral Jellicoe was stationed at Scapa Flow in the Orkneys, and a force of battle cruisers at Rosyth. The German High Sea Fleet was stationed at Kiel. The Germans were reluctant to come out to fight, but eventually emerged and the two main fleets of 28 British and 22 German battleships met on 31 May 1916. The British lost 3 battle cruisers, 3 cruisers, and 8 destroyers, more than the Germans; but the German fleet never again emerged in strength during the war, except for occasional sorties.

Beaconsfield, Earl of, see **Benjamin Disraeli**

Beale, Dorothea (1831–1906), a pioneer of women's education, who became principal of Cheltenham Ladies' College in 1858 and did much to improve educational opportunities for girls. She opened the first residential training college for women teachers at St Hilda's College, Cheltenham, in 1885, which moved to Oxford as St Hilda's Hall of Residence (now College) in 1893. She also campaigned for votes for women.

← FRANCES MARY BUSS: ANNE JEMIMA CLOUGH →

Beaverbrook, Lord (1879–1964), born William Maxwell Aitken in Ontario, Canada. Dynamic newspaperman, owner of the 'Daily Express' and other newspapers; campaigned for Empire Free Trade from 1929; successful Minister of Aircraft Production, 1940–1, and later Minister of Supply and of War Production under Churchill in the Second World War. He was made a Lord in 1917.

← VISCOUNT ROTHERMERE

Beeching Report, 1963, made by Lord Beeching (born 1913), then chairman of the British Railways Board. It recommended cuts in unprofitable railway lines and the introduction of inter-city express trains to meet competition from road transport. Between 1965 and 1970, the length of railway lines was reduced from 14,900 to 11,800 miles and the number of stations from 4,295 to 2,868.

← TRANSPORT ACT, 1947

Beeton, Mrs Isabella Mary (1836–65), writer of the most famous English book on cookery and household management. She was born in London and educated in Heidelberg, Germany. In 1856, she married Samuel Beeton, who published a number of her articles in his magazine, the 'Englishwoman's Domestic Magazine'. These were published in book form as the 'Book of Household Management' in 1861. It was a great success and is still published today. It contained hints on many domestic matters and over 4,000 recipes, which, contrary to popular belief, are not all extravagant. The book gives many fascinating insights into the way in which middle-class Victorians lived.

Belisha crossings see **Zebra crossings**

Bell, Alexander Graham (1847–1922), inventor, born in Edinburgh. In 1870 he emigrated to Canada to teach deaf and dumb people to 'speak' by a method of 'visual speech' invented by his father, Alexander Melville Bell (1819–1905). He became a professor at Boston University in 1873. Although he made many inventions his most important was the *telephone*, which he first demonstrated in March 1876, by phoning his assistant in another room and saying, 'Mr Watson, come here. I want you.' Two years later he demonstrated the telephone to Queen Victoria at Osborne House.

Bell, The Rev. Andrew (1753–1832), educationalist, born in St Andrew's, Scotland, the son of a barber. He went to India in 1787 and two years later he became superintendent of the Madras Male Orphan Asylum, which had been founded by the East India Company. Because of the shortage of teachers, he used the brighter children to teach the others reading and writing. They started by drawing the letters of the alphabet in sand. He returned to England in 1796. In the following year he published 'An Experiment in Education', in which he explained the principles of his *monitorial system* of education. In 1811, he was appointed superintendent of the National Society, which had been founded by the Church of England in that year to provide schools for the children of the poor. He died at Cheltenham in 1832, leaving a fortune of £120,000 to be used for education.

← JOSEPH LANCASTER

Bell, Patrick (1799–1869), invented in 1828 a reaping machine, pulled by a horse, which cut corn mechanically. But the scythe and the sickle continued to be used on most farms until the middle of the nineteenth century when reapers were gradually introduced.

TRACTORS →

Bentham, Jeremy (1748–1832), writer and philosopher, educated at Westminster and Oxford. His chief work, 'Introduction to the Principles of Morals and Legislation' was published in 1789. In his writings, he foreshadowed many of the major reforms of the nineteenth century, including reform of the criminal law, parliament, the Poor Law, prisons, and education. His philosophy, generally called utilitarianism, may be summed up in the phrase, 'the greatest happiness of the greatest number'. He had a major influence on many contemporary reformers such as *Francis Place* and *Sir Edwin Chadwick.*

Benz, Karl (1844–1929), German engineer, who built a motor vehicle driven by a petrol engine in 1885, and a four-wheeled car eight years later.

GOTTLIEB DAIMLER →

Berlin airlift, 1948–9. A major turning point in relations between the Western powers and Russia at the beginning of the *cold war.* After the Second World War, Berlin, the former capital of Germany, was occupied by the Allied powers of Russia, the United States, Britain and France. But it was an isolated city in the Russian zone of occupation (now East Germany), cut off from the three zones of occupation of the Western powers (now West Germany) by a strip of Russian-controlled Germany. In 1948, the Russians stopped the Western powers using roads or railways through this strip of territory, hoping that the blockade would force the Western powers to leave Berlin. But for 323 days the British and Americans flew in all supplies by air. The blockade ended in May 1949. The Allies immediately established the German Federal Republic (West Germany) in their zones of occupation, which became fully independent in 1955, and the Russians set up the German Democratic Republic (East Germany) in 1949.

Bessemer, Sir Henry (1813–98), inventor and engineer, born at Charlton, Hertfordshire, who invented the process named after him, which made large quantities of steel available for the first time. Molten pig iron was run into a converter—a large cylindrical container—and air was blown through it, which oxidized and got rid of most of the unwanted impurities like carbon and silicon. The 'convertor' method, introduced in 1856, produced steel at about one-third of the cost of wrought iron, which it soon replaced for most purposes. Bessemer opened his own steel works in Sheffield in 1859 and in the following year introduced the tilting converter. He made many other inventions, including a type-setting machine used in printing, and was knighted in 1879.
← BENJAMIN HUNTSMAN: SIR WILLIAM SIEMENS →

Best, Charles Herbert (born 1899), a Canadian physiologist, born in Maine, U.S.A., who assisted *Sir Frederick Banting* in his discovery of insulin, a treatment for diabetes, in 1921. He succeeded Banting as director of the Banting-Best Department of Medical Research in the University of Toronto on Banting's death in 1941.

Betting see **Gambling**

Bevan, Aneurin (1897–1960), left-wing Socialist, born in Tredegar, Monmouthshire. He worked as a miner and was elected Labour M.P. for Ebbw Vale in 1929. He was Minister of Health under Attlee and showed great skill in securing the agreement of the medical profession to the *National Health Service Act, 1946*. In 1951, he was appointed Minister of Labour, but he resigned when charges were introduced for dentures and spectacles by the new Labour Chancellor of the Exchequer, Hugh Gaitskell. The Labour party was defeated in that year and Bevan became the leader of a left-wing group within the party (Bevanites), who wanted a more socialistic programme. Bevan commanded great support among many Labour voters and constituency parties, and it seemed at times that he might even split the party. But just before his death he came closer to the official party line and became Labour's spokesman on colonial, and finally, on foreign affairs.

Beveridge, Lord (1879–1963), economist, journalist and civil servant, born in India. He was Director of the London School of Economics from 1919 to 1937, and Master of University College, London from 1937–45. He suggested the idea of *Labour exchanges*, which were set up in 1909; was the author of the *Beveridge report*; and was chairman of other important committees on the social services. He was knighted in 1919 and made a lord in 1946. (See next entry.)

Beveridge Report, 1942. An extremely influential report, published during the Second World War, on which the present *welfare state* is largely based. It was designed to give everyone five freedoms; from want, disease, ignorance, squalor and idleness, through a comprehensive scheme of national insurance. It recommended free medical care, family allowances, increase in old age pensions and unemployment and sickness benefits, and marriage, maternity and funeral grants, so that each citizen would have 'an income sufficient to meet his responsibilities . . . from the cradle to the grave'. Although the Labour government put most of the report into effect after the Second World War, they did not carry out two of its recommendations: that the benefits should be high enough for people to live on and that private insurance companies should be nationalized. The report was called 'Social Insurance and Allied Services'. (See previous entry.)

Bevin, Ernest (1881–1951). After working as a farm labourer and carter, he became a trade union official, and in 1921 was responsible for amalgamating nearly fifty unions into the Transport and General Workers' Union, of which he became general secretary. In May 1940, he was appointed Minister of Labour in Churchill's wartime coalition government and was extremely successful in mobilizing workers for the war effort in factories and mines. From 1945 to 1951 he was Foreign Secretary under Attlee, and was one of the most outspoken opponents of Communist Russia at the start of the *cold war.* He was primarily responsible for Britain becoming a member of the *North Atlantic Treaty Organisation (Nato).*

Bicycle. The first practical safety bicycle, with the rear wheel driven by a chain, was made by J. K. Starley of Coventry in 1885. Pneumatic tyres, which gave a more comfortable ride, were added by *J. B. Dunlop* three years later. The modern bicycle had considerable effect on social life. It allowed working-class people, particularly in the country, to take jobs further away from home, so that many of the brighter sons and daughters of farm labourers started to work in towns. It also gave working-class people greater opportunities for entertainment and a cheap method of transport that they had never had before.
← 'PENNY-FARTHING'

Bills are proposals for legislation presented to the Houses of Parliament. They may be of two main kinds: public and private. Private Bills may be introduced by a body or corporation or an individual or group of individuals to acquire or to vary certain powers: the *Enclosure Acts* were private Bills. The majority of public Bills are now introduced by the government in the House of Commons, though there is also a smaller number of private member's Bills (sponsored by individual M.P.s) most of which never become law. When a Bill is presented to the House it receives its first reading and is then printed and circulated to members. There is then a second reading when the general principles are debated. If passed, it then goes to a committee, usually of the whole House if it is an important measure, or to a smaller committee, where it is considered in detail clause by clause and amendments are made. These amendments then have to be considered by the whole House again, after which it receives its third reading. The Bill is then sent to the other House, where it goes through a similar process. It can be rejected outright by the other House, though the power of the House of Lords to reject money Bills was abolished and to delay other Bills was restricted by the *Parliament Acts.* If the Bill is amended, it then has to go back to the other House again for these to be considered or re-amended. After it has passed through all stages in both Houses it goes to the monarch for the Royal Assent, which can technically be refused, though this has not been done since 1707 in the reign of Queen Anne.

Birth Control. Forms of birth control were used in many ancient civilizations, but it was not until the early nineteenth century that a few reformers, such as *Francis Place*, started to refer to the subject in a guarded way in their books. In 1877, Charles Bradlaugh (1833-91) and Annie Besant (1847-1933) republished an American booklet which gave details of birth control methods. They were both heavily fined and birth control continued to remain an unmentionable subject until the present century. In 1918 *Marie Stopes* published an outspoken book on the subject and three years later opened a birth control clinic in London. The use of contraceptives became more common, particularly among the middle classes in the period between the two world wars. The pill—an oral contraceptive—was introduced in 1961 and six years later *abortion* was made legal under certain conditions in Britain.

Birth rate. The birth rate is thought to have started rising around the middle of the eighteenth century, for reasons which are still not entirely clear. It began to fall in the middle of the nineteenth century and declined sharply in the years between the two world wars, partly as a result of increasing use of *birth control* methods. It has started to fall again recently, partly owing to the legalizing of *abortion.* The birth rate in 1840 was 32.0 per 1,000 of the population (England and Wales only); in 1880, 30.8; in 1900, 28.2; 1920, 25.4; 1930, 16.8; 1940, 14.6; 1950, 16.2; 1960, 17.5; 1970, 16.2.

Black and Tans were men recruited by the British government in 1920 to help fight the Irish Republican Army in Ireland after Irish nationalists had set up their own parliament in Dublin in 1919. Their name came from their half-military, half-police uniform of khaki trousers and tunics and black caps. Their ruthless methods shocked liberal opinion in both Britain and the United States.

'Black Friday', 15 April 1921, when the railwaymen's and transport workers' unions refused to support the miners—fellow members of the Triple Alliance—in their demands for higher wages. The miners, who had been locked out by the employers, hoped that the other workers would strike in their support.
← TRIPLE ALLIANCE: GENERAL STRIKE →

Blackshirts. Members of the British Union of Fascists, founded by Sir Oswald Mosley (b. 1896) in 1931. Although membership was never very large, there were many violent clashes between British Fascists and Communists, particularly in the East End of London, in the years preceding the Second World War. The wearing of political uniforms, such as black shirts, was prohibited by the Public Order Act, 1936. (See also *Fascism.*)

Blackwell, Elizabeth (1821–1910), the first woman doctor in the world, born in Bristol. She emigrated to the United States with her parents in 1832 and became the first woman to qualify as a doctor there in 1849. Eight years later she opened the first hospital with an all-woman staff in New York. She returned to England in 1858 to give a lecture tour and in the following year became the first woman to register as a doctor in England, after the passing of the *Medical Act, 1858*.

Blanketeers. Unemployed hunger marchers from the north of England who planned to walk to London in 1817 to present a petition to the Prince Regent (later George IV). They carried blankets to sleep in overnight—hence the name. But the majority never got further than the assembly point in St Peter's Field, Manchester, where most of them were arrested. (Two years later, this was to be the scene of the *Peterloo* massacre.)

Blenkinsop, John (1783–1831), inventor in 1811 of a steam locomotive, propelled by a cog wheel which fitted into a toothed rail. This system was never developed further.
← RICHARD TREVITHICK: MATTHEW MURRAY →

Blériot, Louis (1872–1946), French airman who made the first flight across the English Channel on 25 July 1909.
← WRIGHT BROTHERS: ALCOCK AND BROWN →

Blitz, The. Popular name for the German air raids against London and other big industrial cities from September 1940 to May 1941. The first raids were made in daylight, but because they lost so many planes, the Germans changed to attacks by night. High explosive and incendiary bombs were used. About 30,000 civilians were killed and over $3\frac{1}{2}$m. houses were destroyed or damaged. *Radar* played a major part in British defences by giving warning of the approaching bombers and by guiding night fighters to their targets. The Blitz failed to break the spirit of the British people, which remained high even among people who slept in London Underground stations every night. The effect on war production was not serious. The attacks were called off as Hitler started to prepare for his attack on Russia in June 1941.
← BATTLE OF BRITAIN

Blitzkrieg (German for 'lightning war'). A method of attack perfected by the Germans in the Second World War, in which dive-bombers and other planes were used against enemy airfields and other targets, while enemy troops were encircled and cut off by rapid tank advances. By these means, Holland was defeated in 4 days, Belgium in 2½ weeks, Poland in 4 weeks and France in 5 weeks.

Board of Agriculture was set up in 1793 to make a county-by-county report on farming to see how it could be improved. *Arthur Young* was the secretary and Sir John Sinclair (1754–1835), a Scottish landowner, was the first president. The Board was dissolved in 1822 after Young had died and Sir John had retired. It was not formed again until 1893. In 1919 it became the Ministry of Agriculture and Fisheries, which absorbed the Ministry of Food in 1954.

Boards of Guardians were set up under the *Poor Law Amendment Act, 1834*, to run workhouses and to supervise relief of poverty in the 590 groups, or unions, of parishes into which the country had been divided. Some Boards, particularly in the north, refused to put men who were temporarily unemployed into workhouses, as the Act provided. They continued to give them cash payments (outdoor relief). The Boards were elected by ratepayers. In 1875 women became eligible for membership and in 1894 the property qualification for membership was abolished, so that some working men became members. The Boards were ended by Neville Chamberlain's Local Government Act, 1929, when their powers were transferred to county, and county borough, councils.

Boer War, 1881, was fought by the Boers in the Transvaal, South Africa, to regain their independence from British rule which had been imposed on them four years earlier. After the Boers' quick victory at the Battle of Majuba Hill, Gladstone granted them independence again by the Convention of Pretoria, 1881. (For the background see *South Africa.*)

Boer War, 1899–1902, shook the self-confidence of the British, as it eventually needed nearly 500,000 British troops to defeat 50,000 Boer farmers in South Africa. The Boer republics of Transvaal and the Orange Free State gained early victories over the small number of British troops stationed in South Africa. British garrisons were besieged in Ladysmith, Natal; Kimberley, Cape Colony; and Mafeking, just over the border from Transvaal in British Bechuanaland (now Botswana). Reinforcements were sent out from Britain under General Sir Redvers Buller (1839–1908), whose armies suffered 3 major defeats in one week in December, 1899. Lord Roberts (1832–1914), was then sent out as commander-in-chief with *Kitchener* as his chief of staff, with new and larger forces. The three garrison towns were relieved—Mafeking on 17 May 1900, after having been defended for 217 days by forces under the command of Col. (later Lord) Baden-Powell, who later founded the Boy Scout movement. Roberts's armies swept on through the Transvaal, capturing Johannesburg on 31 May and Pretoria on 5 June 1900. For almost two more years the Boers conducted a successful guerrilla campaign against the British, and Kitchener replied by burning down Boer farmsteads and moving Boer civilians into *concentration camps*, where many of them died through disease. The war ended with the Treaty of Vereeniging, 1902, under which the two Boer republics became British colonies. British losses were 8,000 killed and another 13,000 deaths from disease. The war revealed the inefficiency of army organization and the diplomatic isolation of Britain, who was opposed by all the great powers. At home, the war had important effects. Many liberal-minded people were shocked by the concentration camps, and the poor health of many army recruits, which was caused by poverty and bad social conditions. The Liberal party was split, and *Lloyd George* became one of the leaders of the pro-Boer section which was opposed to the war. After the war, the British gave the Boers £3m. to rebuild and restock their farms. (For the background see *South Africa*.)

Bondfield, Margaret (1873–1953), the first woman to become a member of the Cabinet as Minister of Labour under Ramsay MacDonald from 1929 to 1931. She started work as a shop assistant at the age of eleven, became a trade union official in 1898, and a Labour M.P. in 1923.
← NANCY ASTOR

Boom, a sudden increase in a country's prosperity and profits, usually associated with an increase in employment, consumption and production.
SLUMP →

Booth, William (1829–1912), founder of the *Salvation Army*, known as 'General' from 1879. He was born at Snenton, Nottingham, and became a Methodist preacher, but broke away from the Methodists and set up an evangelical mission in the East End of London in the middle of the 1860s. The Salvation Army, with its bands and military-style uniforms and ranks, developed from this work in 1878. In 1890, he exposed the terrible conditions of poverty in which a tenth of the

British people were living in his only book, called 'In Darkest England'. As a result, the public subscribed more than £100,000 to his work among the poor.

Borstals. The first was opened at Borstal, near Rochester, Kent, in 1902 to give youths between sixteen and twenty-one a special 'disciplinary and reformatory treatment'. The main aim was to keep young law-breakers separate from older, hardened criminals, in the hope that this would help in their reformation. Previously, they had been put in ordinary prisons.
← REFORMATORIES

Boulton, Matthew (1728–1809), born Birmingham, hardware and coin manufacturer. In 1762 he moved out of Birmingham to the suburb of Soho two miles away, where about 1,000 workers were employed in his factory. In 1775 he went into partnership with *James Watt* and financed his development of the steam engine. He retired in 1800. (See next entry.)

Boulton and Watt, manufacturing firm of Soho, Birmingham. Between 1775 and 1800, when *Watt*'s original patent expired, the firm produced nearly 500 steam engines. Some were used in blast furnaces in the iron industry, others for pumping water out of mines, but most for driving machinery in factories. The firm also pioneered the use of *gas* lighting, through the work of one of its employees, *William Murdock.* It also supplied the Royal Mint with new coin-making machinery. (See previous entry.)

Bow Street Runners. A small group of detectives formed at Bow Street court, London, in the early 1750s by the magistrate Henry Fielding, the writer, to help in the fight against gangs of criminals in London. The force was developed by his blind half-brother, Sir John Fielding, who succeeded him as magistrate. A foot patrol of sixty-eight men to guard London's streets at night was added in the 1780s, and a horse patrol of sixty men to guard the streets for twenty miles around the capital against highwaymen was formed in 1805. It was the first attempt to create a regular police force in the capital.
METROPOLITAN POLICE ACT, 1829 →

Boxer rising, 1900, by a secret Chinese society, called 'Boxers' by Europeans, against European imperialism in China. Britain, and other powers, wanted an 'open door' policy, so that all Chinese ports were open to trade, and had acquired some ports by force and others by treaty. The Boxers, with the support of the Chinese government, murdered foreign ambassadors, missionaries and traders. A combined force of Europeans and Americans went into China, seized Peking and looted the city. Peace was signed with the Chinese in the following year, but the incident helped to recruit many young Chinese for nationalist movements, and started the reawakening of China in modern times.

← OPIUM WAR

Boy Scouts were formed in 1908 by *Lord Baden-Powell.* The Girl Guides were formed in 1910. There are now about 7m. members in 100 different countries. (See next entry.)

Boys' Brigade, the first uniformed youth movement, formed by William Alexander Smith in Glasgow in 1883 to teach boys religion—and discipline, through drill and other activities. There are now about 150,000 members in Britain. (See previous entry.)

Boycott, Captain Charles Cunningham (1832–97), former army officer, who, as a land agent in County Mayo, Ireland, became one of the most famous victims of the campaigns of the *Irish Land League* in 1880. Because of evictions from his estates, local men refused to work for him and local shopkeepers refused to serve him. The campaign was so successful that he had to be placed under police protection and to leave the country temporarily. 'Boycott' became a new word in the English language.

Boyd-Orr, Lord (1880–1971), expert on nutrition, born at Kilmaurs, Ayrshire. He was educated as a doctor at Glasgow and then started to specialize in research into food and nutrition. His report 'Food, Health and Income', published in 1936, showed that the food of 50 per cent of the population was lacking in sufficient vitamins and protein, which was partly responsible for the large number of cases of rickets and tuberculosis. The *food rationing* scheme during the Second World War, which tried to give a balanced, healthy diet, was largely based on his research. After the war he was appointed the first director-general of the Food and Agricultural Organization of the United Nations. He prepared a scheme for a World Food Board to counter the global shortage of food, but resigned in 1949 because of opposition to his scheme by officials. He was awarded the Nobel peace prize in 1949 and was made a lord in the same year.

Bramah, Joseph (1748–1814), inventor, who patented a hydraulic press in 1795. It was based on the principle that water can be used to exert enormous pressure, which was used later in many other aspects of engineering. He also made a lock, named after him, which was very difficult to pick; a spring-winding machine; and a water closet in 1778.
HENRY MAUDSLAY →

Brassey, Thomas (1805–70), railway builder, born at Buerton, Cheshire, who at one time had a force of 45,000 railway navvies at work in Britain and Europe. He was articled to a land surveyor at sixteen and won his first contract to build a railway between Stafford and Wolverhampton in 1834. He then became contractor for the London–Southampton Railway and for the Great Northern Railway which was built between 1847 and 1851. He built railways in many other parts of the world and died a millionaire.
GEORGE HUDSON →

Breathalyzers. Devices used by the police to test whether motorists appear to have been drinking too heavily. If they have, they are taken to the police station where a more scientific test is made. They were introduced in 1967 in an attempt to reduce the number of road accidents caused by drivers under the influence of drink.
← ZEBRA CROSSINGS: ROAD SAFETY →

Bridgewater Canal. The first entirely man-made, modern canal in Britain, which was opened in 1761. It ran from the Duke of Bridgewater's coal mine at Worsley to Manchester, nearly ten miles away, and was used for transporting coal and other goods in barges pulled by mules or horses. It reduced the price of coal in Manchester from 7*d.* to 3½*d.* a cwt. For the times it was a remarkable feat of engineering. The canal ran for a mile underground into the coal mines; crossed the River Irwell over a bridge built of stone at Barton; and was taken over the marshes near Manchester on an embankment. It was planned by the Duke of Bridgewater, his agent, John Gilbert, and *James Brindley.*
GRAND TRUNK CANAL →

Bright, John (1811–89), radical statesman, the son of a Quaker mill-owner. With *Richard Cobden* he formed the *Anti-Corn-Law League* in 1839. He was elected an M.P. in 1843. In 1868, he was appointed President of the Board of Trade in Gladstone's first ministry, but he had to resign in 1870 because of ill health. During his lifetime he supported many proposals for reform, including the abolition of capital punishment, parliamentary reform, the admission of Jews to parliament, the repealing of the game laws, disestablishment of the Church in Ireland and free trade. But towards the end of his life he opposed Gladstone over the Irish Home Rule question. Bright's opposition to the Crimean war caused Palmerston to call him a 'peace at any price' man. He was one of the leaders of the *Manchester school.*

Brindley, James (1716–72), pioneer canal builder, born near Tunstead, Derbyshire. He worked as a millwright at Leek, Staffordshire, and acquired a great local reputation as an engineer. As a result, the Duke of Bridgewater asked him to build the *Bridgewater Canal, 1761*, the first modern canal in Britain. Brindley also designed the *Grand Trunk Canal*, though it was not completed until five years after his death. For a self-taught man, who never even learnt to spell, his achievements were remarkable. He built 360 miles of canal in all, but many of them took a long, winding route as they followed the contours of the land. In the nineteenth century, *Thomas Telford* and others were employed to widen and straighten Brindley's canals.

British Airways, a merger of British European Airways and the British Overseas Airways Corporation, created in 1973.

British and Foreign School Society, created in 1814 to provide *voluntary schools* for poor children. (See also *Joseph Lancaster.*)

British Broadcasting Corporation (B.B.C.) a public corporation, set up by the government, which took over radio broadcasting from the British Broadcasting Company on 1 January 1927, and started experimental television transmissions in 1929. (See also *Radio and Television.*)

British European Airways, formed as a public corporation in 1946. It ran services to Europe, North Africa and the Middle East and internal air services in the United Kingdom.

← BRITISH OVERSEAS AIRWAYS CORPORATION: BRITISH AIRWAYS →

British North America Act, 1867, united four provinces in Canada—Quebec, Ontario, New Brunswick and Nova Scotia—into a federation, and created the first *dominion.* (For the background see *Canada.*)

British Overseas Airways Corporation (B.O.A.C.) was formed as a public corporation in 1939 to take over Imperial Airways and another company, British Airways. The world's first scheduled jet air service was started to South Africa in 1952 with the Comet I. In 1970, B.O.A.C. had a fleet of fifty-seven planes, all of them jets, for its international routes and it also had *Concordes* on order.

← IMPERIAL AIRWAYS: BRITISH EUROPEAN AIRWAYS →

Broadcasting see **Radio and Television**

Brunel, Isambard Kingdom (1806–59), versatile engineer, born in Portsmouth, Hampshire, son of *Sir Marc Brunel*. He always thought in big terms but many of his creations were commercial failures. Between 1835 and 1846 he built 118 miles of the Great Western Railway and nearly another 1,000 miles of railway lines in all. He used a broad gauge of 7 feet 0¼ inches, which was about 2½ feet wider than *Stephenson*'s gauge, so that trains would be faster and more comfortable. But too many narrow gauge lines had already been built and Stephenson's gauge was made standard throughout England and Scotland in 1846. Brunel's gauge was finally abandoned in 1892. He also built three steamships: the *Great Western*, the second steamship to cross the Atlantic in 1838; the *Great Britain*, one of the first all-iron ships with a screw propeller; and the *Great Eastern*, which was much bigger than any other ship that had ever been built before, but was a commercial failure. He also built the Royal Albert bridge across the Tamar at Saltash and designed the Clifton suspension bridge over the Avon Gorge, which was completed after his death. In addition, he constructed many docks; made improvements to artillery, including a floating gun carriage; and helped his father to build a tunnel under the Thames. (See next entry.)

Brunel, Sir Marc Isambard (1769–1849), engineer, born in Normandy, France. He emigrated to the United States and then came to England in 1799. He designed a mechanical plant for making wooden pulley blocks which was built at Portsmouth dockyard by *Henry Maudslay* between 1801 and 1806. It remained in use until the 1930s and was the first use of *mass production* methods in Britain. In 1825, with the help of his son (see entry above), he started to build a tunnel under the Thames, from Rotherhithe to Wapping, which was completed in 1843. He was knighted in 1841.

Bryant, Sophia (1850–1922), the first woman to become a doctor of science at London University in 1884. In 1895 she succeeded *Frances*

Buss as headmistress of the North London Collegiate School. She retired in 1918.

← ANNE JEMIMA CLOUGH

Buchanan report. An important report called 'Traffic in Towns' made by Professor Colin Buchanan in 1963. He estimated that traffic jams in towns then cost the country £250m. a year.

← MOTORWAYS

Building societies were originally self-help societies formed by groups of skilled workers who saved up enough money to buy land and materials and then started to build houses for members of the society. The earliest society that has been traced first met at the Golden Cross Inn, Birmingham, in 1775. These were all temporary societies which were dissolved when all the members had acquired a home. Modern, permanent building societies were started in about 1840. They borrow money from people and lend it out, at a varying rate of interest, to other people who want to buy or build a home. The building societies are a unique British institution, only to be found in Britain and countries where British people have settled in large numbers. Most houses in Britain are bought through mortgages from the societies. The number of people who want their own home, or are in the process of buying one, increased from just over 10 per cent in 1914, to 26 per cent in 1947, and to 51 per cent in 1973.

Bulgarian massacres, 1875–6. Turkey crushed an uprising in her colony of Bulgaria with great cruelty. This led Russia, as the self-appointed defender of the Christians and the Slavs in the Ottoman (Turkish) empire to declare war against Turkey in 1877. Gladstone's attack on Turkey in his pamphlet, 'The Bulgarian Horrors and the Question of the East', 1876, had aroused British public opinion against the Turks. But Disraeli, the prime minister, continued to support the traditional anti-Russian, and pro-Turkish, foreign policy. When Russian troops threatened Constantinople, he ordered a British fleet through the Dardanelles in support of the Turks. The Russo-Turkish war was ended by the Treaty of San Stefano, 1878, which gave Russia gains in Armenia and created a big, independent Bulgaria, stretching from the Black Sea to the Aegean Sea. Britain feared that Bulgaria would become a Russian satellite, thus giving Russia an outlet through the Aegean Sea to the Mediterranean, where British sea routes might be threatened. The Treaty of San Stefano was modified at the Congress of Berlin, when the size of Bulgaria was greatly reduced.

CONGRESS OF BERLIN →

Burdett, Sir Francis (1770–1844), radical politician, who married Sophia Coutts, daughter of a wealthy banker, in 1793. As M.P. for Westminster from 1807 to 1837, he supported parliamentary reform.
← WILLIAM COBBETT: HENRY HUNT →

Burma. Britain fought three wars against Burma in the nineteenth century to protect its Indian empire. The first, in 1824–6, resulted in the occupation of Arakan, a strip of territory on the west coast; the second, in 1852, gave the British the port of Rangoon; and after the third war, 1885–6, the rest of Burma was annexed. It was made part of the Indian empire, but was separated from India in 1937 and given limited self-government. During the Second World War it was occupied by the Japanese, but was recaptured by the British in 1945. It became independent in 1948, but did not join the Commonwealth.

Burns, John (1858–1943), born in London. He helped to organize the London docks strike, 1889, and was elected independent Socialist M.P. for Battersea in 1892. Although he had started as a radical, being a member of the *Social Democratic Federation*, he became increasingly moderate with age and reverted to the old *Lib-Lab* tradition of co-operating with the Liberals. In 1906, the Liberal prime minister, Campbell-Bannerman appointed him President of the Local Government Board, and he thus became the first working-class man to enter the Cabinet. He resigned in 1914, in opposition to the First World War, and retired from public life shortly afterwards.

Buss, Francis Mary (1827–94), pioneer of education for girls, who founded the North London Collegiate School in 1850.
DOROTHEA BEALE →

Butler, the Rev. George (1774–1853), headmaster of Harrow, who was the first headmaster to introduce reforms into the inefficient *public schools* in the nineteenth century. Educated at Cambridge, he was a brilliant mathematician and classical scholar and also an excellent swimmer, skater and fencer. He was headmaster of Harrow from 1805 to 1829. His son, the Rev. H. Montagu Butler, was later headmaster of Harrow, and another son, Arthur, was headmaster of another public school, Haileybury.
THE REV. THOMAS ARNOLD →

Butler, Josephine Elizabeth (1828–1906), leader of a nationwide campaign against the White Slave traffic, in which young girls were bought for a few pounds from their parents and shipped abroad to become prostitutes. It was abolished by law in 1886.

Butler, Lord (born 1902), Conservative M.P., 1929, held minor offices from 1932 to 1941, when he became Minister of Education and was responsible for the Education Act of 1944, which provided secondary education for all. He was Chancellor of the Exchequer from 1951 to 1956, and Home Secretary from 1957 to 1962. He became Master of Trinity College, Cambridge, in 1965, when he was made a life peer.

Buxton, Sir Thomas (1789–1845), Quaker reformer, born at Earl's Colne, Essex. A brother-in-law of Elizabeth Fry, he supported measures for prison reform as M.P. for Weymouth from 1818 to 1837. He also took an even more active part in the anti-slavery movement and helped to form the Anti-Slavery Society in 1823.
← ELIZABETH FRY: MARY CARPENTER →

Byron, Lord (1788–1824), English poet, supporter of liberal and nationalist movements. He died of fever in 1824 in Missolonghi, Greece, while organizing support for the rebels in the Greek War of Independence. His death helped to increase liberal sympathy in Britain for the Greek rebels.

C

Caledonian Canal. A series of inland waterways connecting lochs in the north of Scotland, which run diagonally from Inverness on the east coast to Corran on the west. It was built by *Thomas Telford* between 1803 and 1823 to enable the small warships and merchant ships of those times to avoid the dangerous journey round the north of Scotland. It is now used mainly by fishing vessels.
← LEEDS–LIVERPOOL CANAL: MANCHESTER SHIP CANAL →

Campaign for Nuclear Disarmament (C.N.D.) was formed in 1958 to persuade the government to renounce atomic weapons, even if other powers did not do so. Its slogan 'Ban the Bomb' and its marches from the atomic centre at Aldermaston, Berkshire, to London every Easter became famous. In 1960 a more extreme section broke away to form the Committee of 100, which practised civil disobedience by sit-downs and other means. The campaign lost its force after the easing of the *cold war* in 1963, but it had a lasting effect in persuading other groups to take *direct action.*

Campbell-Bannerman, Sir Henry (1836–1908), born in Glasgow, Liberal M.P., 1868, Secretary for War, 1886 and 1892–5. He became Liberal leader in 1898. Following Balfour's resignation in 1905, he became prime minister and won a resounding victory at the 1906 elections. He succeeded in reconciling the differences between the pro-war and anti-war Liberal leaders, which had developed in the Boer War, 1899–1902. His government started on a programme of social reform, including the Trade Disputes Act, 1906, which safeguarded union funds against employer's claims for damages caused by strikes, and the introduction of free school meals for poor children in the same year. But other reforms were blocked by the House of Lords. He was forced to resign through ill health in 1908.

← EARL OF ROSEBERY: H. H. ASQUITH →

CANADA. Britain took possession of the off-shore island of Newfoundland, its first colony, in 1583. It gained Quebec, Cape Breton and Prince Edward Island from France at the end of the Seven Years' War, 1756–63. After the American War of Independence, United Empire Loyalists, who had fought for Britain, emigrated north and settled in Nova Scotia, New Brunswick and Ontario. In 1791, French-speaking Quebec (Lower Canada) and Ontario (Upper Canada) were given separate governments. But there were increasing demands in both colonies for more representative government and for a fairer distribution of land, much of which was held by long-established settlers and the Church. Following a rebellion by the discontented in 1837, the Earl of Durham (1792–1840) was sent out to investigate and in 1839 he made his important *Durham report.* As a result the two colonies of Quebec and Ontario were united again in 1840. Seven years later, after Lord Elgin had become Governor-General, they obtained responsible self-government in which Canadian ministers ruled and the Canadian parliament controlled revenue. (Britain retained control over defence, foreign affairs, and treaty-making.) The other Canadian colonies of Nova Scotia, New Brunswick and Newfoundland obtained responsible self-government at about the same time. Under the British North America Act, 1867, four of the provinces—Quebec, Ontario, New Brunswick and Nova Scotia—were united in a federation. This was formed to increase trade and improve communications between themselves; to help ease difficulties over language and religion with the French-speaking, Catholic minority in Quebec; and to provide greater unity against the North American States which had just won the American civil war. The building of the Canadian Pacific Railway between 1880 and 1885 opened up the rest of the country for settlement of the vast prairies and between 1896 and 1914 there were over 2½m. immigrants, many of them British. The other provinces of Canada eventually joined the federation: Newfoundland, which had achieved separate dominion status in 1917, was the last to join in 1949. Canada today is a completely independent country, but still a member of the Commonwealth. It has taken an increasingly independent line in foreign affairs since the end of the Second World War; but it is still economically dominated by the United States; still has trouble with French separatists in Quebec; and with its population of only 20m. or so is still underpopulated. (See also *Oregon dispute.*)

CANALS. The first modern form of transport in the industrial age which made the carrying of goods quicker and cheaper. The first modern canal, the *Bridgewater Canal*, was opened in 1761, and by the end of the eighteenth century there were 3,000 miles of canals, many of which had been built by *James Brindley*, *John Rennie*, and *Thomas Telford.* Few canals were built after 1830, except for the *Manchester Ship Canal*, because of competition from railways, and many canals gradually fell into disuse. Most of the remaining canals were nationalized by the Transport Act, 1947.

Canning, George (1770–1827), moderate Tory who shaped British foreign policy into a pattern which was to have an influence to the end of the nineteenth century. He was born in London and educated at Eton and Christ Church, Oxford. In 1794 he became an M.P. and served under Pitt. After a quarrel with *Castlereagh* in 1809, which ended in a duel, he was out of office until 1816 when he became President of the India Office. In 1822, following Castlereagh's suicide, he was appointed Foreign Secretary by Liverpool and held the post for five years. His main aims were to support liberal and nationalist movements abroad, particularly where it was in Britain's commercial interests to do so, and to avoid permanent commitments which would tie Britain's hands too tightly. For this reason he was even more opposed to the *Congress system*, and the way it had developed, than Castlereagh had been in his last years. He refused to support the other great powers at the Congress of Verona, 1822, who wanted to restore King Ferdinand to the Spanish throne. And he refused to send a representative at all to the Congress of St Petersburg, 1825, after which the Congress system finally ended. He supported the colonies in South America which had broken away from Spanish rule, mainly because they had become such an important market for British exports of textiles. He welcomed the *Monroe doctrine, 1823*, which gave the

former Spanish colonies United States' protection. Canning also opposed Spain, which was threatening the constitutional monarchy in neighbouring Portugal, and sent troops and warships to Portugal's capital, Lisbon. Canning's greatest diplomatic triumph was in the *Greek War of Independence*, which started in 1821 and ended in 1830, after his death. He succeeded in helping the Greeks to achieve their freedom, while preventing Russia, which also supported them, from making any gains for itself. He became prime minister in 1827, following *Liverpool*'s illness. Several leading Tories, including *Wellington* and *Peel* resigned, because of Canning's open sympathy with *Catholic emancipation*. But Canning was already a sick man and died within five months.
← LORD LIVERPOOL: DUKE OF WELLINGTON →

Capital gains tax introduced by the Labour government in 1969 to stop speculators from making large tax-free profits by buying and selling shares etc. Some capital gains are exempt, including those from the sale of private motor cars and houses.

Capital punishment see **Death penalty**

CAPITALISM, in its original form, was a system by which the means of production (i.e. factories etc.), distribution and exchange were owned by a small class of people whose main aim was to take the largest possible profit. Capitalism was encouraged in the nineteenth century by the doctrine of *laissez-faire* and the introduction of the *limited liability company*. But there have been great changes in the present century. Governments have played an increasingly bigger part in economic affairs by means of *taxation, nationalization,* and supporting projects such as Concorde. At the same time, the number of people who own shares in companies has become bigger, and managers—rather than owners—now control many firms.
SOCIALISM →

Cardwell, Edward (1813–86), Liberal statesman who carried out drastic reforms of the army as Secretary for War under Gladstone from 1868 to 1874. He abolished flogging as a punishment in peace time and introduced a short service engagement of six years instead of a minimum of twelve, which encouraged recruiting. He also improved the quality of officers by abolishing the purchase of commissions. Cardwell also introduced county regiments, linked with a particular area, and started the 'linked battalion' system. Under this system, a bat-

talion of recruits was trained at home before it was sent out to relieve another battalion of seasoned soldiers in the same regiment serving abroad. He also gave the troops a new and more efficient breech-loading rifle. All of these reforms were made without any extra cost between 1871 and 1872. They were made necessary by the army inefficiency revealed in the *Crimean War*: a great contrast to the efficiency the Prussian armies had demonstrated in their victories over Austria, 1866, and France, 1870–1. Earlier, he had served in various offices under Peel, Aberdeen and Palmerston, when he was responsible for the final ending of *transportation.* He was made a viscount in 1874.
RICHARD BURDON HALDANE →

Carnegie, Andrew (1835–1919), American philanthropist, born in Dunfermline, Scotland. He emigrated to the United States with his parents in 1848. From his humble beginnings as a worker in a cotton factory, he went on to build up a vast commercial empire based on railways, oil and steel. He devoted some of his fortune to setting up *public libraries* in Britain and the United States.

Carpenter, Mary (1807–77), reformer, born in Exeter. In 1846 she opened a ragged school in Bristol and a *reformatory* in 1852. Her book, 'Juvenile Delinquents', 1853, attracted great attention and resulted in a law being passed which allowed magistrates to send children to reformatories instead of prison.
← SIR THOMAS BUXTON

Carson, Edward (1854–1935), lawyer, born and educated in Dublin, who was Conservative M.P. for Dublin University from 1892 to 1918. He was knighted on becoming Solicitor-General in 1900. In 1913 he formed the *Ulster Volunteer Force* to resist Irish Home Rule under the slogan 'Ulster will fight, and Ulster will be right'. He served in the British coalition government during the First World War and was made a life peer on becoming a Lord of Appeal in 1921.

Cartwright, the Rev. Edmund (1743–1823), brother of the political reformer, *John Cartwright,* and inventor of the power-loom for weaving. His first loom of 1787 was driven by horses, but two years later a steam engine was being used. The first machines were not very satisfactory and by 1813, there were only 2,400 in use. But twenty years later, there were about 100,000 improved machines in use. The machines put thousands of hand-loom weavers out of a job, and many of them were reduced to starvation.
← JOHN KAY

Cartwright, Major John (1740–1824), reformer, elder brother of *Edmund Cartwright*, inventor of the power-loom, born at Marnham, Nottinghamshire. He served in the Navy from 1758 to 1770 and was a major in the militia from 1775 to 1790. He was one of the first men to advocate parliamentary reform and originated the phrase 'one man, one vote'. He started *Hampden clubs* in 1812 to campaign for reform.
WILLIAM COBBETT →

Castlereagh, Viscount (1769–1822), son of the first Marquis of Londonderry, and Foreign Secretary from 1812 to 1822. He was largely responsible for the setting up of the *Congress system* at the end of the Napoleonic wars, in which the great powers had regular talks about maintaining peace—the first time this had ever been attempted. At the first congress at Aix-la-Chapelle in 1818 he urged that occupation armies should be withdrawn from defeated France, and that it should be admitted to future congresses, both of which were done. But he became increasingly disillusioned with the Congress system as other members, particularly Alexander I, Tsar of Russia, and Metternich of Austria, tried to use it to keep despotic monarchies in power. They wanted to crush revolts against monarchs in Spain, Portugal, Naples and Piedmont. Castlereagh was opposed to this and sent only officials, instead of a Minister, to the Congresses of Troppau, 1820, and Laibach, 1821. Castlereagh was not a liberal. He was not opposed to great powers crushing revolts in their own country or even in those within their sphere of influence; but he did not want collective action by the great powers which might have disturbed the *balance of power.* Nevertheless, he remained a firm believer in the peaceful settlement of disputes by talks wherever possible. In 1817–18, he settled the boundary dispute between the British colony of Canada and the United States peacefully. Navies of both sides were withdrawn from the Great Lakes and the 49th parallel became the frontier between the two countries from the Lake of Woods, east of Winnipeg, to the Rocky Mountains. At home, Castlereagh supported *Catholic emancipation* and resigned as Chief Secretary for Ireland when George III refused to grant it in 1801. He was Secretary for War and Colonies from 1805 to 1809, when he resigned again after quarrelling with *George Canning* and fighting a duel with him. He was out of office for three years until he became Foreign Secretary. In the popular mind, he was associated with the introduction of the repressive *Six Acts*, and crowds jeered at his funeral in London, after he had committed suicide in 1822.

'Cat and Mouse Act', 1913, popular name for the Prisoners' Temporary Discharge for Health Act, by which the Liberal government under Asquith hoped to avoid having to forcibly feed *suffragettes* on hunger strike in prison. When their health was in danger through lack of food, they were released on licence, and had to report back to prison again after a fixed period. But the Act simply gave them freedom to resume their struggle for women's votes while they were out of prison. Forcible feeding, which had become a national scandal, had to be resumed.

Catholic Association, a mass movement founded in Ireland by *Daniel O'Connell* in 1823 to campaign for Catholic emancipation, so that Catholics could become M.P.s.

CATHOLIC EMANCIPATION. The centuries-old hostility to Popery and Roman Catholicism disappeared only slowly in the nineteenth century. Roman Catholics—and *nonconformists*—had been excluded from holding public office by the *Test and Corporation Acts*, which were not repealed until 1828. In the following year the *Roman Catholic Relief Act* allowed Catholics to become M.P.s. But the reaction to the *Oxford movement* of 1833–45 showed that there was still great opposition to Catholicism. Roman Catholics were not allowed to hold office in the universities of Oxford, Cambridge and Durham until the *Universities Test Act* of 1871.

ECUMENICAL MOVEMENT →

Cato Street conspiracy, 1820, an ill-planned plot by Arthur Thistlewood (1770–1820), who also led the riots after the second *Spa Fields meeting* of 1816. He planned to assassinate some members of the Tory government of Lord Liverpool, and then to set up a provisional government. One of the conspirators, however, was a government agent. Most of the conspirators were arrested by *Bow Street runners* at one of their meetings in the loft of a building in Cato Street, off the Edgware Road, London. Thistlewood killed one of the runners and escaped with several other plotters, but they were arrested within a few days. At the trial, Thistlewood and four others were sentenced to death, and were hanged and then beheaded by a masked executioner—the traditional punishment for treason, but the last occasion on which it was used. Five other men were sentenced to *transportation*. The government used 'discovery' of the plot, about which it had known all the time, to justify having passed the repressive Six Acts in the previous year.

← SIX ACTS

Cayley, Sir George (1773–1857), English inventor, who first formulated the basic principles of flight on which the modern aeroplane is based. In 1809 he predicted that aeroplanes, flying at 20 to 100 m.p.h., would soon be built, but it was not until 1852 that he succeeded in giving his terrified coachman a short flight in a full-size glider.
WRIGHT BROTHERS →

Censorship. Although there has been no official government censorship of books and other publications since 1695, there have always been other strict controls, particularly over obscene publications. In recent times the laws have been made somewhat less strict. The Obscene Publications Act of 1959 and 1964 made the tendency to 'deprave or corrupt' the main test of obscenity, and allowed literary or other experts to be called in court in defence of a book. The censorship of plays by the Lord Chamberlain was abolished in 1969, but they are still subject to the normal laws of the land. Films have to be licensed by councils or magistrates before they can be shown publicly. They usually rely on the certificate given by the British Board of Film Censors, set up voluntarily by the cinema industry in 1912. The British Broadcasting Corporation and the Independent Broadcasting Authority supervise radio and television broadcasts.

Census. The first official government census of the population was made in 1801 by John Rickman (1771–1840). It gave statistics of the number of people, houses, and the number of families in each parish, and tried, unsuccessfully, to give detailed statistics of occupations. A census has been made every ten years ever since, except in 1941 during the Second World War. The range of questions has been increased and the accuracy of the statistics greatly improved so that the census now provides invaluable information for planners in assessing future needs in housing, transport, education etc. Previously all estimates of the population were guesses.
REGISTRATION OF BIRTHS, MARRIAGES AND DEATHS, 1836 →

Chadwick, Sir Edwin (1800–90), reformer with a passion for efficiency, cleanliness and sanitation, born near Manchester. He was trained as a barrister in London and qualified in 1830, though he never practised. He was largely responsible for the report on which the *Poor Law Amendment Act, 1834*, was based. In 1834, he was appointed secretary to the new Poor Law Commissioners, and his attempts to set up new *workhouses* all over the country, soon made him one of the most hated men among the poor of England. But as secretary to the Poor

Law Commissioners, he used his position to write two important reports which drew public attention to the insanitary conditions in which the mass of people had to live. His *Report on Sanitary Conditions, 1842*, exposed the lack of sanitation and adequate water supplies in towns, and in the country. In 1843, his second report on 'The Practice of Interment in Towns' showed that old, overcrowded, insanitary church burial yards were one of the main causes of ill-health and pollution of water supplies in towns. He recommended that new cemeteries should be opened instead, outside the centres of cities. Chadwick lost his job in 1847 when the Poor Law Commission was abolished, following a scandal at Andover workhouse, where starving inmates had been forced to gnaw at old bones just to keep alive. In the following year he was made a member of the new General Board of Health, set up by the *Public Health Act, 1848*, in an attempt to improve sanitation throughout the country. But it, too, had its powers severely restricted in 1854 and was finally abolished in 1858, mainly because Chadwick made so many enemies by his domineering manner. He was a man of great energy and efficiency, who believed firmly in centralized control, long before it became fashionable. The main passion of his life was sanitation and he continued to work for its improvement until his death. He presided over the congress of the Sanitary Institute held in 1878, and was president of the Association of Sanitary Inspectors. His work was greatly influenced by the views of *Jeremy Bentham.* He was knighted a year before he died.

Chamberlain, Joseph (1836–1914), politician who split the Liberal party, allied with the Conservatives, and then split that party, too. A wealthy Birmingham screw manufacturer, he was Lord Mayor of the city from 1873 to 1876 and carried out many reforms and much slum clearance. He was elected Liberal M.P. for Birmingham in 1876 and built up an efficient party machine in the city which was copied in other parts of the country. He was President of the Board of Trade under Gladstone from 1880 to 1885. He helped to win the 1885 elections for the Liberals with his radical 'unauthorized programme' which called for free education, smallholdings with 'three acres and a cow' and other reforms. But in 1886 he broke with Gladstone over *Irish Home Rule.* Chamberlain and ninety-two other Liberals, who wanted to maintain the union between Britain and Ireland, voted against the first Irish Home Rule Bill, 1886, and brought the government down. The Liberal Unionists, as they were known, allied with the Conservatives and in 1895 Chamberlain was appointed Colonial Secretary under Salisbury. His influence in the Conservative party became as great as it had been in the Liberal party. He supported a policy of imperialism and expansion in Africa, and was probably involved to a certain extent in the *Jameson raid* of 1895 designed to overthrow the Boer government in the Transvaal, South Africa. He continued to serve as Colonial Secretary when Balfour succeeded Salisbury in 1902, but resigned in 1903 to campaign for *tariff reform*—import duties on foreign goods. This campaign split the Conservative party and in 1906 it suffered an overwhelming defeat at the elections. Chamberlain became seriously ill in that year and took no further active part in politics.

Chamberlain, Neville (1869–1940), son of Joseph Chamberlain, elected to Birmingham Council in 1911, and Lord Mayor from 1915 to 1916. In 1918 he was elected Conservative M.P. for Birmingham. He was Minister of Health from 1924 to 1929 and by the Local Government Act of 1929 abolished *Boards of Guardians* and transferred their powers to the county authorities. From 1931 to 1937 he was Chancellor of the Exchequer in the *National Government*, first under Ramsay MacDonald and then under Baldwin. He ended free trade by the *Import Duties Act, 1932*, bringing about the tariff reform that his father had campaigned for unsuccessfully thirty years before. He also introduced *imperial preference*, but it came too late to save Britain from her economic troubles in the *depression*. More important than either of these measures was his conversion of the War Loan (over £2,000m. of savings) from an interest of 5 per cent to 3½ per cent, which not only saved money on interest payments, but also helped to bring down interest rates in general, thus encouraging some house building and expansion in new industries. When Baldwin retired in 1937, Chamberlain succeeded him as prime minister. Although he had little knowledge of foreign affairs, Chamberlain believed he could solve international tensions by direct talks with Hitler. He thought that he had obtained lasting peace by the *Munich agreement* of 1938, but he had merely delayed Hitler's ambitions for a few months. Chamberlain, who was particularly associated with the policy of *appeasement*, remained prime minister after the Second World War broke out in 1939. He resigned after the failure of the Norway campaign in 1940 and was succeeded by Churchill. Chamberlain continued in office as Lord President of the Council, but died before the end of the year.
← STANLEY BALDWIN: WINSTON CHURCHILL →

Charge of the Light Brigade. The famous cavalry charge during the *Crimean War* which illustrated the bravery of British soldiers and the incompetence of their leaders. During the Battle of Balaklava, 1854, the

Light Brigade, the 17th Hussars, were sent up a long valley to charge the Russian artillery because of a misunderstanding over instructions. Of the 600 or so cavalrymen, a third were killed or wounded. One of the French allies commented: 'It was magnificent, but it is not war.'

Charlotte Dundas. The first successful British steamboat built by *William Symington,* which was tried out on the Forth and Clyde canal in 1802. It was 56 feet long and had a paddle wheel at the stern. It towed two other loaded boats a distance of $19\frac{1}{2}$ miles in 6 hours.
COMET →

CHARTISM. A radical campaign for *parliamentary reform,* based on the People's Charter, compiled by *William Lovett* and published in 1838. Its six main demands were: votes for all men; the secret ballot; equal electoral districts; abolition of property qualifications for M.P.s; payment of M.P.s; and annual general elections.

The movement was split from the start. The working-class supporters in London wanted the Charter as a first step to other social reforms. The middle-class Chartists of the Midlands, like *Thomas Attwood,* hoped that a reformed parliament would support their proposals for currency reform. And the workers in the north, the most violent group, were mainly concerned with changing industrial conditions.

A mass petition for the Charter which weighed 6 cwt. and had been signed by $1\frac{1}{4}$ million people was presented to the Commons on 12 July 1839, by Attwood, but it was rejected by 235 votes to 46. The National Convention in London, which had organized the presentation of the petition, had threatened to call a 'National Holiday' or general strike if the petition was rejected. But many of the Chartist leaders had already been thrown into prison, and there were disagreements among the supporters. The biggest demonstration was at Newport, Monmouthshire, where Chartists marched on the prison to release one of their imprisoned leaders, Henry Vincent, on 4 November 1839. Troops opened fire and twenty-four Chartists were killed and forty wounded. The rising gave the Government a reason for arresting many other Chartist leaders.

A second petition, with 3 million signatures, was presented in May 1842, but it was also rejected. A third petition, said to contain $5\frac{1}{2}$ million signatures, was presented in April 1848, but was again rejected. Plans had been made for a huge procession to march from Kennington to Westminster with the petition. The Government was alarmed and called in troops, under the Duke of Wellington, to protect the capital. But when the Chartist leader, *Feargus O'Connor,* was told that the march would be resisted, he called it off and presented the petition himself. It was later found that it contained less than 2 million signatures, some of them duplicates and others facetious, like 'the Duke of Wellington', and 'Queen Victoria'. Although the Chartist movement collapsed after that, all but one of its aims—for annual parliaments—were finally achieved.

Chimney Sweep boys had to climb up chimneys to clean them, sometimes while the fire was still burning. A number died through suffocation—at least twenty-three between 1840 and 1860. Lord Shaftesbury was responsible for introducing Bills to stop their employment in 1840 and 1864, but they were evaded. The practice was not stopped until chimney sweeps were made to obtain an annual licence from the police under an Act of 1875.

Chindits, a combined brigade of British and Gurkha soldiers who penetrated deeply into Japanese-held Burma in 1942 to 1943 during the Second World War and carried out many acts of sabotage. They were commanded by General Orde Charles Wingate (1903–44).

Church of England, the *established church*, was shaken out of its complacency in the eighteenth century by the growth of *Methodism* and the new band of *Evangelicals* within the Church itself. It had little contact with the people in the rapidly growing industrial towns of the north, where the Methodists made many converts in the late eighteenth and early nineteenth centuries. The Church tried to regain contact with the people through *Sunday schools* and *voluntary schools.* In 1818, parliament gave the Church of England £1m. to build new churches and another £500,000 six years later. In 1843, the Church was allowed to borrow money from the government to pay the salaries of new clergymen for industrial towns. As a result of these measures, and contributions from wealthy members of the congregations, over 1,700 new churches were built in England and Wales, and another 7,000 rebuilt or restored, between 1840 and 1876. But this failed to attract many of the working classes to church. Usually only about a third of the seats were 'free' for anyone to use, while the rest were reserved for more wealthy members of the congregation. (This also happened in many *nonconformist* chapels.) But the Church of England retained its hold over the respectable middle classes until at least the 1880s, when church-going started to decline.

Churchill, Lord Randolph (1849–94), third son of the 6th Duke of

Marlborough, elected a Conservative M.P. in 1874. In 1880 he tried to form a Fourth party of Conservatives to support a policy of Tory democracy and reform, but got little support. In 1886 he was made Chancellor of the Exchequer by Salisbury, but resigned within a few months in opposition to increased spending on defence. Salisbury, strengthened by the accession of the *Liberal Unionists*, was able to ignore his protest. Churchill became ill shortly afterwards and took no further active part in politics. His wife was American and Sir Winston Churchill was his son.

Churchill, Sir Winston (1874–1965) statesman, soldier, historian, painter, who came into his own as prime minister during the Second World War. He was born at Blenheim Palace, the son of *Lord Randolph Churchill*, and was educated at Harrow and Sandhurst. He joined the Army in 1895 and was on active service in India and the Sudan. During the Boer War, 1899–1902, he acted as a war correspondent for the 'Morning Post' and was captured by the Boers in 1900 but soon escaped. He entered politics as a Conservative M.P. for Oldham in 1900, but became a Liberal in opposition to Joseph Chamberlain's programme of *tariff reform*. In 1906 he was elected Liberal M.P. for Manchester and was President of the Board of Trade from 1908 to 1910, when he set up labour exchanges and introduced the *Trade Boards Act, 1909*, to stop exploitation of workers in sweated industries. He was Home Secretary from 1910 to 1911 and First Lord of the Admiralty from 1911 to 1915 and was largely responsible for the preparedness of the Royal Navy to fight on the outbreak of the First World War. Churchill, however, was blamed for the failure of the *Gallipoli campaign* and resigned in 1915 to serve as a colonel on the Western Front. He was back in office again as Minister of Munitions under Lloyd George from 1917 to 1919 and as Secretary for War and Air from 1919 to 1921.

Churchill broke with the Liberals and was out of parliament for two years from 1922 until 1924, when he was elected a Conservative M.P. He was Chancellor of the Exchequer under Baldwin from 1924 to 1929. He put Britain back on the *gold standard* in 1925 and helped to defeat the General Strike of 1926, when he edited the government newspaper, the 'British Gazette'. From 1929 to 1939, he was out of office. During the period he was politically isolated, opposing any concessions to demands for greater independence in India; supporting King Edward VIII during the abdication crisis of 1936; and calling for rearmament. Although he had long been an admirer of Mussolini, and at first sympathized with Hitler's nationalist aspirations, he became the main voice warning Britain of the new menace from Germany in the years before the Second World War. He was appointed First Lord of the Admiralty by Neville Chamberlain in 1939. In May 1940, he became prime minister for the first time at the age of sixty-five, after Neville Chamberlain had resigned. His restless energy, his courage, and his unshaken faith in final victory helped to bring Britain victory in the war. But in the elections in July 1945, the Conservatives were overwhelmingly defeated by the Labour party, partly because of the bitter memories that most workers had of Conservative pre-war rule, and partly because of the expectation that change would bring a more just society.

In opposition, Churchill warned the world against the new menace from Russia, just as he had warned Britain of the dangers from Germany in the years before the war. In a speech at Fulton, U.S.A., in March 1946, he spoke of the 'iron curtain' which had descended in Europe. He also pledged his support for a United States of Europe at a speech in Zurich, Switzerland, in September 1946, but this promise was forgotten when he got back into power in 1951. His second ministry saw the start of a boom in consumer spending on cars, television sets, radios etc., which had been delayed by Labour's programme of *austerity* and the building up of the *welfare state.* 'Free enterprise' was encouraged by the denationalization of the iron and steel industry and partial denationalization of road transport and the creation of commercial television in 1954. But the basic economic problems of Britain were not really tackled. Churchill resigned as prime minister in 1955 at the age of eighty, but remained an M.P. until 1964. He was knighted in 1953, refusing to accept any higher honour, and died in 1965.

← NEVILLE CHAMBERLAIN: ANTHONY EDEN →

Cinema. The first public cinema show was given by two French brothers, Louis and Auguste Lumière in a Paris café in 1895. The film-making industry developed rapidly in Europe and the United States and even before the First World War a number of spectacular films, such as 'Queen Elizabeth', 1912, and 'Quo Vadis', 1913, had been made. These were all silent films; sound was added in 1928. The cinema really became a major source of entertainment in the years between the two world wars, when many new cinemas were built all over the country, with admission prices of 6*d.* or so, which most people could afford. It soon became one of the main forms of mass entertainment. The way in which film stars talked, dressed and behaved had a great effect on many young people, who tried to copy them. Cinema attendances reached a peak during the Second World

War, but declined after that, mainly owing to the competition from television. In 1946, there were over 4,700 cinemas with 1,635m. tickets sold during the year, but by 1970 there were only 1,529 cinemas with 193m. tickets sold. Many cinemas have been converted into bingo halls.

Civil disobedience. A method of trying to bring about political change by non-violent means, such as non-payment of rates and taxes, sit-ins etc., adopted usually after constitutional means have failed. It was used by Gandhi in South Africa and India, and by many other groups since, including the Committee of 100 during its campaign for nuclear disarmament in the 1960s and by Catholics in Ulster in the 1960s.

Clapham sect, an important group of *Evangelicals*, who lived at the end of the eighteenth century in what was then the village of Clapham in south London. They were mainly responsible for abolishing the slave trade in the British Empire in 1807 and for other reforms, such as the reduction in the amount of duelling. Most of them were rich men who were more interested in saving souls than in changing the structure of society. They thought that the poor should accept their lot with Christian fortitude. One of the members, *William Wilberforce*, wrote that 'the peace of mind, which Religion offers indiscriminately to all ranks, affords more true satisfaction than all the expensive pleasures that are beyond the poor man's reach'. The sect gained much of its strength from the fact that all the members were influential men, who were either closely connected or related by marriage. In addition to Wilberforce, it included his brother-in-law, James Stephen (1758–1832), a prominent lawyer; Henry Thornton (1760–1815), a banker and M.P. for Southwark from 1782 to 1815, with whom Wilberforce resided at one time; Zachary Macaulay (1768–1838), a wealthy merchant; John Shore (1751–1834), the first Lord Teignmouth, former governor-general of India; and *Thomas Clarkson.*
← EVANGELICALS

Clarkson, Thomas (1760–1846), reformer, born at Wisbech. He was educated at Cambridge, where he won a prize in 1785 for an essay opposing slavery. He devoted the rest of his life to the anti-slavery movement, and claimed that *William Wilberforce* had been given too much credit for his part in bringing about the end of slavery.

Clean Air Act, 1956, provided for control of smoke from factory and domestic chimneys and has helped to cut down *pollution* in towns.

Clippers. Fast sailing ships, first built in the United States in the 1890s, which could sail at up to twenty knots. They were first used in the opium trade to China and then for bringing back the new season's crop of tea from China. Early steamships could not compete with them, but after improvements to the marine steam engine by *Alfred Holt* in the 1860s, steamships gradually took over on these routes. Clippers continued to be used on the Australian and New Zealand routes until the 1890s, taking out emigrants and bringing back wool. The most famous British clipper was the *Cutty Sark.*

Clothes rationing was introduced in 1941 during the Second World War and abolished in 1949.

Clough, Anne Jemima (1820–92), pioneer of education for girls, born in Liverpool, sister of the poet, Arthur Hugh Clough (1819–61). She opened a girl's school in Liverpool in 1841 and another at Ambleside in the Lake District when she moved there in 1852. In 1867 she helped to start the North of England Council for Promoting the Higher Education of Women. She became head of the first hall of residence for women in Cambridge, with five students, in 1871. Nine years later it became Newnham College.

←DOROTHEA BEALE: SOPHIA BRYANT→

COAL MINING. Coal played an essential part in the industrial revolution. It was the fuel for steam engines, which were used not only to drive machinery in factories, and locomotives on railways, but also to pump water out of mines so that deeper pits could be sunk. It was also used for making iron and steel, and for producing gas. The output of coal increased slowly from about $2\frac{1}{2}$m. tons a year at the beginning of the eighteenth century to 11m. tons at the end. Thereafter, it expanded rapidly, until it reached 80m. tons a year by 1860 and a peak of 287m. tons, of which one-third was exported, by 1913. Women and children were banned from working underground by the *Mines Act* of 1842. Production, exports and demand all started to fall after the First World War. Other countries, such as Germany and the United States, were producing cheaper coal from more easily-mined seams with modern coal-cutting machinery, while many British miners were still using picks and shovels. The increase in the numbers of cars and lorries also began to reduce the demand for coal for railway locomotives. During the inter-war years, there were many lock-outs and strikes in the coal industry. The miners, always among the most militant of trade unionists, played a leading part in the *General Strike, 1926.* The mines had been put under government control in both world wars and they were nationalized in 1947 when the National Coal Board was established as a public corporation to run the mines. Increasing mechanization since 1946 has greatly increased output per man, but the total output has declined and many pits have been closed and many miners have lost their jobs. In 1970, output from N.C.B. mines was 133m. tons.

Coalition governments are composed of members of normally opposed political parties who, in Britain, usually only unite in times of war or national emergency. There were coalition governments from 1852 to 1855 under Aberdeen and from 1915 to 1922, under Asquith and then Lloyd George, and from 1940 to 1945 under Churchill.

NATIONAL GOVERNMENT →

Cobbett, William (1763–1835), journalist and politician, born in Farnham, Surrey, the son of a small farmer. He served with the Army in England and Canada from 1784 to 1791, reaching the rank of sergeant-major. After he left the Army he accused three of his former officers of fraud. Fearing that he might be unfairly prosecuted for doing so, he went to the United States, where he made a living by teaching and writing pamphlets, in which he attacked the French revolutionaries and other radicals. He was prosecuted for libel and returned to England. In 1802 he started publishing a newspaper, the 'Weekly Political Register', which he wrote almost single-handed until his death. His views gradually changed and he became one of the leading supporters of parliamentary reform. In 1810 he was imprisoned for two years for denouncing the flogging of some soldiers. He fled to the United States again in 1817, fearing that he might be imprisoned for his views, but returned to England two years later. In 1821 and 1826 he tried unsuccessfully to enter Parliament, but was finally elected an M.P., for Oldham, in 1832, after the First Reform Act had been passed. Although he was inconsistent in his views, he always supported the little man against the Establishment and attacked corruption wherever he found it. But he did not want revolutionary change, only the preservation of the old English rural life of the past. He became a farmer himself and of his many books, the most famous is 'Rural Rides'.

← JOHN CARTWRIGHT: SIR FRANCIS BURDETT →

Cobden, Richard (1804–65), politician, born near Midhurst, Sussex, the son of a farmer. In 1819 he started work for an uncle, first as a clerk and then as a commercial traveller in textiles. With two friends he started his own business in Manchester in 1828 and three years later opened a calico-printing works which became one of the biggest in the country. In a pamphlet, 'England, Ireland and America', published in 1835, he made a plea for *free trade*, which he thought would lead to an age of universal peace. Four years later, with a few other manufacturers, he set up the *Anti-Corn-Law League* to campaign for the repeal of the Corn Law. He argued that repeal would lower the price of bread, making it possible for industrial workers to buy more manufactured goods and other foods. The Corn Law was repealed by Peel in 1846. During the campaign, Cobden had neglected his own business, and in gratitude, other manufacturers subscribed to a special fund for him, which raised £76,760.

He was elected M.P. for Stockport in 1841 and remained in the House of Commons for most of the rest of his life. But his opposition to the *Crimean War* lost him much of his former support; some people called him a traitor. He remained a strong supporter of free trade and succeeded in negotiating a commercial treaty with France in 1860. He was one of the leaders of the *Manchester school.*

Cockerell, Sir Christopher (born 1910), British engineer, who designed the *Hovercraft* in 1954. He was knighted in 1969.

Coke, Thomas (1754–1842), 1st Earl of Leicester. In 1776, he inherited the family estates at Holkham, Norfolk. The poor sandy soil had been used mainly for growing rye. He introduced improved breeds of cattle and sheep, and grew turnips for feeding his stock, and wheat instead of rye, showing other landowners that farming could be made to pay even on poor land. He was a master of publicity. The four-day shows, held on his estate every year, were attended by other wealthy landowners from all over Britain and from abroad. There were sometimes 100 people staying in the house and 700 people for dinner. Exhibitions of sheep-shearing, new machinery and cattle were held and lectures were given on the latest developments in farming. He was M.P. for Norfolk from 1776–1806 and from 1807–32.

← ARTHUR YOUNG

Cold war. A state of constant suspicion and tension between the Communist countries of Eastern Europe, under Russia, and the Western nations led by the United States, which started in 1947, and reached a peak in 1962. It led to the *Berlin airlift, 1948–9*, and the formation of the *North Atlantic Treaty Organization, 1949*. In 1962 the world was brought to the brink of nuclear war when the Americans stopped the Russians setting up missile bases on the island of Cuba, off the coast of Florida, U.S.A. Since then there has been a gradual lessening of the tension between the United States and Russia, and in 1973 after the visit of the Russian leader, Leonid Brezhnev, to President Nixon in the United States, the latter announced that the cold war had ended.

Collective security. A system of trying to maintain international peace in which all nations guarantee the security and independence of other states. It was one of the main principles of the *League of Nations*, but it had no armed forces to impose the collective will upon an aggressor, only ineffective *sanctions*. The United Nations has had armed forces for its peace-keeping operations, but the collective will is still lacking.
← BALANCE OF POWER: APPEASEMENT →

Combination Acts, 1799 and 1800, banned workers from combining together to demand higher pay or shorter hours. It became much easier for employers to break strikes, as the Acts allowed strikers to be tried by the local magistrates instead of being taken to the High Court —a much longer and more expensive method. The Acts were repealed in 1824 after a campaign by *Francis Place* and Joseph Hume (1777–1855), a radical M.P. After a wave of strikes, a further law was passed in 1825 banning violence and intimidation by unions.

Combine harvesters, which cut and thresh the corn and thus reduce the labour needed for harvesting, were introduced into Britain during the Second World War. In 1942, there were 1,000 and in 1968, there were over 66,000.
← TRACTORS

Comet. A 51-foot-long, wooden, paddle steamer built by a Scottish engineer, Henry Bell, which started a regular passenger service on the Clyde in 1812—the first in Europe. It had a speed of just under seven knots.
← CHARLOTTE DUNDAS: ROB ROY →

Comet airliner. The de Havilland jet plane with which *British Overseas Airways Corporation* took the lead in the post-war world, becoming the first airline to operate regular scheduled flights by jet aircraft to South Africa in May 1952. Services were also operated to India and the Far East. But crashes caused by metal fatigue in the pressurized cabins caused the Comets to be withdrawn from service in 1954. Though modified Comets were in operation again by 1958, Britain had by then lost its lead in jet airlines.

Common fields see **Open field system**

Common Market see **European Community**

Commonwealth see **Empire and Commonwealth**

Commonwealth of Australia Act, 1901, united the six colonies in *Australia* into a federation.

Commonwealth Immigrants Act, 1962, controlled immigration of Commonwealth citizens into Britain for the first time. Immigrants were restricted mainly to those who had a work voucher from the Minister of Labour for a particular job, their dependants, and students. In practice, the Act affected mainly coloured immigrants.

COMMUNICATIONS. One of the main features of the modern world is the speed and ease with which people can communicate with others in all parts of the world, and now even in outer space. This has been made possible by improvements in the means of transport and the invention of various electronic devices. In the eighteenth century the only way people could communicate with others at a distance was through letters delivered by personal messengers, post-boys, stage coaches, or sailing ships. The first major improvement in the postal services was the introduction of *mail coaches* by *John Palmer* in 1784. With the growth of *railway* networks, the speed and frequency with which letters were delivered was greatly increased. (After the Liverpool–Manchester line was opened in 1830, there were five deliveries of mail a day between the cities instead of two.) The introduction of the cheaper *penny post* in 1840 encouraged correspondence, both business and personal, and the annual number of letters delivered rose from 75m. in 1838 to 207m. in 1842 and to 642m. in 1864. From 1839, a number of *shipping companies* were given government contracts to carry overseas mail, which had previously been carried by naval frigates and Post Office packets (sailing ships) operating from Falmouth. The first *air mail* service opened in 1911 and after the First World War an Empire air mail scheme was started by *Imperial Airways.*

Meanwhile, inventions in the fields of telegraphy and telephony made it possible for people to communicate with each other instantaneously. The invention of the *electric telegraph* in 1837 by a number of people, including *Sir Charles Wheatstone*, was followed by the invention of the *telephone* by *Alexander Graham Bell* in 1876. The first Atlantic cable was laid by Cyrus West Field using Brunel's *Great Eastern* in 1866, but the development of wireless telegraphy by *Marconi* made it possible to send radio signals across the Atlantic and later to any part of the world without the need of a connecting cable. Television was first demonstrated by *John Logie Baird* in 1926. Since the last war the development of *communication satellites* have made it possible to send not only verbal messages, but also television pictures instantaneously to all parts of the world.

The effects of all these developments have been very considerable. Commerce and business has been speeded up; statesmen can communicate with each other direct, instead of having to rely upon their ambassadors; relatives and friends have been brought closer together; and the whole world has become a smaller place in which each country knows the other's business. Radio and other electronic devices have also helped to increase safety in different means of transport; they have also helped to bring about the age of *mass communications*, which with the electronic industry itself, has become one of the major growth sectors in the post-war world.

Communication satellites. The first satellite, Telstar, was sent into orbit round the earth in 1962, followed three years later by the first satellite for commercial use, Early Bird. Since then, many others have been put into orbit. They have made possible instantaneous television transmissions from many parts of the world and have speeded up international telephone communications.

← SPACE TRAVEL

Communist Party of Great Britain was formed in 1920 mainly by former members of the Social Democratic Federation. It has never attracted as much support as Communist parties in most other West European countries. There have never been more than two Communist M.P.s at one time. The last M.P. lost his seat in 1950, when the Communists put up 100 candidates, all of whom were defeated. Many members left the party after the Russians crushed the Hungarian uprising with great brutality in 1956.

← SOCIAL DEMOCRATIC FEDERATION

Comprehensive schools were first set up by some local education authorities after the *Education Act, 1944*, to provide a wide range of education for children of different abilities in one school. In 1965, the Labour government instructed all local education authorities to prepare plans for comprehensive schools, and since then many new ones have been created. There has often been much local opposition to the merging of grammar schools into new comprehensive schools. Through lack of money, suitable accommodation has sometimes not been provided for the new schools, but some comprehensive schools have provided a wide range of options at different levels for pupils of mixed ability.

Concentration camps were first set up by the British in South Africa during the Boer War, 1899–1902, for Boer civilians whose farmsteads had been burnt down to prevent them from aiding Boer guerrillas. Many thousands of Boer women and children died in the camps before sanitation and hygiene was improved. Bad as these camps were, they were quite different from the concentration camps set up by Hitler in 1933. These were first used to detain political and other prisoners, and during the Second World War they were used for systematically exterminating millions of Jews by gassing them.

Concorde. An Anglo-French supersonic aircraft, which made its maiden flight at Toulouse, France, in March 1969. There has been much controversy about the plane, particularly over its supersonic 'bang', and commercial possibilities, and in 1973 two big American airlines decided not to take up their options on the Concorde immediately. It has cost over £1,000m. to develop and employs, directly or indirectly, over 100,000 workers in Britain.

← JET PLANES

Conference of Algeciras, 1906, held in Spain to settle differences which had arisen between Germany and France over *Morocco.*

Congress of Berlin, 1878. An international conference which reduced some of the gains Russia had made by the Treaty of San Stefano at the end of the Russo-Turkish war of 1877–8. The main change was a big reduction in the size of Bulgaria so that it no longer had an outlet to the Aegean Sea. Britain feared that Bulgaria might become a Russian satellite, and thus give Russia an outlet through the Aegean Sea to the Mediterranean, where vital British sea routes might be threatened. The northern part of Bulgaria remained independent; other parts were handed back to Turkey; and a new province of Eastern Roumelia was created, which was under Turkish rule, but had

a Christian governor. Britain obtained the right to occupy Cyprus, the Mediterranean island dominating the Middle East. Austria-Hungary was given the right to occupy Bosnia-Herzegovina (now part of Yugoslavia). The congress appeared to be a diplomatic triumph for Bismarck, the German Chancellor, 'the honest broker' who had arranged it, and for Disraeli, the British prime minister. He had made big changes to the Treaty of San Stefano without going to war; he had checked possible Russian expansion; and he had added Cyprus to the Empire. But the long-term benefits were not so great. Cyprus proved less valuable as a military and naval base after British troops occupied Egypt in 1882; Bulgaria and Eastern Roumelia united in 1885; and Austria-Hungary annexed Bosnia-Herzegovina in 1908, which was one of the links in the chain of events leading to the *First World War*.
← BULGARIAN MASSACRES

Congress system, 1818–25. The first attempt to maintain peace by periodic meetings of the great powers—Britain, Austria, Prussia and Russia. France, defeated in the Napoleonic wars, was also admitted at the first congress held at Aix-la-Chapelle in 1818. There were further congresses at Troppau, 1820; Laibach, 1821; and Verona, 1822. *Castlereagh*, the British Foreign Secretary, became increasingly disillusioned with the system, as other members, particularly Russia and Austria, tried to use it to crush revolts in Europe. *Canning*, who succeeded Castlereagh in 1822, was opposed to the system. He refused to attend a congress held at St Petersburg, in 1825, when the system finally broke up. By that time, too, disagreements had developed between the other members.
← QUADRUPLE ALLIANCE, 1815

Conservative party developed from the Tory party in 1833 after the passing of the First Reform Act. *Peel* revived the party's fortunes by accepting a policy of moderate reform in his *Tamworth manifesto* of 1834 and by setting up a central party organization. Peel was prime minister from 1841 to 1846, when the party was split over the *Repeal of the Corn Law*. They were out of power apart from short ministries until Disraeli became prime minister in 1874. Two years earlier in speeches at the Free Trade Hall, Manchester, and Crystal Palace, Sydenham, he had given the Conservatives a new policy and philosophy: the upholding of the constitution; respect for the Royal Family; support for property as the foundation of independence; practical social reforms, particularly in sanitation; and support of the Empire. After the first Irish Home Rule Bill, 1886, members of the Liberal party, led by *Joseph Chamberlain*, who wanted Ireland to remain part of the United Kingdom, allied with the Conservatives. Later, they formally merged with them when the party became known as the Conservative and Unionist party.

The party was split again in 1903 over the question of tariffs. Joseph Chamberlain wanted *imperial preference* and *tariff reform*, which would have put duties on imported goods, except those from the Commonwealth. But the manufacturers in the Conservative party were dedicated to free trade. The Conservatives suffered an overwhelming defeat by the Liberals in the 1906 elections and were out of office until the First World War, when they became members of the coalition governments. They got back into power in 1922, and apart from short Labour ministries, were in power until 1945—either alone, or as the strongest party in the *National government* and the coalition government during the Second World War. They were in power again from 1951 to 1964 and again from 1970.

← TORY

Conscription was introduced in the First World War in January 1916, and abolished in 1920. It was reintroduced in June, 1939, just before the outbreak of the Second World War. Compulsory military service continued during the cold war. The last National Servicemen, most of whom had served for two years, left the Forces in 1963. Britain was in 1973 one of the few countries not to have conscription.

Conspiracy and Protection of Property Act, 1875, passed by the Conservatives, made peaceful picketing in strikes legal again. It also removed the threat of prosecution for conspiracy against workers who took part in strikes, unless the acts they committed were illegal in themselves.

← CRIMINAL LAW AMENDMENT ACT, 1871

Consumer Council was set up by the government in 1963 to protect consumers against poor workmanship, false advertising etc. It was abolished in 1971.

Container ships. A new way of transporting goods by sea, developed in the 1950s, in which cargo is carried in large pre-packed containers. It saves time in loading and unloading cargo at the docks as the containers can be taken direct to their destinations by road or rail. By 1975 it is planned to have over 160 specially-built container ships in operation.

Containment. The Western policy, originated by the United States after the start of the *cold war*, of surrounding Communist Russia and China by a ring of military alliances—the *North Atlantic Treaty Organization* (NATO), 1949; the South-East Asia Treaty Organization (SEATO), 1954; and the Baghdad Pact, 1955, renamed the Central Treaty Organization (CENTO) in 1959, in the Middle East. SEATO and CENTO, which have no large standing forces, have always been somewhat ineffectual. Britain is a member of all three alliances.
← APPEASEMENT

Convention of Bloemfontein, 1854, under which Britain recognized the independence of the Boers in the Orange river territories. (For the background see *South Africa.*)

Convention of Pretoria, 1881, under which Britain granted the Transvaal self-government after its victory in the first Boer war of that year. (For the background see *South Africa.*)

Co-operative movement started with *Robert Owen*'s schemes for villages of co-operation, where people would live and work in common. In the 1820s and 1830s many co-operative societies were set up to make or to sell goods, but all of them failed. In October 1844, seven handloom weavers set up the Rochdale Society of Equitable Pioneers and in the following December, joined by twenty-one other members, they opened their first shop in Toad Lane, Rochdale. They sold goods to members at about the normal price, but divided up the profit and gave members a rebate, or dividend, once a quarter. Part of the profits were later used for educational and social purposes. By 1851, there were about 130 similar co-operative stores, and by 1875, there were well over 1,000, with a total membership of over 400,000. The Co-operative Wholesale Society was set up in Manchester in 1863, first to buy goods for the shops to sell, and then from 1873 to manufacture them. The Co-operative party was set up in 1917 to sponsor M.P.s, who sat with the Labour party. In 1946, it was agreed that they should be known as Co-operative and Labour candidates.

Copyholders. Farm tenants who originally held a copy of the agreement to rent their land, which had been inscribed in the manorial court roll. As many of their descendants no longer had a copy of the agreement, or held their land only for a fixed number of years, they were easy to evict when landlords passed *Enclosure Acts.*

Corn Law, 1815, tried to maintain the prosperity that farmers had gained in the Napoleonic wars by keeping the price of wheat high. Foreign grain could be imported only when the price of home-grown wheat was more than 80*s*. a quarter. But the law did not have the intended effect. Farmers did not benefit as much as they had hoped, because bread was so dear that people could not afford to buy other food that farmers produced. The law was one of the main causes of social unrest. The new manufacturing classes were also opposed to it, as they wanted cheap food so that they could keep wages low. A sliding scale was introduced in 1828, under which duties on foreign corn were lowered as the price of British wheat rose. There were no duties after the price of home-grown wheat reached 74*s*. a quarter.
ANTI-CORN-LAW LEAGUE →

Corn Production Act, 1917, gave farmers a guaranteed minimum price for the first time to encourage them to grow more corn. Many merchant ships bringing in food had been sunk in the German submarine campaign, which started in March 1917. The Act was repealed in 1921.
WHEAT ACT, 1917 →

Corresponding societies were set up by working men, mainly artisans, to campaign for parliamentary reform towards the end of the eighteenth century. The first, the London Corresponding Society, was formed by a bootmaker, Thomas Hardy (1752–1832) in 1792. The societies, which issued pamphlets and kept in touch with each other, had a great influence among radicals. They were banned by the Corresponding Act, 1799.
HAMPDEN CLUBS →

Cort, Henry (1740–1800), who introduced a new process of making wrought iron at his works in Fareham, Hampshire, in 1784. Previously, workmen had had to keep on hammering and heating the pig iron which was produced in the furnace, to get rid of all the carbon which made the iron too brittle to be used for wrought iron. Cort put the pig iron into a special kind of furnace (a reverberatory furnace) where the iron was melted but did not come into contact with the coke or coal so that no more carbon was added to it. Then workmen stirred or 'puddled' the iron with long bars so that all parts of it were exposed to the heat, burning out the carbon. The 'puddler' then formed the iron into balls or 'blooms', which were taken out of the furnace with a pair of long tongs. They were then passed, while still red-hot, between grooved rollers so that the iron came out in the shape of bars. 'Puddling' was fifteen times quicker than the old process, and helped to give Britain a great lead over other countries in the production of wrought iron, which was the main metal used in making machinery before steel was produced in large quantities. A similar method had probably been used earlier by Peter Onions, a foreman at a Welsh ironworks, and by the Cranage brothers at *Darby*'s Coalbrookdale works, but it was Cort who really developed the process.

County and Borough Police Act, 1856, made it compulsory for all counties to set up police forces and appointed three Inspectors of Constabulary to check on their efficiency. By then many boroughs had set up police forces under the *Municipal Corporations Reform Act, 1835*.
← METROPOLITAN POLICE ACT, 1829: POLICE ACT, 1919 →

County Clare election, 1828, was won by Daniel O'Connell and led to the passing of the *Roman Catholic Relief Act, 1829*.

'Coupon election' held by Lloyd George in December 1918, in which Conservative and Liberal candidates who supported the wartime coalition government were given a letter of support signed by Lloyd George and Bonar Law, the Conservative leader. Asquith, the former Liberal prime minister, denounced the letters as a 'coupon', but the coalition gained an overwhelming victory, and continued in office until 1922.

Crimean War, 1854–6. A war which could probably have been avoided, or settled much more quickly by military means or negotiations once it had started. But Britain feared that if it did not prop up the Turkish Empire, the Russians might take it over and gain an outlet to the Mediterranean, where Britain's sea routes would be threatened. The immediate cause was Russia's claim to protect the Christians in the Turkish Empire. In 1853, the Russians invaded Moldavia and Wallachia (which united as Rumania shortly after the war). Turkey declared war against Russia, and Britain and France sent warships into the Black Sea as a warning to Russia. After Russia had destroyed a squadron of Turkish warships off Sinope, the capital of a Turkish island in the Black Sea, Britain and France declared war on Russia in 1854. Russia withdrew from Moldavia and Wallachia, and the war might have been ended at that stage. But the government of Lord Aberdeen was divided and British public opinion was by then extremely hostile to Russia. The British and the French landed in the Crimea and attacked Sebastopol, Russia's naval base in the Black Sea. If they had followed up their initial successes they could probably have taken the city, but they hesitated and the chance was lost. The city was besieged for a year, with cholera and the cold winters killing more Allied soldiers than Russian bullets did. The war revealed the astonishing incompetence of the British army in strategy, supplies and care of the sick and wounded, which was exposed by the 'Times' under *John Delane.* These reports led to *Florence Nightingale* being sent out to the British military hospitals at Scutari, a suburb of Constantinople. Further incompetence—in the giving of orders—was revealed during the Battle of Balaklava, October 1854, which led to the famous *Charge of the Light Brigade.* Parliament demanded an inquiry into the conduct of the war and *Aberdeen* was replaced by *Palmerston* as prime minister in 1855. Sebastopol was captured in August of that year and the war ended in 1856. As a result, the Black Sea was neutralized, though Russia re-established a fleet there during the Franco-Prussian War of 1870, and Moldavia and Wallachia united as Rumania in 1862. The Turkish empire had, however, been propped up to become a new source of friction in the future.

Criminal Justice Act, 1948, allowed courts to put people on *probation* for a much wider range of offences, instead of sending them to prison.
← PROBATION: CRIMINAL JUSTICE ACT, 1967 →

Criminal Justice Act, 1967, allows courts to give suspended prison sentences, which are not put into effect unless the convicted person commits another serious offence within a specified period. (See previous entry.)

Criminal Law Amendment Act, 1871, passed by the Liberals, made picketing and intimidation in strikes illegal. It followed a number of cases in which blacklegs, who had refused to join strikes, had been injured or killed by fellow workers.
← TRADE UNION ACT, 1871: CONSPIRACY AND PROTECTION OF PROPERTY ACT, 1875 →

Cripps, Sir Stafford (1899–1952), brilliant left-wing lawyer, ambassador to Moscow from 1940 to 1942, and Minister of Aircraft Production, from 1942 to 1945. He made a wartime mission to India but failed to secure Indian leaders' agreement on terms for self-government. As Chancellor of the Exchequer under Attlee from 1947 to 1950 he introduced the policy of *austerity.* He resigned in 1950 because of ill health.

Crompton, Samuel (1753–1827), born Bolton, Lancashire, who invented the spinning 'mule' in 1779. It was called a mule because it combined the advantages of two other inventions, *Hargreaves*'s spinning jenny and *Arkwright*'s spinning frame. It produced a thread which was not only strong but was also fine enough to be used for making the finest cotton cloths, like muslin. At first, it was used by workers at home, but larger models were soon installed in factories, where they were driven by water or steam power. Crompton was unable to patent it, because Arkwright still had a patent for his spinning frame. In 1812, the House of Commons gave Crompton a grant of £5,000.
← SIR RICHARD ARKWRIGHT: RICHARD ROBERTS →

Cross, Viscount (1823–1914), Conservative, who as Home Secretary under Disraeli from 1874 to 1880 carried through major social reforms, including the *Public Health Act*, the *Artisans and Labourers Dwellings Improvement Act*, and the *Conspiracy and Protection of Property Act*, which legalized peaceful picketing. They were all passed in 1875. He was made a viscount in 1886.

Curie, Marie (1867–1934), born in Warsaw, Poland, and **Pierre** (1859–1906), born in Paris, France, brilliant scientists who were married in 1895 and worked as a husband and wife team. In 1898 they discovered the highly radioactive element of radium, which with *X-rays*, has been used in the treatment of some cancers.
← WILHELM KONRAD VON RÖNTGEN

Curragh incident, 1914, showed the support of some British army officers for Ulstermen who were prepared to fight to remain part of the United Kingdom. Fifty-seven officers of the Third Cavalry Brigade, stationed at headquarters in Curragh, Dublin, said they would resign their commissions rather than impose Home rule on Ireland. The War Office gave them written assurances that they would not be asked to do so, partly because it wished to avoid any trouble in the Army on the eve of the First World War.

CURRENCY. The *gold standard* was suspended during the Napoleonic wars, but Britain went back on it again in 1816. This meant that the £ had a fixed value and that banks were obliged to change notes for gold sovereigns. The sovereign (which was then worth £1) became the main coin, or unit of currency, in 1817, in place of the gold guinea (which was then worth £1 1*s*.). Private and joint-stock banks could issue their own bank notes, but this was restricted by the *Bank Charter*

Act, 1844, so that Bank of England and Treasury notes gradually became the only legal ones. At the beginning of the First World War, the gold standard was suspended and no new gold coins have been issued since, except for collectors. Treasury notes were abolished in 1928. The £ was equivalent to 20 shillings or 240 pennies. The main coins were half-crowns (2*s.* 6*d.*); florin, or two shillings (2*s.*); one shilling (1*s.*); sixpence (6*d.*); threepence (3*d.*); penny (1*d.*); halfpenny (½*d*); and the farthing (¼*d.*). The farthing went out of circulation in 1961. In 1971 the coinage was decimalized, when the £ became equivalent to 100*p*.

Cutty Sark. A 963-ton *clipper*, launched at Dumbarton on the Clyde in 1869, for use in the tea trade from China. It was sold to the Portuguese in 1895 and is now on display at Greenwich.

D

D Day, 6 June 1944, when Allied troops landed on the beaches of Normandy, France, to liberate Europe during the *Second World War*. An immense force had been built up of 4,000 assault craft, 13,000 planes, and an army of 3½m. men. On the first day, over 150,000 men were put ashore. The supreme commander was *General Eisenhower*, and *General Montgomery* was operational commander of all troops until 1 September. After fierce fighting Cherbourg was taken on 27 June and Caen was captured by the British and Canadians on 9 July. Paris was liberated on 25 August and Brussels on 3 September 1944.

Daimler, Gottlieb (1834–1900), pioneer German motor-car manufacturer. As a young man he worked in *Whitworth*'s factory in Manchester and then returned to Germany. In 1885 he built a vehicle driven by a petrol engine, and soon started producing motor-cars. A Daimler Motor Company was founded in England in 1896.
← KARL BENZ: JOHN BOYD DUNLOP →

Dalton, John (1776–1844), chemist, who established the principle of atomic weight, born at Eaglesfield, Cumberland, the son of a handloom weaver. It had long been known that matter was made up of very small particles, or atoms, but Dalton showed that atoms of the same element are identical in all ways, including weight, and that they combined in whole units (i.e. not halves, quarters etc.). He also made

discoveries about the weather and about colour blindness, from which he himself suffered.
SIR JOSEPH THOMSON →

Dandy horse. The earliest form of bicycle produced at the beginning of the nineteenth century. It had no pedals. The rider sat on a saddle between the two wheels and propelled the machine by kicking his feet against the ground.
VELOCIPEDE →

Darby, Abraham, I, (1677–1717), who revolutionized the iron industry by discovering in 1709 that coke could be used as a fuel for making iron instead of charcoal. Because much wood was needed for ships, furniture and houses, charcoal was becoming scarce. Other ironmasters had tried using coal, but the sulphur in it made the iron too brittle. Darby used coke instead, which has a lower sulphur content. The cast iron which he produced was particularly suitable for making cooking pots, stoves and firebacks, and his works at Coalbrookdale, Shropshire, became one of the most famous in Britain. As a result of his discovery, the iron industry moved away from the wooded areas of south and south-west England to the coal-mining areas of the north of England, Wales and Scotland.
JAMES BEAUMONT NEILSON →

Darby, Abraham, III, (1750–1791), grandson of the above, who with *John Wilkinson*, built the first cast-iron bridge across the River Severn in 1779.

Darwin, Charles Robert (1809–92), scientist who put forward a theory of evolution which caused a sensation in the Victorian world. He was born at Shrewsbury and educated at Edinburgh and Cambridge. He was appointed naturalist in the Government discovery ship the 'Beagle' which visited South America and the Pacific from 1831 to 1836. From his discoveries on this voyage and from twenty years of further research, he formed his theory of evolution which was published in 1859 as 'The Origin of Species'. He argued that no two members of the same species of animals are exactly the same, but have minor differences in size, speed, colour, strength etc. There was a continuous struggle for existence in which many would die before they could reach maturity and have offspring. Therefore, those who were best adapted through their minor differences would live and produce others like them. Over the centuries, this would produce new species, such as, for example,

long-necked giraffes, which had been able to reach the food that shorter-necked members of the same species could not reach. The theory of evolution was not new. Darwin's contribution was his emphasis on 'natural selection' and the idea of the 'survival of the fittest'. His theory produced a sensation as most religious people at that time still believed that the story of Adam and Eve was literally true and that man and woman had been created by God in one day. It also had a great effect on attitudes to social questions. Some people saw it as a proof of continuing and inevitable progress, while others saw it as a warning that Nature's law of the survival of the fittest should not be interfered with by introducing reforms. Darwin also wrote many other works on botany, zoology, and geology.
THOMAS HUXLEY →

Davy, Sir Humphry (1778–1829), a scientist, many of whose discoveries were not developed until after his death. He was born at Penzance, Cornwall, the son of a wood carver. While making some experiments in 1798, he breathed in some nitrous oxide, or 'laughing gas', which made him feel happy and then sent him to sleep. He suggested that it might be used to relieve pain in surgical operations, but his suggestion was not followed up at that time. In 1801, he isolated a new metal, potassium, by passing an electric current through potash, and also discovered sodium by similar means. Shortly afterwards he produced an arc light by passing an electric current through two charcoal rods which were nearly touching, but this was not used for lighting by *electricity* until much later. At about the same time as George Stephenson, he also invented a miner's safety lamp which was much more widely used. He was made director of the chemical laboratory at the Royal Institution, London, in 1801, and knighted in 1812.
MICHAEL FARADAY →

De Gaulle, General Charles (1890–1970), French soldier and politician, who went to London after the fall of France in 1940 and built up the Free French forces from Frenchmen who had escaped from France to continue the fight against Hitler. He was president of France from 1945 to 1946 and again from 1958 to 1969, when he successfully opposed Britain's entry into the European Community, largely because it might have destroyed the dominating position he had built up inside the Community.

De Valera, Eamon (born 1882) in New York. He joined the *Irish Volunteers* in 1913 and was commandant in charge of a section of

Dublin during the *Easter Rising, 1916*. He was captured by the Birtish but was released under an amnesty in 1917 and was elected president of *Sinn Fein* in the same year. In 1926, he founded his own party Fianna Fáil, and he was prime minister of the *Irish Free State* (now the Republic of Ireland) from 1932 to 1948. He was elected president in 1959 and retired in 1973.

Death duties see **Estate duties**

Death penalty. It was abolished in Britain in 1965 (except for treason and piracy). At the beginning of the nineteenth century, there were still over 200 offences which could be punished by death. In 1808, *Sir Samuel Romilly* persuaded parliament to abolish capital punishment for picking pockets. In 1832 it was abolished for stealing cattle and in 1833 for housebreaking. Four years later the number of capital offences was reduced to fifteen and in 1861 to four—murder, treason, piracy and setting fire to warships and dockyards. The last public execution took place in 1868, when Daniel Barrett was hanged for his part in blowing up part of the wall at Clerkenwell prison in an attempt to free a *Fenian* prisoner.

Death rate. It has declined greatly in the United Kingdom since the 1840s mainly owing to improvements in *sanitation*, *water supplies*, *food*, *medicine*, and *social services* in general. In 1840, it was 22.9 per 1,000 of the population (England and Wales only); in 1880, 20.3; 1900, 18.4; 1910, 14.0; 1920, 12.9; 1930, 11.7; 1940, 14.4; 1950, 11.8; 1960, 11.5. The number of deaths by natural causes in 1970 was 629,100, of which 161,400 were caused by heart disease, and 131,000 by cancers of various kinds, which were the main fatal diseases. Some diseases, like tuberculosis, which was the main cause of death in 1900, have been virtually eliminated.

DEFENCE. The most important service during the nineteenth century was the *Royal Navy.* It gave Britain security against invasion, protected its overseas possessions, and allowed Britain to dominate many smaller powers by naval bombardments or by sending a gunboat as a threat. The Army, on the other hand, tended to stagnate after its victories in the Napoleonic wars. It was usually successful—in the end—in its actions against native tribesmen, but its general inefficiency was strikingly revealed in the *Crimean War* and in the second *Boer War.* It was completely reformed by *Edward Cardwell* between 1871 and 1872 and further reforms were carried out by *Richard Haldane*, as

Secretary of War from 1905 to 1912. During the First World War, Britain relied upon its regular Army and volunteers until 1916 when conscription was introduced.

The Royal Flying Corps was formed in May 1912 and it expanded greatly during the First World War. At the beginning of the war there were only 200 military aircraft in all, but by the end there were over 3,000 first-line aircraft ready for immediate service and over 20,000 in all. In 1918 it was amalgamated with the Royal Naval Air Force to form the Royal Air Force.

Just before the outbreak of the Second World War conscription was reintroduced. All three services expanded greatly during the war. The strength of the Royal Navy and the Commonwealth navies increased from just over 400 warships in 1939 to nearly 3,500 in 1945. The R.A.F. with its 2,600 aircraft in 1939 grew to 9,200 first-line planes by 1945 with over 1m. British, Commonwealth, and allied officers and airmen. It proved its effectiveness in the *Battle of Britain*, the night air raids on Germany, and support of land forces on all fronts. The numbers in the Army increased from over 200,000 in 1939 to nearly 3m. by 1945 and many branches like the *Eighth Army* and the *Chindits* proved their valour.

There was a fundamental change in British defence policy after the Second World War, when Britain was no longer able to compete with the super powers of the United States and Russia, and had to adopt a more limited role. It has its own nuclear deterrent with its four *Polaris* submarines, but the number of warships has been greatly reduced and many army regiments have been amalgamated. The main defence commitment is to the *North Atlantic Treaty Organization.* Since the end of the war British forces have been almost ceaselessly involved in action, as Britain handed over power to native governments in newly independent countries of the Commonwealth. The strength of the forces in 1972 was Royal Navy and Royal Marines, 83,000; Army, 177,700; Royal Air Force, 111,500. Defence cost nearly £3,000m. in 1972. (See also *First World War*, *Second World War*, and individual wars and generals.)

Delane, John (1817–79), outstanding newspaper editor, born in London, the son of a barrister. He was educated in London and Oxford. At the age of twenty-three he was appointed editor of *The Times*, a post he held for thirty-six years. Under him the paper attained an enormous political influence, which no other British paper has had before or since. It exposed the financial corruption during the railway speculations of the 1840s. The reports by its correspondent, Howard

Russell, on the sufferings of British soldiers during the Crimean War, 1854–6, shocked the country and led to Florence Nightingale being sent out to tend the sick and the wounded. And its outspoken views prevented Britain from assisting Denmark in its war against the Prussians and the Austrians over the Schleswig-Holstein provinces in 1864.
<— JOHN WALTER

Density of population. The United Kingdom is one of the most densely populated countries in the world with 588 people to the square mile in 1968. This was surpassed only by West Germany, 604 to the square mile; Japan, 707; Belgium, 800; and Holland, 977.

Department of Education and Science. Education was supervised from 1839 to 1899 by the Vice-President of the Education Committee of the Privy Council. In 1899 the powers were transferred to the Board of Education, headed by a president, and in 1944 to a Ministry of Education. In 1964 the Ministries of Education, and of Science, were merged to form the present Department of Education and Science.

Depressed areas. Places where *unemployment* is particularly high because of the decline of traditional industries such as mining, shipbuilding and textiles. During the 1930s, Scotland, South Wales, Tyneside and West Cumberland were designated depressed areas and were given small government grants to set up industrial estates to provide new factories. In 1945, the Labour government passed a Distribution of Industry Act which gave greater financial aid to these and similar areas and in 1960 a Local Employment Act gave firms which set up in any areas where employment was particularly high, special government aid. But the problem is still far from solved.

Depression. Periods marked usually by falling profits and prices, rising *unemployment*, and political, industrial and social friction. There were industrial depressions in the 1830s, and 1840s, between 1873 and 1896, and in the 1920s and 1930s. There was an *agricultural depression* from about 1875 to 1895.

Derby, Earl of (1799–1869). He became a Whig M.P. in 1822, supported parliamentary reform, and as Colonial Secretary introduced the Bill to abolish slavery in the British Empire in 1833. He left the Whigs in the following year over the question of Ireland and from 1841 to 1845 served under the Conservative, Peel. As a landowner he supported protection and strongly opposed the Repeal of the Corn Law,

1846. He became leader of the Conservative party after the downfall of Peel and formed short-lived ministries in 1852 and in 1858 to 1859. He became prime minister again in 1866, but resigned in 1868 and was succeeded by Disraeli. He was known as Lord Stanley until he succeeded as the fourteenth earl in 1851.
BENJAMIN DISRAELI →

Devaluation has reduced the value of the £ in relation to other currencies. The £ was devalued in 1949 so that it became worth 2.80 dollars instead of 4.03 dollars. Many other countries devalued at the same time. In 1967 the £ was devalued by just over 14 per cent from 2.80 to 2.40 dollars. And in 1972 it was allowed to float so that it found its natural level in relation to other currencies. Devaluation has the temporary effect of making a country's exports cheaper and its imports dearer.
← GOLD STANDARD

Development areas see **Depressed areas**

Dieppe raid, 1942, was made mainly by Canadian forces to test German defences around the French port of Dieppe during the Second World War. It was a failure, mainly because of bad planning, and over half of the 5,000 Canadian troops were killed or taken prisoner.

Diesel, Rudolph (1858–1913), German engineer, who invented an engine in 1897, which ran on heavy oil instead of petrol. Although the Diesel engine, which is used in lorries, locomotives and motor vessels, is named after him, many changes and developments have been made in modern engines.

Direct action, a method of trying to gain political ends when constitutional means of doing so appear to have failed. Direct action may involve violence, as with the *suffragettes*, or be non-violent, as with *civil disobedience.* Its use has increased greatly in recent years.

DISARMAMENT. The increase in the destructive power of weapons (from Maxim's automatic machine gun in 1899 to the *atom bomb* in 1945) has led to increased efforts by both governments and groups of individuals to control armaments and to limit the horrors of warfare. From 1864 a series of international agreements—the *Geneva Conventions*—have tried to impose 'rules of war'. Attempts were made at the *Hague Conferences* of 1899 and 1907 to stop the arms race, which was one of the causes of the First World War, but without much success. After the war renewed attempts were made to bring about some naval disarmament at the *Washington Conference* of 1921 to 1922 and the *London Naval Conferences* of 1930 and 1936 and these had slightly more success, until *Hitler* came to power in Germany and the Japanese walked out of the London conference. A *Disarmament Conference*, held from 1932 to 1934 in Geneva, failed for similar reasons. Political attempts to limit or prevent war by means of *collective security*, *sanctions*, and *appeasement*, all failed. Ordinary people, however, in most countries, including a considerable proportion even in Germany, had no desire for war: opposition to war was shown in Britain by the *Peace Ballot* of 1935. But mutual fears and suspicions, economic greed, lack of statesmanship, the arms race itself, the weakness of the West, isolationism in the United States, and the aggression of the European dictators and of the ruling class in Japan, brought about the long-drawn-out destruction of the Second World War.

After the war attempts were made by the *United Nations* to secure conventional and nuclear disarmament through the work of the *Disarmament Commission*. Many of the long-established pacifist organizations (in which the *Quakers* have always had a prominent role) continued their attempts to secure disarmament and world peace, joined by new-style organizations like the *Campaign for Nuclear Disarmament*. Unfortunately, no attempts to secure disarmament by either governments or private organizations have been particularly successful yet. In fact, the quantity and power of weapons is now greater than it has ever been, with the development of *hydrogen bombs*, *Polaris missiles*, and in the early 1970s, a laser beam weapon. Although the nuclear deterrent has preserved an uneasy peace in Europe since the end of the war, elsewhere in the world there have been some of the most destructive wars of all times, notably in Vietnam. The one really encouraging feature has been, perhaps, the growing opposition to the idea of war among many ordinary people, and the renewed attempts in the early 1970s to secure some disarmament following the easing of the *cold war*.

Disarmament Commission of the United Nations has had very limited success since it was formed in 1952. It was set up as the result of a merger of two previous U.N. bodies which had dealt with nuclear disarmament and conventional disarmament separately. Originally Russia proposed that conventional armed forces should be reduced by a third, that atomic weapons should be banned, and a control organization for inspecting the changes should be set up later. The West wanted the control organization to be set up first, and also feared that reductions in conventional forces would benefit Russia most, because of the large size of its forces and their nearness to Western Europe. Since then, there have been many proposals and counter-proposals for new methods of aerial inspection and control, non-aggression pacts between the North Atlantic Treaty Organization and the Warsaw Pact countries of Eastern Europe and the creation of atom-free zones in Europe, but with no results so far. After the easing of the *cold war*, a *Test Ban Treaty* was signed in Moscow in 1963 and in the same year the United States and Russia agreed not to put atomic weapons into outer space. In 1972 a convention banning the use of biological weapons of warfare was signed by over ninety nations and in the same year Britain, the United States and Russia agreed not to put nuclear weapons on the seabed, outside a 12-mile zone around their own coastlines. These agreements, however, have failed to halt the growth of enormous nuclear arsenals in the United States and in Russia. Until 1959 the Commission contained only representatives of the major powers and Canada. In 1959, it was renamed the Committee on Disarmament and its membership was expanded to include smaller nations.

Disarmament Conference of 1932 to 1934 held in Geneva under the auspices of the League of Nations. It was attended by sixty nations, but failed to bring about any significant reductions in armaments. After Hitler came to power in 1933 the Germans walked out, and France wanted a system of *collective security* to be set up before it disarmed.

Disestablishment. In the nineteenth century, the special position of the Anglican, or established, Church caused great resentment in Ireland, where the majority of the population was Catholic, and in Wales, where the majority was nonconformist. The Church of Ireland was disestablished by Gladstone in 1869, which came into effect in 1871, and the Church in Wales by the Liberals in 1914, which came into effect after the First World War. Both Churches lost their special position in the State and some of their endowments.
← ESTABLISHED CHURCH

Disraeli, Benjamin (1804–81), man-about-town, novelist, wit and Conservative statesman of Jewish ancestry—the most unusual prime minister of the nineteenth century. He stood for parliament three times before he was elected Tory M.P. for Maidstone in 1837. He was disappointed that Peel did not offer him a post in his government in 1841, and five years later had his revenge when he opposed Peel over the

Repeal of the Corn Law, 1846, and brought the government down shortly afterwards. Disraeli soon became leader of the Conservatives in the Commons. He had brief spells as Chancellor of the Exchequer in 1852 and 1858–9 under Derby. From 1866 to 1868 he held the same post again and as leader of the House of Commons showed great skill in successfully steering the Second Reform Act (the *Representation of the People Act, 1867*) through the House. In February 1868, Derby resigned for health reasons and Disraeli succeeded him as prime minister; but Disraeli was defeated in the elections in the same year when Gladstone came into power.

Disraeli got back into power in 1874 and his second ministry lasted until 1880. In one of his earlier novels 'Sybil', published in 1845 he had criticized the division of the country into 'two nations—the rich and the poor'. To help remedy this, several important measures of social reform were carried through in 1875, including the *Artisans' and Labourers' Dwellings Improvement Act*, the *Sale of Food and Drugs Act*, and the great *Public Health Act.* Peaceful picketing during strikes was legalized by the Conspiracy and Protection of Property Act of 1875.

But Disraeli's main concern was with the Empire and foreign policy. He was responsible for making imperialism an important part of *Conservative party* policy. By the Royal Titles Act, 1876, he made Queen Victoria Empress of India—much to her delight. In 1877, he annexed the Boer province of Transvaal in *South Africa.* He was also personally responsible for borrowing £4m. in 1875 to buy shares for Britain in the *Suez Canal.* His greatest success in foreign policy was at the *Congress of Berlin, 1878*, when he claimed to have achieved 'peace with honour' by checking Russian ambitions and gaining the right for Britain to occupy the island of Cyprus. He was made Earl of Beaconsfield in 1876 and was Queen Victoria's favourite minister. (See also *Conservative party.*)

← EARL OF DERBY: MARQUIS OF SALISBURY →

Divorce. Before 1857 a woman in England and Wales could not obtain a divorce at all, and a man could get one only by special Act of Parliament. The Matrimonial Causes Act, 1857, set up new courts to grant divorces, but they were still difficult to obtain. A man could get one only on the grounds of his wife's adultery, while a woman had to prove not only her husband's adultery but some other cause as well, such as cruelty. In 1923 women were allowed to get a divorce on the ground of adultery alone. In 1937 A. P. (later Sir Alan) Herbert (1890–1971) successfully introduced a private member's Bill which extended the grounds for both men and women to desertion and insanity. From 1971 divorces have been much easier to obtain as the courts now grant them on any grounds which show that there has been an 'irretrievable breakdown' in a marriage. Until fairly recent times, divorce was too expensive for the poor and too shameful for other classes. (In 1890, divorce ended the political career of Parnell, the Irish nationalist leader, and in 1936 it was the cause of the *abdication crisis.*) The number of divorces in Great Britain increased from 801 in 1910 to 3,747 in 1920, to 32,516 in 1950, and to nearly 55,000 in 1969. The proportion of marriages which will end in divorce is now about 10 per cent.

Dole. A contemptuous name for the small assistance payments given to men who had been out of work for long periods in the 1930s. 'Dole' originally meant a miserly gift.

Domagk, Gerhard (1895–1964), German chemist who provided doctors with the first sulphonamide drug in 1936. Later versions have cured thousands of people of pneumonia and other infections.
← SIR FREDERICK BANTING: SIR ALEXANDER FLEMING →

Domestic servants. This was one of the main traditional occupations for women until the Second World War. The number of women in domestic and personal service reached a peak of over 2m. by 1911, when it started to decline, because of the low wages, lack of freedom, and the increase of other jobs for women.

Domestic system of manufacturing goods, particularly textiles, at home. Women and children spun the wool or cotton which was then woven into cloth by a weaver on a hand loom. The system started to die out in textiles with the growth of the factory system at the end of the eighteenth century and had disappeared by about 1830. But it continued much longer for women in many other trades, including glove-making, straw-plaiting, tailoring etc. (See also *Sweated industries.*)
FACTORY SYSTEM →

Dominion. Self-governing member-nations of the Commonwealth which gradually achieved full independence from Britain. The first dominion was Canada, created in 1867, and other 'white' colonies were given a similar status—Australia in 1901 and New Zealand in 1907. South Africa (where the white minority ruled) was a dominion from 1909 to 1961; Newfoundland, from 1917 to 1933; and the Irish

Free State (now the Republic of Ireland) from 1921 to 1948. The status of dominions was defined by the *Imperial Conference, 1926*, and the *Statute of Westminster, 1931*. The term fell into disuse after the Second World War when 'black' colonies started to become independent.

'Don Pacifico' affair, 1850. Following an attack on his home in Athens, Greece, Don Pacifico, a Portuguese-Jewish moneylender claimed £31,000 damages from the Greek government. Palmerston, who was then Foreign Secretary, supported him, because he was technically British having been born in Gibraltar. Palmerston ordered Greek ports to be blockaded and Greek ships seized, to force the Greeks to pay compensation. His action was criticized by many British statesmen, including Gladstone, but Palmerston successfully defended himself in a 5-hour-long speech which ended with the words: 'as the Roman, in the days of old, held himself free from indignity when he could say "Civis Romanus sum"; so also a British subject, in whatever land he may be, shall feel confident that the watchful eye and the strong arm of England, will protect him against injustice and wrong'. The affair represented one of the peaks of Palmerston's 'gun-boat' diplomacy.

Douglas-Home, Sir Alec (born 1903), former 14th Earl of Home, Conservative statesman, who disclaimed his peerage in 1963 and became prime minister for twelve months. It had by then become unacceptable for a prime minister to sit in the House of Lords.

← HAROLD MACMILLAN: EDWARD HEATH →

Dreadnoughts. A new class of British battleship introduced in 1906. (For further details see *Royal Navy*.)

Drinking was one of the main social problems in Victorian industrial towns. Gin palaces opened at seven in the morning and sold gin for 2*d*. a glass. In an attempt to restrict the drinking of gin, beerhouses were set up.

From 1830 any householder in England was allowed to take out a licence from the Customs and Excise to sell beer, without having to get another licence from the magistrates also. But this did not have the intended effect, as people simply drank more beer as well. A heavy duty was put on gin in 1861 and from 1869 all beerhouses had to get a licence from the magistrates. The hours at which public houses could open were restricted by the *Licensing Act, 1872*, which was passed partly through pressure from *temperance societies*. Other restrictions on drinking were introduced later in the century. In 1886 it was made illegal for children under thirteen to drink in public houses. During the First World War, public houses were forced to close during the afternoon to stop war workers spending too much time and money on drink. There are now plans to liberalize drinking again by allowing public houses to stay open longer.

Dunkirk. A Channel port in northern France, from which nearly 350,000 British, French and Belgian soldiers were evacuated to England between 27 May and 4 June 1940, after they had been cut off by the German advance through the Low Countries. Although ceaselessly bombed on the beaches, the majority escaped safely, but they had to leave behind most of their equipment, sometimes even their rifles. A total of 860 ships was used, many of them fishing boats, yachts and pleasure steamers. The name of Dunkirk became a symbol of the British ability to wrest victory out of defeat.

Dunlop, John Boyd (1840–1921), inventor, born at Dreghorn, Ayrshire. He was a veterinary surgeon and moved to Belfast in 1867. Twenty years later, when his small son complained that the solid rubber tyres of his tricycle jolted him about, Dunlop made a pneumatic tyre. He took out a patent in 1888 and his pneumatic tyres were first used on bicycles at a sports meeting at Queen's College, Belfast. The competitors using Dunlop's tyres all won. A company was formed in the same year to manufacture the tyres, but Dunlop sold his patent for a relatively small sum. The pneumatic tyre revolutionized bicycles and cars by making them safer, faster and more comfortable.
← GOTTLIEB DAIMLER: FREDERICK LANCHESTER →

Durham report, 1839. An influential report on Canada which set a pattern for the transformation of other 'white' colonies into self-governing dominions, too. It recommended that Canada should be governed by its own ministers and parliament in internal affairs, and that foreign relations and defence should remain in British hands. The report was made by the Earl of Durham (1792–1840) after he had visited Canada for five months to investigate unrest among British and French-speaking settlers. He was accompanied by Edward Gibbon Wakefield. (See also *Canada*.)

E

E.E.C. see **European Community**

E.F.T.A. see **European Free Trade Association**

East India Company, formed by Royal Charter in 1600 to trade with the Far East. By about 1620 it had been ousted by the Dutch from what is now Indonesia, and it established itself in India. It lost its trading monopoly with India in 1813 and with China in 1834, and was finally abolished in 1858. (See also *India.*)

Easter rising, 1916. A rebellion in Dublin by Irish nationalists against British rule to set up an Irish republic. It was led by *Irish Volunteers,* James Connolly's Citizen's Army of working-class nationalists, and members of *Sinn Fein.* There was heavy street fighting and the rebels seized the General Post Office. They surrendered after a week and fifteen of their leaders, including Connolly, were shot, which outraged Irish feeling.
SINN FEIN →

EASTERN QUESTION dominated British foreign policy during the nineteenth century and led to the only major European war in which Britain was involved—the Crimean War. The problem was caused by the decline of the Turkish, or Ottaman, empire which at the beginning of the century included Albania, Bulgaria, Greece, Crete and what is now Rumania, and most of Yugoslavia, Syria, Palestine and Egypt. As a result of the weakness of Turkey—the 'sick man of Europe'—these subject nations rose in revolt. Britain feared that Russia would use the chance to expand its influence in the area and advance towards Constantinople, and the straits of the Dardanelles and Bosphorus. This would have given the Russian fleet in the Black Sea an outlet to the Mediterranean, where British trading interests and the route to India might have been threatened. Normally Britain supported Turkey as it did against Mehemet Ali in 1839 and in the *Crimean War, 1854–6,* against Russia: the *Greek War of Independence, 1821–30,* was a major exception.

The Eastern question continued to play a leading part in European politics right down to the First World War. After the *Bulgarian massacres* by the Turks in 1875–6, Russia again attacked and defeated Turkey, making gains of territory by the Treaty of San Stefano.

Disraeli succeeded in reversing some of these gains by his diplomatic skill at the *Congress of Berlin, 1878.* The Eastern Question was one of the immediate causes of the *First World War.* By then Turkey had turned to Germany instead of Britain for support and entered the war on the German's side in November 1914. The Turkish empire finally collapsed after the war and a republic was set up in 1923 under Kemal Atatürk (1881–1938), a dictator who tried to modernize and westernize the country.

Ecumenical movement. A world-wide movement to reunite all the Christian churches, which were split in 1054 by the secession of the Eastern Orthodox Church and again in the Reformation. Three of the main *Methodist* churches were reunited in 1932; the World Council of Churches was formed in 1948; and in 1960, Lord Fisher became the first Archbishop of Canterbury to visit the Pope in Rome since the Reformation. But in 1972, the General Synod of the Church of England failed to approve a scheme for Anglican–Methodist unity, which had already been approved by the Methodists.

Eden, Anthony (born 1897), Conservative M.P. for Warwick and Leamington from 1923 to 1957. He resigned as Foreign Secretary in 1938 over a proposed pact with the Italian dictator, Mussolini, but was Foreign Secretary again from 1940 to 1945 and from 1951 to 1955 under Churchill. He became prime minister in 1955 following Churchill's resignation at the age of eighty. He was responsible for Anglo-French intervention during the crisis over the *Suez canal* in 1956 and resigned for health reasons in the following year. He was made the first Earl of Avon in 1961.

← SIR WINSTON CHURCHILL: HAROLD MACMILLAN →

Edison, Thomas Alva (1847–1931), an American, whose many inventions included the incandescent electric lamp and the gramophone.

EDUCATION. In the eighteenth century most people could not read or write. *Grammar schools, public schools,* and the *universities* of Oxford and Cambridge were reserved mainly for the rich or the very bright. Some poorer children were educated at charity schools and other working-class parents, like some Scottish shepherds, clubbed together to pay for a private tutor for their children. But these were exceptions. Most ordinary people who wanted education had to teach themselves, as did some of the pioneers in industry and communications, like *James Brindley* and *Sir Richard Arkwright.*

The first attempt to provide *elementary education* on a national basis was made by the *Sunday school* movement at the end of the eighteenth century. Its aim was just as much to give children a grounding in religion and to make them well-behaved as to teach them to read and write. This kind of education became more widely available with the opening of *voluntary schools*, run by the churches, in the early years of the nineteenth century. Attempts were also made in the first half of the century to reform the long-established institutes of education. Headmasters, like the *Rev. George Butler*, of Harrow, and *Thomas Arnold*, of Rugby, made great changes in the old inefficient public schools, and the universities were reformed by government intervention and the work of some university teachers themselves. Frances Mary Buss, who opened the North London Collegiate School in 1850 and *Dorothea Beale*, who became principal of Cheltenham Ladies' College in 1858 provided educational oppurtunities for some middle-class girls.

But the main feature of education in the last hundred years has been the growth of the State system. Although the State started to give the voluntary societies limited sums of money from 1833, education was provided on the cheap by the use of the *monitorial system*, and then by the *pupil–teacher* system. The State system of education began after the passing of the *Education Act, 1870*, which eventually provided some elementary education for all children. Increased opportunities for *secondary education* were made possible by the *Education Act, 1902*, and secondary education for all by the *Education Act, 1944*, increasingly in recent years in *comprehensive schools*. The *school-leaving* age has been progressively raised; *school fees* have been abolished in State schools; and more and more school-leavers now obtain some form of qualification through the introduction of the Certificate of Secondary Education in 1965. (The General Certificate of Education replaced the old School and Higher Schools Certificate in 1951.)

The State has not only provided formal education but has also given increasing attention to the general needs of children in many other ways, notably with the introduction of *school meals* and the *school medical service*. Although education is supervised by the *Department of Education and Science*, it is run by the local education authorities of councils, and schools and teachers have much more individual freedom in methods and subjects than they do in many other countries. The State also provides large sums of money for the remaining grammar and voluntary schools and for universities and other higher institutes of education.

Since the end of the last war, following the *Robbins report, 1963*, there has been a great expansion of *further education*. Opportunities for adult education, which were started with *mechanics' institutes* (the first opened in 1822), *university extension lectures*, and the *Workers' Educational Association*, have been further expanded by the creation of the *Open University* in 1971.

Education Act, 1870. The first major education Act, which eventually made it possible for all children to receive some full-time *elementary education.* The existing 20,000 *voluntary schools* were not abolished, but were given slightly increased grants. In places where there were insufficient schools, as in many large cities, new school boards, elected by ratepayers, could be set up to build schools, which were paid for partly out of the rates. These Board schools could provide religious instruction so long as it was not 'distinctive of any particular denomination'. *School fees* of a few pence each week were charged, but poorer parents could be excused from paying them. Between 1870 and 1876, over 1,600 Board schools were built. The Act was the work of William Edward Forster. (See next entry.)

Education Act, 1880, made it compulsory for children to go to school. They had to attend from the age of five to ten, when they could be exempted to work as *half-timers* in factories, if they had reached a certain educational standard. (See next entry.)

Education Act, 1902, made it possible for some poorer children to get *secondary education.* School boards were abolished and replaced by new local education authorities, which were allowed to 'supply or aid' secondary education. Many of them did so by building new secondary schools and giving grants to *grammar schools.* From 1907, all secondary schools which received grants from the local education authorities had to reserve 25 to 40 per cent of their places for children from elementary schools, who could attend free of charge. This free-place system allowed some of the brighter children, whose parents were too poor to afford secondary school fees, to receive a secondary education. The Act is often known as *Balfour*'s Act, though a civil servant, Sir Robert Morant (1863–1920), also played a large part in drafting it. (See next entry.)

Education Act, 1918, raised the *school-leaving age* to fourteen and abolished the remaining school fees for elementary education in some voluntary schools. The most important part of the Act, providing for compulsory part-time education for young people of fourteen to eighteen, was never carried out, because of economies in government spending after the First World War. The Act is sometimes known as Fisher's Act, after H. A. L. Fisher (1865–1940), the politician and historian, who was then President of the Board of Education. (See next entry.)

Education Act, 1944, raised the school-leaving age to fifteen and provided free secondary education for all children. The State system was divided into three stages—primary, secondary and *further education.* Most local education authorities used an 11+ examination to decide whether a child should go to a grammar school, a secondary modern school, or a technical school, where one existed. With the introduction of *comprehensive schools* and middle schools, this examination has been abolished in many areas. The Act was designed to give each child an education 'appropriate to his age, aptitude and ability'. It is often known as Butler's Education Act, after *Lord Butler,* who was then Minister of Education.

Edward VIII (1894–1972), who reigned from 20 January to 11 December 1936, but was never crowned, because of his *abdication.*

Edwards, Sir George (1850–1933) founded the National Union of Land Workers in 1906, which still exists as the National Union of Agricultural and Allied Workers. He was Labour M.P. for South Norfolk from 1920 to 1922 and from 1923 to 1924, and was knighted in 1930.
← JOSEPH ARCH

Eighth Army. A famous British Army in the *Second World War* which showed for the first time that the Germans were not unbeatable by its victory at El Alamein in 1942. It was formed in November of the previous year during the North African campaign and *General Montgomery* was appointed its commander in August 1942. After the victory over the German general, Rommel, at El Alamein, it went on with other Allied forces to defeat all the Germans and Italians in North Africa. Some of the Eighth Army then fought in Italy, including the 7th Armoured Brigade—known after their emblem as the 'Desert Rats'. The 'Desert Rats' were withdrawn to take part in the *D day* landings in France.

Eire, the name adopted by southern Ireland in 1937, in place of the *Irish Free State,* after it had declared itself independent of Britain. In 1948, it adopted the name of the Republic of Ireland.

Eisenhower, General Dwight (1890–1969), Supreme Commander of the Allied Forces in Western Europe, 1944–5, who had the difficult task of trying to keep a balance between the strategies and personalities of the British and American generals involved in the fight against Germany. He insisted on an advance on a broad front so that all armies would participate. He was president of the United States, 1953–1961.

Elder, John (1824–69), shipbuilder, who developed the improved compound, or expansion, steam engine in 1854. The steam first entered a small cylinder, where it expanded partially, and drove one piston, and then a second, larger cylinder, where it expanded more and drove a second piston. This made more efficient use of the steam and allowed ships to carry a smaller amount of coal and, therefore, more cargo.
ALFRED HOLT →

Electric telegraph, the first modern means of communication, which allowed messages to be sent almost instantaneously along a wire to a receiving instrument. It was invented by a number of scientists in different countries at about the same time and was patented in Britain by *Sir Charles Wheatstone* and Sir William Fothergill Cooke in 1837. In the following year it was adopted by the Great Western Railway. The telegraph attracted great attention in 1845 when it was used to send a message from Slough to London, saying that a suspected murderer had boarded a train bound for London. He was arrested as he got off. It was installed by other railway companies, and private companies were set up to provide a telegram service for business and urgent personal messages. The telegraph was also used by *Julius Reuter* to provide a service of foreign news for British newspapers, after telegraph cables to the Continent had been laid. It was also used to send the standard *time* from London to cities throughout the country. The telegram service was taken over by the Post Office in 1870.

Electric trains. The first electric train was used on Volk's Railway at Brighton in 1883, and the first section of the London Tube, which opened in 1890, also used them. A small number of surburban lines had been electrified before the First World War, but it was not until the 1930s that Southern Railways (now Southern Region) started to carry out widespread electrification of their system. Since the end of the last war all steam locomotives have been replaced by electric or diesel trains by British Railways.

Electricity. The pioneers of electricity were *Sir Humphry Davy* and his assistant, *Michael Faraday.* At the beginning of the nineteenth century, Sir Humphry succeeded in producing a brilliant bluish-white arc light, by passing an electric current through two charcoal rods which were nearly touching. In 1831, Faraday discovered the principle of the dynamo, which is used to generate electricity. But it was some years before their work was put into effect. In 1858, the South Foreland lighthouse became the first in Britain to use arc lights. They were also used experimentally for street lighting in parts of London between 1878 and 1884. The modern electric lamp was invented independently by an American, Thomas Edison, and *Joseph Swan* in 1878. From the 1880s electricity gradually started to be used for lighting streets and in some well-to-do homes. The invention of the steam turbine by *Sir Charles Parsons* in 1884 allowed abundant supplies of electricity to be produced. The first modern power stations were built at Deptford to supply parts of London in 1889, and at Wallsend, Northumberland, in 1901. Many small power stations were built by councils and private companies and there continued to be chaos in the supply of electricity, with different voltages being used by separate companies in the same towns, until the Central Electricity Board was formed in 1926 to build a national grid. Britain used electricity to drive *trams* from 1895, but lagged far behind the United States and Germany in industrial uses. In 1920, there were still only about 750,000 consumers of electricity. In the years between the two world wars, electricity was more commonly used in factories, on the railways —the Southern Railways started to electrify the main lines in the 1930s—and in the home, where it could be used not only for lighting, heating and cooking, but also for labour-saving devices, such as vacuum cleaners. By 1938 there were nearly 9m. consumers and in 1970 there were 17m.

Elementary education. In the early part of the nineteenth century, elementary education—mainly in reading, writing, arithmetic, and religion—was provided for poor children mainly in *voluntary schools*, *Sunday schools*, and 'dame's schools', which were sometimes run by the local curate. After the *Education Act, 1870*, it was gradually provided for all children in State or voluntary schools. The *school leaving age* was raised by stages from ten to fourteen. Elementary education was abolished by the *Education Act, 1944*, and replaced by primary and *secondary education.*

Emancipation of women see **Women's emancipation**

EMIGRATION. Since the Napoleonic wars more people have emigrated from the British Isles than from any other European country. Between 1815 and 1930 about 24m. people emigrated. The largest number—about 9m., of whom over half were Irish—went to the United States. Another 3m. went to Canada, and the rest to Australia, New Zealand, South Africa and other countries. In the 1820s the government and charitable organizations began making small grants to poor, unemployed people to help them emigrate. In the 1830s *Edward Gibbon Wakefield* started a system of planned emigration to Australia, under which some of the money from the sale of land in the colony was used to help pay the fares of other emigrants. A similar system was later applied in New Zealand. *Gold rushes* induced many people to emigrate, but the main cause in the mid-century was the *Irish famine.* As a result about 2m. Irish people left for North America between 1846 and 1861.

All government-assisted passages were stopped in 1878. By then emigration had become a self-sustaining process with settlers in the United States and in the colonies often paying for their relatives and friends to come out to join them. *Shipping companies* were keen to encourage emigration as it meant more business. From 1887 to the First World War emigration went on at an annual rate of about 300,000. A government free-passage scheme for emigrants to the Dominions was operated for ex-Servicemen between 1919 and 1922, and an assisted-passage scheme for all emigrants from 1922 to 1931. After the Second World War, some of the dominion governments, notably Australia, started their own assisted-passage scheme to attract new British settlers. There is now an annual emigration of British and Commonwealth citizens of about 250,000.

IMMIGRATION →

EMPIRE AND COMMONWEALTH. After the loss of the 13 American colonies, following the American War of Independence, 1775–1783, Britain built up a new empire—the largest there has ever been. It still had settlements and trading stations in *Canada*, Newfoundland, *India*, the Caribbean, and on the West African coast. *Australia* was first developed as a convict settlement, but later attracted free emigrants. The settlement of *New Zealand* led to conflict with the native tribes in the Maori wars. In *South Africa* British settlers came into conflict with the Boers who had already been there for many years. Rhodesia was created by *Cecil Rhodes* after 1890. During the *scramble for Africa*, Britain acquired extensive territories in East and West Africa, occupied Egypt in 1882, and the Sudan by 1898, though not without conflict with the French in the *Fashoda incident*. During the nineteenth century, too, Britain acquired an extensive empire in the Far East. It included Malaya, Singapore, North Borneo (now Sabah), Sarawak, Brunei and Hong Kong, which was taken after the *Opium War* with China. To link this vast empire, which comprised about one-fifth of the total land area of the world, there was the *Empire lifeline* of ports, islands and bases.

The motives for creating the empire were many and varied. They included a desire for new land for *emigration*; markets for manufactured goods; a source of raw materials and the hope of easy profits by finding gold, silver and diamonds. Behind it all was a genuine, if mistaken belief that the British had a divine mission to give the benefits of their rule and civilization to less developed countries, as they did in the abolition of *slavery*. Imperialism, which had been encouraged by Disraeli, reached its peak in the last thirty years of the nineteenth century. By the end of the century, Joseph Chamberlain was advocating a policy of *imperial preference*, which would have strengthened the traditional links with the older white colonies with stronger economic bonds.

But long before this, there had been a counter-tendency for the empire to dissolve. The Durham report, 1839, advocated the grant of internal self-government to Canada, and before the First World War, Canada, Australia, New Zealand and South Africa had all become self-governing dominions. Their status was defined by the *Imperial Conference, 1926*, and the *Statute of Westminster, 1931*. Independence for India was long delayed, but the sub-continent, split into India and Pakistan, became the first coloured country to be granted independence in 1947. *Burma* became independent in 1948. Malaya was given its independence in 1957 and in the same year the Gold Coast and neighbouring territories in West Africa also gained its freedom as the new country of Ghana. Other African countries gained their independence shortly afterwards. Practically all of Britain's former colonies and dominions are now independent members of the Commonwealth, many of them as republics.

Burma never joined the Commonwealth and South Africa left in 1961 over the question of *apartheid*. *Rhodesia* made its own unilateral declaration of independence in 1965. Many Commonwealth organizations still exist and a new Commonwealth secretariat was formed in 1965 to maintain better contacts between members. It is based in London, but the secretary-general is a Canadian. Commonwealth links are less close than they once were and they can be expected to weaken further, following Britain's entry into the European Community in 1973.

Empire lifeline. A chain of ports, islands and bases which gave Britain a secure sea route to her Indian empire and the Far East. It consisted of Gibraltar (acquired in 1713); Malta, 1814; Cyprus, 1878; Egypt, 1882; the Suez Canal (a financial interest acquired in 1875); Aden, 1839; Ceylon, 1802; Singapore, 1819; and Hong Kong, 1841.

Employment exchanges see **Labour exchanges**

Enclosure Acts were private Acts of Parliament which allowed landowners to make compact, unified farms, enclosed by hedges, ditches or fences, out of common and waste land, and land which had been previously split up into separate strips in *open fields*. Local landowners, sometimes just one or two of the wealthiest, presented petitions to parliament for the change to be made. Permission was usually given for a Bill to be introduced, as parliament was then dominated by the landowners. When the Bill was passed, commissioners were appointed to share out the land into compact farms, in the same proportion as the strips of land had been held before. Although most of the commissioners did their work fairly, many of the smaller farmers could not afford the high cost of fencing or hedging, which might be £3 an acre, and were forced to sell out to larger landowners. They also lost their right to graze a cow or pig on the common land, as it was also enclosed.

Between 1730 and 1820 about 3,500 Acts were passed (1730–59, 212 Acts; 1760–89, 1,291; 1790–1820, 2,169). It is estimated that about a quarter of all land suitable for cultivation was enclosed by these Acts; by 1820, only two counties still had more than 5 per cent of their land in open fields. Enclosure had been going on for many centuries by different means and these Acts completed the process. They did not cause a sudden evacuation of the countryside, as more workers were needed to clear the commons, to build fences, and to dig ditches: the number of farm workers went on rising until the middle of the nineteenth century. Those who lost their land suffered greatly, as labourers' wages were very low. The *Speenhamland system* was introduced in 1795 to provide relief for farm workers with low wages. One of the main advocates of enclosures was *Arthur Young*.

← OPEN FIELD SYSTEM

ENTERTAINMENT. During the eighteenth and nineteenth centuries, the rich had many different ways in which to amuse themselves. There were frequent dinners and balls in their large houses; there were many home entertainments, such as musical recitals, plays, charades and *reading*; there were hunting and shooting parties; and they could visit fashionable places in England, such as Bath and the seaside, or go on the Grand Tour of Europe. In addition there were a number of traditional forms of entertainment shared by men of all classes, particularly *drinking*, *gambling*, and 'blood sports', such as cock-fighting, bear-baiting, and pugilism—boxing with bare hands. During the Victorian age, all of these traditional entertainments came under stricter legal controls or were officially abolished, as cock-fighting was in 1849, though it still went on in secret. The Churches and *temperance societies* were largely responsible for stricter legal controls over the hours at which public houses could open. The Lord's Day Observance Society, formed in 1831, was largely responsible for the Victorian Sunday, when shops, public houses and places of entertainment were forced to close for part or the whole of the day. The introduction of *excursion trains* allowed many working-class people to escape from the grim forbidding industrial towns for a day, and by the end of the century *Association football* matches were attracting thousands of spectators every Saturday. During the present century increased *holidays*—and wages—have allowed many more people to have a week or more away from home. The motor-car, particularly since the age of *mass-motoring*, has given ordinary people a freedom of movement they have never had before. In the 1920s and 1930s, the *cinema* became one of the main forms of entertainment in the towns, but it has been replaced for many people by television, which is now the main form of entertainment for all classes of people. In 1971, the British spent almost seventeen hours a week, on average, watching television. The next most popular entertainments for men were gardening, excursions, reading, and visiting friends and relatives, in that order. (See also *mass communications*.)

EPIDEMICS of various diseases, which killed thousands of people, have been common in Britain until recent times. Smallpox was one of the major causes of death in the late eighteenth century, followed closely by typhus fever, and there were many epidemics. The introduction of *vaccination* against smallpox by *Edward Jenner* in 1796–8 helped to control the disease. Vaccination of babies was made compulsory in 1853, but it was not until there was another severe epidemic of the disease in 1871–2, which caused 42,000 deaths in England and Wales, that local authorities tried to ensure that all babies were vaccinated. Typhus, which is transmitted by body lice, flourished in the dirty towns of the eighteenth century and was also very prevalent in the overcrowded slums of the industrial *towns*. With a general improvement in living conditions and greater personal cleanliness made possible by increased *water supplies*, typhus started to disappear in the second half of the nineteenth century.

There were four serious epidemics of Asiatic cholera in Britain in 1831–2, 1848–9, 1854, and 1865–6, which killed an estimated total of 150,000 people in England and Wales, of whom 53,293 died in the second, and most serious, epidemic. Cholera is caused by a bacteria, which is transmitted in water supplies polluted by human sewage. Although the bacteria was not discovered by *Robert Koch* until 1883, the improvements in *water supplies* and *sanitation* from the middle of the nineteenth century prevented any large-scale epidemics after 1866. Typhoid fever is also transmitted by contaminated water supplies. Epidemics of this disease have also disappeared, though there have been isolated cases in modern times including one at Croydon in 1937–8 in which forty-three people died. It can also be carried in polluted milk, but the introduction of pasteurization, following the discoveries of *Louis Pasteur*, prevented milk from being a source of infection, except, again, for isolated cases.

There were a number of big epidemics of influenza in the nineteenth century, including one in 1847–8 and another in 1891–2, in which many people died. In 1918–19 there was an epidemic of influenza which was one of the biggest and most fatal of all times. It also affected practically all other countries in the world. In England and Wales 157,000 people died. There was also a serious epidemic of Asian 'flu' in 1957. Since the end of the last war, there have been four epidemics of polio(myelitis), between 1947 and 1955, but the number of deaths was reduced after the development of an effective vaccine in the 1950s. Although general improvements in *medicine*, living conditions and *public health* have helped to reduce the number of epidemics, it is still not fully understood why some diseases should suddenly acquire a particularly virulent form.

Equal Pay Act, 1970, to prevent discrimination between men and women in wages and conditions of employment, is due to come into force by December 1975.

Established Church is the one recognized by the State as the official Church. In England, it is the Church of England and in Scotland the presbyterian Church of Scotland. The monarch, who must be a member of the Church of England, is officially 'Defender of the Faith'; the archbishops of Canterbury and York and twenty-four bishops sit in the House of Lords; and the Church is not free to change its form of worship, as laid down in the Prayer Book, without parliament's con-

sent. The Church of England became established as a result of the long struggle against Catholic powers and doctrines in earlier centuries. The Church of Scotland was established by the Treaty of Union, 1707, but it has no bishops and is free from parliamentary control, so that its links with the State are not so close.
DISESTABLISHMENT →

Estate duties are charged on the total value of the property and assets left by a person on his death. They were introduced by the Liberals in 1894 to level out differences in wealth. Estates valued at £15,000 or less are now exempt, but after that the rate rises from 25 per cent to 75 per cent—on that part of an estate over £500,000.

European Community of nine West European nations which hopes to establish a complete economic union by 1980 in the hope that this will lead eventually to some form of political union or United States of Europe. It is based on the Treaty of Rome, signed on 25 March 1957, which came into force on 1 January 1958. The original members were Belgium, France, West Germany, Italy, Luxemburg and Holland. The first step was to create a European Economic Community, or Common Market. This involved abolishing tariffs or duties on industrial goods of member nations and establishing a common duty against goods imported from foreign countries. Both were done by 1968. At the same time, a common agricultural policy was created. Under this system the price of food is kept high so that farmers can make a reasonable living. All member countries put the same high duties on imported foods, so that home farmers will not be undercut in price. Some of the money from the duties is used to form more efficient farms by combining smaller peasant holdings into larger units. In addition, there has been integration in many other spheres. There is freedom of movement, so that members of one country can live and work freely within any other country in the Community. A start has been made in achieving a common transport policy—for example in the maximum size of lorries—and a common energy policy. Common trade policies have also been adopted towards East European countries and the Community has negotiated as a whole over trading questions with non-members. It is now planned to move towards a full monetary and economic union, possibly with a single currency. A first step towards harmonizing taxes has been made by the introduction of *Value Added Tax* (V.A.T.) in all member countries.

The European Community was formed in 1967 out of a merger of the Common Market with two other bodies. These were the European

Atomic Energy Community, set up in 1958, by the same six original members, to deal with the production of nuclear power for peaceful purposes; and the European Coal and Steel Community, formed in 1952, to control the marketing and the production of coal and steel in the six countries. The Community is controlled by a number of commissioners (international civil servants) who put forward proposals, based on the original Treaty of Rome. The decisions whether these should be put into effect are taken by the Council of Ministers, one from each country, who have a veto on all important matters. Once a proposal has been accepted it is the task of the commissioners to see that it is put into operation in all the countries. There is also a European parliament, which, however, still has very limited powers.

Britain first applied to enter the Common Market in 1961, but its application was rejected by General de Gaulle, the French president, in 1963, mainly because he feared that Britain might destroy the dominating position he had built up inside the Common Market. Britain applied to join again in 1967, but this was again blocked by de Gaulle and it was not until after his death that Britain finally became a member in 1973. It left the *European Free Trade Association* in the same year. Denmark and Ireland also joined the Community at the same time as Britain.

European Free Trade Association (E.F.T.A.) formed by seven West European states, including Britain, in 1960, to eliminate tariffs, duties and trade restrictions between themselves in industrial goods. Agriculture was excluded. By 1967 all industrial duties had been abolished. The other original members were Austria, Denmark, Norway, Portugal, Sweden and Switzerland. Finland became an associate member in 1961 and Iceland became a full member in 1970. In 1973 Britain and Denmark left the Association and joined the *European Community.* Tariffs and duties on industrial goods between the European Community and the remaining members of E.F.T.A. are to be abolished by 1977.

Evangelicals were the counterparts to the *Methodists* inside the Church of England. They, too, believed in personal salvation through good works, strict standards of conduct, and the importance of reading the Bible. *Lord Shaftesbury* and *William Wilberforce* were both evangelicals.

CLAPHAM SECT →

Excursion trains. The first cheap-fare excursion by train was organ-

ized by Thomas Cook (1808–92) for people from Leicester to attend a *temperance* meeting in Loughborough in 1841. He went on to build up a huge travel and tourist business. Many excursion trains were run for visitors to the *Great Exhibition, 1851*, and after that they became increasingly common and were used by many working-class families to have a cheap day at the seaside.
RAILWAYS ACT, 1844 →

Expectation of life. The average expected length of life has risen very considerably during the present century from 46 for men and 50 for women in 1900 to 68 for men and 74 for women in 1970. This has been brought about mainly by improvements in *medicine*, *public health*, *food*, and the development of the *welfare state.* As a result of this, and the falling birth rate, there is now a much higher proportion of old people in the population. The percentage of people over 60 rose from 7.5 in 1900 to about 14 in 1970, which has resulted in increased demands on housing, hospitals, and social security payments.

F

Fabian Society of middle-class intellectuals, founded in 1884, which has had a profound effect on the development of the *Labour party* as a party of moderate reform. The Fabians believe that socialism can only be achieved gradually by democratic means and not by sudden, or violent, change. The society became famous in 1889 with the publication of a series of tracts. In 1900 it helped to form the Labour Representation Committee, which became the Labour party in 1906. Its members have included many prominent politicians, for example, Harold Wilson, and many intellectuals, such as George Bernard Shaw (1856–1950), the playwright; Herbert George Wells (1866–1946), the novelist and science-fiction writer; and *Beatrice and Sidney Webb.* It still publishes essays which have a considerable influence on the thinking of the Labour party. The name came from the Roman general, Quintus Fabius Maximus, who fought slow, delaying actions against Hannibal.

FACTORY ACTS. Conditions in eighteenth-century factories—mainly cotton mills—were extremely bad. They were usually unhealthy and insanitary; the machinery was unprotected and, therefore, dangerous; and hours of work were long, twelve or more a day, even for small children of seven or eight years of age. The first factory act—

the *Health and Morals of Apprentices Act, 1802*,—was introduced by Sir Robert Peel, whose son became prime minister. It provided that no apprentice should work more than twelve hours a day, but was ineffective as there was no efficient means of inspection. This also applied to the next Factory Act of 1819, which banned the employment of children of under nine years of age in cotton mills. Later Acts were:

Factory Act, 1831, gave a 12-hour day to all factory workers under eighteen, but there was still no efficient means of inspection to see that this was carried out.

Factory Act, 1833. The first effective factory act which provided for four full-time factory inspectors to be appointed. It applied to the textile industry. Night work by workers under eighteen was banned, except in lace factories; the employment of children under nine was prohibited, except in silk factories; the hours of work of children under thirteen were limited to nine a day; and children from nine to eleven years of age (later raised to thirteen) had to have two hours' compulsory education every day. The last clause was often ignored, because of the shortage of schools. It was also often difficult to prove a child's age, before the *Registration of Births, Marriages and Deaths* in 1836.

Factory Act, 1844, applied to all textile factories and provided that women, and young persons between thirteen and eighteen, were not to work more than twelve hours a day. Hours of work for children under thirteen were reduced from nine to six and a half hours a day with three hours' education, but the age at which children could start work was lowered from nine to eight.

Factory Act, 1847, restricted the hours of work for women and young persons in textile factories to ten a day. The supporters of the *ten hours' movement* hoped that this Act would restrict the hours of all workers to ten a day, as the men were unable to do their work without the help of young persons and women. But factory owners made the latter do shift work, so that many men still had to work a 15-hour day or more.

Factory Act, 1850, specified the hours during which women and young persons could work in textile factories to prevent them from doing shift work. They were allowed to work only from 6 a.m. to 6 p.m., with a one-hour meal break. Work finished at 2 p.m. on Saturday. Their hours of work were therefore extended from ten to ten and a half a day, but it was hoped that these changed hours would also now apply to men. But factory owners got round the law by employing children (who were not mentioned in the Act) to do shift work to help the men.

Factory Act, 1853, closed the loophole in the 1850 Act by giving children the same hours of work as women and young persons. All textile workers now had a ten and a half hours' working day.

Factory Acts (Extension) Act, 1864, made special regulations for health and safety in six 'dangerous' industries, including match-making, cartridge-making, and pottery manufacture where there was a danger of lead poisoning. Existing factory acts were made to apply to these industries, which were the first non-textile industries to be covered by law, apart from the *Mines Act, 1842*.

Factory Acts (Extension) Act, 1867, extended existing laws to all factories where more than fifty people were employed.

Factory Act, 1874, reduced working day from ten and a half hours to ten for women and young persons in the textile industry.

Factory and Workshops Act, 1878, divided workshops—where no mechanical power was used—into different categories and made separate regulations for them.

Factory and Workshops (Consolidation) Act, 1891, concentrated on safety and sanitary regulations and raised minimum working age in factories to eleven.

Factory and Workships Act, 1901, raised minimum working age to twelve.

Factories Act, 1937, gave women and young persons a 48-hour week, limited overtime, and made many new regulations on lighting, ventilation, and cleaning.

Factory Act, 1961, the last major consolidating Act, covering safety, conditions of employment etc.

Wages in *sweated industries* were controlled by the *Trade Boards Act* of 1909. (The introduction of the early Acts was due mainly to the work of Lord Shaftesbury, John Fielden, Michael Sadler and Richard Oastler.)

Factory farming. A method of intensive production developed since the end of the Second World War, which has been extensively applied in chicken farming. Many chickens are now kept permanently in small wire cages, or batteries; they are fed and watered and the eggs are collected automatically. Other chickens are reared in large units and slaughtered and made ready for freezing on production lines, before they are sent to shops in plastic bags.

Factory system, in which goods are made by groups of workers using machinery, developed in the nineteenth century. The first British factory was set up in Derby by John and Thomas Lombe between 1717 and 1721; but *Richard Arkwright* was the first man to set up a

large number of cotton mills or factories towards the end of the eighteenth century. He is usually acknowledged as the founder of the factory system, which has profoundly changed the way in which many workers live, and provides vast quantities of cheap goods.
← DOMESTIC SYSTEM

Family Allowances of 5*s*. (25p.) a week were introduced in 1945 for all children except the eldest in a family. In 1970 the allowance was 90p. a week for the second child and £1 for the third or subsequent children. There were over 4m. families receiving the allowances in 1970, which are paid to the mother direct to help ensure that they are spent on the children for whom the money is intended.

Faraday, Michael (1791–1867), scientist, born in London the son of a blacksmith. In 1813, *Sir Humphry Davy* made Faraday his assistant and he succeeded him as professor of chemistry at the Royal Institution, London, in 1833. He made many discoveries, but his most important were the principles of the electric motor and the dynamo. In 1821, he succeeded in making a circle of wire with a current flowing through it rotate around the pole of a magnet, the principle on which the electric motor is based. Ten years later he conducted another experiment in which a metal disc was rotated between the poles of a magnet, and produced an electric current. Using this principle, a Belgian engineer, Théophile Gramme, made the first effective dynamo, which is used to produce electricity, in 1870.
← SIR HUMPHRY DAVY

Farming see **Agriculture**

Fascism, a nationalist, authoritarian, anti-Communist movement founded by *Mussolini* in Italy after the First World War. Fascist movements were founded in many other countries. One was formed in Britain in 1931. The name was derived from the 'fasces'—bundles of rods with an axe in the middle, carried in front of Roman consuls as a symbol of their authority. (See also *Blackshirts*.)

Fashoda incident, 1898. British troops, under Kitchener, had occupied much of the Sudan, including Khartoum. They were marching south to occupy the rest of the country and to secure control of the upper waters of the Nile, when they met French forces at the small town of Fashoda on the Upper Nile. For a time there was great tension between Britain and France, with both countries claiming the region for itself. But after intense diplomatic activity, the French agreed to withdraw and renounced their claim. Britain then set up a joint government with Egypt to rule the Sudan.

Fellow traveller. A term applied to those socialists who are said to be secret sympathizers with, or members of, the Communist party. Fear of fellow travellers was partly responsible for the fall of the Labour government in 1924 following the publication of the *Zinoviev letter*.

Fenians. A secret, revolutionary Irish movement founded in 1858 by James Stephens (1824–1901), a former member of the Young Ireland movement. It had two branches: the Irish Republican Brotherhood in Ireland and the Fenian Brotherhood in the United States, composed of emigrants who had left Ireland following the Irish famine. Its aim was to organize secret 'circles' of revolutionaries in Ireland, who would overthrow British rule by force and set up a republic. A small uprising in Ireland in 1867 was easily crushed by British troops. There were a number of incidents in England at the same time. They included an attempt to seize Chester castle and an attempt to release a Fenian prisoner from Clerkenwell prison, London. Part of the prison wall was blown up and twelve neighbouring residents were killed. (Daniel Barrett, who was sentenced to death for his part in this bomb attack, was the last man to be hanged in public.) The movement's main importance was that it persuaded Gladstone that something must be done about Ireland. It also established the link between Irish emigrants in the United States and nationalist movements in Ireland. Its name came from the féinne, legendary Irish warriors.
← YOUNG IRELAND: IRISH LAND LEAGUE →

Festival of Britain was held in 1951 on the centenary of the much more successful Great Exhibition of 1851. The Festival Hall and Battersea Pleasure Gardens, London, are the main legacies.
← GREAT EXHIBITION

Field, Cyrus West (1819–92), American businessman who used Brunel's steamship, the *Great Eastern*, to lay the first successful transatlantic telegraph cable from Valentia, off the coast of Kerry, to Newfoundland in 1866. It speeded up, and increased commerce, between Britain and North America. He also built the New York elevated railway.
← SAMUEL MORSE

Fielden, John (1784–1849), wealthy cotton manufacturer of Todmorden, Yorkshire, who supported factory reform. As M.P. for Oldham, he introduced the Factory Act of 1847, which is often called

Fielden's Act. He was one of the leaders of the *Ten Hours' Movement.*
← MICHAEL SADLER: RICHARD OASTLER →

Fifth column. Secret, or underground, fighters who try to destroy a state from within. The term originated in the Spanish Civil War, 1936–1939, when the rebel General Franco attacked Madrid with four columns, while the fifth column of his supporters inside the city tried to bring the government down by sabotage and spying.

First Reform Act, 1832. During the first half of the nineteenth century many reformers like *William Cobbett*, *John Cartwright*, and *Henry Hunt* believed that parliamentary reform would open the way to other, much-needed, social reforms. They campaigned for the abolition of *rotten* and *pocket boroughs* and for the extension of the vote to the working classes. In November 1830, when the Whigs came into power, their leader, *Earl Grey*, introduced two Bills which were both defeated. The third Bill was passed in 1832, after a threat to create new peers if the House of Lords continued to reject it. (The same tactic was employed later with the controversial *Parliament Act, 1911*.)

Fifty-six 'rotten boroughs' lost both M.P.s, and thirty lost one M.P. Some of these seats were given to the new industrial towns, which were formerly unrepresented in parliament. The vote was given to all men in boroughs whose property was rated at £10 or more a year. Potwallopers in thirteen boroughs, who could vote if they had their own fireplace where they could cook for themselves, and scot and lot voters in thirty-six boroughs who qualified by paying local taxes, were allowed to continue voting for the rest of their lives. After that, these franchises were abolished. In the counties, the 40*s*. freeholders retained their vote and it was also given to men who held land on a long lease to the value of £10 a year, and to men who rented, or held land on a short lease, to a value of £50 a year. Similar Acts were passed for Scotland and Ireland, but the vote for 40*s*. freeholders in Ireland, which had been abolished in 1829, at the same time as the Roman Catholic Relief Act was passed, was not restored. The Act gave the vote to about 300,000 of the upper middle classes and benefited mainly the new manufacturers. The disappointed working-class radicals turned to a new radical movement, *Chartism*.
REPRESENTATION OF THE PEOPLE ACT, 1867 →

FIRST WORLD WAR, 1914–18. The basic cause was the German desire, as a new nation unified by Bismark only in 1871, to achieve a place in the world equal to that of the long-established powers of Britain and France. It wanted colonies for prestige, emigration and trade; a strong navy to challenge British mastery of the seas; and a dominating position on the mainland of Europe. The situation was made more dangerous by the arms race; the division of Europe into two rival blocs represented by the *Triple Alliance* and the *Triple Entente*; and the crumbling of the Turkish (Ottoman) empire under the forces of nationalism. In 1908, Austria-Hungary annexed Bosnia-Herzegovina, formerly part of the Turkish empire (now part of Yugoslavia). This caused resentment in Serbia, which had wanted to take over the two provinces itself. The Balkans were set alight by the two Balkan Wars of 1912 to 1913. In the first war, Serbia, Bulgaria, Greece and Montenegro defeated Turkey and in the second some of the victors fought over the spoils. On 28 June 1914, the Archduke Franz Ferdinand, heir to the Austro-Hungarian throne, visited Sarajevo, capital of Bosnia, where he was assassinated by a Serbian student. Austria-Hungary declared war on Serbia in July 1914. Russia then mobilized in support of its fellow Slavs in Serbia. Germany declared war on Russia on 1 August 1914, in support of Austria-Hungary, and two days later on France, which had begun to mobilize in support of its ally, Russia. There was still some hope in Britain that it could remain outside the war, as it had no firm, formal obligation to support either France or Russia. But this hope was shattered when Germany invaded Belgium on 3 August 1914. Under a treaty of 1839, Britain, and other great powers, including Prussia, had guaranteed Belgian neutrality. Furthermore, it was a traditional interest of Britain to stop any hostile power from dominating the Low Countries, which could act as a springboard for an invasion of Britain. On 4 August 1914, Britain declared war on Germany. Japan, an ally of Britain, declared war on Germany on 23 August. Italy, which had always been the least enthusiastic member of the Triple Alliance, did not declare war, as France had not attacked Germany. Instead, in May 1915, it entered the war on the Allied side, partly through gratitude for British support in Italian reunification in the nineteenth century. The United States entered the war in April 1917, following German submarine attacks on neutral shipping. After the Bolsheviks came into power in Russia, following the October revolution of 1917, they made a separate peace with the Germans. The main events affecting Britain were:

The Western Front. The initial German advance brought them within a few miles of Paris, but they were beaten back at the Battle of the Marne in September 1914. By the end of the year both sides were established in trenches, which ran from the borders of Switzerland to the English Channel. The trenches were sometimes only a few yards apart, but on average were separated by about 350 yards of 'no-man's-land'—a barren wilderness of barbed wire, mud, shattered trees, and rotting corpses. For nearly four years the armies attacked each other, never gaining more than a few miles, and achieving no decisive results. *General Haig*, who threw his men recklessly into these battles, took over as British commander-in-chief on the Western Front in December 1915. Some of the main battles were: Ypres, 1915, when the Germans used poison gas for the first time; Somme, 1916, when the British suffered 420,000 casualties; Passchendaele, nearly 250,000 British casualties. In 1918, the Germans again broke through to the Marne, but were thrown back, and the Allies then made successful advances. The vast majority of British and Commonwealth casualties in the war—over 1m. killed—occurred on the Western Front. Aeroplanes were used by both sides, first for reconnaissance and then for bombing troops and bases, and tanks were first used by the British in 1916.

War at Sea. The Royal Navy bottled up the German navy in its ports from 1915 and started a successful blockade of Germany, capturing German merchant ships and stopping neutral ships from taking war materials to Germany. The main naval encounter was at the *Battle of Jutland*, in the North Sea, after which the German High Seas Fleet never again ventured out to sea in strength. Instead the Germans relied mainly on submarine attacks. In March 1917, they opened an unrestricted submarine campaign, in which they sank all ships, including neutrals, on sight. This brought the United States into the war against them and caused *food rationing* to be started in Britain. The convoy system helped to reduce Allied shipping losses, but Britain lost nearly 8m. tons of shipping during the war—almost half the total tonnage it had possessed in 1914.

Home Front. The first *air raid* against Britain occurred in 1914; *conscription* was started in 1916 to supplement *Kitchener*'s volunteers; and food rationing began in 1918. Women were increasingly used to replace male workers in factories, which helped the cause of *women's emancipation*. Following a scandal over the shortage of shells and other munitions, Asquith formed a coalition government in 1915, and was replaced as prime minister by *Lloyd George* in the following year.

Middle East. Turkey entered the war on Germany's side in November, 1914. The British failed in their attempt to force a passage through the Dardanelles straits during the *Gallipoli campaign*, 1915–16, but later gained victories over the Turks in other parts of the Middle East, capturing Jerusalem in 1917 and Damascus, Syria, in 1918.

The war ended in 1918 and the total estimated cost for Britain was over £6,000m.

TREATY OF VERSAILLES →

Five freedoms—from want, disease, ignorance, squalor and idleness—which were the aims of the *Beveridge report, 1942.*

Fleming, Sir Alexander (1881–1955), discoverer of penicillin, born at Lochfield, Darvel, Scotland. He was educated as a doctor. In 1928, while working in his laboratory at St. Mary's Hospital, London, he noticed a green mould growing on a tray of bacteria, with which he was working. He found that the fungus killed many kinds of bacteria but was harmless to animals. Just before the Second World War, two Oxford scientists—Sir Howard (later Lord) Florey (1898–1968) and Dr (later Sir) Ernst Chain (born 1906)—succeeded in producing the drug penicillin in a pure form which was suitable for human beings to take. It was manufactured on a large scale in the United States during the Second World War and helped to save the lives of many Allied servicemen, who might otherwise have died of pneumonia and infections of various kinds. Fleming was knighted in 1944.
← GERHARD DOMAGK

Fleming, Sir John (1849–1945), electrical engineer, born in Lancaster and educated at Cambridge. He helped to introduce electricity into Britain in the 1880s. In 1904 he made the first modern valve, which played an important part in the development of radio telephony. He was professor of electrical engineering at London University from 1885 to 1926 and was knighted in 1929.
← G. MARCONI: JOHN BAIRD →

Floating voters, estimated at up to 25 per cent of the total electorate who either abstain or vote for a different party from the one they supported in the previous general election. There are a large number of 'safe' seats, which are won almost invariably by either Labour or Conservative candidates. The floating voters in the more marginal seats are therefore usually the ones who really decide which party gets into power at general elections.

Flying bombs see **V.1**

FOOD. Up to the middle of the nineteenth century, the main food of the working classes was bread, potatoes and weak tea or beer. This was supplemented by the small amounts of sugar, cheese, vegetables, boiling bacon and meat that they could afford to buy or any vegetables they could grow for themselves. The middle classes had a much richer and more varied diet, illustrated in the menus published by *Mrs Beeton.*

They usually had a three- or four-course dinner every day consisting of soup, fish, meat and vegetables, and a pudding.

The food of the working classes started to improve from about the middle of the nineteenth century. Following the *Repeal of the Corn Law* in 1846, and the building of railways in the United States and Canada, cheap wheat started to be exported from the vast prairies of the New World to Britain (and the rest of Europe) in the 1870s. At about the same time the development of the *food canning* industry brought in supplies of cheaper tinned meat from abroad. Better quality meat became available with the introduction of *refrigeration* in 1880. Tinned and refrigerated food—and much later *frozen food*—made it possible to buy out-of-season foods and thus gave people a much greater variety in their diets. The increase in the efficiency of home *agriculture* and improvements in breeds of cattle and sheep also helped to make food more plentiful and nutritious.

The growth of the *co-operative movement* helped to cut the cost of food in the shops and there was even greater competition after the opening of chains of grocery shops by a Glasgow grocer Sir Thomas Lipton (1850–1931) and John James Sainsbury (1844–1928), who opened his first shop in Drury Lane, London, in 1869. There were also stricter controls over the quality of food: the first clean food law—the *Adulteration of Food, Drink and Drugs Act*—being passed in 1872. The discoveries of *Louis Pasteur* made milk a safer drink through the process of pasteurization (named after him). Later advances in the science of nutrition, such as the discovery of vitamins, and the research of *Lord Boyd-Orr* between the two world wars made people far more conscious of the nutritious value of the food they ate.

The introduction of *school meals* by some local authorities from 1906 helped to improve the diet of many neglected children, and improvements in *gas* and *electricity* supplies made it easier for mothers to cook at home. But, because of *unemployment* and low wages many families were still undernourished in 1939. *Food rationing* and higher wages during the Second World War gave the majority of people a much better diet than they had ever had before.

Food canning, which was first tried out experimentally in the Royal Navy in 1813, brought about great changes in people's diet. Previously the only way of preserving meat was by salting it, but in 1870 tinned meat from the United States and Australia started to arrive in Britain. Although it was initially of poor quality, it was about 50 per cent cheaper than fresh meat and was available throughout the year. By 1918, tinned soup, salmon and fruits were also available and by 1939

there was a wide choice of canned foods, which allowed people to have a much more varied diet.
REFRIGERATION →

Food rationing. In the First World War rationing of sugar began on 1 January 1918, and it was soon extended to butter, margarine, jam, tea, bacon and meat. It was introduced mainly because of the success of the extended German U-boat, or submarine, campaign which started in 1917. Rationing was abolished in 1921. It was started again in January 1940, during the Second World War. The system was based on the research into food values by *Sir John* (later Lord) *Boyd-Orr*. The ration varied according to supplies, ranging from ¼ lb. to ½ lb. of bacon per person per week, 2 oz. to 4 oz. of tea; 1 oz. to 8 oz. of cheese; 8 oz. of sugar; and 1*s.* to 2*s.* worth of meat. In 1941, a 'points' rationing system was introduced for other items of food such as tinned fruit and meat and sweets. Some food, like bread, flour, potatoes, fish and fresh vegetables, was never rationed during the war. Restaurants were allowed to serve only 3-course meals and to charge a maximum of 5*s.* British restaurants were set up early in the war, at first only in bombed areas, and later more generally, to provide hot meals for the general public and factory workers for 1*s.* or so. In the economic crisis after the end of the war, food continued to be rationed and bread was also rationed from 1946 to 1948 and potatoes in 1947. All rationing finally ended in 1953. In both world wars, the mass of people were better fed than they had been in the pre-war years, because food was more fairly distributed and full employment gave them money to buy food. As a result the general standard of health was also higher. A Ministry of Food was set up from 1917 to 1921 and again from 1939 to 1954, when it was amalgamated with the Ministry of Agriculture.

Ford, Henry (1863–1947), American motor-car manufacturer, born at Greenfield, Michigan, the son of a farmer. He made motor cars available to millions, instead of being a rich man's luxury, by using *mass production* methods. He produced his first 4-horsepower car in 1896 and in 1903 founded the Ford Motor Company. Five years later he made the first T model car—or 'Tin Lizzie' as it was affectionately known. Between 1908 and 1927, when a new A model car started to be produced, over 15m. 'Tin Lizzies' were sold. He started making Fordson tractors in 1915 and in the 1920s expanded his business greatly by setting up factories in many foreign countries, including Britain. He was a man of immense vision and strong opinions and during the First

World War he led a mission in his 'Peace Ship' to various European capitals in an unsuccessful attempt to stop the war.

← HENRY ROYCE: VISCOUNT NUFFIELD →

FOREIGN POLICY. The main aims of British foreign policy in the nineteenth century were to maintain a *balance of power* in Europe: to safeguard the sea routes and the *Empire lifeline* on which Britain's overseas trade and imperial possessions depended; and to avoid intervention in the internal affairs of other nations, unless Britain's own vital interests were involved, or there was a direct threat to peace. One major fear was that Russia might expand through the Balkans towards the Aegean, thus giving the Black Sea Fleet an outlet into the Mediterranean where British trading and Empire routes might be threatened. The *Eastern Question* therefore played a dominant part in British foreign policy in the nineteenth century and led to the *Crimean War, 1854–6,* the only major European war in which Britain was involved.

After the defeat of Napoleon, *Castlereagh* helped to set up the *Congress system,* the first attempt to maintain peace by international agreement between the major powers; but he had become increasingly disillusioned with the working of the system before his death in 1822, and his successor, *Canning,* finally rejected it. British foreign policy was dominated by *Palmerston* from 1830 to his death in 1865. Although he was quite willing to use the big stick against what he called 'half-civilized' nations like China, he was not a warmonger and was cautious in dealing with other big powers. After the Crimean War, Britain tried to avoid major commitments by relying on the strength of the *Royal Navy,* then the undisputed master of the seas, and by a policy of 'splendid isolation', sometimes falsely attributed to *Salisbury.* But Britain's vast Empire sometimes brought it into conflict with other European powers, notably with France in the *Fashoda incident* of 1898, and also involved it in a long succession of colonial wars in *India, Burma, Afghanistan, South Africa* etc. The military weakness of Britain and its isolation was revealed in the second *Boer War* of 1899–1902, when practically all other countries were opposed to Britain. This opposition and the growing suspicions of German intentions made Britain rearm, with Army reforms being carried out by *Viscount Haldane* and the launching of the first *Dreadnought* in 1906. It also brought about a big change in foreign policy, with a greater willingness to form commitments, symbolized by the *Anglo-Japanese alliance* of 1902, and in Europe the *Anglo-French Entente* of 1904 and the *Anglo-Russian Entente* of 1907.

After the First World War Britain gave support to the *League of Nations* (set up as a result of Woodrow Wilson's *fourteen points*) and a policy of *collective security.* When this failed, a policy of *sanctions* was tried, which was equally unsuccessful, and Britain then adopted a policy of *appeasement* towards the European dictators *Mussolini* and *Hitler*. This also ended in failure—and the Second World War.

After the war the decline in Britain's position as a great power brought about a great change in foreign policy. Britain no longer had the money, strength or authority to act as the world's policeman as it had done during most of the nineteenth century. The change was strikingly illustrated in 1951 when Britain was excluded from the *Anzus pact*, a defence treaty between the United States and two members of the Commonwealth, Australia and New Zealand. The limits of Britain's independent military and diplomatic actions, when they ran counter to American wishes, were manifested in the *Suez* crisis of 1956. For twenty-five years or so, after the Second World War, Britain vainly tried to maintain a special relationship with the United States, leadership of the Commonwealth, and a superior attitude in Europe, but it was no longer strong enough to do so. The world was now dominated by the new super powers of the United States and Russia—and the *cold war*. As a member of the *North Atlantic Treaty Organization*, and one of the strongest members still of the American-led Western alliance, Britain took a big part, particularly in the *Berlin airlift* and the general policy of *containment*. The final acceptance of Britain's new status came with the entry into the *European Community* in 1973, when Britain accepted that it could no longer exist in isolation from its more powerful neighbours in Western Europe.

Forster, William Edward (1818–86), Liberal M.P. for Bradford, 1861 to 1886. He carried the *Education Act, 1870*, and the *Ballot Act, 1872*, through the House of Commons. In 1880 he was appointed Chief Secretary for Ireland but resigned two years later because of Gladstone's *Kilmainham pact* with Parnell. He later opposed *Irish Home Rule*.

Fourteen points. Declaration of peace aims made by Woodrow Wilson (1856–1924), President of the United States, in January 1918, during the First World War. They included the end of secret diplomacy and treaties; freedom of the seas; reduction of trade barriers; arms reductions; 'self-determination' for new countries created out of the former Austro-Hungarian and Ottoman (Turkish) empires; and a new association of nations to guarantee the independence of all states. As a result of the last point, the *League of Nations* was formed, and its

Covenant (constitution) was written into the peace treaties at the end of the First World War, though because of domestic opposition, the United States never became a member.

TREATY OF VERSAILLES →

FREE TRADE. A system in which no duties or tariffs were charged on foreign goods imported into a country, in the hope that other countries would then also reduce or abolish their duties. (This is now usually done by trade agreements between groups of countries.) The purpose is to increase international trade. For most of the nineteenth century, Britain was the leading supporter of free trade. It was the first country to industrialize and did not therefore need duties and tariffs to protect its industries from foreign competition. It also had a surplus of manufactured goods, particularly textiles, for export to its empire and South America in particular. Additionally, it needed to import cheap raw materials so that it could produce manufactured goods at a low cost, and cheap food so that the wages of industrial workers could be kept down. *William Huskisson* started to abolish some duties in the 1820s. This was continued by *Peel*, notably with the Repeal of the Corn Law in 1846, and by *Gladstone* in the 1850s. The peak of the free trade movement in Britain was reached in 1860 when *Richard Cobden* negotiated a commercial treaty with France. Britain abolished all duties on manufactured goods from France and reduced the duties on brandy and wine, while France reduced its duties on many British goods.

Britain remained a supporter of free trade until 1932. But during the depression of 1873 to 1896 many foreign countries, including Germany, France and the United States introduced tariffs to protect their new, growing industries. At the beginning of the present century, *Joseph Chamberlain* campaigned for a policy of tariff reform, but it was not until 1932 that his son Neville Chamberlain successfully introduced the *Import Duties Act*, which ended British free trade, as a result of ever-increasing foreign tariffs, growing unemployment and a world depression. After the Second World War an international attempt was made to return to a free trade policy through the *General Agreement on Tariffs and Trade* (G.A.T.T.) of 1948. In 1958, six West European countries started the Common Market, now the *European Community*, to bring about free trade amongst themselves. But Britain with its links with the Commonwealth and its large imports of cheap food from abroad, preferred to stay outside. Instead it helped to form the *European Free Trade Association*, which allowed cheap food still to be imported. But as Britain's trade with the Commonwealth rose more slowly than its trade with the members of the European Community,

Britain applied to join the Community, and eventually succeeded in doing so in 1973.

Freud, Sigmund (1856–1939), Austrian doctor who founded the science of psychoanalysis by investigating the nature of dreams and of sexual impulses. His discoveries opened up a whole new aspect of man—the unconscious mind.

Friendly societies were formed by skilled workers in the seventeenth and eighteenth centuries to provide members with insurance benefits for sickness, unemployment, old age and death. They were given full legal recognition by the Friendly Societies Act, 1793. Before the repeal of the *Combination Acts* in 1824, they were sometimes used illegally to provide benefits for members during strikes. Trade unions were allowed to register as friendly societies by the *Trade Union Act, 1871.* By 1875, there were nearly 32,000 societies with nearly 4m. members in England and Wales. They were incorporated in the State insurance scheme by the *National Insurance Act, 1911.*

Frozen foods were developed in the United States by Clarence Birdseye (1886–1956). The first commercial packs were being sold in the United States in 1925, but they did not gain great popularity there—or in Britain—until after the Second World War. The increase in the number of working married women has helped to increase sales.
← REFRIGERATION

Fry, Elizabeth (1780–1845), prison reformer and nursing pioneer, born in Norwich, the daughter of a *Quaker* banker, John Gurney. At the age of twenty she married Joseph Fry, a Quaker merchant in London. She had eleven children. In 1813 she paid her first visit to *Newgate prison*, London, and was shocked by the insanitary, ragged state of the women prisoners, who were herded together with their little children into what they called 'The Hell above Ground'. Four years later she formed an Association for the Improvement of Female Prisoners in Newgate. She, and her band of helpers, visited the prison regularly, organizing needlework, knitting and spinning classes for the women prisoners, providing them with clean clothes, and reading the Bible to them. She also visited the ships taking women to serve their sentence of transportation in Australia. On one of her frequent visits to study prisons abroad, she visited Kaiserswerth in Germany, where the first training hospital for nurses had been established. In 1840 she founded

the Institute of Nursing Sisters in Whitechapel to train nurses to care for poor people in their own homes.
← JOHN HOWARD: SIR THOMAS BUXTON →

Fuel crisis, 1947. The worst winter for more than sixty years caused an increased demand for coal and electric power, which neither the mines nor the generating stations could meet. Many factories had to close because of power cuts and unemployment rose to over 2m. in March. Transport was dislocated by heavy falls of snow. People shivered in their homes and potatoes were rationed for the first time. Double summer-time was introduced to save fuel. The fuel crisis greatly delayed Britain's recovery from the Second World War, and resulted in the introduction of a policy of austerity.
AUSTERITY →

Further Education. Since the end of the last war there has been a very great increase in the number of young people receiving further education after they have left school. In 1970–1, about 40 per cent of men and just over 20 per cent of girls between the ages of eighteen and twenty were either full-time students in universities, colleges of education, or some other further education institute, or were attending part-time courses during the day or in the evenings. Other opportunities for study were provided originally by the *Workers' Educational Association* and more recently by the *Open University.*

G

Gallipoli campaign, 1915–16. An unsuccessful attempt by British and Commonwealth forces in the First World War to create a second front, by concentrating on the defeat of Turkey, Germany's ally. They hoped to force a way through the Dardanelles Straits, take Constantinople, and thereby free Russian forces in the Caucasus for operations elsewhere, and allow Russian warships and merchant ships free access to the Mediterranean. In March 1915, French and British warships bombarded the Turkish forts in the Straits, but after several Allied ships had been sunk, the rest withdrew. British, Australian and New Zealand troops then made two landings on the northern shores of the Straits—the Gallipoli peninsula—in April and August 1915, but suffered heavy casualties in several battles with the Turks. The remainder of the Allied forces were then evacuated without loss between December 1915, and January 1916. Churchill, who had been First Lord of the

Admiralty since 1911, was made the scapegoat and resigned from the government.

Gambling. The Betting Act of 1853 prohibited ready-money betting in homes or offices. This encouraged people to bet in the streets, but this was also made illegal in 1906. Betting shops were established in 1960. There are now more than 15,000 betting shops in Britain. Many cinemas have been converted into Bingo halls. The total amount of money staked on horse and greyhound racing is well over £1,000m. a year.

Game laws against poaching have existed for many centuries. The Night Poaching Act, 1829, imposed stricter penalties. For a third offence of poaching at night the offender could be punished by transportation (changed to seven years' imprisonment in 1844). The Poaching Prevention Act, 1871, gave policemen powers to search suspected poachers. Poaching is still punishable by law.

Gandhi, Mohandas Karamchand (1869–1948), commonly known as Mahatma (Saint) Gandhi, an Indian nationalist who led the fight for Indian independence and introduced a new method of campaigning—civil disobedience. He was educated as a lawyer in London and returned to India in 1891. Two years later he went to South Africa where he led the Indian community there in a successful non-violent fight against racial discrimination. He returned to India in 1914 and went to London to organize an Indian ambulance corps during the First World War. Afterwards he went back to India to lead the fight for self-government. He used non-violent methods, boycotting British goods, organizing marches and meetings, and fasting. He was imprisoned in 1922, 1930, 1933 and finally in 1942 for organizing protests against the British war effort. By that time, he believed that only full independence could satisfy India and this was granted in 1947. In the following year he was assassinated by a Hindu fanatic, who was opposed to Gandhi's acceptance of the sub-continent being divided into a mainly Hindu India and a Moslem State of Pakistan.

Garden cities. A revolutionary idea, put forward by *Ebenezer Howard* in 1898, for small self-contained towns, where, in his own words, 'the most energetic and active town life' would be combined with 'all the beauty and delight of the country'. The towns, which were to be owned by the residents, would have a central park containing public buildings, such as hospitals, churches, and the town hall, surrounded by

arcades of shops and houses and communal gardens. Factories, workshops, and warehouses would be situated on the outskirts of the towns, which would be cut off from other towns by a green belt of farmland, orchards, and forests. The towns, which would have 30,000 inhabitants, would be self-supporting. Howard started the first garden city at Letchworth in 1903 and a second at Welwyn (both in Hertfordshire) in 1920. They provided models for the development of new towns after the Second World War.
NEW TOWNS →

Gas. Coal gas lighting, which was invented by *William Murdock*, was first used in his house at Redruth, Cornwall in 1792. Six years later he used it to illuminate *Boulton and Watt*'s factory at Soho, Birmingham. A few years later it started to be used for lighting in some textile mills, and by 1814 some streets in Westminster had gas lighting. By the middle of the nineteenth century it was being used for lighting in the streets of many towns and in middle-class homes. Gas cookers were first sold in the 1850s, though it was not until the 1890s that they started to become common as replacements for the old coal-burning kitchen range. Coal gas was supplied by private or municipal companies, and these were all nationalized by the Gas Act, 1948. In 1967, following the discovery of four large natural gas fields off the east coast of England, conversion of all gas appliances to North Sea gas was started, first of all in Burton-on-Trent. The work of conversion throughout the whole country is expected to be finished by 1978–9.

'Geddes Axe'. Economy measures introduced in 1922 following a report by a government-appointed committee headed by Sir Eric Geddes (1875–1937). The main effect was on education, with cuts in teachers' salaries and the abandoning of the compulsory part-time education from fourteen to eighteen, provided for in the *Education Act, 1918.*

General Agreement on Tariffs and Trade (G.A.T.T.), an agreement between the world's leading trading nations to reduce tariffs or duties so that international trade is encouraged. There have been six conferences since 1948, the last in 1964–7—the so-called Kennedy round, named after President Kennedy of the United States.

General Board of Health was set up in 1848 with Lord Shaftesbury and Edwin Chadwick as members to supervise sanitation and public health throughout the country. But because of local opposition to central control its powers were severely restricted in 1854 and it was finally abolished in 1858.

LOCAL GOVERNMENT BOARD →

General Strike, 1926, was defeated by the Baldwin government in only nine days. It started as a result of a pledge by the Trades Union Congress in 1925 to support the miners who were threatened with lower pay and longer hours by the mine owners. After the miners had been locked out by the employers on 30 April 1926, the T.U.C. called a general strike which started on 4 May. The first workers to be called out were in the transport, printing, building, and iron and steel industries. There was almost a 100 per cent response, and as a result there were no national newspapers, and scarcely any buses, trams, or trains on the first day. Docks, mines and power stations were all deserted. But the government had made plans to beat the expected strike and opened recruiting stations for special constables and for volunteers to run essential services. Skeleton services of buses and trains, run by volunteers, started on the second day; and troops and volunteers were used to unload ships in the docks and to maintain food supplies. The government issued its own official newspaper, the 'British Gazette' and the T.U.C. published a rival 'British Worker'. Engineering and shipbuilding workers were called out a week after the strike had started. But on 12 May, the T.U.C. suddenly surrendered, without obtaining any concessions for the miners, who did not go back to work until November. The strike failed partly because the T.U.C. was not willing to go far enough by calling all workers out at the same time. Some union leaders feared that more extreme members of their unions, who had formed Councils of Action in many areas, might take over the union movement if the strike went on too long. The government had well-prepared plans for beating the strike and could make its views known to the nation on the radio. The middle-class volunteers, who ran essential services, were keener to preserve the established order, than most union leaders were to have a radical change in society. (In Plymouth, strikers and policemen played a football match with each other.) General strikes were banned in the following year by *Trade Disputes and Trade Unions Act*, and the membership of unions fell as a result of the failure of the strike.

← BLACK FRIDAY

Geneva Conventions. A series of international agreements, the first being signed in Geneva, Switzerland, in 1864, which lay down 'rules of war' to protect Servicemen, prisoners of war, and civilians. Not all countries have signed the conventions, and even those who have, sometimes ignore them.

George, David Lloyd see **Lloyd George**

Gilchrist-Thomas process allowed iron ores containing phosphorus (as many of them do) to be used in steel-making. The process was invented in 1878–9 by Percy Gilchrist (1851–1935), a chemist in an ironworks and his cousin Sidney Gilchrist Thomas (1850–85), a clerk in a London magistrates' court. They found that if they lined a *Bessemer* converter with a basic substance, the common mineral, dolomite, the phosphorus in the ore was absorbed. The process was later applied to *Siemen*'s open hearth process, and electric furnaces, too.
← SIR WILLIAM SIEMENS

Gladstone, William Ewart (1809–98), great Liberal statesman with a missionary zeal to bring about reforms at home, free trade and peace abroad, and stability in Ireland. He was born in Liverpool, the son of a wealthy merchant. He was educated at Eton and Christ Church, Oxford, but spoke with a strong Lancashire accent to the end of his life. Originally, he had intended to enter the Church, but he became a Tory M.P. for Newark in 1832. He held minor offices in Peel's short government from 1834 to 1835 and was President of the Board of Trade from 1843 to 1845 during Peel's second ministry. He supported Peel's free trade policies and was out of office until 1852, when he became Chancellor of the Exchequer in Aberdeen's coalition government of Whigs and Peelites. In 1853 he introduced the first of his free trade Budgets, which cut duties on many foods and manufactured goods. He also hoped to abolish income tax by the 1860s but was unable to do so largely because of increased government spending during the Crimean War, 1854–6. He resigned when Palmerston became prime minister in 1855. Gladstone finally broke with the Conservatives in 1858 when he refused to serve under Derby, and in the following year, he and other Peelites agreed to serve under Palmerston. Gladstone was Chancellor again from 1859 to 1866. During this period he repealed the paper tax—the last of the *Taxes on Knowledge*—in 1861 and in the same year set up the Post Office Savings Bank (now the National Savings Bank) for small savers. He also swept away most other duties so that Britain became virtually a free trade nation. Following Palmerston's death, Gladstone became leader of the Liberal party which had emerged as a fusion of Whigs, Peelites and radicals in 1867, and in the following year he became prime minister for the first time.

His first ministry, from 1868 to 1874, was distinguished by a large number of reforms which had been blocked by Palmerston. They included the *Education Act, 1870*, which started the State system of elementary education; the *University Tests Act, 1871*, which finally ended the discrimination against nonconformists in universities; the *Ballot Act, 1872*, which made voting secret; and the *Trade Union Act, 1871*. *Edward Cardwell*, Secretary of State for War, introduced radical reforms in the Army. *The Licensing Act, 1872*, controlled public houses and limited their opening hours. The Civil Service was also reformed by the introduction of competitive entry examinations. In foreign affairs, Gladstone agreed to settle the *Alabama dispute* with the United States by arbitration—an important step forward in internationl relations. But his main mission, as he himself said, was 'to pacify Ireland'. He made his first attempts (which were to occupy much of the rest of his life) during his first ministry. An Act of 1869 brought about the *disestablishment* of the Irish Church, so that it lost its special status. The *Irish Land Act, 1870*, tried but failed to give Irish tenants some protection against eviction.

All of these reforms, however, offended some sections of the population. The upper classes were offended by the Army and Civil Service reforms; the Church of England by the disestablishment of the Anglican Church in Ireland and the University Tests Act; and the industrial workers by the *Criminal Law Amendment Act of 1871*, which made picketing in strikes illegal. The public as a whole disliked the settling of the Alabama dispute by arbitration and the Licensing Act—which also offended brewers and publicans. Gladstone himself thought that the Licensing Act was the main cause of his defeat in the 1874 election: he wrote, 'we have been borne down in a torrent of gin and beer'.

Gladstone resigned his leadership of the Liberal party in 1875, but he could not keep out of politics for long. In the following year he launched a massive onslaught against Turkey—and Disraeli's foreign policy—over the *Bulgarian massacres.* He became prime minister again in 1880, following his own great personal triumph in the *Midlothian campaign* in his new constituency.

During his second ministry, from 1880 to 1885, the main domestic reform was the Third Reform Act (the *Representation of the People Act, 1884*), which gave the vote to male farm workers. Imperial affairs took up much of his time. He gave self-government to the Boers in the Transvaal, after Britain had been defeated in the short Boer War of 1881. He failed to prevent the death of *General Gordon* at Khartoum in 1885. Both of these events made him unpopular with large sections of the public. But his main concern was still with Ireland. His *Irish Land*

Act of 1881 gave tenants the security they wanted, but it came too late to prevent continued disturbances. This Act, and his *Kilmainham pact* with the Irish nationalist leader Parnell, in 1882, offended many of his own supporters. During his third-short-lived ministry of 1886, Gladstone introduced his first *Irish Home Rule Bill*, which split the Liberal party and led to Joseph Chamberlain and other Liberal Unionists (who wanted to retain the link between Britain and Ireland) voting with the Conservatives and bringing Gladstone down. Gladstone was back in power from 1892 to 1894, when he introduced a second Irish Home Rule Bill, which was defeated in the House of Lords.

During his lifetime, Gladstone was regarded by many people as an extremist. Queen Victoria once described him as a 'half-mad firebrand'. But he was in reality much more moderate than some of his contemporaries believed. He supported reform, but he did not want fundamental changes to be made in the structure of society.

EARL OF ROSEBERY →

Gold rushes. The discovery of gold-fields at various times in the nineteenth century stimulated *emigration* to the United States and the empire. There was a gold rush to California in 1848; to Australia, where gold was found at Bathurst, New South Wales, in 1851, and at Ballarat, Victoria, where the largest nugget ever found, weighing over 180 lb., was discovered in 1858; and to the Klondike district of the Yukon, Canada, in 1896. The largest gold-field in the world—the Rand—was discovered in the Transvaal, South Africa, in 1886.

Gold standard. A system operating in Britain from 1816 to 1914 in which the main coin, or unit of currency, was the gold sovereign of a fixed weight which was worth £1. It meant that banks were obliged to change notes for sovereigns and that the £ had a fixed value in relation to other nation's currencies. Britain abandoned the gold standard in the First World War, but it was restored in part by Churchill, as Chancellor of the Exchequer, in 1925. This had no effect internally, where Bank of England notes, and Treasury notes (which were abolished in 1928), continued to be used; but it meant that the Bank of England bought and sold gold at a fixed price in dealings with other countries. The gold standard was finally abandoned in September 1931, during the world depression, so that the £ no longer had a fixed relation to other currencies, but could vary in value.

DEVALUATION →

Gordon, General Charles (1833–85), who was killed by Sudanese rebels in Khartoum in 1885, two days before a British relief force arrived from

Egypt. His death became part of the folk-lore of the British empire. Gladstone, the prime minister, was much criticized for not sending help earlier. The British evacuated the Sudan, but it was conquered by *Kitchener* in 1896–8.

Grammar Schools. Until the twentieth century, grammar schools and *public schools* provided most of the *secondary education* for those who could afford to pay the fees. After the *Education Act, 1902*, a number of grammar schools were given financial assistance by the State and in return they had to provide a minimum of 25 per cent of free places for children from elementary schools. In the 1960s a large number of grammar schools were merged with *comprehensive schools*, often in the face of much local opposition.

Grand National Consolidated Trade Union, formed in 1834, under the influence of the ideas of Robert Owen, to combine all workers, skilled and unskilled in one union. It was claimed that 500,000 workers joined within a few weeks. But there was more enthusiasm than intelligent planning. The union collapsed within a year owing to shortage of funds; lack of support by one group of strikers for other groups; and lock-outs by employers. The final blow was the prosecution of the *Tolpuddle Martyrs* in 1834, which showed how far the government was prepared to go in resisting unions.

Grand Trunk Canal. One of the most important canals, linking the Trent and Mersey rivers, designed by *James Brindley*, and partly financed by *Josiah Wedgwood*, who used it for transporting his pottery and clay. The canal, which was ninety-three miles long, was opened in 1777, five years after Brindley's death. It involved building the longest tunnel that had been constructed, the 2,800-yard Harecastle tunnel. The canal formed part of Brindley's grand design to link up four great rivers the Trent, Mersey, Severn and Thames. The Staffordshire and Worcestershire canal, which linked up with the Severn at Stourport, was opened in 1771, and the Oxford and Coventry canal, which linked up with the Thames in 1790.

← BRIDGEWATER CANAL: LEEDS–LIVERPOOL CANAL →

Great Britain. An all-iron steamship built by *I. K. Brunel* and launched at Bristol in 1843. It was one of the first ships to have a screw propeller instead of paddle wheels. It continued in service until 1866. In 1970, it was towed back from the Falkland Islands, where it had been beached and brought back to Bristol, where it is now on display.

← GREAT WESTERN: GREAT EASTERN →

Great Eastern. A steamship of nearly 19,000 tons, 692 feet long, built by *I. K. Brunel.* It was many times larger than any other ship that had been then built and was not surpassed in size for nearly forty years. It had both a screw propeller and paddle wheels; it could cruise at 15 knots; and it was designed to carry 4,000 passengers and 5,000 tons of cargo to the United States in seven days and to Australia in thirty-five days. The ship was dogged by ill luck from the start. In 1857, the first attempt to launch it on the Thames—sideways because of its weight and size—failed, and it was not successfully launched until the following year. On its maiden voyage, there was a serious explosion on board, which killed ten people and injured many more. Brunel died after receiving news of this disaster. The ship made several voyages to the United States, but they did not pay. In 1866, it was chartered by Cyrus West Field, an American businessman, to lay the first successful transatlantic cable. It was used to lay several more telegraph cables before it was broken up in 1888.
← GREAT BRITAIN

Great Exhibition (of the Works of Industry of all Nations), 1851, was held in Hyde Park, London, in the specially built Crystal Palace, which was made of glass and about a third of a mile long. There were over 7,000 British exhibitors and nearly as many foreign exhibitors. About 1m. articles had been entered. British exhibits won many of the prizes. The exhibition symbolized the material progress Britain had made as the first industrial nation in the world: it represented the height of Victorian prosperity. Over six million people visited the exhibition, many of them travelling by *excursion trains.* This idea of the exhibition was put forward by *Albert, the Prince Consort,* and *Samuel Plimsoll* was the honorary secretary. The Crystal Palace was later moved to a site at Sydenham, south London, where it was destroyed by fire in 1936.
FESTIVAL OF BRITAIN →

Great Trek see **South Africa**

Great Western. A British paddle steamer of 1,340 tons built by *I. K. Brunel,* which left Bristol with seven passengers aboard on 8 April 1838, to sail across the Atlantic. It reached New York in fifteen days, and was the second ship to cross the Atlantic using steam all the way, the first being the Sirius.
← SIRIUS: GREAT BRITAIN →

Greek War of Independence, 1821–30. This was one of the few occasions when Britain allied with Russia against Turkey in the nineteenth century—partly owing to the pressure of British public opinion. The Greeks in the Morea, southern Greece, rebelled against Turkish rule. This was followed by Turkish massacres of Greek Christians. The Greek revolt attracted great public support in Britain, and volunteers went out to help the Greeks, including Lord Byron, the poet, who died of fever at Missolonghi in 1824. But *George Canning*, the British Foreign Secretary, wanted to remain neutral. He feared that if Britain intervened, Russia (who also supported the Greek rebels) would do so too, and thus extend her power in the Balkans. The Turks then obtained help from *Mehemet Ali*, governor of Egypt, which was then part of the Turkish empire. He sent an army under his son Ibrahim Pasha to assist the Turks in 1825, and more massacres of Greek Christians took place. Neutrality then became impossible, as British public opinion was inflamed and it was certain that Russia would intervene. To forestall this, Canning, who had become prime minister, called the London Conference of 1827, under which Britain, Russia and France agreed to use force if the Turks would not give the Greeks their freedom. The Allies sank the Turkish and Egyptian fleets at the Battle of Navarino Bay, 1827, off the Morea, the last major battle under sail; Russian armies defeated the Turks; and the French defeated Ibrahim. Greece became independent in 1830 and a monarchy was established under Otto of Bavaria, who reigned from 1832 to 1862.

Grey, Earl (1764–1845), Whig statesman, born in Northumberland. During the Napoleonic wars, he supported parliamentary reform and Catholic emancipation. He resigned as Foreign Secretary in 1807 as a result of the refusal of George III to grant Catholic emancipation, and was out of office until November 1830, when he became prime minister. After a two-year-long struggle he succeeded in passing the *First Reform Act, 1832*, and retired two years later.

VISCOUNT MELBOURNE →

Grey, Sir George (1812–98), colonial governor who did excellent work in Australia, New Zealand and South Africa. After serving as an army officer, he became Governor of South Australia from 1841 to 1845 and built up the colony's finances and attracted better-class settlers. He was Governor of New Zealand from 1845–53 and from 1861–7, where he won the respect of the native Maori people and helped to settle the land question. He settled in New Zealand and was prime minister from 1877 to 1879, but returned to England four years before his death. He was also Governor of Cape Colony, South Africa, from 1853 to 1859.

Grey, Viscount (1862–1933), long-serving Liberal foreign secretary, from 1905 to 1916, who concluded the *Anglo-Russian Entente* of 1907, and insisted that Britain had a duty to help Belgium at the outbreak of the First World War. He was made a viscount in 1916.

Gross national product (g.n.p.), an estimate of the total value of all goods and services, plus profits and rents, produced in a country in a year. In 1970 the British g.n.p. was over £42,000m.

H

Habeas Corpus Act, one of the main defences of individual liberty, which prevents any person (except a prisoner of war) from being held in prison without trial. A person who has not been charged can demand after a certain period of time a writ of habeas corpus from a judge. The gaoler is then obliged to produce the prisoner in court and to state why he has been imprisoned or to release him. The Act, which was passed in 1679, has been suspended in times of war and in times of emergency, for example, in 1817 after the *Spa Fields meetings*, and by some *Irish Coercion Acts.* Habeas corpus (Latin) means literally 'you must have the body'.

Hague Conferences, of 1899 and 1907, were held in the Hague, Holland, in an attempt to stop the arms race. The first conference was attended by 26 nations and the second by 44, but little was achieved, apart from some conventions designed to stop the use of new weapons, such as expanding bullets. As a result of the first conference, which was called by Nicholas II, Tsar of Russia, a Court of International Arbitration (now the *International Court of Justice*) was set up in the Hague in 1901.

Haig, Earl (1861–1928), British commander-in-chief on the Western front during the First World War. He mistakenly believed that he could beat the Germans by massive artillery attacks followed by assaults by troops on their trenches. In the third battle of Ypres, for example, in 1917, over 4m. shells were used in the initial bombardment. But the British lost about 300,000 men in their assault and won very little ground. Lloyd George, who was prime minister from 1916, was highly critical of his methods and the consequent loss of men. In 1919 Haig was made an earl and given £100,000 by parliament. He was president of the British Legion from 1921 to his death and launched the 'Poppy Day' appeal for disabled ex-Servicemen.

Haldane, Richard Burdon (1856–1928), born in Edinburgh. As Secretary for War from 1905 to 1912 he carried out important reforms in the Army. He established an efficient general staff in 1906 and made plans for an expeditionary force which could be sent to Europe quickly to meet any threat from Germany. He also formed the Territorial Army out of the former volunteers, and a special reserve out of the former militia, so that well-trained reserves were always available. In addition he created the Officers' Training Corps in schools to provide a large group of young future officers with some basic military training. As a result of his planning, Britain was able to send an efficient, highly-trained expeditionary force of seven divisions to France within a few weeks of the outbreak of the First World War. He was made a viscount in 1911.

Half-timers. From 1880, children over the age of ten could be exempted from school to work part-time in factories if they had reached a certain educational standard. The age at which they could start work was gradually raised by successive Factory Acts and the raising of the *school-leaving age.* The half-time system was finally abolished by the Education Act, 1918.

Hampden Clubs were founded in 1812 by *Major John Cartwright* for rich and influential radicals to discuss reform. The first club, which met at the Thatched House Tavern, London, had an annual subscription of 2 guineas and was a failure. Cartwright then reduced the subscription to 1*d.* a week and set up clubs in the north, where they attracted support from skilled workers and were responsible for organizing much radical protest between 1815 and 1825. They were named after John Hampden (1594–1643) who refused to pay the 'ship money' tax to Charles I.
← CORRESPONDING SOCIETIES

Hardie, James Keir (1856–1915) was mainly responsible for creating the Labour Representation Committee (later the *Labour Party*) in 1900. He was born in Lanarkshire, the illegitimate son of a miner, but his mother later married a ship's carpenter. He started work as a messenger boy at the age of eight, and two years later went to work in the mines. He soon became a union leader and in 1892 was elected an independent Socialist M.P. for West Ham, London. He later denied stories that he was accompanied to the House of Commons by a drummer and a trumpeter, and that he was wearing a cloth cap: it was a deerstalker. In 1893 he founded the Independent Labour Party, which put up 28 candidates in the 1895 elections, but all of them were defeated, including Hardie. He became an M.P. again—for Merthyr Tydfil—in 1900. In 1906 when 29 Labour M.P.s were elected he became chairman of the parliamentary Labour party, but gave up the post in 1908. A convinced pacifist, he opposed Britain's entry into the First World War. He was an idealist in his support for pacifism, women's votes, and the rights of Indian workers, but a realist in his careful work in building up a coalition between the socialist parties and the trade union movement.

Hargreaves, James (died 1778), carpenter and weaver, born at Standhill, near Blackburn, Lancashire, inventor of the 'spinning jenny', named after his wife, which speeded up the spinning of wool and cotton greatly. The old spinning wheel had only one spindle worked by a treadle, but the spinning jenny, invented in about 1765, had eight spindles, driven by a big wheel at the side. At first, it was used by women spinners in their cottages, but larger versions, with up to 120 spindles, were later used in factories.

SIR RICHARD ARKWRIGHT →

Health and Morals of Apprentices Act, 1802, the first *factory act* prohibiting apprentices (pauper children from workhouses), from working more than twelve hours a day in the textile industries. Millowners had to provide them with at least one new suit of clothes a year, and a little elementary education. The Act also provided that all factories employing more than twenty people should be adequately ventilated and disinfected twice a year. (This was to prevent further outbreaks of 'factory fever' which had occurred in Manchester a few years before.) But as there was no efficient system of inspection, the Act was largely ignored.

Heath, Edward Richard George (born 1916), who became leader of the Conservative party in 1965 and prime minister in 1970. A dedicated European, he successfully took Britain into the European Community in 1973. His government has introduced many measures, including the *Housing Finance Act* and the *Industrial Relations Act*, which have aroused great opposition from the unions.

← SIR ALEC DOUGLAS-HOME

Hess, Rudolf (born 1896), Hitler's deputy, who flew alone to Scotland in May 1941, with proposals for a compromise peace to end the Second World War. They were rejected. He was sentenced to life imprisonment at the *Nuremberg trials, 1946*, and in 1973 was the only former Nazi leader still held in Spandau prison, Berlin.

High farming. A period of great prosperity for British farmers, though not for farm workers, which lasted from about 1850 to 1875. Farm workers' wages were low; British farmers were among the most skilful in the world in breeding sheep and cattle; the farms had been made into large, compact units by the *Enclosure Acts*; and Britain was well advanced in producing agricultural machinery and also in agricultural science, through the work of such men as *Patrick Bell* and *Sir John Bennet Lawes*. ('High' refers both to the high level of investment in farming and to the high level of achievements.)
AGRICULTURAL DEPRESSION →

Hill, Octavia (1838–1912), housing reformer, born at Wisbech, Cambridgeshire, daughter of a corn merchant. As a young woman she taught *ragged school* children in London, which opened her eyes to the bad housing conditions of the working classes. In 1865, she persuaded John Ruskin, the art critic, to provide £750 to buy three slum houses in Paradise Place, Marylebone, of which she became the manager. Ten years later she was managing fourteen other slum properties. She made repairs, planted trees, opened playgrounds, and persuaded the tenants to clean up their homes and to pay their rent regularly. In 1884 she was asked by the Ecclesiastical Commissioners, who ran the estates owned by the Church of England, to manage many of their slum properties in Southwark. Her housing reforms had little general effect and her creation of the *National Trust*, which she helped to found in 1895, was a much bigger achievement, as it has preserved thousands of acres of countryside for visitors from overcrowded towns.
← GEORGE PEABODY

Hill, Sir Rowland (1795–1879), campaigner for the *penny post*, son of a Birmingham school master. In 1827 he opened a school at Bruce Castle, Tottenham, which is now preserved as a postal museum. The campaign for the penny post had been started by Robert Wallace, M.P. for Greenock, and in 1837, Hill joined it by publishing a book 'Post Office Reform', which attracted much attention. Two years later he was given an appointment in the post office to put the scheme into effect. The penny post started in 1840, but Hill was dismissed in 1842 after the Conservatives came into power. From 1843 to 1846 he was chairman of Brighton railway, where he introduced *excursion trains*. He was appointed secretary to the Postmaster-General in 1846 and retired from the post office in 1864 for reasons of health. He was knighted in 1860.
← JOHN PALMER

Hire purchase was first introduced for buying goods such as furniture, pianos, and bicycles: one of the first schemes was started by the bicycle manufacturers W. A. Starley, in 1900. Hire purchase increased in the years between the two world wars, but many of the poor still feared it, because their goods could be taken away entirely if they fell behind with their instalments, and the lower middle classes feared what their neighbours might think—and had their goods delivered in plain vans. Hire purchase has increased greatly since the Second World War; the total debts outstanding in 1970 were £1,384m., about £85 per household.

Hitler, Adolf (1889–1945), born in Austria, German Führer (leader), who created a Third Reich (empire), which he hoped would last a thousand years but which collapsed in ruins after twelve. He was appointed Chancellor of Germany in 1933. He played upon the resentment of the German people at the *Treaty of Versailles*, particularly the clause which blamed the German nation for the First World War. In defiance of the treaty, he rearmed, and reoccupied the Rhineland in 1936. In 1938 he occupied Austria and in 1938–9, Czechoslovakia. His attack on Poland in 1939 led to the *Second World War*. After conquering most of Europe, he made a grave error in 1941 by attacking Russia, and was gradually defeated by the overwhelming strength of the Allies—the United States, Russia and Britain. He killed himself in his underground bunker in Berlin on 30 April 1945. Before the war, the British government had given in to many of Hitler's demands through its policy of *appeasement*, but the nation, under a new leader, *Churchill*, fought the Second World War against Hitler and the Germans with great determination. After the war the British and other nations were horrified by the revelations about German concentration camps, where an estimated 6m. Jews had been deliberately killed in gas chambers.

Holidays. Textile workers obtained a free Saturday afternoon (from 2 p.m.) after the Factory Act of 1853. During the rest of the century this was gradually extended to other workers, though many still had to work all day on Saturdays, particularly shop assistants, farm labourers, and transport workers. Christmas Day, and in some occupations Good Friday, were traditional holidays, and in 1871 the Bank Holiday Act established Boxing Day, Easter Monday, Whit Monday and the first Monday in August as free days, too. Paid annual holidays of one week for manual workers were first given by one firm in 1884, but it took many more years before this became general through agreements between employers and trade unions. In 1925 there were still only 1½m. manual workers entitled to a paid annual holiday but this had risen to 11m. by 1939. In that year, about 15m. people in all had a week's holiday or more away from home. Unlike most other countries in the European Community, there was still in 1973 no legal minimum annual holiday in Britain. But practically all workers are entitled to a fortnight's annual holiday or more under agreements with employers. About 30m. people now have a holiday away from home—5½m. of them abroad.

Holt, Alfred (1829–1911), engineer and shipowner. In 1864 he designed a new improved compound steam engine, which allowed steamships to compete with *clippers* on the long run to China. They could do the trip in sixty-five days instead of the ninety days normally taken by clippers. As a result, steamships ousted sailing ships on the profitable tea route from China. Holt founded the Ocean Steamship Company, also known as the Blue Funnel line.
←JOHN ELDER: SIR CHARLES PARSONS→

Home Guard, originally called Local Defence Volunteers, which was formed in May 1940, to help protect Britain from a possible German invasion. About 1m. men quickly volunteered, many of them First World War veterans. At first, they had little equipment, apart from shotguns, pikes and swords. But by the end of the war, the Home Guard was much better equipped, and included younger men, who were also doing essential war work in factories and other places. The Home Guard, which was never called into action, was re-formed from 1951 to 1957 during the *Cold War.*

Home rule see **Irish home rule**

HOSPITALS. At the beginning of the nineteenth century, there were two kinds of hospitals: voluntary hospitals and poor law infirmaries. Some of the voluntary hospitals, which were supported mainly by public charity, had been founded in the Middle Ages, like St Bartholomew's in London. The Poor Law infirmaries had been set up by *Boards of Guardians* to care for the 'destitute sick'. Standards of hygiene, medicine and nursing were very low in all hospitals, with filthy wards, untrained nurses and surgeons in bloodstained coats. Sir James Young Simpson, who introduced chloroform as an anaesthetic, wrote in the 1840s: 'The man who lies on the operation table in one of our hospitals runs a greater risk of dying than did the British soldier on the battlefield of Waterloo.' Hospital conditions started to improve after the reforms of *Joseph Lister* and *Florence Nightingale.* In 1929 poor law infirmaries were taken over by the municipal authorities and many of them were modernized before the Second World War. But many of the voluntary hospitals suffered from a great lack of funds and conditions in them varied greatly. In 1948, under the *National Health Service Act*, the existing 1,143 voluntary and 1,545 municipal hospitals were taken over by the State. (See also *Medicine.*)

HOUSING. The conditions in which the majority of British people lived had always been bad enough, but the housing problem became even worse with the increase in *population* and the growth of the new industrial *towns* in the second half of the eighteenth century. There was almost a total neglect of *public health*, with impure *water supplies* and inadequate *sanitation*, and the building of huge areas of badly ventilated back-to-back houses, which resulted in a very high *death rate* in many towns. These Victorian slum conditions were exposed in a number of official reports, including that of the *Select Committee on the Health of Towns, 1840*; Chadwick's *Report on Sanitary Conditions, 1842*; and the *Royal Commission on the Housing of the Working Classes, 1885.*

The first attempts to improve working-class housing in the towns were made through the formation of *building societies* by skilled workers as a form of self-help; the provision of blocks of flats by philanthropists like *George Peabody* in the 1860s; and the improved management of slum properties by *Octavia Hill.* But these changes, valuable though they were in themselves, were on such a small scale that only a very small minority of people benefited. As the population continued to increase, and more and more people flocked into the towns, the slums became even more overcrowded, particularly in London. The tendency of housing conditions to worsen was counteracted to a certain extent by the introduction of *trams* and cheap *workmen's fares* on the railways, and the building of *underground railways*, which enabled some of the skilled workers at least to move out into slightly better working-class suburbs further away from the city centre. (The repeal of the *window tax* in 1851 meant that new houses were better ventilated.)

Governments attempted to introduce better housing conditions by law through a number of Acts such as the *Artisans' and Labourers' Dwellings Act* of 1868 and the *Public Health Act* of 1875. But no really significant general improvements could be made until the State became prepared to give local councils subsidies to build better homes.

This was first done by the *Housing and Town Planning Act, 1919*, and by 1939 over 1,100,000 council houses and flats had been built in England and Wales—almost a quarter of the total number constructed between the two world wars. Improvements in *gas* and *electricity supplies* provided greater amenities within homes and a start was made on slum clearance, particularly after the *Housing Act* of 1930. But by 1939, when the Second World War broke out, much still remained to be done.

During the Second World War 200,000 homes were totally destroyed and another 3½ million were damaged. To help solve the immediate housing shortage, *prefabs* were put up. The State had by then accepted responsibility for housing as a social service: the building of private houses was strictly controlled by licence and until 1959 the majority of homes built every year were constructed by councils with the aid of government subsidies. A major attempt to control the development and expansion of towns, was made under the *Town and Country Planning Act, 1947*, with local councils trying to keep a balance between housing, amenities and industry. *New towns* were also built, based on *Ebenezer Howard's garden cities*, the first of which had been started at Letchworth, Herts, in 1903. Since the end of the war more people have started to buy their own homes, mainly through mortgages from building societies, and in recent years there has been an attempt to make people who live in rented accommodation pay a more economic rent through the *Rent Act, 1957*, and the *Housing Finance Act, 1972*.

Between 1945 and 1970 about 7½m. new homes were built in the United Kingdom. In 1970, 30 per cent of families lived in rented council houses or flats; 50 per cent owned their own home, or were in the process of buying it; 15 per cent rented their home from a private landlord; and another 5 per cent had tenancies of various kinds, mainly 'tied houses', which are occupied free, or for a low rent, by some workers like farm labourers, who have to give up their house when they leave their job. In recent years about 70,000 to 80,000 slum houses have been demolished every year, but many still remain, and there is still a considerable housing shortage, particularly in London and the overcrowded south-east of England.

Housing Act, 1924, a major landmark in the history of housing, which started council house building on a large scale. The Act, passed by the Labour government under Ramsay MacDonald, gave local authorities increased subsidies for houses built to let.

← HOUSING AND TOWN PLANNING ACT, 1919: HOUSING ACT, 1930 →

Housing Act, 1930, gave increased government subsidies to local authorities for slum clearance. By 1939, over 250,000 slum houses had been demolished and the residents rehoused; but at least 250,000 more slums, and even more overcrowding, still remained when the Second World War broke out.

← HOUSING ACT, 1924

Housing and Town Planning Act, 1919, gave government subsidies for building houses to local authorities (and private builders) for the first time. It also ordered local authorities, with populations of over 20,000, to draw up a plan for the development of their area.

← HOUSING OF THE WORKING CLASSES ACT, 1890: HOUSING ACT, 1924 →

Housing Finance Act, 1972, ordered local councils to charge 'fair rents' for their $4\frac{1}{2}$m. houses and flats, which had previously been subsidized. The increase in rents would be made in stages, the first in 1972. Those who could not afford to pay the higher rents were given rent rebates, or allowances, by local authorities.

← RENT ACT, 1965

Housing of the Working Classes Act, 1890, gave local councils greater powers to close insanitary houses and to build council houses. But because the money to build council houses had to come out of the local rates very little was done. By 1906, only 20,000 council houses had been built in the whole country—by 142 different local authorities.

← ARTISANS AND LABOURERS DWELLINGS ACT, 1875: HOUSING AND TOWN PLANNING ACT, 1919 →

Hovercraft was invented by *Sir Christopher Cockerell* in 1954. Although the idea of a vessel riding on a cushion of air was proposed by a Swedish scientist in the eighteenth century, Cockerell was the first man to design a satisfactory vehicle which entered regular service in 1959. There are now hovercraft operating across the Channel, in the United States, Germany and other countries. Some hovercraft have already reached speeds of well over 70 knots, much faster than any conventional ship. Many marine engineers believe that the hovercraft will eventually carry much of the *container ship* traffic at high speeds of 70 knots or more and that new hovercraft will allow passengers to cross the Atlantic in twenty-four hours or less.

Howard, Sir Ebenezer (1850–1928), founder of *garden cities*, born in

London, the son of a confectioner. He started work as a clerk, emigrated to the United States in 1872, and on his return to England in 1879, worked for the rest of his life as a shorthand writer, mainly in the law courts. In 1898 he published 'Tomorrow', which was reissued in 1902 under the title 'Garden Cities of Tomorrow'. In the following year, he founded a company to develop the first garden city at Letchworth, Herts, as a self-contained town combining the advantage of town and country, and industry and agriculture. It now has a population of about 30,000. A second garden city was started at Welwyn, Herts, in 1920, which became a *new town* in 1948. He was knighted in 1927.

Howard, John (1726–90), prison reformer. He became High Sheriff of Bedfordshire in 1773, when he exposed the insanitary conditions of prisons and the unjust treatment of prisoners. Prisons were then run by gaolers for their own private profit. As a result of Howard's work, they were paid a regular wage and some improvements were made in cleanliness. But gaolers continued to charge prisoners up to 6*d.* a night for the use of a bed and to sell them food and drink at a profit. Convicts wêre given a free allowance of bread each day, but debtors, who could then be imprisoned, had to provide their own food. Most of them were forced to beg from passers-by through the bars of the windows.

ELIZABETH FRY →

Hudson, George (1800–1871), businessman, known as the 'Railway King', who made a fortune—and then lost it—out of railways. He was born at Howsham, near York, and as a young man built up a thriving drapery business in York. In 1827 he inherited £30,000 from a great-uncle, which he invested in banks and railways. In 1833 he helped to found the York Union Bank and four years later became chairman of the directors of the newly-formed York and North Midland Railway Co. During the 'railway mania' of the 1840s, when many competing lines were being built, Hudson succeeded in raising over £4m. to form the Great Midland Railway, of which he became chairman in 1844. He was also managing the Eastern Counties and the York, Newcastle and Berwick railways. By 1849 he controlled 1,450 miles of railway lines—over a quarter of the total length that had then been built. His financial empire started to collapse in 1849 when his shareholders accused him of publishing false balance sheets and manipulating accounts, offences of which he was guilty. He had to resign his chairmanships and he lost most of his money. But Sunderland, which had elected him as a Conservative M.P. in 1845, remained loyal to him, and continued to elect him until 1859. He also helped to develop Scarborough as a seaside resort.

← THOMAS BRASSEY

Hunger marches made by unemployed workers to draw public attention to their plight. There have been many marches from the *Blanketeers' march* in 1817 onwards. One of the most famous in recent times was the Jarrow 'crusade' to London in 1931, from the Durham shipbuilding town, where about two-thirds of the men had been out of work for almost ten years.

Hunt, Henry (1773–1835), outspoken reformer, known as 'Orator Hunt'. He always wore a white hat—then the colour of reform—at his meetings. He worked on his father's farm at Upavon, Wiltshire, before taking up the cause of parliamentary reform. He spoke at the *Spa Fields meetings, 1816*, and was the chief speaker at *Peterloo, 1819*, where he was arrested and later sentenced to two years' imprisonment. While he was in prison he wrote his 'Memoirs', which were first published in fortnightly parts. He was M.P. for Preston from 1830 to 1833.

← SIR FRANCIS BURDETT: FRANCIS PLACE →

Huntsman, Benjamin (1704–76), a clockmaker, born in Doncaster, who invented a method of making better steel in about 1740. Previously steel had been produced by heating high-quality iron bars and charcoal in a furnace for a number of days. This produced 'blister' steel which had small swellings on the surface. Huntsman put 'blister' steel, and other ingredients including charcoal, in a sealed clay container (or crucible) which was heated in a furnace. This produced a higher-quality cast steel, which was stronger and more flexible, so that it could be used for making watch springs and razors. But steel was still very expensive to produce and remained a scarce metal for many more years.

SIR HENRY BESSEMER →

Huskisson, William (1770–1830), born at Birch Moreton, Worcestershire, Tory statesman. He was President of the Board of Trade from 1823 to 1827, when he abolished a number of tariffs or duties and started a *free trade* policy. He halved the duties on many raw materials, such as copper and tin, and cut the duty on some foreign manufactured goods. He became Colonial Secretary under Wellington, but quarrelled with him and resigned in 1828. He was killed by a locomotive, Stephenson's 'Rocket', at the opening of the Manchester and Liverpool railway in 1830, as he was walking over to Wellington to patch up his quarrel with him.

Huxley, Thomas Henry (1825–95), scientist, who strongly supported Darwin's theory of evolution by natural selection. He defended it, in print and words, against bishops, clergymen and politicians.
← CHARLES DARWIN

Hydrogen bomb. A much more powerful weapon than the atom bomb, which was first tested by Britain in 1957 in the Christmas Isles. Five nations—Britain, the United States, Russia, China and France—now have hydrogen bombs.
← ATOM BOMBS: POLARIS →

I

Identity cards were introduced in Britain in 1939 during the Second World War, but were abolished after the end of the war. They are used in many European countries.

IMMIGRATION. There has always been a long tradition of immigration into Britain of political and religious refugees; of Jews; and, in the nineteenth century, of Irish people. But until 1945, there had been very few black immigrants—mainly slaves in earlier times, and later seamen and students. Since then, there has been a large-scale immigration of West Indians, Pakistanis, Indians and other coloured people from the Commonwealth, so that the coloured population is now estimated at around 1m. Most of them came because of unemployment at home. They were admitted freely until the *Commonwealth Immigrants Act* was passed in 1962. Three years later, the first *Race Relations Act* was passed in an attempt to end discrimination against coloured people.
← EMIGRATION

Imperial Airways was formed in 1924 out of four small British companies and given a government grant of £1m. to develop services for passengers and *air mail.* Passenger services were started to India in 1929, to Central Africa in 1931, and to Australia in 1935. Seaplanes, which need no airports, were used on many routes. By 1939, the routes flown totalled 25,000 miles.
BRITISH OVERSEAS AIRWAYS CORPORATION →

Imperial Conference, 1926, where Arthur James Balfour, Lord President of the Council, defined the status of *dominions* as 'autonomous communities' which were 'equal in status' and 'freely associated as members of the British Commonwealth of Nations'. By the end of the First World War, the dominions had already obtained independence of Britain in foreign affairs by making separate peace treaties; becoming individual members of the League of Nations; and setting up their own legations abroad.

STATUTE OF WESTMINSTER, 1931 →

Imperial Conferences. The first—known as a Colonial Conference—was held in London in 1887 by the prime ministers of Britain and the *dominions* and 'white' colonies to increase co-operation between member-nations of the empire in defence, trade, communications etc. They became known as imperial conferences in 1907, when it was agreed to meet every four years, and as prime ministers' meetings from 1944. They are still held at intervals.

Imperial preference, a system under which Britain and the *dominions* and colonies gave each other preferential rates of duties so that Commonwealth trade was encouraged. The idea was first put forward in the 1890s by *Joseph Chamberlain*, who hoped that Britain could supply most of the manufactured goods, while the dominions and colonies would supply cheap food and raw materials. In this way he hoped that the empire might become a self-sufficient economic unit. By the time imperial preference had been established by his son Neville Chamberlain, under the *Ottawa agreements, 1932*, it was too late to benefit Britain much as the dominions were no longer content merely to supply Britain with cheap raw materials, and wanted to buy cheaper manufactured goods from other countries.

Imperial War Cabinet of prime ministers from the *dominions* and Britain was set up by Lloyd George in 1916. He hoped that it would take military and diplomatic decisions for the whole empire, but the dominion prime ministers insisted that they must remain responsible to their own governments at home. *General Smuts*, of South Africa, was a permanent member from 1917 to 1919. India, which had 500,000 troops fighting in the First World War, was represented in the Cabinet. This increased its hopes that it would be given self-government after the war, but it was disappointed. The Imperial War Cabinet ended in 1919.

Imperialism see **Empire and Commonwealth**

Import Duties Act, 1932, ended Britain's century-old *free trade* policy by putting a minimum 10 per cent duty on most foreign goods. Commonwealth goods, food and raw materials were exempted. The Act was made necessary by the depression, massive unemployment and tariff barriers in foreign countries.
OTTAWA AGREEMENTS, 1932 →

Income tax was first introduced by Pitt in 1798 as a temporary measure during the Napoleonic wars, and was abolished in 1816. It was reintroduced by Peel in 1842 at the rate of 7*d.* in the £ on incomes over £150 a year for a three-year period, but it has remained in force ever since. Gladstone hoped to abolish it, but only succeeded in reducing it to 2*d.* in the £ by 1874. By 1900, it had risen to 1*s.* in the £. In 1907 the Liberals introduced a new principle by giving a lower rate of 9*d.* in the £ on earned incomes below £2,000 a year (i.e. wages or salaries, not profits, rents or dividends). In 1909, Lloyd George introduced a new supertax (later renamed surtax) on incomes of over £2,000 a year, which was payable in addition to ordinary income tax. The standard rate of income tax rose to a peak of 10*s.* in the £ in 1941–2 and 1944–6, when people with very large incomes had to pay 19*s.* 6*d.* in the £, including surtax. The rate was 30p. in the £ in 1973. (See also *Taxation.*)
PAY AS YOU EARN →

Independent Labour Party (I.L.P.), a Socialist party, formed by *Keir Hardie* in 1893, which helped to set up the Labour Representation Committee (later the *Labour party*) in 1900. The I.L.P.—whose members included *Ramsay MacDonald* and *Margaret Bondfield*—retained its own separate organization and policies. Under James Maxton (1885–1946), it became increasingly socialist and critical of the policies of the Labour party. It broke with the Labour party in 1932 and in 1935 gained only four seats, all in Glasgow, which had dropped to three by 1945. No I.L.P. candidates have been successful in general elections since then.

Independent Television Authority (I.T.A.) was set up in 1954 to supervise television broadcasting by the commercial programme companies. In 1972 its name was changed to the Independent Broadcasting Authority (I.B.A.). It now supervises the fifteen TV companies and the sixty or so commercial radio stations which are being set up.

INDIA with its ancient civilization, its strange customs and religions, and its great natural beauty was always the brightest jewel in the crown for imperialists. From the beginning of the seventeenth century, the East India Company gradually established itself along the coasts by setting up forts and trading stations. These included Bombay; Madras and a small area of surrounding territory; the Circars around the port of Masulipatam; and Bengal, the largest territory in the north-east, with its main port of Calcutta. The French, who also had possessions there, were defeated by the British in the eighteenth century. In 1784, Pitt's India Act put the company's possessions under the dual control of the Crown and the company. By the middle of the nineteenth century, Britain had become the undisputed ruler of India, mainly through a series of wars against the Marathas, 1803–5 and 1816–19; Nepal, 1814–16; and the Sikhs, 1845–6 and 1848–9. The Indian princes who remained in power did so only under British protection. The protection of the Indian empire led Britain into other wars with neighbouring countries—two against *Afghanistan* and three against *Burma*.

India was of enormous economic importance to Britain, as it was one of the chief markets for the main British exports, textiles, throughout the nineteenth century. There was also a profitable export trade in drugs from India to China, which led Britain into the *Opium War, 1840–2*. Nevertheless the British believed that they had a mission to civilize India and to introduce the benefits of the Western way of life. In the first half of the nineteenth century Britain introduced railways, the electric telegraph, canals, cheap postage, better roads, English education for the upper classes, the Christian Church and abolished a number of Indian customs. These included suttee—the Brahman practice of the widow being burnt alive on her husband's funeral pyre. Relations between the British and the Indians were drastically changed by the *Indian mutiny, 1857–8*, which left hatreds and suspicions on both sides. Under the India Act, 1858, the East India Company, which had lost its monopoly of trade in 1813, was abolished. Its powers were transferred to the Crown, represented by a viceroy, and its troops were taken over by the Army. The country was run by British officials, members of the Indian Civil Service, which had been recruited by competitive examinations since 1853, and by the Secretary of State for India in Whitehall. In 1876 Queen Victoria assumed the title of Empress of India. Vast profits from the sale of textiles and the Indian railways continued to flow into Britain, but there were frequent famines and plagues in the country in which millions of Indians died. The approach to any form of self-government was very slow. By the India Councils Act, 1892, a few Indians were admitted to the legislative councils of the Viceroy and provincial governors, but they could only voice their grievances, and still had no real control. In 1909 under the India Councils Act—the *Morley-Minto reforms*—Indians were given greater representation in the legislative councils and also representation in London, where two Indians were added to the council of the Secretary for India. But they still had little real power.

During the First World War, India provided 500,000 troops, and was given representation in the *Imperial War Cabinet.* This increased Indian hopes that they would be given some form of self-government after the war, and they were bitterly disappointed by the India Act of 1919. This provided that in both the central legislative council and also in the provincial councils, there was to be a majority of elected Indians, though some would still be nominated by officials. In the provincial councils, some subjects like education, agriculture and public health were to be entirely controlled by Indian ministers; but more important matters, like revenue and law and order were still to come under the control of the executive council. The central government continued to be controlled by the viceroy and his executive council. This did not go far enough, or fast enough, for Indian nationalists. Led by *Gandhi* they conducted a ceaseless campaign for self-government, and when this was not granted, they started to demand complete independence. This was finally granted in 1947 when the Indian sub-continent was partitioned into two countries: India, which was mainly Hindu; and Pakistan, which was mainly Muslim. There were clashes between Hindus and Muslims during the partition and an estimated 300,000 to 500,000 were killed.

Indian Mutiny, 1857–8. The immediate cause was the refusal of native sepoy soldiers, employed by the East India Company, to use the cartridges for the new Enfield rifles. These had to be bitten before they could be loaded. The rumour spread that they were greased with cow-fat or pig-lard. As the cow is sacred to Hindus and the pig is unclean to Muslims, both religious communities in India were offended. The deeper causes of the mutiny were resentment at Westernization and fears that native customs, religions, and social structures would be destroyed by the British. The mutiny began at Meerut in May 1857, when the sepoys shot their British officers. It soon spread to Delhi, which was captured by the rebels; Lucknow was besieged; and the British surrendered at Cawnpore. British troops, helped by Sikhs and Gurkhas fought back, and the last rebels were captured in 1858. There were great cruelties on both sides. At Cawnpore over 200 British women and children were hacked to pieces and thrown down a well. Some Indian rebels were tied to cannons by the British and blown to pieces. (For the background see *India.*)

Industrial Relations Act, 1971, passed by the Conservatives to put industrial relations within a framework of law by creating a new National Industrial Relations Court. The Act provided for a code of industrial practice, protection of workers against unfair dismissal, legally binding contracts between employers and employees, strike ballots, 'cooling off' periods in disputes, and the registration of trade unions. But the majority of trade unions were opposed to the Act, preferring voluntary agreements between unions and employers.

INDUSTRIAL REVOLUTION. In spite of its name, the industrial revolution was a long, complicated process spread over many years. It not only involved the replacement of the *domestic system* by the *factory system* but also profoundly changed the way in which the majority of people lived. The *textile industry* was the first to be mechanized, but developments in *coal mining*, in the *iron and steel industry*, and in *mechanical engineering* were equally important. The *steam engine* provided a new, and much greater, source of power, which was used in mines for pumping out water, so that deeper seams could be mined, and in factories for driving machinery. It was also used to drive locomotives and ships, thus improving communications and transport by rail and sea, which were an essential part of the industrial revolution. By 1851, the year of the *Great Exhibition*, Britain had been transformed from a largely agricultural country, to an industrial country, with the majority of people living in *towns*. But there were still many people employed at home or in small workshops, and not all of industry had been mechanized.

The industrial revolution occurred first in Britain for a number of reasons, not all of which are clear even now. They included the rich deposits of coal and iron; a long tradition of commerce and banking; the growth of population; internal peace and security; and a great burst of inventiveness and technical progress, particularly in Scotland. But by about 1870 a number of foreign countries were beginning to overtake Britain in some spheres, particularly the United States and Germany. The reasons again are not entirely clear, but they included greater natural resources; exploitation of new industries, such as chemicals, and later, electricity and motor-cars; greater state support; larger industrial units; better technical education; and bigger internal markets. (See also *Free Trade.*)

Industrial Training Act, 1964, provided for industrial training boards to be set up to supervise the training of workers in their industries. Employers had to contribute towards the cost, unless they ran their own training schemes.

Infant mortality. The number of children who die under one year of age has declined dramatically in the present century. In 1900 it was 130 per thousand live births; in 1930, 70; in 1960, 25; and in 1970, 18. This decline has been brought about mainly through the curing and prevention of many infectious diseases by new drugs and inoculation; the introduction of ante-natal clinics during the First World War; and general improvements in *public health* and *food*, including the introduction of *school meals*.

Inflation, is in simple terms, a rise in prices, which causes the value of the £ to decline, because it will buy fewer goods. This results in demands for higher wages, and if these are granted, prices tend to rise again. As a result of inflation the £ of 1960 was worth only 69 p. in 1970 (i.e. it would buy only that amount of goods). There has been a considerable inflation in most countries since the end of the Second World War.

International Court of Justice was established at the Hague, Holland, in 1901, under the name of the Court of International Arbitration. It has had some success in settling minor disputes between nations and became one of the organs of the League of Nations and is now part of the United Nations Organization.
← ALABAMA DISPUTE

Invisible exports, earnings from foreign countries for services such as banking, insurance, shipping, and payment on debts and capital invested overseas. Britain has to pay other countries for similar services (invisible imports), but usually makes an overall profit of several hundred millions a year on 'invisibles'. This is an important factor in Britain having a surplus on its *balance of payments*.
← VISIBLE EXPORTS

IRELAND. The English have been making attempts to subdue Ireland ever since the first Anglo-Norman invasion in the twelfth century. There have been many rebellions and reconquests, notably under Elizabeth I, Cromwell and William III. By the end of the eighteenth century the country was dominated by the Protestant minority.

Three-quarters of Irish land was owned by the English or Anglo-Irish Protestant families. Many of them were absentee landlords, some of whom had never visited Ireland, but lived in England on the rents they drew from their vast Irish estates. There were constant evictions of Irish tenants to make way for pastures for grazing sheep and cattle, most of which were exported. There was an Irish parliament in Dublin, but it had few powers. The established church was Protestant, and the Roman Catholic majority had to pay *tithes* to a church, whose doctrines they did not support. In 1798 the United Irishmen, led by Wolfe Tone (1763–98) and aided by the French, rebelled against British rule, but they were defeated at the Battle of Vinegar Hill in June 1798. Two years later the *Act of Union* made the whole of Ireland part of the United Kingdom, ruled from Westminster. Although *Catholic emancipation* had been promised by *Pitt*, George III refused to grant it and it was only after a long fight by *Daniel O'Connell* that the *Roman Catholic Relief Act* was passed in 1829 which allowed Catholics to become M.P.s But most Catholics remained dissatisfied by this late concession of what had been promised to them thirty years before and agitation for further reforms continued unabated. There were continual outbreaks of violence and *Irish Coercion Acts* were frequently introduced to maintain order.

The situation in Ireland took a turn for the worse when the *Irish famine* of 1845 to 1849 caused the death of at least 1m. people and forced many others to emigrate. It left a legacy of bitterness and hatred for the British, who were blamed for not doing more to provide relief; but an attempt by the *Young Ireland movement* to promote a rebellion in the midst of this dreadful suffering was not unnaturally a total fiasco. The demand for reforms among the Irish Catholics had now greatly increased. Tithes had been abolished in Ireland in 1838 and a fixed charge substituted, but the Catholics wanted the Anglican Church to be disestablished. Land reform was being demanded to stop evictions. Some extremists, like the *Fenians*, founded in 1858, wanted a republic. The violent campaigns by the Fenians—a mere foretaste of what was to come—convinced *Gladstone* that something must be done to solve the Irish problem. After he came to power in 1868, he introduced two reforms: the *disestablishment* of the Church in 1869 and the first *Irish Land Act* in 1870. But this latter measure failed to stop evictions. The *Irish Land League* was formed in 1878–9 and introduced a new method of protest which was first successfully used against *Captain Boycott*, an English land agent. A second *Irish Land Act* passed by Gladstone in 1881 was more successful in stopping evictions, but it came too late to satisfy Irish demands and violence continued. *Charles Stewart Parnell*, an Irish M.P., who was both leader of the Home Rule Association and president of the Irish Land League, was arrested in 1881 for allegedly inciting members of the League to violence. He was released in the following year after the *Kilmainham pact* had tried to secure more moderate policies on both sides. But hopes of a reconciliation disappeared when an Irish 'underground' group committed a new outrage in 1882—the *Phoenix Park murders*.

Gladstone persisted in his efforts to solve the Irish problem and introduced his first *Irish Home Rule Bill* in 1886, but it was defeated by the defection of many members of his own party led by *Joseph Chamberlain*. Home rule was eventually forced through the Westminster parliament by the Liberals in 1914, but it was suspended for the duration of the First World War. By then Ireland was on the brink of civil war, with the protestant *Ulster Volunteer Force* pledged to resist home rule—supported by some members of the British Army as the *Curragh incident* showed—and the Catholic *Irish Volunteers* pledged to home rule, at least, or complete independence. Once again, delays in introducing reforms increased violence: in the *Easter Rising, 1916*, Irish nationalists tried to set up a republic by force. The rebellion was crushed by the British, but in 1919, *Sinn Fein*, the Irish nationalist party, established a republic, based on Dublin; the Irish Republican Army (I.R.A.) was formed to defend it against British regular troops, the Irish constabulary, and the *Black and Tans*. As a result of negotiations between *Lloyd George* and Irish nationalist leaders, an *Irish Free State* was set up for twenty-six counties, while six counties in the north-east remained part of the United Kingdom. Demands for a united Ireland, ruled from Dublin, continued to be made, particularly by members of the I.R.A. In the 1960s a civil rights movement started to campaign for fairer treatment of the Catholic minority in *Ulster* and disturbances broke out in 1969 which were still continuing in 1973.

Irish Coercion Acts. During the violent disturbances in Ireland in the nineteenth and twentieth centuries, British governments passed many Acts, usually for short periods, which denied the Irish some of their civil liberties. The Acts gave the authorities various powers, including the right to impose curfews, or to arrest on suspicion, or to arrest without a trial, or to try accused people without a jury. Seventeen Acts were passed between the Act of Union, 1800, and the Irish famine, 1845–9. The Acts were passed by both Conservative and Liberal governments, including Gladstone's in 1881 and 1882.

Irish famine, 1845–9, was caused by a fungus which attacked potatoes and turned them into an uneatable, black pulp. The fungus, or potato blight, first appeared in 1845, when some crops were affected, and in 1846 and 1848 there were almost total failures of the potato crops. The potato was the only food of almost half the population of Ireland. People ate weeds just to keep alive. Starving bands roamed the countryside or begged for food from workhouses, which were already greatly overcrowded. It is estimated that more than 1m. people died (out of a total population of about 8m.) either directly of starvation, or through typhus or fever. Within five years at least 800,000 Irish people emigrated, mainly to the United States. Thousands of them died of disease in the overcrowded ships. The famine left a legacy of bitterness in Ireland and among the Irish community in the United States, who blamed the English for not providing greater relief. The famine was one of the factors which converted Peel to the *Repeal of the Corn Law, 1846.*

Irish Free State was set up in 1922 by the Anglo-Irish Treaty signed by Lloyd George and representatives of the Irish nationalists in the previous year. It gave the twenty-six counties of southern Ireland self-government as a *dominion*: the six counties of *Ulster* in the north-east remained part of the United Kingdom. The settlement was opposed by a minority of the *Sinn Fein* party in southern Ireland, who wanted a republic, and there was civil war from 1922 to 1923. In 1937, the country was renamed Eire, and declared itself to be 'sovereign' and 'independent', though still retaining an 'external association' with the Commonwealth. It remained neutral in the Second World War and severed the last links with Britain and the Commonwealth in 1948, when it became the Republic of Ireland. Both Britain and the Republic became members of the European Community at the same time in 1973.

Irish Home Rule. Demands, mainly by Catholics, for the repeal of the *Act of Union, 1800*. After a long struggle, the twenty-six counties of southern Ireland were given self-government as the *Irish Free State* in 1922.

Irish Home Rule Bill, 1886, proposed that the whole of Ireland should be given responsible self-government by its own parliament in Dublin, while Britain would have retained control over defence, foreign affairs and external trade. This would have given it a similar status to other *dominions*. The Bill was introduced by *Gladstone*, who had been converted to home rule by the growing Irish support for *Parnell.* The Bill split the Liberal party; Joseph Chamberlain and ninety-two other Liberal Unionists, who wanted to keep Ireland part of the United Kingdom, voted against it. The Bill was defeated by thirty votes and Gladstone resigned. (See next entry.)

Irish Home Rule Bill, 1893, a modified Bill, introduced by *Gladstone.* It provided for some Irish M.P.s to continue to sit at Westminster, in addition to those in the Irish parliament at Dublin. It was forced through the House of Commons, but was heavily defeated in the Lords. (See next entry.)

Irish Home Rule Bill, 1912–14, introduced by *Asquith* and forced through the House of Lords under the *Parliament Act, 1911.* The Protestants in Ireland formed the *Ulster Volunteer Force* in 1913 to resist home rule and the Catholics then formed the *Irish Volunteers.* The Bill became law in 1914, but was suspended for the duration of the war. An *Irish Free State* was set up in 1922.

Irish Land Act, 1870, passed by Gladstone, was the first attempt to try to solve the land problem in Ireland. It made landlords pay compensation to tenants who were evicted after they had made improvements. But it was easily evaded. Landlords raised the rents to impossibly high levels so that the tenant left. Evictions of other tenants, who had not made improvements, still continued, and this led to the formation of the *Irish Land League.* (See next entry.)

Irish Land Act, 1881, passed by Gladstone, gave tenants much greater security by making it illegal for them to be evicted if they paid their rent. It also set up special courts to assess 'fair rents'. Leaseholders could sell their lease, without their landlord's permission, so that they could profit from any improvements they had made. But it came too late to solve the Irish problem, and violent agitation still continued.
IRISH LAND PURCHASE ACT, 1903 →

Irish Land League, formed in 1878–9 by Michael Davitt (1846–1906), a former Fenian, to stop evictions by new means. Local people refused to work for, or have any dealing with, the landlord or agent responsible and the new tenant. The successful use of these methods against *Captain Boycott,* a land agent, attracted great attention—and also added a new word to the language. These boycotts often led to violence, with ricks being burnt, cattle being injured, and new tenants being wounded or murdered.

← FENIANS: IRISH VOLUNTEERS →

Irish Land Purchase Act, 1903, passed by the Conservatives in a final attempt to settle the land question in Ireland. The government provided up to £5m. a year for tenants to buy their land, repaying the mortgage to the government over a 68-year period. Many tenants took advantage of the scheme, but it came too late to solve the Irish question and to stop the demands for home rule or independence. The Act was introduced in 1902 by George Wyndham (1863–1913), then Chief Secretary for Ireland, and is sometimes known as Wyndham's Act.

← IRISH LAND ACT, 1881

Irish Republican Army (I.R.A.). A guerrilla force formed in 1919 to establish a republic for the whole of Ireland by force. After *Sinn Fein* set up a republic in southern Ireland in 1919, the I.R.A. defended the republic against the British Army, the Royal Irish Constabulary and the *Black and Tans.* When the *Irish Free State* was set up in the south of Ireland in 1922, the I.R.A. split. Some members left the I.R.A. and supported the Irish Free State; others, who were eventually defeated, fought against it in the civil war in southern Ireland from 1922 to 1923. The members of the I.R.A. never gave up their aim of a united republic for the whole of Ireland, north and south. In the 1930s it organized a series of bomb attacks in London and Manchester and in the 1950s carried out a succession of armed raids against police stations and Army barracks in Ulster. It has taken a leading part in the disturbances in Ulster which started in August 1969.

← IRISH VOLUNTEERS: SINN FEIN →

Irish Volunteers, a private army formed by Catholic nationalists in 1913, in opposition to the *Ulster Volunteer Force*, which opposed home rule for Ireland. Its members were mainly responsible for the *Easter rising* in Dublin in 1916, and many of them later became members of the I.R.A.

← IRISH LAND LEAGUE: IRISH REPUBLICAN ARMY →

IRON AND STEEL INDUSTRY. In the Middle Ages small quantities of pig iron were produced in primitive blast furnaces using a draught of air provided by large bellows driven by a water wheel. Pig iron contains impurities, such as carbon, silicon, manganese, sulpher and phosphorous, which had to be removed by reheating the pig iron in a second furnace and hammering it until all the impurities were removed. The fuel used in both furnaces was charcoal, the residue of partly-burnt wood. With the increasing shortage of timber, ironmasters started to experiment with other fuels, such as coal. But this has a high sulphur content, which made the iron too brittle. The problem was solved in 1709 when *Abraham Darby I,* started to use coke, from which much of the carbon has already been expelled. But it was still a lengthy process to produce wrought iron as the pig iron still had to be repeatedly heated and hammered. A much quicker method—the 'puddling process'—was introduced by *Henry Cort* in 1784 which gave Britain a great lead in the production of wrought iron, one of the essential elements in the *industrial revolution.* In the last quarter of the eighteenth century, the great ironmasters like *John Wilkinson* started to use iron to make a great variety of objects, including bridges, barges and machines. Production of iron was cheapened by *James Neilson's* introduction of the hot blast in 1829.

Steel, however, which is much stronger than iron and can be used for many more purposes, was still being produced only in very small quantities, mainly by *Benjamin Huntsman's* crucible process. In 1856, *Sir Henry Bessemer* invented the converter named after him which allowed steel to be produced cheaply in great quantities. An alternative open hearth method was invented by *Sir William Siemens* in 1866 and the introduction of the *Gilchrist-Thomas method* allowed a greater variety of iron ores to be used in both processes. During the last quarter of the nineteenth century steel started to replace wrought iron for most purposes.

Iron was the essential material in the industrial revolution, being used for *railways, ships,* and in *mechanical engineering.* The production of pig iron in Britain rose from 68,000 tons in 1788 to 250,000 tons by 1806. By 1850, 2½m. tons of cast and wrought iron were being produced and twenty years later Britain was the biggest producer in the world of iron and steel. But it had been overtaken before the First World War by both the United States and Germany. In 1970, Britain produced 27m. tons of steel.

The industry was nationalized by the Labour government in 1951, but was partly denationalized by the Conservatives two years later. Steel was renationalized in 1967 by the Labour government when a British Steel Corporation was set up to run most of the industry. In 1972, the Conservatives announced a £3,000m. plan for modernizing the state-controlled industry.

Iron Curtain, a phrase used by Churchill in a speech at Fulton, U.S.A.

in March 1946, to warn of the growing divisions of Europe into two physically and politically separated parts—the East and the West.

J

Jameson raid, 1895. Part of a plot by *Cecil Rhodes* to overthrow the government in the Transvaal, a Boer republic in South Africa. A friend and employee of Rhodes, Dr (later Sir) Leander Starr Jameson (1853–1917), led a group of about 500 horsemen into the Transvaal, hoping that it would provoke a rising by British workers in the Johannesburg gold-fields, who were dissatisfied with Boer rule. But the raiders from Rhodesia were all captured soon after they crossed the border. The raid was a dismal failure, but it hardened Boer suspicions of the British and helped to lead to the second Boer War.

Jenner, Edward (1749–1823), doctor who introduced *vaccination,* born at Berkeley, Gloucestershire. After being trained by the great London surgeon, John Hunter (1728–93), he returned to Gloucestershire, where he became interested in the belief among many countrywomen that if he caught cowpox from cattle they would not get smallpox. Both diseases produce small blisters on the face and body; but cowpox is only a mild disease whereas smallpox is often fatal. In 1796 Jenner inoculated an eight-year-old boy with cowpox by taking some of the fluid from the blisters on the hands of an infected dairymaid and injecting it into the boy's arm. He later inoculated the boy with real smallpox, but he failed to get the disease. In 1798 Jenner published the results of his experiments in 'An Enquiry into the Causes and Effects . . . of Cow Pox'. Although his methods were at first opposed, they were soon adopted, not only in Britain but also in many other European countries and in the United States. Parliament gave him £10,000 as a reward for his work in 1802 and another £20,000 in 1807.

LOUIS PASTEUR →

Jet planes were developed in Britain in 1941 by *Sir Frank Whittle* and were being used before the end of the Second World War. The German firm of Heinkel had already successfully tested a jet plane by 1939, but Hitler gave little encouragement to the production of jet fighter planes. He preferred to use jet propulsion for his 'secret weapon'—the *V1*, or flying bomb. Jet passenger planes were developed after the war and the British were the first to run a regular service from London to Johannesburg, South Africa, with a de Havilland *Comet* jet airliner. The service started in 1952.

← SIR FRANK WHITTLE: CONCORDE →

Johnson, Amy (1903–41), pioneer airwoman who made a number of spectacular solo flights and joint flights with her husband, James Mollison (1905–60). In 1930, she flew from England to Australia in nineteen days; and in 1936 she flew from London to the Cape and back, beating the existing records on both journeys. Her flights not only helped to pioneer the development of world air routes but also did much to raise the status of women, by showing that they could succeed in a sphere, which had been thought of almost exclusively as man's.

← ALCOCK AND BROWN

Justices of the Peace (J.P.s) are part-time, unpaid magistrates who have helped to maintain *law and order* and carried out administrative functions since 1361. During Tudor times they were given many new administrative functions, including responsibility for administering the *Poor Law.* They also appointed surveyors of highways, were responsible for weights and measures, administered justice, and kept order by calling in troops if necessary. They lost many of their administrative functions after county councils were established in 1888 though they still have some, such as licensing public houses and granting special licences for drinking after permitted hours at dinners and dances and other occasions. The 20,000 or so J.P.s are appointed by the Lord Chancellor. They still have important legal functions as 98 per cent of criminal cases in England and Wales are dealt with summarily in their magistrates' courts. In general they can deal with cases where there is a maximum sentence of six months' imprisonment or a £400 fine. They also conduct preliminary hearings to see if there is a sufficient case for an accused person to be sent for trial in a higher court on a more serious charge. There are also forty-eight stipendiary magistrates—who work full time and are paid and trained—in London and some other big cities.

K

Kay, John (died 1764?), born in Bury, Lancashire, inventor of the 'flying shuttle' which speeded up the weaving of cloth. Previously two men had been needed to weave broadcloth on a hand loom by passing the shuttle, which carries the weft, or horizontal thread, between them.

In 1733, Kay patented the flying shuttle, which ran on wheels and was knocked from one side of the loom to the other by pulling a cord. It allowed one man to do the work of two. Kay's house was attacked by weavers, who believed that his invention would make them unemployed. He fled to France, where he died. His flying shuttle started to come into general use about 1760.
EDMUND CARTWRIGHT →

Kilmainham Pact, 1882, between Gladstone and Parnell, who had been imprisoned without trial in Kilmainham prison, Dublin, in an attempt to stop outrages by the *Irish Land League*, of which he was president. Gladstone agreed to introduce a Bill to wipe out arrears of rents of Irish tenants and to release Parnell, if he would call off the League's campaign. Parnell was released, but this attempt to introduce more moderate policies failed because of new violence by another Irish organization, the Invincibles, in the *Phoenix Park murders, 1882.*

Kitchener, Lord (1850–1916), famous British military commander, whose poster campaign with the pointing finger and the caption 'Your Country needs YOU', helped to persuade over 2½m. men to volunteer for the Forces during the First World War. Kitchener joined the Army in 1871. He served in the Sudan and Egypt and was appointed a major-general in 1890. In 1896 he set out to reconquer the Sudan, which he finally did after the *Fashoda incident, 1898.* During the Boer War, 1899–1902, he was at first chief of staff under Lord Roberts, and from 1900, commander-in-chief. He was greatly criticized by some Liberals at home for his use of *concentration camps* during the war. In August 1914, he was appointed Minister of War. He was generally popular with the public, but he did not get on well with some of his colleagues in the Cabinet, who blamed him for the shortage of shells on the Western Front in 1915. He was drowned in June 1916, when the warship in which he was travelling to Russia struck a mine. He was made a lord in 1898, a viscount in 1902, and an earl in 1914.

Koch, Robert (1843–1910), German doctor who identified, under the microscope, the bacteria which cause anthrax (1876), tuberculosis (1882), and cholera (1883), and thus helped to lay the foundations for the science of bacteriology.
← LOUIS PASTEUR

Korean War, 1950–3, the only full-scale war officially waged by the United Nations. In 1950, Communist North Korea invaded South

Korea and the United Nations—which was then being boycotted by Russia—condemned North Korea as an aggressor. Although troops fought under the United Nations flag, the main brunt of the fighting was borne by the United States, which suffered 25,000 casualties. Britain lost 600 men.

L

Labour exchanges were originally places where craftsmen could exchange the goods they produced with each other, so that middlemen did not make a profit. They were established by *Robert Owen* in the early 1830s. The modern labour exchange, where people go to find a job, was suggested by *William* (later Lord) *Beveridge*. They were set up by Churchill in 1909. They are now known as employment exchanges and in 1972 the Conservative government announced that they would be modernized over the next few years to get rid of their old-fashioned image.

Labour party was originally known as the Labour Representation Committee. This was formed in 1900 out of a combination of trade unionists; intellectuals in the *Fabian Society*; and two socialist parties, the *Social Democratic Federation* (*S.D.F.*) and the *Independent Labour party* (*I.L.P.*). The Committee favoured a policy of moderate social reform, which caused the more extreme S.D.F. to leave in 1900. (The I.L.P. left for similar reasons in 1932.) *Keir Hardie* played a prominent part in setting up the Committee and the first secretary was *Ramsay MacDonald*. In the 1906 elections 29 out of the 50 candidates were successful. The name of the Labour party was adopted, by which it was already popularly known. The party was hampered by shortage of money, particularly after the *Osborne judgment* of 1909, which stopped unions from contributing to the funds of political parties. The party was helped by the introduction of payment for M.P.s in 1911 (£400 a year), and the *Trade Unions Act, 1913*, which allowed unions to contribute to party funds again under certain conditions. Both of these measures were passed by the Liberals in return for Labour party support of social reforms. A number of Labour party M.P.s, particularly those from the I.L.P., opposed Britain's entry into the First World War; but the Labour party leader, Arthur Henderson (1863–1935), served in Asquith's coalition government and was also a member of Lloyd George's war cabinet from 1916 to 1917. Other Labour M.P.s held minor posts.

Until 1918, the party was dominated by the trade unions. There were scarcely any local constituency parties and in the 1918 election 49 of the 57 Labour M.P.s were sponsored by unions. In 1918 the party was reorganized. Local Labour parties were formed and a new, more radical constitution was adopted, which supported *nationalization*, or as the constitution said, 'the common ownership of the means of production' to secure 'the most equitable distribution' of wealth. The party grew rapidly in the depression after the First World War and won 191 seats in the 1923 election. In 1924 it formed a minority government under Ramsay MacDonald which lasted only eleven months. In 1929 it became the biggest party with 287 seats, but it was still in a minority as the Liberals and Conservatives together could outvote it. Ramsay MacDonald became prime minister for the second time in 1929. In 1931, he split the Labour party, when he and some of his colleagues decided to form a National government including both Conservatives and Liberals to deal with the growing economic crisis. In the 1931 election the Labour party was reduced to 46 M.P.s, but it had trebled its strength to 154 M.P.s by 1935. *Attlee* became leader of the party in 1935 and, with other members of the party, served in the coalition government under Churchill during the Second World War. Attlee became the first Labour prime minister with a clear majority in 1945. He was defeated in 1951. Labour was in power again under *Wilson* from 1964 to 1970.

Labourers' revolt, 1830, see **Swing riots**

Laissez-faire, describes a belief widely held in the nineteenth century that there should be no government interference in economic affairs. The Factory Acts were one of the first breaches of this doctrine, which is now discredited.

Lancaster, Joseph (1778–1838), Quaker educationalist, born in London. In 1798 he opened a school for 1,000 pupils in Borough Road, London, using a *monitorial system* of education, in which the older children taught the younger ones. He claimed that he could teach up to 10,000 children to read fluently in three months. Although he never hit children, he had some even more terrifying punishments, such as tying them to a pillar, or hoisting them to the ceiling in a cage. He lectured widely on his methods and in 1805 George III gave him an interview and subscribed to his work. Three years later, some nonconformists who supported his methods founded the Royal Lancasterian Society, which opened a number of *voluntary schools* for poor

children. When the name of the society was changed to the British and Foreign School Society in 1814, Lancaster was greatly insulted that his own name had been dropped. Four years later, he emigrated to North America, where he opened a number of schools.
THE REV. ANDREW BELL →

Lanchester, Frederick (1868–1946), car manufacturer, born in Lewisham, the son of an architect. In 1895 he built the first successful British motor-car, and six years later started manufacturing a 10-horsepower car in his factory at Sparkbrook, Birmingham. Its design was far in advance of its time, as it had automatic lubrication and an air-cooled engine. He also made experiments with gliders, but failed to receive the recognition he deserved until the end of his life. He died a relatively poor man.
← JOHN BOYD DUNLOP: HENRY ROYCE →

Land League see **Irish Land League**

Law, Arthur Bonar (1858–1923), born in New Brunswick and educated in Canada and in Glasgow. He became an iron merchant in Glasgow and was elected a Conservative M.P. in 1900. He succeeded Balfour as leader of the Conservative party in 1911 and served in the coalition governments during the First World War. He became Conservative prime minister in 1922, but resigned after five months because of ill health.
← ARTHUR JAMES BALFOUR: STANLEY BALDWIN →

LAW AND ORDER. In the eighteenth century there were few efficient forces to maintain law and order: only parish constables and nightwatchmen in the towns and *justices of the peace* who could call in troops if there were serious troubles. The first attempt to create a regular police force was made in the early 1750s when Henry Fielding started the *Bow Street runners* in London. *Peel* created the first modern police force, again in London, by the *Metropolitan Police Act, 1829.* Other towns were obliged to establish forces under the *Municipal Corporations Reform Act, 1835*, and they were set up throughout the country by the *County and Borough Police Act, 1856.*

At the beginning of the nineteenth century punishments were very severe, even for what would now be considered minor offences. Over 200 offences carried the *death penalty*; men, women and children were confined to overcrowded unhealthy prisons; and the sentence of *transportation* was extensively used for minor and political offences.

Attempts were made to improve prison conditions by reformers like *John Howard*, and *Elizabeth Fry* who started work at *Newgate* prison in 1813. After transportation to New South Wales, Australia, was stopped in 1840, many new prisons were built in Britain on the same pattern as *Pentonville*, which was opened in 1843.

From the middle of the century increasing attempts were made to provide alternatives to prison, particularly for children and young people. After a campaign conducted by *Mary Carpenter*, juvenile delinquents were allowed to serve most of their sentence in *reformatories* instead of prison from 1854 onwards. In 1887 magistrates were allowed to put young people on *probation* for first offences. The first *Borstal* was opened in 1902 and juvenile courts were established under the Children's Act of 1908. The first *open prison* was established in 1936.

Since the Second World War, attempts have been made to provide different kinds of sentences for different classes of offenders. In 1948, magistrates were allowed to put people of all ages on probation for a much wider variety of offences and the *Criminal Justice Act, 1967*, made it possible to give suspended sentences. But in recent years much longer sentences of twenty or thirty years have been given to professional criminals, particularly those who have used violence, and new top-security prisons were created, following the escape of a spy from Wormwood Scrubs prison in 1966. The death penalty was abolished in 1965. Attempts to improve the efficiency of prison forces were made by the *Police Act, 1946*, which merged many forces, and by the *Police Act, 1964*, which encouraged the formation of regional crime squads. To speed up the hearing of criminal cases, the old quarter sessions and Assizes, which heard cases only from one area, were replaced in 1971 by Crown courts, which can sit anywhere. They are presided over by a judge or a recorder.

As in most other countries there has been a considerable increase in the amount of crime in recent years. The number of prisoners in England and Wales rose from 53,852 in 1960 to 85,509 in 1970 and in Scotland from 11,128 to 15,340 during the same period. In 1970 there were 89,200 policemen and 3,600 policewomen in England and Wales and 10,000 policemen and 400 policewomen in Scotland—a total of 16,300 below the authorized strength.

Lawes, Sir John Bennet (1814–1900), developed the first artificial fertilizer, superphosphate. He was educated at Eton and Oxford and studied chemistry. With the assistance of John Gilbert, he conducted agricultural experiments on his family estates at Rothamsted, Hertfordshire, and found that superphosphate—made from treating bones with sulphuric acid—greatly increased crop yields. He set up a factory at Deptford in 1844 to manufacture it. He was made a baronet in 1882. Rothamsted Experimental Station is still one of the main centres for agricultural research in the country.

League of Nations. A new attempt, after the failure of the *Congress system*, 1818–25, to settle disputes and prevent war by international co-operation. In contrast to the Congress system, which included only the great powers, the League was open to all nations. An elaborate organization was set up in Geneva in 1920, with a Council containing the great powers, who were permanent members, and smaller nations, changed every three years, and an Assembly of all member states. The League settled a number of minor disputes in the Balkans and in South America, but failed to stop the major aggressors—Japan in Manchuria, 1931; Italy in Abyssinia, 1935; and Germany in Europe, 1936–9. Its policy of *sanctions*—restricting exports to aggressors—was totally ineffective. The League was weakened from the start by the refusal of the United States to join, because of its growing desire after the First World War to avoid international involvement (isolationism) and its resentment that it would have had only one vote compared with six for Britain and the Dominions. Russia did not become a member until 1934; Germany and Japan left in 1933, and Italy in 1937, by which time the League was discredited. However, it continued to do some useful work in helping refugees, supervising former German and Turkish colonies under the *mandate* system; and improving working and social conditions in member countries, through the International Labour Organization, now associated with the *United Nations*.
← TREATY OF VERSAILLES: UNITED NATIONS →

Leeds–Liverpool canal. An important 127-mile-long canal, opened in 1816, linking the clothing city of Leeds with the port of Liverpool.
← GRAND TRUNK CANAL: CALEDONIAN CANAL →

Lend–Lease was started by President Roosevelt in March 1941, before the United States entered the Second World War. It enabled the American government to lend or lease any defence materials to the Allies. The British Commonwealth received over £7,875m. in goods and services during the war. Lend–Lease was abruptly stopped by President Truman on 2 September 1945, when the war against Japan ended, which helped to bring about an economic crisis in Britain.
AMERICAN LOAN →

Lib-Labs. The name given to working-class M.P.s, who sat with the Liberals in the House of Commons. The first two were elected in 1874 and there were eleven by 1885. The collaboration died away after the formation of the Labour party, though *John Burns* accepted office under the Liberals in 1906, and became the first working-class Cabinet minister.

Liberal party emerged under Gladstone as a fusion of *Whigs*, '*Peelites*' and *radicals.* During his first ministry, from 1868 to 1874, he introduced many reforms which had been blocked by the Whig prime minister, Palmerston. (For details of these reforms see *Gladstone.*) He also supported *free trade*, settled the *Alabama dispute* by arbitration, and cut government spending, under his policy of 'peace, retrenchment and reform'. The Liberals were the first party to build up a highly efficient party machine—initially in Birmingham by Joseph Chamberlain in 1878. This model was soon copied in other parts of the country. Its efficiency was revealed in Gladstone's *Midlothian campaigns.* The Liberal party split over Irish Home Rule in 1886, when Joseph Chamberlain and other *Liberal Unionists* left the party. It was split again to a lesser extent in the second Boer War, when there was a large anti-war section led by Lloyd George. The Liberal party got into power in 1905 and carried out many reforms before the First World War. These included *The Trade Disputes Act, 1906*; *old-age pensions, 1908*; *Trade Boards Act, 1909*; *labour exchanges, 1909*; the *Parliament Act, 1911*; *payment of M.P.s, 1911*; the *National Insurance Act, 1911* and the *Irish Home Rule Act, 1912–1914.*

Liberal prime ministers, first Asquith and then, from 1916, Lloyd George, headed the coalition governments during the First World War. Lloyd George's coalition government remained in office until 1922. But the party had been severely damaged by the feud between Lloyd George and Asquith and in the 1922 elections only 54 Liberals were elected (plus 62 National Liberals who favoured the coalition with the Conservatives). The Liberals got 159 seats in the 1923 election, but only 40 in the election in the following year. They have never been in power since. During the nineteenth century, the party was supported by big business; the urban middle classes, particularly nonconformists; and some workers. But in the present century, big business has become increasingly associated with the Conservatives and workers with the Labour party.

Liberal Unionists, led by *Joseph Chamberlain*, who wanted Ireland to remain part of the United Kingdom and left the Liberal party after the first *Irish Home Rule Bill, 1886.* They allied with the Conservative party, which became officially known as the Conservative and Unionist party.

The Liberator, nickname of *Daniel O'Connell,* whose campaign in Ireland resulted in the granting of Catholic emancipation.

Licensing Act, 1872 (amended 1874), restricted the hours at which public houses could open in England. They were not allowed to open until 12.30 a.m. or 1 p.m. on Sundays and had to shut again in the afternoons. But on weekdays they were allowed to open from 6 a.m. to 11 p.m. in towns (5 a.m. to 12.30 p.m. in London) and from 6 a.m. to 10 p.m. in the country. The Act was passed by Henry Austin Bruce (1815–95), later Lord Aberdare, Home Secretary under Gladstone. The law, which was unpopular with the general public and publicans and brewers, was a major cause of Gladstone's defeat in 1874. (See also *Drinking.*)

Life Peerages Act, 1958, allowed peers to be created for their lifetime only, so that the titles could not be inherited by their heirs. It also admitted women to membership of the House of Lords. Life peerages were first suggested in 1870 and have been granted to some judges (Lords of Appeal) since 1876.
← PARLIAMENT ACT, 1949

Lighting. Oil lamps, candles and rushlights—made by stripping rushes of their outer leaves and dipping them into melted fat—were the only means of artificial lighting in the eighteenth century. As a result many people went to bed soon after it was dark. Gas lighting was invented by *William Murdock* in 1792. It was first used in factories and textile mills and was installed in some streets of Westminster in 1814. By the middle of the nineteenth century, gas lights were common in the streets of many towns and in middle-class homes. The gas came straight out of a burner, shaped like a fishtail or a bat's wing, and gave a yellow, smoky light. In 1885 an incandescent gas mantle was introduced, which gave a much whiter, brighter light. *Electricity* started to be used for lighting streets and in some well-to-do homes from the 1880s. The first town in the world to install electric street lights was Godalming, Surrey, but the experiment was abandoned after three years because of the high cost. Electric lighting gradually replaced gas lighting in the streets and in the homes as more power stations were built and electricity became cheaper, but this did not happen until after the First World War.

Limited liability company. Firms in which the shareholder is liable only for the money he has invested if the firm fails or goes into liquidation. Limited liability companies were authorized by the Joint Stock Companies Act, 1856 and the Companies Act, 1862. Previously, with a few exceptions, owners, partners or investors had been liable to lose all their money and possessions if their firm failed. As a result of the Acts, many more people became willing to invest their savings in firms, so that it became much easier for industry to obtain money and to expand. This was one of the causes of the expansion in the size of firms during the later years of the century. Between 1856 and 1862, nearly 2,500 firms registered as limited liability companies.

Lister, Joseph (1827–1912), later Lord Lister, a surgeon who made operations much safer by using antiseptic methods. He was born at Upton, Essex, and educated at University College, London. Following the discoveries made by *Louis Pasteur*, he started using antiseptic methods in his operations from 1865, by soaking all his operating instruments and surgical dressings in a solution of carbolic acid, which kills 'germs'. As a result most of his patients recovered, though previously up to half had died after an amputation. Antiseptics also helped to wipe out gangrene and other diseases in his wards, which in his own words had been 'among the unhealthiest in the whole surgical division of Glasgow Royal Infirmary'. Surgeons at that time still wore old bloodstained coats, used unsterilized instruments, and employed other patients to make up surgical dressings out of pieces of old linen. Lister's methods were at first opposed, but were eventually adopted with the saving of many lives. He was made a lord in 1897.

← SIR JAMES SIMPSON

Liston, Robert (1794–1847), surgeon, born Ecclemachan, Linlithgow. He performed the first operation in Britain using an anaesthetic (ether) at University College Hospital, London, in 1846. After the operation, the patient woke up and asked 'When are you going to begin?' Liston was noted for the speed of his operations, which was necessary in the days before anaesthetics, to save the patient pain. It was said of him that 'the gleam of his knife was followed so instantaneously by the sound of sawing as to make the two actions appear almost simultaneous'.

← CRAWFORD LONG: SIR JAMES SIMPSON →

Liverpool, Earl of (1770–1828), prime minister for fifteen years, the longest term of office in the nineteenth century. He was educated at Charterhouse and Christ Church, Oxford, and became a Tory M.P.

in 1790. He was Foreign Secretary from 1801 to 1804; Home Secretary from 1804 to 1806 and from 1807 to 1809; and Secretary for War from 1809 to 1812, when he became prime minister. He remained in office until 1827, when he resigned after a stroke. Although his years in office were some of the most reactionary in modern British history, he did introduce progressive Tories into his government, including Canning, Peel and Huskisson. He had the gift of maintaining harmony between ministers of widely differing views. He succeeded to his father's title in 1808.

← VISCOUNT SIDMOUTH: GEORGE CANNING →

Livingstone, David (1813–73), best-known of the Victorian *missionaries* whose journeys in the interior of Africa did much to open up the continent to European settlers and also exposed the evils of the continuing slave trade. He was born at Blantyre, Lanarkshire, and worked in a cotton mill from the age of ten to twenty-three, when he left to enter Anderson's College, Glasgow. He studied medicine, and qualified in 1840 when he left England as a missionary for the London Missionary Society. He worked at a mission station in Bechuanaland and in 1849 discovered Lake Ngami, north of the Kalahari Desert. He set out on his first major journey of exploration in 1853, accompanied only by a group of Africans. It lasted three years. During the journey, he discovered the Victoria Falls on the Zambezi river, and by the time he returned to England he had become famous. In 1858, he set out on his second journey in Africa, during which he discovered Lake Nyasa. The Royal Geographical Society then asked him to try to discover the sources of the Nile and he set out on his third, and final, journey in 1866. Nothing was heard of him for five years until he was 'found' by H. M. Stanley. Livingstone continued his search for the source of the Nile unsuccessfully. Worn out by his exertions and ill-health, he died in 1873. His body, which had been embalmed by Africans, was carried by them to the coast and then sent to England for burial in Westminster Abbey.

HENRY MORTON STANLEY →

Lloyd George, David (1863–1945), Liberal reformer, born in Manchester, but brought up in Caernarvonshire after his father's early death. He attended a village school and became a solicitor in 1884. In 1890 he was elected Liberal M.P. for Caernarvon and held the seat until 1945. He attracted great attention by his 'pro-Boer' speeches during the Boer War, 1889–1902. In 1905 he was made President of the Board of Trade by Campbell-Bannerman and in 1908 he became

Chancellor of the Exchequer. Lloyd George created the beginnings of the welfare state with the introduction of *old age pensions* in 1908 and the *National Insurance Act, 1911*. In 1909 he introduced his radical '*People's Budget*', which proposed a supertax on large incomes and a tax on land. When the Budget was rejected by the House of Lords, the *Parliament Act, 1911*, was passed, which took away their powers to hold up other Bills. During the First World War there was a serious shortage of shells on the Western Front by 1915, and Lloyd George was put in charge of a new Ministry of Munitions and succeeded in ending the shortage of war supplies. After increasing criticisms of Asquith's leadership, Lloyd George combined with the Conservatives to overthrow him, and became prime minister of a new coalition government in 1916. He prosecuted the war with great vigour through a small war cabinet of five men. Following the *coupon election* of 1918, his coalition government retained power after the end of the war. *A Housing and Town Planning Act* was passed in 1919; unemployment insurance was extended to most workers; and the railways were amalgamated into four major companies. In 1921 Lloyd George persuaded representatives of the Irish nationalists to sign the Anglo-Irish Treaty, which set up the *Irish Free State* in southern Ireland. This and other policies offended the Conservatives, who left the coalition. Lloyd George resigned. After an election in 1922 the conservatives got into power under Bonar Law. Lloyd George's personal feud with Asquith over the leadership and the coupon election had wrecked the Liberal party and it has never held power again. Lloyd George remained an M.P. until 1945 and was made Earl Lloyd George of Dwyfor just before his death.

← H. H. ASQUITH

LOCAL GOVERNMENT. At the beginning of the nineteenth century there was great confusion, corruption and inefficiency in local government. Justices of the Peace (magistrates), were responsible for many local matters, such as law and order, weights and measures etc. Some public services, such as *turnpike roads*, were controlled by local trusts which had been set up by special Act of Parliament. Some older towns were governed by mayors and corporations, who were often corrupt, but most of the big new industrial towns, like Manchester, had no local council at all. The *Municipal Corporations Reform Act, 1835*, replaced the old borough corporations by new, elected councils, and allowed big industrial towns to apply to become boroughs with councils of their own. At first the new councils were not given many powers, except over police forces, which they were obliged to set up. But the councils in some big industrial towns, like Liverpool and Manchester, applied to Parliament for special Acts of Parliament to be passed, which gave them powers to introduce much-needed reforms in sanitation, housing and the appointment of *medical officers of health.* Under the influence of *Edwin Chadwick* an attempt was made in the 1830s and 1840s to reverse the trend towards local government by establishing uniform national control of the relief of poverty under the *Poor Law Amendment Act, 1834,* and of sanitation under the *Public Health Act, 1848,* but neither was entirely successful.

Modern local government, with elected councils controlling a wide range of public and social services, developed during the last quarter of the nineteenth century. County councils, elected by ratepayers, were set up under the Local Government Act, 1888, to run local government services in the whole county. Towns with populations of 50,000 or more were made into county boroughs to control services in their own urban areas, and a special council was set up in the capital—the London County Council (L.C.C.). Another Local Government Act, passed in 1894, set up rural and urban district councils, and parish councils, with smaller powers. In the present century, the larger councils, county and county boroughs, have been given control over many more matters, such as education and midwifery (1902), maternity and child welfare (1918), and libraries (1919). The Local Government Act of 1929 passed by Neville Chamberlain, then Minister of Health, gave county and county borough councils control over public assistance to the poor and sick, and the old poor law hospitals, and abolished *Boards of Guardians.*

In 1965 a new two-tier system of local government was introduced in London. A new Greater London Council was set up, which is responsible for general services such as fire and ambulance and overall planning. At the same time 85 borough councils were merged into 32 larger units to cover much wider areas. In 1971 it was proposed to introduce a similar system throughout Britain. There will be 6 'metropolitan counties' in England and Wales to run all the local government services in these major conurbations and 39 county councils which will control most transport, education and personal social services and make the major planning decisions in their areas. There will also be 375 district councils, for areas with populations from 40,000 to 100,000, which will provide local services such as housing, refuse collection and the provision of parks and other amenities. These new councils will replace 1,200 councils of various kinds; but 7,000 smaller parish councils will remain in existence. Elections for the new councils were held in England and Wales in 1973 and they will assume power in 1974. Elections are due to be held in Scotland in 1974 and the councils will take over in 1975.

The main problem in local government, which is still far from solved, is how to keep a proper balance between large units, which are needed for more efficient planning, and the desires of ratepayers to have some control over what happens in their own street or town.

Local Government Board was set up in 1871 to supervise both the poor law and public health. This meant that the provision of better sanitation and housing was sometimes treated as if it were poor law charity rather than an urgently needed reform. The Board was abolished in 1919.
← GENERAL BOARD OF HEALTH: MINISTRY OF HEALTH →

Lock-out, the opposite of a strike, in which an employer tries to force workers to accept lower wages, longer hours, or the closure of a factory or plant by refusing to allow workers to come into the factory to work. There were many lock-outs in factories from the early years of the industrial revolution. There were also lock-outs by farmers in the 1870s following the campaign by *Joseph Arch* for higher wages for farm labourers, and frequent lock-outs in the mining industry throughout the nineteenth and twentieth centuries until it was nationalized in 1947. The modern answer to a lock-out is a *work-in.*

Locomotive Act, 1865, also known as the 'Red Flag' Act, made it compulsory for any mechanically propelled vehicle on the roads to have a person walking in front carrying a red flag to warn pedestrians and horsemen. It also introduced a speed limit of 4 m.p.h. The Act, which was passed under pressure from the railway companies, was designed to stop any competition from *steam carriages.* It also affected the first motor-cars. (See next entry.)

Locomotives on Highways Act, 1896. Motor-cars, or light locomotives as they were then called, no longer had to have a person walking in front of them. The speed limit was raised to a maximum of 14 m.p.h., which was usually fixed at 12 m.p.h. by Local Government Boards. The raising of the speed limit was celebrated by delighted pioneer motorists with a drive from London to Brighton, which is still held for veteran cars every year.
← LOCOMOTIVE ACT, 1865: MOTOR-CAR ACT, 1903 →

London Docks Strike, 1889, the first major strike by unskilled workers, who succeeded after a 5-week struggle in gaining their demand for 6*d.*

an hour pay, and 8*d.* an hour for overtime. They were led by *Tom Mann, John Burns, and* Ben Tillett (1860–1943), first secretary of the Dockers' Union which was formed after the strike. The success of the strike resulted in a growth in union membership, and new unions for unskilled workers were formed.

London Naval Conferences were held in 1930 and 1936. The first conference of big naval powers agreed that the building of capital ships (battleships or cruisers) should be suspended for six years, and that Britain, the United States and Japan should reduce the number of capital ships to 15, 15 and 9 respectively. At the second conference, it was agreed that warships should be limited to 14-inch guns and that the size of aircraft carriers should be reduced. But Japan withdrew; France and Italy refused to co-operate; and mounting international tension made the agreement ineffective.
← WASHINGTON CONFERENCE

Long, Crawford (1815–78), American doctor, who first used ether as an anaesthetic in an operation at Jefferson, Georgia, in 1842. Previously, patients had been held down on the operating table by assistants or tied to it by ropes, and given a drink of rum in an attempt to alleviate the pain.
ROBERT LISTON →

Lovett, William (1800–77), Chartist, born at Newlyn, Cornwall. He was apprenticed to a ropemaker in Penzance, but went to London in 1821 and became a cabinet maker. He soon became associated with the *co-operative movement* and the campaign for parliamentary reform. In 1832 he was arrested and accused of rioting, but he was acquitted. Disappointed by the failure of the *First Reform Act* to give the vote to the working classes, he helped to found the London Working Men's Association in 1836 to carry on a new campaign for parliamentary reform. He drew up the People's Charter, which formed the basis of *Chartism.* In 1839 he was imprisoned for a year for publicly condemning the conduct of the police in breaking up a Chartist meeting at the Bull-ring, Birmingham. After the failure of the Chartist movement in 1848, he devoted himself to education and eked out a living by writing science textbooks and teaching.
← FEARGUS O'CONNOR

Lowe, Robert (1811–92), Whig statesman, who as Vice-President of the Education Department, 1859–64, started '*payment by results*' in schools. He led the *Adullamites* in the Liberal party who opposed plans for parliamentary reform in the 1860s. As Chancellor of the Exchequer from 1868 to 1873, he introduced an unpopular tax on matches. He was made Viscount Sherbrooke in 1880.

Luddites. Weavers, and other hand workers in the textile industries, who feared that the introduction of machinery would make them unemployed. They wrecked machinery and burnt down factories and mill-owners' houses. The riots started in the Midlands in 1811, spread to Lancashire and Yorkshire, and continued until 1817. It was thought that the movement was controlled by a master mind, 'General Lud', who wrote illiterate letters to newspapers, justifying the Luddites' actions. The name of Luddite is now sometimes used to describe those who resist industrial change.

Lunacy Act, 1845, set up a Board of Commissioners to inspect asylums, hospitals and workhouses where the mentally ill were detained. Some patients were still kept permanently in chains in cells with filthy straw-covered floors, in spite of the more humane methods of treatment, pioneered by *William Tuke*. The Act, which was passed after a long campaign by *Lord Shaftesbury*, resulted in some improvements. (See next entry.)

Lunacy Act, 1890, made it necessary to get an order from a magistrate before a person could be detained in a mental asylum, to prevent cases in which sane people had been wrongfully detained.
← LUNACY ACT, 1845: MENTAL TREATMENT ACT, 1930 →

M

McAdam, John Loudon (1756–1836), road builder, born in Ayr, Scotland. After his father died in 1770, he went to live with an uncle in the United States and became a merchant. In 1793, he returned to Scotland as a wealthy man and bought an estate there. He was appointed deputy lieutenant for Ayrshire and took a special interest in the county's roads. In 1798 he moved to Falmouth, Cornwall. Between 1798 and 1814 he claimed to have travelled along 30,000 miles of British roads to see how they could be improved. In 1815 he was appointed Surveyor-General for Bristol, which put him in charge of 149 miles of roads in the area, and twelve years later he was made Surveyor-General to the Commissioners of Metropolitan Turnpike Roads, which gave him responsibility for roads throughout the country. He revolutionized the building of roads. Instead of using large stones, which were displaced by the wheels of vehicles, he used small stones which were bound together by the weight of the traffic. He said that any stone which was more than an inch in any of its dimensions was 'mischievous'. Macadamized roads (named after him) were built in other countries throughout the world. At the beginning of the twentieth century they were tarred, because of the dust problem caused by fast-moving motor traffic.

← THOMAS TELFORD

MacDonall, James Ramsay (1866–1937), one of the founders of the Labour party who was eventually expelled for collaborating with the Conservatives and Liberals and forming a National government with them in 1931. He was born of poor parents in Lossiemouth, Scotland, and worked on a farm and then as a *pupil teacher*. He moved to London and became a journalist and private secretary to an M.P. He joined the *Independent Labour party* soon after it was formed in 1893 and in 1900 became the first secretary of the Labour Representation Committee, which became the *Labour party* in 1906. He was elected an M.P. in 1906 and was leader of the Labour party from 1911 to 1914, but lost that position when he opposed Britain's entry into the First World War. He lost his seat in the 1918 *coupon election,* but became an M.P. again in 1922 and was re-elected leader of the Labour party. In 1924 he became the first Labour prime minister. A *Housing Act* was passed in 1924, which started Council house building on a large scale. But MacDonald did not have a clear majority. He was dependent on Liberal support, and his first ministry lasted only eleven months. He was defeated in the 1924 election, partly because the *Zinoviev letter* convinced some voters that the Labour party included fellow travellers who sympathized with Communist Russia. He became prime minister again in 1929 and appointed Margaret Bondfield as Minister of Labour—the first woman ever to be a Cabinet minister. But MacDonald was still dependent on Liberal support and resigned in 1931 in the midst of the depression and the ever-worsening economic crisis. In August 1931, he agreed to lead a National government, which included Conservatives and Liberals. Although three other Labour ministers agreed to serve under him, most of the party thought MacDonald was a traitor and expelled him. He led the government, which was dominated by Conservatives, until 1935, when he resigned in favour of Baldwin.

CLEMENT ATTLEE →

Macmillan, Harold (born 1894), Conservative statesman and publisher, educated at Eton and Balliol College, Oxford. He succeeded Eden after the crisis over the *Suez canal* and was prime minister from 1957 to 1963. During his period in office there was a considerable increase in the standard of living, which helped to give the Conservatives an increased majority in the 1959 election fought under Macmillan's slogan 'You've never had it so good'. But the basic economic problems were not solved. In 1963 Britain's application to join the European Community was rejected by General de Gaulle. Macmillan obtained the *Polaris* missile from the United States for nuclear defence and played some part in obtaining agreement to the *Test Ban Treaty* of 1963. He also took an active role in Commonwealth affairs. In 1960, in an address to the South African parliament in Cape Town, he gave a warning that Britain could no longer condone *apartheid* as a 'wind of change' was blowing through Africa. In 1962 his government passed the *Commonwealth Immigrants Act*, which restricted free entry for Commonwealth citizens into Britain for the first time.

← ANTHONY EDEN : SIR ALEC DOUGLAS HOME →

Maginot line of strong fortifications, erected along France's border with Germany, from Luxemburg to Switzerland, between the two world wars. The Germans got round the line by attacking France through Belgium and Holland. The line, named after a French minister of war, became a symbol of a defensive state of mind which was unprepared for the unexpected.

Mail coaches. Fast coaches with a Post Office armed guard which carried both passengers and mail. They were introduced by *John Palmer* on the London–Bath–Bristol route in 1784 to replace the post-boys who travelled much more slowly on horseback. The service was extended to all parts of the country and at one time there were over twenty mail coach routes from London alone, In the 1830s contracts to carry the mail were given to the *railways* and the last London mail coach was withdrawn in 1846.

← STAGE COACHES : PENNY POST →

Malthus, Thomas Robert (1766–1834), clergyman and economist, who published an influential 'Essay on the Principle of Population' in 1798. His theory was that the population, when unchecked, increased more rapidly than the means of subsistence and food supplies and that it was only wars, famine, plague and poverty that kept the two in balance. The theory was used by some people to justify the payment of low wages to workers on the grounds that they would then be unable to afford to have large numbers of children, and the reduction in outdoor relief brought about by the *Poor Law Amendment Act, 1834*. But Malthus failed to foresee the enormous increase in food production which was made possible by the application of science and technology to agriculture and the development of lands in the Empire; and also the effects of increased demands from workers in the towns in stimulating agricultural growth. His theory that better living conditions would necessarily cause an increase in the *birth rate* has also not been borne out.

Manchester school. Radical politicians, from the new manufacturing classes in and around Manchester, who believed in *free trade*, '*laissez-faire*', and international collaboration. They were opposed to war. They flourished from the 1840s onwards and were the mainstay of the radical wing of the Liberal party in the middle of the century. *Richard Cobden* and *John Bright* were the main leaders.

Manchester ship canal. A 35-mile-long canal, opened in 1894, which allows ocean-going vessels to reach Manchester, which is the country's biggest inland port. In 1970, Manchester was the seventh largest port for foreign trade in Britain.
← CALEDONIAN CANAL

Mandate system of government, established by the *League of Nations*, under which the former colonies of the defeated powers of Germany and Turkey were put under the control of one of the Allied powers after the First World War. The countries had to be made ready for independence, and annual progress reports had to be given to the League. Britain became responsible for Palestine, Iraq, Transjordan and Tanganyika.

Mann, Tom (1856–1941), Socialist leader, born at Foleshill, Warwickshire. He started work on a farm at the age of nine and then became an apprentice engineer. He joined the *Amalgamated Society of Engineers* in 1881 and was one of the younger members who tried to make it adopt more radical policies. In 1889 he took a leading part in the *London Dockers' Strike* and was president of the Dockers' Union from 1890 to 1893. He was secretary of the Independent Labour Party from 1894 to 1896. From 1902 to 1908 he worked in Australia as a Socialist agitator. On his return to England he took a leading part in the Socialist campaign to persuade working men not to fight in the

First World War. He was secretary of the Amalgamated Society of Engineers from 1918 to 1921 and joined the Communist party of Great Britain when it was formed in 1920. He continued to campaign for Socialist reforms until the end of his life and in 1932 was sentenced to two months' imprisonment for agitating among the unemployed in London.

Mao Tse Tung (born 1893), Chinese Communist leader, whose little red book of his thoughts and whose theories of guerrilla warfare have had a great influence on many modern revolutionaries. He helped to found the Chinese Communist party in 1921; organized the Red Army in 1927; and led the 3,000-mile Long March from Kiangsi to Shensi in China between 1934 and 1935 when the Red Army was attacked by the Chinese nationalists. After the Americans had failed to patch up a peace between the two sides at the end of the Second World War, during which China fought on the Allied side against the Japanese, civil war broke out in China. The Communists, under Mao, finally expelled the Chinese nationalists to the offshore island of Formosa, or Taiwan. The Chinese nationalists continued to represent China in the United Nations until 1971. Mao's claim to represent the true voice of Marxist-Leninist Communism, his theory that revolution never ends, and his great achievements in building up his country, have made him the hero of many Communists throughout the world, who are opposed to what they consider to be Russian 'revisionism'.

Maori Wars of 1843 and 1860 to 1870 were fought by the native inhabitants of New Zealand against the British over the land question. (For the background see *New Zealand.*)

Marconi, Guglielmo (1874–1937), Italian pioneer of radio. He conducted his first successful experiments with radio telegraphy in 1896 by sending a message in Morse code a distance of nearly two miles without using a connecting cable between the transmitter and the receiver. Three years later he sent signals from England to France. On 12 December 1901, he succeeded in sending a wireless signal across the Atlantic, though many scientists thought this would be impossible because of the curvature of the earth. He shared the Nobel prize for physics with K. F. Braun in 1909.
SIR JOHN FLEMING →

Markievicz, Countess (1868–1927), born Constance Gore Booth, an Irish revolutionary married to a Polish count, who was the first woman to be elected an M.P.—for Dublin in 1918. But like other members of *Sinn Fein* she refused to take her seat.

NANCY ASTOR →

Married Women's Property Acts. The first Act in 1870 gave a wife the right to keep her own earnings, and a second Act in 1882 gave women the right to keep property they owned on marriage, or acquired later. Previously the wife's property and earnings had belonged to her husband by law.

Marshall Aid, 1948–51. United States aid, totalling 13,000m. dollars, which was given to Western Europe after the start of the *cold war* to help restore its economic strength which had been greatly weakened by the Second World War. Originally, the aid was also offered to Russia and other East European countries, but none of them accepted it. The aid helped to put Western Europe back on its feet and to reduce the support for Communism, which was strong in many West European countries after the war. The idea was put forward by General George Marshall (1880–1959), who was U.S. Secretary of State from 1947 to 1949.

← AMERICAN LOAN

Marx, Karl (1818–83), German-Jewish historian, economist and philosopher, whose theories have had a lasting effect on world history, and resulted in the founding of modern Communism. In 1848 he wrote the Communist Manifesto in collaboration with Friedrich Engels (1820–1895), which called for world revolution and for the 'proletarians of all countries' to unite. He then went to London, where he spent much of the rest of his life working in the reading room of the British Museum on his major work 'Capital'. His main theory was that *capitalism* created within itself the means of its own destruction. He argued that big firms would swallow up smaller firms; there would be economic crises; and the conditions of the working classes would gradually worsen, so that a class of poor workers—the proletariat—would be created. These would eventually rise in revolt and destroy capitalism and the 'bourgeois' (middle class) society. A dictatorship of the proletariat would follow, in which industries would be taken over by the people under a programme of *nationalization*, and large private fortunes would be taken away. But eventually, the State would 'wither away' and there would be a true Communist society based on the principle 'from each according to his ability, to each according to his needs'.

MASS COMMUNICATIONS is the communication of the same information and views to millions of people at the same time. In the eighteenth century when most people could not read, and books, *newspapers* and magazines were scarce and expensive, the majority of people depended for information and news on their neighbours and the occasional visitors, travellers and pedlars who visited the villages and small towns where they lived. Only in London and some of the larger ports and cities was there a more lively flow of information—and rumour.

The age of mass communications started with the growth of the *popular press* towards the end of the nineteenth century which was made possible by the repeal of the *Taxes on Knowledge*, and the increase in the number of people who could read after the passing of the *Education Act, 1870*. For twenty years or more, most people relied mainly on newspapers and magazines for outside views and information, but the development of *radio and television* broadcasts between the two world wars provided an alternative source. The mass communications age on a world scale has developed only since the end of the last war, with technical improvements in *communications* making it possible for millions of people in many different countries to watch and hear the same thing at the same time. This has helped to make attitudes, aspirations and ideas more uniform in urban areas throughout the world. Mass communications has now become an industry in its own right.

Mass consumption, the buying of a large number of similar or identical goods—produced in factories by *mass production* methods—by millions of people. If people were not encouraged to buy the goods by advertising, *hire purchase*, and other means, the factories would be unable to sell many of their goods and there would be unemployment. The mass consumption age started in Britain in the 1950s. By 1970, 52 per cent of all households had a car, 65 per cent a washing machine, and 66 per cent a refrigerator. Practically all homes had radios and television sets. As these goods sometimes do not live up to the buyer's expectations, various means of protecting the consumer have had to be introduced.
CONSUMER COUNCIL →

Mass motoring started in Britain in the 1950s. In 1955 there were only about 2½m. cars (only ½m. more than in 1939), but by 1965 there were nearly 9m. In 1968 there were over 11m. and it is estimated that by 1980 there will be 19m. motor-cars in Britain and an additional 8m. commercial vehicles.
MOTORWAYS →

Mass production, the making of identical goods in factories by machinery. The earliest example in Britain was the plant for making wooden pulley blocks at Portsmouth dockyard, built by *Henry Maudslay* between 1801 and 1806 to the designs of *Sir Marc Brunel.* But modern mass production methods in metal goods could not be used until *Sir Joseph Whitworth* improved engineering techniques so that parts could be made which were exactly alike and therefore interchangeable. (Previously most parts of machines had been made individually and if one broke another similar part had to be made so that it fitted.) In mass production methods thousands or millions of identical parts are made by machines and then put together on an assembly line. The United States was the first country to use mass production methods on any large scale, first for the production of muskets and clocks, and then, by the middle of the century for revolvers. *Henry Ford* was the first motor-car manufacturer to use mass production methods. The extension of these methods to other industries led to the age of *mass production.*
AUTOMATION ⟶

Match girls' strike, 1888, by women workers at Bryant and May's factory in London for better working conditions and higher wages. It was one of the first successful strikes by unskilled workers. Mrs Annie Besant (1847–1933), a socialist and a freethinker, helped to organize it.
⟵ EMMA PATERSON

Maudslay, Henry (1771–1831), engineer, who pioneered new standards of accuracy in mechanical engineering and trained many of the great engineers of the nineteenth century. He started work in Woolwich Arsenal at the age of twelve and was employed by *Joseph Bramah* from 1789 to 1797, when he left to found his own engineering firm in London. In 1800 he invented a screw-cutting lathe which could produce metal screws of identical size. Previously they had been made by hand. He also invented a micrometer which could measure up to 1/10,000th of an inch. From 1801 to 1806 he was employed by *Sir Marc Isambard Brunel* in constructing machinery to make wooden pulley blocks at Portsmouth dockyard—the first example of *mass production* methods in Britain. In 1810 he set up a firm at Lambeth in partnership with Joshua Field (1787–1863), which specialized in making steam and marine engines.
⟵ JOSEPH BRAMAH: JAMES NASMYTH ⟶

Mauretania. A Cunard line steamship of 31,000 tons which held the

record for the fastest Atlantic crossing at an average speed of over 26 knots from 1909 to 1930.
QUEEN MARY →

Means test was introduced in 1931 to save money on public assistance payments to men who had been out of work for a long time. The unemployment insurance scheme, first introduced by the *National Insurance Act, 1911*, had broken down almost completely with the massive *unemployment* during the *depression.* In assessing the amount that a man should receive, the earnings or pensions of other members of his family living in the same house were taken into consideration. As a result, payments to many men were reduced and fathers had to live off their son's or daughter's earnings, and elderly relatives living on pensions were forced to move out so that the man could draw his full allowance. The payments in the 1930s amounted to 12*s.* 6*d.* a week for a single man, 23*s.* for a couple, 4*s.* for the eldest child and 3*s.* for each other child. The household means test, which aroused much bitterness and anger among the working classes, was not officially ended until 1941, when unemployment was no longer a problem because the Second World War had provided increased opportunities for work.

MECHANICAL ENGINEERING was an essential part of the industrial revolution. The growth of the *iron and steel industry*, the development of the *steam engine*, and the use of machinery in factories, all created a demand for skilled mechanical engineers who could work to fine limits. Many millwrights, who had built and maintained windmills and water mills, became mechanics; clockmakers and mathematical instrument makers became toolmakers, who made precision tools, such as lathes, which were used in making the parts for other machines. Some of the great engineers of the nineteenth century were *Henry Maudslay*, *Richard Roberts*, *James Nasmyth* and *Sir Joseph Whitworth.* The growth of the industry was reflected in the formation of the *Amalgamated Society of Engineers*—the first of the new model unions—in 1851. Britain led the world in mechanical engineering for much of the nineteenth century, but by the end of the century the United States had taken over the lead in the production of new machine tools and *mass production* methods. In 1970, over 1,200,000 workers were employed in mechanical engineering in Britain.

Mechanics' Institutes provided instruction in English, arithmetic, elementary science and other subjects for thousands of workers, mainly skilled craftsmen, in the nineteenth century. They were started in 1800 when Dr George Birkbeck (1776–1841) gave a course of lectures at the Andersonian Institute, Glasgow. In 1822 he founded the London Mechanics' Institute in Chancery Lane and by 1850 there were over 700 other institutes in various parts of the country. Their importance declined after the passing of the *Education Act, 1870*.

UNIVERSITY EXTENSION LECTURES →

Medical Act, 1858, greatly improved medical standards by setting up a General Medical Council (G.M.C.) to supervise the work of universities and other colleges which trained doctors. The Council was also allowed to keep an annual register of doctors and to remove the name of any doctor who was guilty of unprofessional conduct, which meant that he could no longer practise. (See next entry.)

Medical Act, 1886, made it necessary for doctors to take an examination before they could register with the General Medical Council. (See next entry.)

Medical Act, 1950, gave the General Medical Council powers to appoint Visitors to inspect the work of medical schools.

Medical Officers of Health. The first, Dr William Duncan, was appointed by the city of Liverpool under a special Act of Parliament in 1847. The *Public Health Act, 1848,* allowed the new local boards of health to appoint medical officers of health. This was made compulsory in 1872, but most of them were only part-time. It was not until 1929 that county and county borough councils were required to appoint full-time officers. Medical officers of health have played a big part in trying to maintain high standards of *public health* in their area.

MEDICINE. Developments in medicine in modern times have made a major contribution to the general welfare of the mass of people by helping them to live longer and healthier lives and by taking much of the pain out of illness and operations. The use of anaesthetics in operations was suggested by *Sir Humphrey Davy* in 1798, but they were not used until 1842 by an American, *Crawford Long.* Four years later ether was used as an anaesthetic in Britain by *Robert Liston* and in 1847 *Sir James Simpson* started using a stronger anaesthetic, chloroform. But many people still died in *hospitals* as a result of the unhygienic conditions. The first attempts to improve hygiene were made by *Florence Nightingale* during the Crimean War, 1854–6, who was also responsible for big improvements in *nursing.* There was a general raising of medical standards after the *Medical Act, 1858.* In 1865 *Joseph Lister* started to use antiseptic methods in his hospital at Glasgow, which resulted in a great reduction in the number of deaths during operations.

Lister's work was based on the discoveries of a Frenchman, *Louis Pasteur,* who revolutionized the whole approach to medicine—and *public health*—by showing that some diseases were caused by 'germs' or bacteria. His pioneering work led on to many other important discoveries in bacteriology by *Robert Koch.* Pasteur also showed how inoculation with a mild form of a disease could safeguard people against it. (In 1796–8, *Edward Jenner* had successfully used *vaccination* against smallpox—inoculation with a similar disease, cowpox.)

The discovery of X-rays by *Wilhelm Konrad von Röntgen* in 1895 and of radium by *Marie and Pierre Curie* in 1898 have had many important applications in medicine, including the treatment of some cancers. In 1897 *Sir Ronald Ross* discovered how malaria was transmitted to people by the bite of a particular kind of mosquito. As a result of his work it became possible to start controlling one of the most widespread and fatal diseases, which was prevalent in marshy areas of Britain in earlier times.

In recent years one of the most important developments in medicine has been in the discovery of new drugs. Insulin was discovered by *Sir Frederick Banting* and *Charles Herbert Best* in 1921; sulphonamide drugs were first provided by *Gerhard Domagk* in 1936; and penicillin, discovered by *Sir Alexander Fleming* in 1928, was developed into a safe drug by Lord Florey and Sir Ernst Chain just before the Second World War. There have also been notable advances in the treatment of mental disorders—and public attitudes towards them. The theories of *Sigmund Freud* helped to give a better understanding of the mind and led to the development of psychoanalysis. It was made easier for people to receive treatment for mental disorders in hospitals after the *Mental Treatment Act, 1930.* (Earlier reforms had been made by *William Tuke* and *Lord Shaftesbury,* who was primarily responsible for the *Lunacy Act, 1845.*) Since the last war, considerable advances have been made in *spare part surgery.*

In the present century medical care and attention have gradually become more widely available. *School medical services* were introduced by local authorities from 1907. The *National Insurance Act, 1911,* provided medical attention for many workers. But it was not until the passing of the *National Health Service Act, 1946,* that a full range of all kinds of medical treatment became available—free at first—for the whole population.

Mehemet Ali (1769–1849), appointed Pasha (Governor) of Egypt, then part of the Turkish Empire, in 1811. He built up a powerful army and navy. In 1825, he sent an army to help the Turks fight the Greek rebels during the *Greek War of Independence.* As a reward, the Turkish Sultan made him Pasha of Crete in 1830, but he was not satisfied and invaded and captured Palestine and Syria from the Turks, 1831–3. The Turks, who feared an Egyptian advance towards Constantinople, appealed to the Russians for help, who halted the Egyptian armies. As a reward to the Russians, the Turks agreed to close the Bosphorous and Dardanelles to foreign warships whenever Russia asked them to do so, which increased Russian influence in the area. Just before his death in 1839, the Sultan of Turkey tried to regain the lost provinces from Mehemet Ali. Palmerston, the British foreign secretary, decided to help the Turks, so that Russian influence over them would be lessened. British warships bombarded Beirut and threatened Alexandria in Egypt. Mehemet Ali gave up his conquests but was recognized as the hereditary ruler of Egypt. Palmerston obtained a new Straits Convention in 1841, under which Turkey agreed to close the Bosphorous and Dardenelles to foreign warships in times of peace.

Melbourne, Viscount (1779–1848), Whig statesman, who became an M.P. in 1806, served under the moderate Tory, Canning, in 1827 but rejoined the Whigs in 1830. He succeeded Earl Grey as prime minister in 1834 and was in power until 1841 apart from a few months of Conservative rule by Peel in 1834 to 1835. Under Melbourne, a number of reforms were carried out, including the *Municipal Corporations Reform Act, 1835*, the *Registration of Births, Marriages and Deaths, 1836*, and the introduction of the *penny post* in 1840. But these were passed more through the initiative of others than through the efforts of Melbourne himself. His main achievement was to set the feet of the young Queen Victoria (who came to the throne in 1837) on the paths of constitutional monarchy. He succeeded to his father's title in 1829.
← EARL GREY: LORD JOHN RUSSELL →

Mental Health Act, 1959, made it easier for patients to get treatment for mental ill-health or disorder on an informal basis, by going to an outpatient's department in a hospital like any person suffering from a physical illness. Compulsory orders of detention for the mentally ill, who might be of harm to society, could still be made on the recommendation of two doctors, one of whom had to be a psychiatrist.
← MENTAL TREATMENT ACT, 1930

Mental Treatment Act, 1930, tried to end the sense of shame people then felt about mental illness, by making it possible for people to enter hospitals as voluntary patients. Previously, people could only get treatment if they had been certified as insane by one or two doctors. This had been introduced as a safeguard to prevent people from being wrongfully detained in asylums when they were not insane.
← LUNACY ACT, 1890: MENTAL HEALTH ACT, 1959 →

Mercantile Marine Act, 1850, instituted examinations for masters and mates of foreign-going vessels in an attempt to reduce some of the dangers at sea caused by incompetent navigation and seamanship. It also set up a Mercantile Marine Department within the Board of Trade to supervise maritime affairs. Discipline was tightened up on merchant vessels with strict penalties being imposed for desertion, insubordination and any act that was likely to endanger the vessels or its cargo. (See next entry.)

Merchant Shipping Act, 1854, gave the Board of Trade greater control over ship construction and improved conditions for crews by making it compulsory for them to have nine square feet of living space, and a daily ration of lemon or lime juice to counteract scurvy, caused by lack of fresh meat and vegetables in their diet. (See next entry.)

Merchant Shipping Act, 1876. A major attempt to increase the safety of ships at sea by preventing overloading. It was made compulsory for every ship to have a load-line painted on the side, which had to remain visible above water after the cargo had been taken on board, to show that the ship was not overloaded. The Act was mainly the work of *Samuel Plimsoll*, and the load-line is often known as the Plimsoll line or mark. But shipowners were allowed to put the line at any level they liked, and the Act did not become really effective until 1890, when the load-line had to be approved by a Board of Trade official. (See next entry.)

Merchant Shipping Act, 1906, increased the living space for each merchant seaman to 120 cubic feet and laid down minimum rations, which remained unchanged until 1939. (See previous entry.)

Metcalf, John (1717–1810), road builder, born at Knaresborough, Yorkshire. He lost his sight at the age of six and was commonly known as 'Blind Jack'. In spite of this handicap he fought at Culloden in 1746 during the Jacobite rising; dealt in horses; and established a stage

coach service from Knaresborough to York in 1754. Later he started building roads. He prodded a long stick into the ground to make his surveys. He built his first road between Minskip and Fearnsby. In all, he built over 180 miles of *turnpike roads* in the north of England.
THOMAS TELFORD →

Methodism, founded by *John Wesley* and his brother Charles, in the late eighteenth century. It emphasized the possibility of personal salvation and rebirth by reading the Bible, thrift, prayer, and hard work. The structure of the Methodist Church was more democratic than that of the *Church of England* as there were no bishops and the congregation helped to run the local chapel. It had a great appeal to the new middle classes and to the more ambitious members of the working classes. The Methodist Church split into different sects during the nineteenth century, but three of them were reunited into the United Methodist Church in 1907. In 1932 the three largest groups—the United, Weslyan and Primitive Methodists—were reunited. In 1791, there were over 130,000 Methodists; in 1870, there were about 350,000; and in 1970, about 700,000. (See also *Ecumenical Movement.*)

Metropolitan Police Act, 1829, established the first professional police force in the capital, except for the City of London, which still has its own force. Originally, there were 3,000 policemen, who wore blue tailcoats and black top hats, with a thick leather crown, and carried a rattle and a truncheon. They were known as 'Peelers' or 'Bobbies' after Sir Robert Peel, who was responsible for passing the Act. He had set up a similar Peace Preservation Force in Ireland when he was Chief Secretary there from 1812 to 1818. One of the main initial tasks of the Metropolitan police was to control political demonstrations and riots, which became common in the next few years during the battle over the First Reform Act, 1832. The use of unarmed police avoided calling in troops, which might have caused bloodshed.
← BOW STREET RUNNERS : COUNTY AND BOROUGH POLICE ACT, 1856 →

Midlothian campaigns were undertaken by Gladstone who was M.P. for this Scottish constituency from 1880 to 1895. The first, from 1879 to 1880, was a triumphant success, and the new Liberal party machine which had just been set up, was responsible for persuading thousands of Liberals to attend Gladstone's meetings. The second in 1884 was less successful, even though his meetings were packed with Liberal supporters from other parts of the country. These were the first occasions on which a party leader had set out, with his wife, to make a direct, highly-organized appeal to the voters in his constituency—and through them to the whole country.

Mines Act, 1842, prohibited women and girls and boys under ten years of age from being employed in coal mines underground. Previously, children, some of them only five or six years of age, had been used to open and close ventilation doors in coal mines for twelve or more hours a day, while girls had had to pull loaded coal tubs by means of a chain attached to a girdle round their waist. Women and girls had carried the coal in baskets up ladders in the shaft to the surface. The invention of stronger wire ropes in the 1840s allowed coal tubs to be brought to the surface in a cage, or lift, drawn up by a steam engine. The Act was the work of *Lord Shaftesbury.*

Ministry of Agriculture see **Board of Agriculture**

Ministry of Education see **Department of Education and Science**

Ministry of Food see **Food rationing**

Ministry of Health was set up in 1919 to deal with all matters 'promoting the health of the people', while the Poor Law became the responsibility of the Home Office. In 1968, the ministry was merged with the Ministry of Social Security to form a new Department of Health and Social Security, thus linking health and social welfare again.
← LOCAL GOVERNMENT BOARD

Ministry of Transport was set up in 1919 to supervise land and sea transport. County and county borough councils continued to be responsible for road building as they had been since 1888, but the Ministry took over responsibility for 4,459 miles of trunk (main) roads in 1936.
← ROAD BOARD

Missionaries. There was a great revival of missionary work from the end of the eighteenth century as a result of the influence of the *Evangelicals* and nonconformists. The Baptist Missionary Society was formed in 1792; the London Missionary Society, inter-denominational, in 1795; the Church Missionary Society, Anglican, in 1799; and the Methodist Missionary Society in 1813. The British and Foreign Bible Society, inter-denominational, was founded in 1804 to distribute copies of the Bible in foreign languages (now more than 500 languages). There was a great expansion of activity after 1858 when three different events in separate continents provided bigger opportunities for missionaries. In that year, *David Livingstone* set up the Universities' Mission to Central Africa; the East India Company, which had never been very favourable to missionaries, was abolished; and the interior of China was opened to missionaries. The work of missionaries in exploring the interior of unknown countries and continents stimulated imperialism and the conquest of these countries. In addition to religion, missionaries brought education and medicine to millions of people in primitive countries. The Roman Catholics had long been involved in missionary work and a specifically British society was started in 1866. There are still many missionaries at work in underdeveloped countries.

Monitorial system. A cheap method of education in which the older, cleverer children were supposed to teach the younger ones how to read and write. It was used in some *Sunday schools* in the eighteenth century, but it was developed into a national system by the *voluntary societies* in the early nineteenth century. It was based on the work of the *Rev. Andrew Bell* and *Joseph Lancaster.*
PUPIL TEACHER SYSTEM →

Monroe doctrine, 1823, under which European powers were warned not to try to establish new colonies, or to interfere with colonies which had already gained their independence, in the whole of the American continent, north and south. It was proclaimed by the American president, *James Monroe* (1758–1831), mainly to prevent the Spanish from trying to reimpose their rule on their former colonies in South America. Canning had suggested that Britain and America should jointly guarantee the independence of these colonies, but Monroe refused the offer.

Montgolfier brothers, Joseph Michel (1740–1810) and Jaques Etienne (1754–99), sons of a paper manufacturer of Annonay, France. They sent up the first balloon, filled with hot air, in 1783, and in the same year, a balloon carrying two passengers. This was the first time human beings had ever left the earth.

Montgomery, Field-Marshal Viscount (born 1887), British General who became a legend in his own lifetime during the Second World War. He joined the Army in 1908 and served in the First World War. In 1939, he was put in command of the Third Division and was present at the *Dunkirk* evacuation, 1940. He became widely-known after he took over the *Eighth Army* in August 1942, and won a brilliant victory over the

Germans at the Battle of El Alamein, Egypt, in October–November, 1942. From the *D day* landings in France in June 1944, to September 1944 he was operational commander of the Allied forces in Western Europe. He led the 21st Army Group when it crossed the Rhine into the German Reich in March 1945.

More, Hannah (1745–1833), writer, born at Stapleton, Gloucestershire. She wrote plays, opened a Sunday school at Cheddar, 1789; and wrote some pamphlets which led to the formation of the Religious Tract Society in 1799.

Morley-Minto reforms, in the government of India made by Viscount Morley (1838–1923), Secretary for India, and the Earl of Minto (1847–1914), Viceroy of India. The India Councils Act of 1909, for which they were responsible, gave the Indians greater representation in legislative councils in India and some representation in the Secretary for India's council in London, but still no real power. (For the background see *India.*)

Morocco was at the centre of two international crises before the First World War, which were provoked by the Germans in the hope that they would weaken the *Anglo-French Entente, 1904.* Under the Entente, Britain had given France a free hand in Morocco, but the Germans insisted that an international conference should be called to decide Morocco's future. This was held at Algeciras, Spain, in 1906, when the British gave strong support to the French. The second crisis occurred in 1911 when the Germans sent a gunboat to *Agadir,* on the Moroccan coast, allegedly to protect German interests in the country. The effect of the German moves was the opposite to that intended, as they helped to strengthen the Anglo-French Entente.

Morris, William (1834–96), poet, craftsman and Socialist, who wanted to set up workshops in small towns to produce beautiful hand-made goods, instead of the ugly objects produced in factories. He also wanted to make existing factories, in his own words, 'centres of intellectual activity', where workers spent part of the day growing food, painting, or studying. In 1861 he set up a firm in London with some partners to make wallpapers, embroideries etc. In 1883 he joined the *Social Democratic Federation,* but left two years later to found the Socialist League. In 1891, he founded the Kelmscott Press, which produced hand-printed books, at Hammersmith. Although his work had a considerable influence on improving design, his ideas have had relatively little effect on the development of society as a whole or of socialism.

Morris, William Richard see **Viscount Nuffield**

Morse, Samuel (1791–1872), American inventor and painter and sculptor, who invented an *electric telegraph* at about the same time as Sir Charles Wheatstone. In 1838, he developed the Morse code, which is named after him.
← SIR CHARLES WHEATSTONE: CYRUS WEST FIELD →

Motor-Car Act, 1903, raised the speed imit from 12 m.p.h. to 20 m.p.h., though it could be reduced to 10 m.p.h. in towns. Cars had to be licensed and to carry number plates. Police laid speed traps for motorists in many towns, and the Automobile Association was formed in 1905 to protect motorists' interests.
← LOCOMOTIVES ON HIGHWAYS ACT, 1896: ROAD TRAFFIC ACT, 1930 →

Motorways. The first in Europe from Milan to Varese, a distance of 31 miles, was built by the Italians in the 1920s. Germany had built over 1,000 miles by 1939. Construction of motorways began in Britain in the late 1950s, much later than in most other European countries. By the early 1970s, there were 1,000 miles of motorway, out of a total of over 200,000 miles of all types of roads in Britain.
← MASS MOTORING: BUCHANAN REPORT →

Mountbatten, Lord (born 1900), uncle of Queen Elizabeth II. He was Supreme Allied Commander, South East Asia, 1943–6, and Viceroy and Governer-General of India, 1947–8, when it was given independence and partitioned into India and Pakistan.

Munich agreement, 1938. removed the immediate threat of war as the British and the French gave in to *Hitler's* demands to occupy the Sudetenland—part of Czechoslovakia which contained about 3m. German-speaking people and ½m. Czechs. *Neville Chamberlain,* the British prime minister, returned by plane to London declaring that he had got 'peace for our time'. But Hitler soon occupied the rest of Czechoslovakia. Chamberlain then abandoned the policy of *appeasement* and offered an alliance to Poland. When the Germans attacked Poland in 1939, Chamberlain declared war on Germany.

Municipal Corporations Reform Act, 1835, was passed by the Whigs. It swept away the old, inefficient and often corrupt corporations in 178 boroughs and replaced them by councils elected by male ratepayers. The mayor and alderman were elected by the councils. The Act did not give the new councils many powers at first, though they did have to set up watch committees to maintain a police force in the borough and the surrounding area. New industrial towns, without charters, could apply to parliament to become boroughs so that they could set up councils, as Manchester did in 1838, Birmingham in 1839, and Sheffield in 1843. The Act was the first step in the reform of *local government.*

Murdock, William (1754–1839), engineer, who invented *gas* lighting, born at Auchinleck, Ayrshire. He started work with the manufacturing firm of *Boulton and Watt* of Soho, Birmingham, in 1777, and became their chief steam engine erector in Cornwall. In 1792, while living in Redruth, Cornwall, he used coal gas to light his house and, six years later, on his return to Birmingham, he built a gas plant to illuminate the factory. By 1804 he had installed the first big gas lighting plant in a cotton mill at Salford, Lancashire. Murdock was also said to have developed a *steam carriage* and he also made several improvements to *Watt's* steam engine.

Murray, Matthew (1765–1826), engineer, who opened his own firm in Leeds to produce steam engines. He invented the inlet and exhaust valve (the D-slide valve) and built several locomotives. Earlier, he had made several improvements to flax spinning machinery.
← JOHN BLENKINSOP: GEORGE STEPHENSON →

Mussolini, Benito (1883–1945), founder *of Fascism,* dictator of Italy from 1922. He attacked Abyssinia in 1935; formed an '*Axis*' with Hitler in 1936; but did not enter the Second World War until June 1940, when France was virtually defeated. He resigned in 1943 after a coup by the Italian king and Marshal Badoglio and was imprisoned. But he was rescued by German parachutists in the same year and set up a Republican Fascist government in northern Italy, which was under German control. He was shot by Italian anti-Fascist partisans in 1945.

N

Napoleon, Bonaparte (1769–1821), born in Corsica, military genius, who became First Consul of France in 1799, Emperor of France in 1804, and master of much of Europe shortly afterwards. Britain fought two wars against France from 1793 to 1802 and from 1805 to 1814. Napoleon's plans to invade Britain in 1805 were defeated by the Royal Navy, which intercepted the Franco-Spanish fleet off Vigo, Spain, and, finally, by Nelson at the Battle of Trafalgar, 1805, when the French and Spanish lost about two-thirds of their fleets. Napoleon then tried to defeat Britain by economic warfare, starting a Continental system, under which all British exports were banned from European countries under French control. Britain, with its superior sea power, replied by blockading Continental ports. From 1809 some of the Continental countries started to evade the Continental system and to trade with Britain again. From 1808 Napoleon was weakened by the victories of the *Duke of Wellington* in the Peninsular War in Spain and Portugal. His failure to defeat the Russians and his retreat from Moscow in 1812 was an even more crippling blow. After being defeated by the Russians, Prussians and Austrians at the Battle of Leipzig, he abdicated in 1814, and was made emperor of the island of Elba. He escaped to France in 1815, and raised an army, but was defeated by the Duke of Wellington and a Prussian army, under Blücher, at the Battle of Waterloo, near Brussels, Belgium, on 18 June 1815. He was exiled to the island of St Helena, in the South Atlantic, where he died in 1821.

Britain emerged from the Napoleonic wars as the strongest power in the world, with the largest empire and the most powerful navy. Industry had been stimulated and agriculture expanded. Britain had saved itself from invasion and Europe from domination by one man. But the French Revolution, and Napoleon's reforms in law, currency, tariffs and administration, had created a new climate of opinion, and awakened a new sense of nationalism in Europe. In Britain, after the end of the war, renewed demands for parliamentary reform in the midst of economic chaos, were to dominate political and economic life until the 1840s.

Nasmyth, James (1808–90), engineer, who invented the steam hammer in 1839. The hammer was driven down with much greater force by steam power, which allowed much larger iron plates and beams to be forged on the anvil. He also made many other inventions, including a hydraulic punching machine. He was a pupil of Henry Maudslay and set up his own engineering business at Patricroft, near Manchester, in 1834.
← HENRY MAUDSLAY: SIR JOSEPH WHITWORTH →

National Assistance Act, 1948, finally ended the *Poor Law*, which had existed since 1601. It provides cash payments for those in real need

such as old age pensioners with no other source of income, deserted wives etc. The initial hope that the number of people needing financial aid would decrease, has not been fulfilled, partly because of *inflation.* In 1948 there were about 1m. people receiving national assistance which had increased to 2,791,000 by 1970, at an annual cost of £568m.
← POOR LAW AMENDMENT ACT, 1834

National Economic Development Council was set up in 1962 to suggest ways in which economic growth could be increased. Its members include government ministers, trade unionists and employers.

National Government was formed by the Labour prime minister, *Ramsay MacDonald*, in August 1931, to deal with the financial emergency created by the world depression and to save the £. It included Conservative, Liberal and Labour ministers, but the Labour party as a whole opposed it, and expelled MacDonald and the other Labour ministers from the party. The National government survived in name until 1940, but it was dominated by the Conservatives who won 472 seats in the October 1931 elections. *Stanley Baldwin* became prime minister in 1935 and *Neville Chamberlain* in 1937. The National government was succeeded in 1940 by Churchill's wartime coalition government.
← COALITION GOVERNMENTS

National Health Service Act, 1946, provided a free medical service for everyone, thus making Britain the first country in the world to have a fully comprehensive national health service. It gave free medical and hospital treatment, free dental treatment, including false teeth, and free optical care and spectacles. The Act was passed by *Aneurin Bevan*, then Minister of Health, and came into operation in 1948. Hospitals were nationalized and doctors and dentists were given the opportunity to work for the Health Service, though they could continue to have private, paying patients as well. Owing to the heavy costs of the service, Hugh Gaitskell, Labour Chancellor of the Exchequer, introduced charges for dentures and spectacles in 1951, which caused Bevan to resign from the government. In the following year, when the Conservatives were in power, they started charges for medical prescriptions. The National Health Service has produced immense benefits in general health and welfare, but it has been criticized for its heavy cost (nearly £2,000m. in 1970–1); for splitting up responsibility for patients between the family doctor, the hospital, and the local authority welfare services; and for not concentrating enough on preventive medicine.

National Insurance Act, 1911, introduced by *Lloyd George*, took the first steps towards the present *welfare state* by setting up a State scheme of compulsory insurance for most workers against sickness. It also covered workers in some industries, such as building, ship-building and engineering against unemployment. Workers who earned less than £160 a year—then the majority—had to pay 4*d.* a week into a national fund, while their employers contributed 3*d.* and the State 2*d.* If they were ill they received sickness benefit of 10*s.* a week and free medical care. Workers in seven industries insured against unemployment, paid in 2½*d.* a week, while their employers and the State paid the same amount. If they were out of work they could draw unemployment benefit of 7*s.* a week for a maximum of fifteen weeks in a year. The main defects were that the worker's family were not covered for medical treatment and that the payments were too small to live on. The unemployment insurance scheme was extended to most other workers in 1920. (See next entry.)

National Insurance Act, 1946. A comprehensive Act providing compulsory insurance for unemployment and sickness and maternity benefits and also for retirement and widow's pensions, and funeral grants. It was introduced by the Labour government and was based on the *Beveridge report* of 1942. It employed the same principle of contributions from the worker, his employer, and the State as in the Act of 1911. (See entry above.) In 1961 a graduated pension scheme was introduced in addition to the flat-rate *old age pension*, and in 1966 a system of earnings-related supplements for unemployment and sickness benefits, under which higher-paid workers contributed more each week and received higher benefits.

National Prices and Incomes Board was set up by the Labour government in 1965 to investigate changes in pay and prices and make recommendations to the government. It was abolished in 1971 by the Conservatives, who announced in 1973 that they were setting up a new pay board and prices commission.

National Society (for promoting the Education of the Poor in the Principles of the Established Church) was set up by the *Rev. Andrew Bell* in 1811 to provide elementary education in *voluntary schools*.

National Trust was founded in 1895 by *Octavia Hill*, Sir Robert Hunter and Canon Rawnsley to preserve the countryside and houses of architectural or historic interest for the benefit of the public. It now administers more than 400,000 acres of land in England, Wales and Northern Ireland; over 180 miles of coastline; and many old houses, parts of which are open to the public. A National Trust for Scotland was formed in 1931.

NATIONALIZATION. The taking over of an industry, services (such as transport), or the land by the State, which then runs them in the public interest. Nationalization was advocated by *Karl Marx* and is one of the major doctrines of *socialism.* It was adopted as a policy by the *Labour party* in 1918. Early examples of nationalization were the Port of London Authority, 1909; the Central Electricity Board, 1926, set up to control the national grid; the British Broadcasting Corporation, 1927; the London Passenger Transport Board, 1933, to control the capital's buses, trams and tubes; and the *British Overseas Airways Corporation, 1939.* The mines and the railways were controlled temporarily by the government in both world wars. The main period for nationalization was during the *Attlee* administration from 1945 to 1951 when the following industries and services came under State control: Bank of England, and civil aviation, 1946; coal, and Cable and Wireless, 1947; health service, and transport, including road haulage, 1948; electricity and gas supplies, 1949; and the iron and steel industry, 1951. In most cases, they are run by a public corporation, such as the National Coal Board, with a chairman appointed by the government. In 1953, the Conservatives, under Churchill, restored private ownership to most road haulage and also partially in the iron and steel industry, though an Iron and Steel Board was set up to fix maximum prices and to supervise supplies of raw material. Steel was nationalized again by the Labour government under Wilson in 1967, when the British Steel Corporation took over fourteen of the major steel companies.

Nationalization has not fulfilled all the hopes of its supporters for a number of different reasons. Many nationalized corporations have proved to be no more efficient than private firms; the compensation paid to private owners left a heavy debt; and because many of the industries were in a poor state or extremely unprofitable, large investments have been necessary to bring them up to date. The State also owns shares in some private companies (e.g. in the oil industry) and this method of 'partial nationalization' is now one that finds favour with some members of the Labour party.

Nationalism. One of the major forces in the modern world which was awakened in Europe by Napoleon's attempts to impose his rule throughout the continent. Nationalism is usually based on a sense of a common history, traditions and attitudes. Most nationalist movements have first been manifested in the cultural fields. Nationalism has had a great effect on British history, indirectly through the rise of the nation-state of Germany in the nineteenth century, which then became the main European challenger of British power; and more directly in *India* and *Ireland*. After the Second World War strong nationalist movements developed in Africa and Asia, which resulted in the British colonies there demanding their independence. There are also nationalist movements in Wales and in Scotland.

Navigation Acts. A long series of Acts (the first two being passed in 1651 and 1660) making it compulsory for all imports to and exports from Britain and the Empire to be carried in English ships, in which three-quarters of the crew had to be English. The Acts were designed to increase the number of merchant seamen (who could be seized in times of war by the *press gang* and forced to serve in Royal warships) and to strike a blow at the Dutch, who were then one of Britain's main maritime rivals. The main Acts were repealed in 1849, which stimulated some British shipowners to become more efficient by exposing them to foreign competition. The last Acts, relating to the coastal trade were repealed in 1854.

Neilson, James Beaumont (1792–1865), Scottish inventor of the hot blast method of making iron. Previously a cold blast of air had been used in the furnace, but while experimenting with Scottish coal (which does not coke very well) Neilson found that it could be used satisfactorily with a hot-air blast. His method was first used at Clyde Ironworks, Glasgow, in 1829, and was soon adopted in other parts of the country, as it also trebled the amount of iron that could be made with the same amount of fuel. He also invented the fishtail burner for gas lighting.

← ABRAHAM DARBY

New towns started to be built in Britain after the Second World War to relieve overcrowding in existing cities. By 1970, thirty-two had been built, or were in the process of construction, accommodating well over 500,000 people. There are plans for others, particularly in the crowded south-east of England. New towns have provided much better houses and surroundings than those in which residents formerly lived. But many of them have failed to develop a communal spirit, as they are too large, and the population is often unbalanced, with too many young people and too few of the middle classes.

← GARDEN CITIES

NEW ZEALAND. At the beginning of the nineteenth century the few white inhabitants were mainly missionaries, traders, and convicts who had escaped from Australia. There was a large native population, the Maoris, living mainly in the north island. British settlers started to arrive in greater numbers in the 1830s through *Edward Gibbon Wakefield*'s New Zealand Association. In 1840, under the Treaty of Waitangi, the Maori chiefs accepted British sovereignty, but retained their lands. This treaty led to endless disputes over Maori claims to wastelands, and the price of land sold by Maoris to settlers. There were two Maori wars, in 1843, and from 1860 to 1870, following which the Maoris were allowed to keep about half of the north island. The south island had been bought from the Maoris by the government when *Sir George Grey* was governor of New Zealand from 1845 to 1853. New Zealand was given self-government in 1856 and attained *dominion* status in 1907. It is mainly an agricultural country. The *Ottowa agreements, 1932*, increased exports of butter, lamb, cheese and other farm products to Britain. Since the end of the Second World War, New Zealand has come to develop closer ties with Australia and the United States, symbolized by the *Anzus Pact, 1951*, which excluded Britain. The population in 1973 was about 3m.

Newcomen, Thomas (1663–1729), blacksmith, born at Dartmouth, Devon, who invented the first widely-used steam engine in 1706. It was used for pumping water out of coal mines so that deeper seams could be mined. Steam was let into a cylinder which was then cooled by a jet of cold water. This created a vacuum and the piston was forced down by the pressure of the atmosphere. The 'atmospheric' steam engine was expensive to run, as heat was wasted in alternately cooling and heating the cylinder.
JAMES WATT →

Newgate prison. An ancient, notorious prison in the City of London, where *Elizabeth Fry* started her work of prison reform in 1813. Public executions were held in the square outside until 1868. Newgate prison was demolished in 1904 and the Central Criminal Court—the Old Bailey—was built on the site.
← TRANSPORTATION: PENTONVILLE PRISON →

Newman, John Henry (1801–90), a leader of the *Oxford movement*, later a cardinal. He was made a fellow of Oriel College, Oxford, in 1822, and vicar of St Mary's, Oxford, in 1828. He helped to found the Oxford movement and wrote many of their 'Tracts for the Times' to publicize the movement's views. His Tract No. 90, published in February 1841, caused a storm of protest because it seemed to imply that it was possible for Church of England clergymen to believe in the doctrines of the Roman Catholic Church. In spite of some *Catholic emancipation*, there was still a great fear of Popery in England. Newman gave up the living of St Mary's in 1843 and became a Roman Catholic in 1845. He went to Rome in the following year, where he was ordained a Catholic priest, and returned to England as a member of a Roman Catholic Order—the Congregation of the Oratory of St Philip Neri. He founded the oratory at Maryvale, Birmingham, in 1847 and was created a cardinal in 1879.

Newsom Report, 1963, entitled 'Half our Future', was concerned with the education of 'pupils aged 13 to 16 of average and less than average ability'. It recommended raising the *school leaving age* to sixteen in two years' time; less concentration on external examinations like G.C.E.; and an education more related to adult life in the final year at school. The chairman, Sir John Newsom, was appointed head of the Public Schools Commission in 1965.

NEWSPAPERS. The first printed news sheet was published in Britain in 1513 and the first dated and numbered paper, 'The Weekely Newes' appeared in 1622. In 1702 the first daily paper, the 'Daily Courant' was published in London. During the second half of the eighteenth century many other daily newspapers were started, including *The Times* which first appeared as the 'Daily Universal Register' in 1785. The invention of the *electric telegraph* in 1837 and the establishment of the news agency—*Reuters*—in London in 1851 helped to speed up the reporting of foreign news. Newspapers reached the peak of their influence in the nineteenth century, under such editors as *John Delane* of 'The Times'. Their readership, however, was confined mainly to the middle and upper classes and the more educated and intelligent members of the working classes. Some radical working class papers, like the *Weekly Political Register* and *Feargus O'Connor*'s 'Northern Star' had also appeared in the first half of the century, but their circulations too were relatively small. The *popular press* as we know it today, read by millions of people, did not develop until the repeal of the *Taxes on Knowledge* made it possible to produce papers at a price people could afford, and the *Education Act* of 1870 had created a larger number of people who could read and were thirsting for information and entertainment. The popular press was founded by *Viscount Northcliffe* who started the 'Daily Mail' in 1896; other chains of popular papers were created later by his brother *Viscount Rothermere* and by *Lord Beaverbrook.* The popular press was the first of the *mass communications* media, but it has become less important since the advent of *radio and television.*

Nightingale, Florence (1820–1910), nursing reformer, daughter of wealthy parents, named after the city of Florence, Italy, where she was born. She was educated at home, and as a young woman travelled on the continent with her parents and married friends. In 1851, she studied for three months at a Protestant hospital in Kaiserswerth, Germany, which had pioneered the training of nurses. (*Elizabeth Fry* had also studied there more than ten years before.) Two years after she returned to England, Florence Nightingale became superintendent of a small hospital for women in London. After the outbreak of the *Crimean War* in 1854, thousands of British soldiers were dying of wounds and disease in the filthy, understaffed and overcrowded hospitals at Scutari, Turkey. In 1854, Florence Nightingale was sent out in charge of a party of forty British women who had volunteered to act as nurses. Florence Nightingale's untiring work in caring for the sick, cleaning up the wards, and improving supplies of food, water and clothing, made her famous throughout Britain. Largely as a result of her work the mortality rate was reduced from 42 to 2 per cent. In 1855, a grateful nation opened a Nightingale Fund, which had reached a total of £44,000 by the time she returned to England in 1856, travelling as 'Miss Smith' to avoid publicity. She used the money to establish the first training school for nurses in Britain at St Thomas's Hospital, London. In 1860 the first fifteen probationer nurses started work there, at a salary of £10 a year, plus free food, accommodation and white and brown uniforms. After training, some of the nurses went to other hospitals, so that within ten years or so, practically all big hospitals had at least one trained 'Nightingale' nurse. With their emphasis on neatness and cleanliness, they were far ahead of most surgeons, who continued to wear bloodstained coats, until the reforms of *Joseph Lister* began to take effect. Florence Nightingale had always been particularly concerned about the welfare of babies and infants. In her 'Notes on Nursing' (1858) she asked, 'Might we not make the home a healthy place and so lessen the need for children's hospitals?' As a result of the campaign she conducted in her later years, the first training course for health visitors was started in Buckinghamshire in 1892. Her work not only improved the standards of nursing, but also helped to raise the status of women.

Nobel prizes are awarded annually for outstanding achievements in physics, chemistry, medicine, literature and international peace. They were started by Alfred Bernhard Nobel, Swedish discoverer of dynamite, and the first prizes were awarded in 1901, after his death. In 1968, the Swedish Riksbank provided the money for a new Nobel prize in economics.

Nonconformists. Protestants who do not conform to the customs and doctrines of the established Church of England. They have their own form of worship, and the congregation plays a much bigger part in running the Church than it does in the Church of England. The original dissenters or nonconformists were the 2,000 Puritan ministers, who refused to accept the Act of Uniformity of 1662 and left the Church of England. They were banned from taking university degrees and from holding public offices, but this discrimination was legally abolished by the repeal of the *Test and Corporation Acts*, in 1828, and by the *Universities Tests Act, 1871*. By the nineteenth century, there were many nonconformist sects, including *Methodists*, *Quakers*, Baptists, Unitarians etc. The nonconformists were strong in Wales and in Scotland, where the presbyterian Church of Scotland had been the *established church* since the Treaty of Union between England and Scotland in 1707. Nonconformists, with their emphasis on piety, peace and *temperance*, had a great influence on the Liberal party in the nineteenth century.

Normandy landings see **D-day**

North Atlantic Treaty Organization (N.A.T.O.) set up in 1949 to protect Western Europe against any possible attack from Russia. Under Article 5 of the Treaty, the members declare that they will regard an attack on one of them as an attack on all. It has been Britain's main defensive military alliance in the post-war world and the most far-reaching to which it has ever committed itself in times of peace. The United States, with its massive nuclear deterrent, and its large number of troops in Germany, became the main protector of Western Europe against any Russian attack. The original members were Canada, and the United States, Belgium, Britain, Denmark, France, Holland, Iceland, Italy, Luxemburg, Norway and Portugal. Since then Turkey, Greece, and West Germany have become members, and France has left the military side of the organization, but has not renounced the treaty. *Ernest Bevin* was mainly responsible for Britain becoming a member of N.A.T.O., and played a large part in its being set up. British troops of occupation remained in West Germany as members of the alliance, after West Germany became independent in 1955 and was admitted to N.A.T.O.

Northcliffe, Viscount (1865–1922), born Alfred Harmsworth, son of a barrister, the founder of the *popular Press.* In 1888, he started publishing a magazine called 'Answers to Correspondents' which reached a circulation of 1m. copies a week fours years later. On 4 May 1896, he published the 'Daily Mail', the first popular ½*d.* daily newspaper. It sold 400,000 copies on the first day and its circulation had risen to nearly 1m. four years later. He started many other newspapers and magazines and acquired others, including *The Times*, which he controlled from 1908–22. He was appointed Director of Propaganda in the First World War and was made a viscount in 1917.
VISCOUNT ROTHERMERE →

Northern Ireland see **Ulster**

Nuclear power see **Atomic energy**

Nuclear-powered ships. The first nuclear-powered merchant ship, the American 'Savannah', entered service in 1962. Nuclear power is also used for the submarines which carry *Polaris* missiles.

Nuffield, Viscount (1877–1963), born William Richard Morris. He started work in a bicycle shop at the age of sixteen and became a multi-millionaire and Britain's biggest car manufacturer. At the age of seventeen he set up his own bicycle-repairing business in a shed at Cowley, near Oxford, on a borrowed £4. He soon started to make his own bicycles, and then motor-bicycles. Just before the First World War, he opened a factory to produce motor-cars. After the war, he introduced *mass production* methods. By 1926, the Morris Cowley car (which sold at £165 so that it was cheap enough for many of the middle classes to buy) was being produced at the rate of 1,000 a week. By the time the Second World War broke out, he had produced over one million cars. In 1952, his business and the Austin Motor Co. were merged to form the British Motor Corporation, which later became part of British Leyland. He gave much of his money away to charity. In 1927 to 1930, he gave thousands of pounds to many hospitals and in 1937 founded Nuffield College, Oxford, for graduate research. In 1943 he established the Nuffield Foundation with a capital of £10m. for medical, social and industrial research and the care of the aged.
← HENRY FORD: HERBERT AUSTIN →

Nuremberg trials held by the Allies in Germany between November 1945, and October 1946, to try twenty-two German leaders after the Second World War. They were accused of planning and waging wars of aggression, of war crimes, and of crimes against humanity, involving the deaths of 12m. men, women and children. Only three were acquitted. Twelve were sentenced to death by hanging; three to imprisonment for life; and four to shorter terms of imprisonment. Hermann Goering (1893–1946), creator of the German Luftwaffe (Air Force), committed suicide just before he was due to be hanged. In 1973 *Rudolf Hess* was the only one still in prison.

Nursing. An Institute of Nursing Sisters was started by *Elizabeth Fry* in 1840 to train district nurses to visit poor people in their own homes, but the main reforms came about through the work of *Florence Nightingale.* After a long campaign, an Act was passed in 1919, which set up a General Nursing Council to establish a general standard of training. Qualified nurses had to register with their Council in the same way as doctors had to register under the *Medical Act, 1858.*

O

Oastler, Richard (1789–1861), Yorkshire land agent, who claimed that 'slavery' in the mills of Yorkshire was far worse than the slavery in the West Indies in the early 1830s. He was one of the leading supporters of the *ten hours' movement* for reducing hours of work in textile factories.
← JOHN FIELDEN

O'Connell, Daniel (1775–1847), lawyer, born in County Kerry, known as the 'Liberator' for his part in securing *Catholic emancipation.* In 1823 he formed the Catholic Association as a mass movement to campaign for emancipation. It was financed mainly by subscriptions of 1*d.* a month from Irish peasants. In the 1828 elections, O'Connell came top of the poll in the County Clare constituency, but he was not allowed to take his seat because he was a Catholic. There were great disorders in Ireland, and, fearing a civil war, the Tory government, under Wellington, passed the *Roman Catholic Relief Act, 1829,* which allowed Catholics to become M.P.s. O'Connell took his seat in the House of Commons at Westminster, after another by-election in County Clare, at which he returned unopposed. His long-term aim was the repeal of the *Act of Union, 1800.* In 1842 to 1843 he held a series of mass meetings throughout Ireland in support of this demand. The last meeting, which was due to be held at Clontarf, Dublin, in October 1843, was banned by the British government and O'Connell cancelled it. He was sentenced to a year's imprisonment for conspiracy and served part of his sentence before the rest of it was quashed on appeal. He died a few years later—a sick and broken man—discredited with many Irish extremists, who thought that he should have gone ahead with the Clontarf meeting, in defiance of the British government.

YOUNG IRELAND →

O'Connor, Feargus (1794–1855), lawyer and Chartist leader. In 1837 he founded the radical newspaper the 'Northern Star', in Leeds, which soon achieved the large circulation for those days of 60,000 copies a week. It was the main voice of *Chartism.* O'Connor presented the third Chartist petition to the House of Commons in 1848. There was a history of insanity in his family and in 1852 he became insane and was detained in an asylum.

← THOMAS ATTWOOD: WILLIAM LOVETT →

Oil tankers. The first real oil tanker, a German vessel, was launched in 1886, since when they have increased greatly both in size and total number because of the world-wide demand for oil as a fuel for road travel and other purposes. The closing of the *Suez canal* in 1967, which meant that some tankers had to take a much longer route, stimulated the construction of super tankers. The Japanese tanker 'Nisseki Maru' launched in 1971 is 184,855 gross tons. Tankers are now one of the most important forms of merchant shipping in all countries. In 1970 they accounted for nearly one quarter of all 1,977 British merchant ships of over 500 tons, and almost a half of the total carrying capacity. Although oil tankers are the best known, other tankers are used to carry chemicals, cleaning fluids and methane gas —and even semi-liquid pulp, fruit juice and wine. Oil slicks from tankers have caused much *pollution* of beaches.

Old age pensions, introduced by *Lloyd George* in 1908, were the first social security benefits given to the poor as a right and not as charity. Men and women over 70 received 5*s*. a week if their income from all sources was £21 or less a year and a smaller amount if their income was between £21 and £31 10*s*. Above that they received nothing. The pensions were non-contributory, and all the money was provided by the State. In 1919 the pension was raised to 10*s*. a week. In 1926, pensions were made contributory and all workers had to contribute a few pence each week towards their future pension. At the same time the qualifying age was reduced to 65 for men and 60 for women. Although the pensions were small, they helped to keep many old people out of the *workhouse*. Under the *National Insurance Act, 1946*, everyone, with the main exception of married women, had to contribute to the State scheme and on retirement received a flat-rate pension of 26*s*. (£1.30) a week in 1946 for a man at 65 and for an insured woman at 60. A graduated pension scheme was introduced in 1961, under which higher-paid workers contributed more and received a higher pension when they retired. In 1970, there were over 7½m. people receiving the flat rate pension of £5 for a single person and £8.10 for a married couple. Many of them, who had no other source of income, were also receiving supplementary pensions, but the amounts were still too low for them to live on comfortably. In 1972 the Conservative government introduced a scheme under which pensions rise automatically with increases in the cost of living.

'Open door' policy. In the nineteenth century, the United States and European powers wanted China to open all its ports to trade, instead of making foreign countries sign a treaty of permission to use the ports. Chinese resistance to these demands resulted in the *Boxer rising, 1900*, against Europeans in China.

Open field system. An ancient system of farming, used over much of England, particularly in the broad central area, in which the farmland was divided into three or more large fields, which were cultivated in common. Farmers had a number of scattered strips in each field and also had the right to graze their cattle, sheep and pigs on the surrounding common and wasteland. There was usually a three-course rotation of crops, with all the farmers growing wheat in one field, oats, or barley, in another; and with the third being left bare, or fallow, so that it could regain heart. The open field system had gradually been disappearing throughout the centuries as the land was enclosed into compact, unified farms by agreements between landowners or by the use of force or threats against small landowners. The remaining open fields almost entirely disappeared as a result of the *Enclosure Acts* of 1730–1820. *Arthur Young* was one of the main critics of the open field system. He argued that time and labour were wasted in moving men and tools from one strip to another; the grazing of animals together spread diseases; and new crop rotations, which included the use of turnips and clover to provide winter fodder, could not be introduced because the farmers were 'bound to the courses of crops entailed by custom on a common field'.

There was much truth in his arguments, but recent research has shown that not all open field farmers were as backward as he claimed. Some in Oxfordshire had introduced the new crop rotations.
ENCLOSURE ACTS →

Open prisons. The first prison without bars, where prisoners were also paid for their work for the first time, was opened at New Hall Camp, in a wooded area eight miles from Wakefield prison, in 1936. The 100 prisoners worked on a pig and poultry farm in the camp. Another open prison was opened at Maidstone in 1944, and a third in Gloucestershire in 1946. There are now a number of open prisons, mainly for men and women who have not committed serious offences.
← PENTONVILLE PRISON

Open University uses radio and television broadcasts and correspondence to teach adult students at home. It is designed mainly to meet the needs of those who failed to have the opportunity to take a degree as a full-time student. The degree courses usually last five years, though some students who have had a longer period of formal education are allowed to take shorter courses. The university opened in January 1971 and the first students (those who had been able to claim exemptions for part of the course) graduated in 1973.
← WORKERS' EDUCATIONAL ASSOCIATION

Opium War, 1840–2. In the nineteenth century, merchants in India did a profitable trade selling opium to the Chinese. In 1839, the Chinese government, which wanted to end the drug trade, confiscated some British cargoes of opium at Canton. Palmerston ordered Canton to be bombarded, and Hong Kong was occupied. By the Treaty of Nanking, 1842, Hong Kong was ceded to the British; five Chinese ports were opened to British traders; and compensation was paid for the confiscated drugs.
BOXER RISING →

Oregon dispute between Britain and the United States in the early 1840s over the boundary between the British colony of Canada in Oregon and the United States—a vast area, west of the Rocky mountains, which had only been populated by white men in the previous twenty years. After long negotiations, Peel and his foreign secretary Aberdeen, convinced the Americans that the boundary should be on the 49th parallel. This continued the boundary which had been fixed for the territories east of the Rockies by *Castlereagh* in 1817–18. Under a treaty signed in 1846, the United States acquired what are now the states of Oregon, Washington and Idaho, while Britain obtained Vancouver Island.

Orange Order was formed in Ireland in 1795 to support the Protestant religion against 'popery' and to defend the Protestant succession to the throne established finally by William III (of the Dutch House of Orange), at the Battle of the Boyne, 1690.

Osborne judgment, 1909. A legal ruling which struck a great blow at the new Labour party, formed in 1906, and the trade unions. W. V. Osborne, secretary of the Walthamstow branch of the Amalgamated Society of Railway Servants, brought a court case challenging the right of his union to give money to political parties. The case, which eventually went to the House of Lords, went in Osborne's favour. The 'judgment' had a great effect on the finances of the Labour party, which depended almost entirely on contributions from trade unions.
TRADE UNION ACT, 1913 →

Ottowa agreements, 1932, under which Britain and the *dominions* accepted a limited policy of *imperial preference.* Britain exempted some imports, mainly food and raw materials, from duties, while the dominions gave preferential tariffs to British manufactured goods. A similar system was applied to the colonies in the following year. But imperial preference came too late to benefit Britain greatly. British imports from the Commonwealth rose from 25 per cent to nearly 38 per cent between 1930 and 1938, but British exports to the Commonwealth rose less rapidly, from 37.5 per cent to 45.6 per cent during the same period.
← IMPORT DUTIES ACT, 1932

Owen, Robert (1771–1858), social reformer, born at Newtown, Montgomeryshire, the son of a postmaster and saddler. He left home at the age of ten to seek his fortune and became apprenticed to a draper at Stamford, Lincolnshire. At the age of fourteen he set up as a manufacturer in Manchester on a borrowed £100, and six years later he became the manager of a large spinning mill employing 500 people. In 1799, he married the daughter of a wealthy millowner, David Dale, and shortly afterwards, with some other partners, bought his father-in-law's business for £60,000. His work at the New Lanark Mills, Scotland, made him internationally famous. He reduced the hours of work, provided a free medical service, and opened the first nursery infant school in Britain. To solve the unemployment problem, he suggested that villages of co-operation should be set up all over the country, where 300 to 2,000 people could live in common. These villages, built in the shape of a parallelogram, would contain communal kitchens, and dormitories for the children, while the private apartments would have central heating and air conditioning. This communistic scheme had a mixed reception and his attack on 'all the religions of the world' in 1817 lost him further support. He went to the United States and in 1825 set up a community, New Harmony, on the lines he had suggested, but it was a failure. He lost £40,000—four-fifths of his capital. On his return to England, he became involved in a number of schemes for social reform, including equitable labour exchanges, where workers could exchange the goods they produced, and, in 1834, the *Grand National Consolidated Trades Union*, which soon collapsed. From 1834 to 1841 he published his own newspaper 'The New Moral World' to expound his views on social and moral questions, but people listened to him less and less. Towards the end of his life he became a spiritualist.

Oxford movement, a group within the Church of England which tried to restore some of the ancient traditions, by emphasizing ceremonial, the authority of the clergy, and the divine mission of the Church. The movement started in 1833 when the Whigs abolished some Anglican bishoprics in Ireland. The movement feared further interference by the State in Church affairs, and started publishing a series of 'Tracts for the Times' in which they emphasized the independence of the Church and its importance as a body inspired by God. As a result of these tracts, the members were sometimes known as Tractarians. The leaders, who were all fellows of Oriel College, Oxford, were: Edward Bouverie Pusey (1800–82), appointed regius professor of Hebrew in 1828; John Keble (1792–1866), after whom Keble College, Oxford, is named; and *John Henry Newman.* After Newman became a Catholic in 1845, the Oxford movement lost much of its force. The members who remained within the Church of England became known as High Churchmen or Anglo-Catholics. They created 'settlements' to do social work in poor parts of cities; started Anglican monasteries and nunneries; and introduced ceremonial into services in the churches.

P

Pacifico, Don see **'Don Pacifico' affair**

Palmer, John (1742–1818), son of a Bath theatre owner, who introduced the first *mail coach* on the London–Bristol route in 1784. Mail

coaches, which travelled much faster than other coaches, were soon introduced in many other parts of the country. Palmer was made comptroller-general of the Post Office in 1786 and retired in 1793, when he was given a pension of £3,000 a year. Parliament gave him a further £50,000 in 1813 for his introduction of the mail coach scheme.
SIR ROWLAND HILL →

Palmerston, Viscount (1784-1865) dominated foreign policy from 1830 to his death in 1865. He became a Tory M.P. in 1807, and held the minor office of Secretary at War, responsible for Army administration and finance, from 1809 to 1828. (The office was merged with the more important office of Secretary of State for War in 1863.) He supported Catholic emancipation and some parliamentary reform and broke with the Tories in 1828 and became a Whig. He was appointed Foreign Secretary by Earl Grey in 1830. He held the office until 1841, apart from a few months in 1834-5 when Peel was in power, and was Foreign Secretary again from 1846 to 1851. In foreign affairs he was a Canningite, with an added touch of arrogance. He supported national independence movements, particularly when they could be of advantage to Britain's trade; he wanted to avoid wars with major powers so that British commerce could flourish; and he also wanted to make British power felt throughout the world, mainly by bullying small powers. In 1830, he supported the Belgian revolt against Dutch rule which had been imposed by the Treaty of Vienna, 1815. He succeeded in putting Leopold, uncle of the future Queen Victoria, on the Belgian throne. In 1834 he formed the *Quadruple Alliance* in the hope of creating constitutional monarchies in Spain and Portugal, but without much success. In 1839 to 1841, Palmerston helped the Turks against *Mehemet Ali*, who had occupied the Turkish provinces of Palestine and Syria. Palmerston was also responsible for the *Opium War, 1840–2*, against what he called in private the 'half-civilized government' of China. This policy of bullying weaker nations reached a peak with the *Don Pacifico affair* of 1850, when he ordered Greek ports to be blockaded and Greek ships to be seized in support of the claim against the Greek government by a Portuguese-Jewish money lender, who was only technically British. These actions were immensely popular with many of the Victorian middle classes. Palmerston was one of the first statesmen deliberately to use the newspapers to gain public support for his policies, by holding Press conferences at a convenient time and place for journalists—even, if necessary, in his own hotel bedroom—so that they could get their story in the following morning's paper. But his attitudes found less favour with some of his colleagues and with Queen Victoria.

She was immensely annoyed when Palmerston approved the coup by Louis Napoleon in France in 1851, before she had been consulted. It was this incident that led to his dismissal by Russell in the same year.

But Palmerston had such a large personal following in the country that Aberdeen appointed him Home Secretary in 1852. Palmerston took over as prime minister from Aberdeen in 1855, following the disastrous failures in the early stages of the *Crimean War, 1854–6.* He brought the war to a successful conclusion, suppressed the *Indian Mutiny* in the following year, but his government was defeated in 1858. He was prime minister again from 1859 to his death in 1865. He supported Italian progress towards reunification, but sympathized with the losing side—the Confederates—in the American Civil War, 1861–5. At home, he blocked many much-needed reforms, which were not put into effect until Gladstone came into power in 1868. He was born Henry John Temple and succeeded to the Irish title of viscount in 1802.

← LORD JOHN RUSSELL

Pankhurst, Mrs Emmeline (1859–1928), leader of the *suffragette movement*, born in Manchester. She married a Socialist lawyer, who died in 1898. In 1903, with her daughter Christabel (1880–1958), she formed the Women's Social and Political Union, which used increasingly violent means in its campaign for votes for women. Mrs Pankhurst was arrested many times and was sentenced to three years' penal servitude in 1913 after a house which was being built for Lloyd George was blown up by a bomb, but was soon released on licence. On the outbreak of the First World War, she immediately stopped her campaign and later helped to recruit women workers for munition factories. She joined the Conservative party in 1918 and just before her death was adopted as Conservative candidate for Whitechapel, London.

Paperbacks. The modern paperback was created by Sir Allen Lane in 1936, when he started publishing Penguin books, which originally sold for 6*d*. each. There had been paper-covered books before that, but these were the first which sold in many thousands. They made it possible for many more people to own their own small library of fiction, and, later, non-fiction works.

Parliament Act, 1911, stopped the House of Lords from rejecting any 'money Bill' involving taxation (e.g. the Budget) and allowed the Lords to delay the passing of any other Bill for only two years, after which it automatically became law. The House of Lords, which was dominated by the Conservatives at that time, had rejected many of the Liberal reforms, including the *People's Budget.* The Bill was only passed after a threat to create sufficient new peers to get it through the House, as had been done also with the *First Reform Act.* At the same time the duration of a parliament was reduced from seven years to five. (See next entry.)

Parliament Act, 1949, passed by the Socialists to reduce the delaying powers of the House of Lords to one year.
LIFE PEERAGES ACT, 1958 →

PARLIAMENTARY REFORM. In the first three decades of the nineteenth century the main demands of radicals like *John Cartwright, William Cobbett* and *Henry Hunt* was for reform of parliament. They were joined in these demands by some of the wealthier men in the new manufacturing towns, most of which had no M.P.s to represent them. Only about 3 per cent of the population had the vote. Both Houses of Parliament were dominated by the landowning classes, who controlled the *rotten* and *pocket boroughs* and who could bribe and influence electors through the open voting system in which the elector had to call out his choice of candidate. The agitation for parliamentary reform drew thousands of people to the *Spa Fields meetings* in London 1816. Three years later at a meeting for parliamentary reform in Manchester, eleven people were killed and hundreds injured by yeomanry at the *Peterloo* massacre. The government clamped down on agitation by passing the *Six Acts* in the same year, and used the *Cato Street conspiracy* as an excuse for having done so.

But agitation for parliamentary reform could not be so easily squashed and in 1830 the *Whigs* came into power, with their leader *Earl Grey* pledged to reform. After a two-year-long struggle, inside and outside parliament, in which *Thomas Attwood*'s Birmingham Political Union of working- and middle-class reformers played a big part, the *First Reform Act* was passed. But it was of most benefit to the wealthy manufacturers in the new industrial towns, and the disappointed working-class reformers turned to a new movement, *Chartism*, instead. This failed to achieve any of the six reforms demanded and it collapsed in 1848.

It was not until 1867 that the *Representation of the People Act* (the Second Reform Act) gave the vote to most working men in the towns. Successive Acts of the same name gave the vote to most farm workers, 1884; all men and some women, 1918; and all women over twenty-one, 1928. Secret voting to stop bribery was introduced by the

Ballot Act, 1872; constituencies were made more equal in size by the *Redistribution of Seats Act, 1885*; and the powers of the House of Lords were curbed by the *Parliament Acts* of 1911 and 1949. The first woman to be elected an M.P. was *Countess Markievicz* in 1918; the first woman M.P. to take her seat was *Nancy Astor* in 1919; and the first woman Cabinet minister *Margaret Bondfield* was appointed in 1929. Life peers were created and women were admitted to the House of Lords under the *Life Peerage Act, 1958*. The voting age was reduced from twenty-one to eighteen in 1969.

Although all but one of the original six demands of the Chartists have now been achieved—that for annual parliaments—universal suffrage in itself has not brought as many benefits as the early reformers thought it would. Owing to the constituency system, many Conservative votes are 'wasted' in safe Labour seats and vice versa. This applies even more to the Liberals, who collect millions of votes in total at most general elections, but usually end up with only a handful of seats. The party in power has frequently polled a minority of the total votes cast, and sometimes has won fewer votes than the Opposition. *Floating voters* exercise a great influence on which party gets into power. The party manifestoes issued before the elections often bear little relation to the actions of the government once it is in power. Furthermore, M.P.s are reluctant to vote against their own government and bring it down, except on really major issues, as it means that they have to fight a new election, in which the party might be defeated. *Pressure groups* of many different kinds exercise a great influence on politics behind the scenes. In recent years there has also been a considerable lessening of the credibility of M.P.s and ministers, particularly since television has brought them face to face with a much more highly-educated and critical public. For these reasons, and others, there has been an increasing tendency to turn to *direct action* instead of constitutional means of change and reform.

Parnell, Charles Stewart (1846–91), Protestant landowner in Ireland who championed the Irish Catholics in their demand for *Irish Home Rule*. His family were anti-British: his great-grandfather had been one of the Protestant patriots who voted against the *Act of Union, 1800*, with Britain, and ancestors of his American mother had fought against the British. He was elected M.P. for County Meath in 1875 and succeeded Isaac Butt (1813–79) as leader of the Home Rule Association in 1880, and was elected president of the *Irish Land League* when it was formed in 1878–9. Parnell used his skill in parliamentary affairs to obstruct the normal business of the House of Commons, to draw attention to the need for reform in Ireland. In October 1881, he was arrested for allegedly inciting the members of the Irish Land League to violence and was held in Kilmainham prison, Dublin. He was released in May 1882, after the *Kilmainham pact* with Gladstone, which was designed to secure more moderate policies on both the English and Irish sides. After the *Phoenix Park murders, 1882*, Parnell re-formed the Irish Land League as the National League, which tried to use parliamentary, rather than violent, means to bring about change in Ireland. In the 1885 elections, Parnell's supporters won 86 of the 105 Irish seats and thus held the balance of power between the Liberals and Conservatives in the House of Commons. With Parnell's support, Gladstone brought in his first *Irish Home Rule Bill* in 1886, which was defeated by the defection of the *Liberal Unionists*, led by Joseph Chamberlain. In the following year *The Times* accused Parnell of condoning the Phoenix Park murders, even though he had already condemned them. He won a libel action against the newspaper by proving that the story had been based on forged documents, which greatly increased his political stature. But his political career was abruptly ended when he was cited in a divorce case brought in 1890 by one of his former colleagues, Captain O'Shea. Divorce was then considered shameful and he was discredited with most of the Irish voters, Gladstone, and the Catholic Church. He lost his hold on his party, and was dismissed as chairman. He died in the following year, five months after he had married the former Mrs O'Shea.

JOHN REDMOND →

Parsons, Sir Charles (1854–1931), engineer, born in London, son of the third Earl of Rosse. His steam turbine, invented in 1884, was used to generate electricity in power stations and to increase the speed of ships. Unlike the old steam engine with its pistons, the steam turbine has jets of steam which are directed on to the blades of a rotating shaft. It is mechanically simpler and far more powerful. At first, it was used to drive a dynamo to provide lighting in ships, but it was soon put into more general use in power stations. In 1897 Parsons fitted the steam turbine to a small 100-foot-long vessel, the Turbinia. It reached a speed of 34 knots, much faster than that of conventional steamships. Soon afterwards the steam turbine was used in both Royal Navy and merchant ships. Parsons was also responsible for 300 other inventions, including an improved form of optical glass, the gun silencer, and the auxetophone, which amplified the sound of musical instruments. He was knighted in 1911.

← ALFRED HOLT

Passfield, Lord, see **Sidney Webb**

Pasteur, Louis (1822–95), French chemist and biologist, who originated the 'germ' theory of disease. In 1854 he made some experiments proving that all kinds of microbes, some of which can cause disease, are present in the air in great quantities. This was a revolutionary discovery as previously most doctors had believed that microbes were caused by decaying matter and that diseases were transmitted by smells. They therefore took no antiseptic precautions in their operations. Pasteur also showed how most bacteria could be killed or weakened by heat or by using an antiseptic, like carbon acid. (Pasteurised milk, which has been heated for 30 minutes to kill bacteria, is named after him.) In the 1880s he showed that protection against a disease could be provided by inoculation with a milder form of the same disease. He successfully inoculated sheep against anthrax and a boy against rabies. His discoveries not only made surgery safer through the use of antiseptics, but also led on to the use of inoculation against many diseases. His work was based on the principle, expressed in his own words, that there are two opposed forces in society, one 'a law of blood and of death' which led to wars and the creation of new means of destruction and another 'law of peace, work and health' which puts 'human life above any victory'.
ROBERT KOCH →

Paterson, Mrs Emma (1846–86), born in London. She formed the Women's Protective and Provident League in 1874 to start trade unions for women workers and in 1875 became the first woman delegate to the Trades Union Congress. Although women's trade unions died out, she did much to gain greater equality for women in the union movement. She also campaigned for women factory inspectors to be appointed.
MATCH GIRLS' STRIKE, 1888 →

Pay as You Earn (P.A.Y.E.), a method of collecting income tax, introduced during the Second World War, under which employers had to deduct tax week by week from the wages of their workers. With increased wages during the war, more people became liable to pay tax and this simplified its collection. Previously, employees had been individually assessed by the income tax authorities and had had to pay their tax direct to them twice a year.
← INCOME TAX

Payment by results was introduced by *Robert Lowe* in 1862 to reduce the government grant to voluntary schools, which then totalled over

£800,000 a year. The grant to each school was made to depend mainly on how many children passed the annual examination conducted by inspectors. The system was not totally abolished until 1900.
← VOLUNTARY SCHOOLS

Payment of M.P.s was introduced by the Liberals in 1911, and came into effect in 1912. It was of greatest benefit to working-class Labour M.P.s. They were paid £400 a year, which has been progressively inscreased to £4,500. In 1957 members of the House of Lords (who now include many former Labour M.P.s) were given an expense allowance of three guineas a day, in addition to travelling expenses which had been granted in 1946.

Peabody, George (1795–1869), a rich American draper, who settled as a banker in London in 1843. He gave £500,000 to provide homes for the poor in the capital. The first block of four-and five-storey Peabody flats was opened in Spitalfields in 1864, and more were built in other districts, including Chelsea, Islington and Bermondsey. The really poor did not benefit, as the rents were too high for anyone but skilled craftsmen to afford. The problem of providing better *housing* for the working class was not solved until councils were given government subsidies to build council houses for the first time by the *Housing and Town Planning Act, 1919.*
OCTAVIA HILL →

Peace Ballot, 1935, of all households in Britain was organized by the League of Nations Union. Of the 11½m. replies, over 10m. wanted all-round disarmament and the use of economic *sanctions* against aggressors. Over 2m. were opposed to any war against an aggressor, even if sanctions failed. The result of the ballot had some influence in persuading the government to adopt a more moderate line towards aggressors, like Mussolini and Hitler, and led on to the policy of *appeasement*, even though this was not the intention of the sponsors of the ballot.

Peel, Sir Robert (1788–1850), statesman who adapted Conservatism to the changed conditions of the new industrial age, but split his party by doing so. He was born near Bury, Lancashire, the son of a wealthy cotton manufacturer, and was educated at Harrow and Christ Church, Oxford. He became a Tory M.P. in 1809 at the age of twenty-one. From 1812 to 1818, he was Chief Secretary for Ireland, under Liverpool, where he fulfilled all Tory hopes of him by firmly opposing

Catholic emancipation and setting up a police force to maintain law and order—the Peace Preservation Force. He was Home Secretary from 1822 to 1827 and made some improvements in prisons and reduced the number of crimes which could be punished by death by over one hundred. The *Combination Acts* were repealed in 1824, during his term as Home Secretary, which made it somewhat easier for workers to form trade unions. After a wave of strikes, Peel introduced a law which made it illegal for strikers to use intimidation or threats of violence. When Canning got into power in 1827, Peel resigned, fearing that he would introduce Catholic emancipation. But he was back in office again from 1828 to 1830 as Home Secretary and Leader of the House of Commons, under Wellington. During this period, he passed the *Metropolitan Police Act, 1829*, which established the first police force in the capital, and which was later used as a model for police forces in the rest of the country. Then came the first of Peel's abrupt changes of policy, which split the Conservative party. *Daniel O'Connell* won the County Clare election in Ireland, but could not take his seat at Westminster as an M.P. because he was a Catholic. Fearing that there would be a revolution in Ireland if O'Connell was not allowed to do so, Peel piloted the *Roman Catholic Relief Act, 1829*, through the House of Commons. This was not a radical reform, as Pitt had promised Catholic emancipation almost thirty years before, but many Tories were opposed and in revenge they brought down the government, which ended nearly fifty years of Tory rule. Many Tories never forgave Peel for his change of mind and always distrusted him afterwards. Many of the more moderate Tories, however, soon forgave him.

Peel justified his philosophy of new Conservatism, which accepted necessary, moderate reform, in an address to his electors in 1834—the *Tamworth manifesto*. He was prime minister for four months in 1834–1835, and again from 1841 to 1846. His second ministry brought about the settlement of wars and disputes abroad, and financial reforms at home. The *Opium War* with China was concluded by the Treaty of Nanking, 1842, and the first unsuccessful war against *Afghanistan* was ended in the same year, after the failure of the British to replace the popular ruler, Dost Mohammed, by the exiled Shah Suja. With the aid of his Foreign Secretary, Aberdeen, Peel established closer relations with France and settled the *Oregon dispute* with the United States over its boundary with Canada in 1846. At home, *income tax* was reintroduced at 7*d.* in the £ in 1842 and in 1844 a *Bank Charter Act* was passed to prevent the over-issuing of bank notes and the consequent failure of many banks. Peel supported a *free trade* policy and in all 600 duties were abolished and over 1,000 reduced. This culminated in the

Repeal of the Corn Law in 1846, which offended the great landowners in the Conservative party and split the party even more deeply than Catholic emancipation had done. The government was brought down in the same year by a combination of Whigs and Conservatives, led by Disraeli, who were opposed to the repeal of the Corn Law. The Conservatives were out of effective power for another twenty years. Peel succeeded his father as a baronet in 1830.
← DUKE OF WELLINGTON: LORD ABERDEEN →

'Peelites', Conservatives who continued to support Peel's free trade policies after the party had been split by the *Repeal of the Corn Law, 1846*. Many of them, notably Gladstone, eventually became members of the Liberal party.

'Penny-farthing'. An early type of bicycle with a large wheel at the front and a smaller wheel at the back, used in the second half of the nineteenth century. The rider sat on a saddle above the front wheel, about four or five feet above the ground.
← VELOCIPEDE: BICYCLES →

Penny Post. A uniform charge for sending inland letters introduced in 1840 owing to the campaigns by Robert Wallace, M.P. for Greenock, 1831–46, and *Sir Rowland Hill.* Previously it had cost up to 8*d.* to send a letter. Adhesive stamps were introduced at the same time, the first being the Penny Black. The number of letters increased from 75m. in 1838 to 642m. in 1864. The penny post was welcomed by businessmen and by reformers, like Francis Place and Richard Cobden, who also supported the campaign, because they saw the advantage of being able to send their propaganda cheaply all over the country. The penny post lasted until 1918, when the charge was raised to 1½*d.*
← MAIL COACHES

Pentonville Prison. A new 'model' prison, with 540 separate cells, opened in 1843 after *transportation* to New South Wales, Australia, had been abolished. Long-term prisoners started their sentence with a period of up to eighteen months' solitary confinement, so that they had a chance to think about their sins and to repent. Fifty-four similar prisons, to hold a total of 11,000 men and women, were built in the next six years, including Holloway (1851) and Parkhurst (1854). Most of them are still in use today, which severely restricts attempts at the reformation of criminals, as they are out of date and also overcrowded.
← NEWGATE PRISON: OPEN PRISONS →

'People's Budget', 1909, introduced by the Liberal Chancellor of the Exchequer, Lloyd George. It reduced tax for parents with young children; introduced a new supertax (later renamed surtax) on incomes over £2,000 a year; and put a 20 per cent tax on the increase in the value of land whenever it was sold. The land tax infuriated the House of Lords, which was still dominated by large landowners, and it rejected the Budget. Lloyd George planned to use the money to pay for social services and rearmament.
PARLIAMENT ACT, 1911 →

Perkin, Sir William (1837–1907), chemist, born in London, who discovered how to make the first synthetic dye—mauve—from coal tar in 1856. Previously dyes had to be obtained from extracts of vegetables, such as madder (red); woad (blue); and weld (yellow). Other dyes were soon discovered by German chemists, and Germany built up a massive dye-producing industry.

Peterloo. A massacre of peaceful men, women and children at a meeting in support of parliamentary reform held in Manchester on 16 August 1819, when eleven people were killed and at least 500 injured. The Manchester magistrates sent the local yeomanry into the crowd of 80,000 to arrest the principal speaker, *Henry Hunt.* The horsemen then turned upon the crowd, slashing at them with their swords. The incident in St Peter's Field, became known as Peterloo, in ironic contrast to the bravery that the yeomanry had displayed at the Battle of Waterloo four years previously. *Viscount Sidmouth*, the Home Secretary, later sent a letter of congratulation to the Manchester magistrates. It was one of the most repressive acts in the troubled years after the Napoleonic wars, and became part of the folk history of the working classes.
← SPA FIELDS MEETINGS: SIX ACTS →

Phoenix Park murders, 1882, in Dublin, had a great influence in worsening relations between England and Ireland. An underground group, the Invincibles, murdered Thomas Burke, the permanent under-secretary for Ireland and Lord Frederick Cavendish, the Chief Secretary for Ireland, who had just been appointed by Gladstone to carry out a more moderate policy. *Parnell* had just been released from prison under the *Kilmainham pact.* English opinion hardened and a new Prevention of Crimes Act was passed which allowed trial without a jury in Ireland.

Pitt, William (1759–1806), son of the Earl of Chatham (1708–78), many of whose measures had a long-lasting effect. He became prime minister in 1783, at the age of twenty-three. He introduced a number of reforms, including a Bill for parliamentary reform in 1785, which was defeated, and urged *William Wilberforce* to take up the cause of abolishing slavery. In 1784 his India Act set up a system of dual control by the Crown and the East India Company in India, and in 1791 his Canada Act gave separate governments to Ontario and French-speaking Quebec. After the French revolution and the outbreak of the war with France in 1793 he became increasingly conservative, passing the *Combination Acts* of 1799 and 1800 and banning *Corresponding societies* in 1799. In 1800 he passed the *Act of Union* which made Ireland part of the United Kingdom, but resigned in the following year when George III refused to give the Irish the *Catholic emancipation* that Pitt had promised. He was prime minister again from 1804 to 1806.

Place, Francis (1771–1854), reformer, born in London. He started work as a breeches maker, and organized a strike among other London workers in the same trade in 1793, and was unemployed for nine months as a result. In 1799 he opened his own tailor's shop at Charing Cross, which was so successful that he was able to hand over control of the business to his son ten years later, and devote most of his time to political activity. The library behind his shop became one of the main meeting places for *radicals.* He was involved in the campaigns for the repeal of the Combination Acts, the First Reform Act, the penny post and Chartism. He also gave guarded support to the then unmentionable subject of birth control in a book 'Illustrations and Proofs of the Principle of Population', published in 1822. Although Place was a good organizer and knew how to run committees, his importance as a reformer has been somewhat exaggerated. He was no revolutionary, but was more interested in increasing the prosperity of skilled craftsmen and small businessmen—like himself—than in helping the really poor working classes.

← HENRY HUNT: THOMAS ATTWOOD →

Plimsoll mark, or load line, on ships, named after *Samuel Plimsoll.* The Merchant Shipping Act, 1876, made it compulsory for merchant ships to have a load line painted on the hull, which had to remain above water after the ship had taken on its cargo, to show that it was not overloaded. But, owing to a defect in the law, shipowners could paint the mark (a circle bisected by a straight line) at any level they liked.

The Act did not become effective until 1890, when the position of the line on the hull had to be approved by a government official. Modern merchant ships have other load lines showing the safety level for various areas and sea conditions.

Plimsoll, Samuel (1824–1898), M.P. for Derby, 1868–80, who was mainly responsible for the Merchant Shipping Act, 1876. He was also honorary secretary of the *Great Exhibition, 1851*. (See previous entry.)

Plowden report, 1967, recommended that more nursery schools should be provided and better primary schools should be built in the poorer areas of large cities.

Plug plot, a name given to the strikes which occurred in many parts of the north of England, Scotland and Wales, at the same time as the presentation of the second Chartist petition. In factories where other workers would not come out in their support, the strikers pulled the plugs out of steam engines so that production stopped. Many of the leaders were sentenced to transportation.

Pocket boroughs, which were small enough for the local lord or landowner to influence voters or to bribe them to vote for the candidate he supported. The practice did not end entirely until the Ballot Act, 1872, made voting secret.

Polaris. A missile which can be fired underwater from a nuclear-powered submarine, successfully tested by the Americans in 1960. Britain has four submarines equipped with Polaris missiles. The theory is that they provide a deterrent against a surprise attack, because the aggressor would know that his own country could be devastated by the missiles, even after Britain had been obliterated.
← HYDROGEN BOMB

Police Act, 1919, was passed following a strike by 6,000 Metropolitan policemen in 1918, and a second strike by policemen in other parts of the country, for recognition of their union and better pay. The Act created the Police Federation and gave the Home Secretary powers to make pay and conditions the same throughout the country.
← COUNTY AND BOROUGH POLICE ACT, 1856: POLICE ACT, 1946 →

Police Act, 1946, amalgamated forty-five smaller police forces with larger forces in the interests of great efficiency. (See next entry.)

Police Act, 1964, encouraged police forces to set up joint crime and traffic squads. Two years later, more police forces were amalgamated, reducing the number in England and Wales from 117 to 49. Because of growing concern about police corruption, the Act laid down that public complaints had to be investigated by an officer from an outside police force.

POLITICAL PARTIES have been repeatedly split and re-formed throughout the nineteenth and twentieth centuries, as their members have reacted to changed circumstances: the idea that parties represent rigid, fixed attitudes will not bear historical examination. In 1829, the old *Tory party* was split by the passing of the *Roman Catholic Relief Act* by *Wellington and Peel*, though most Tories remained uncompromisingly opposed to *parliamentary reform.* After the *Whigs* came into power in 1830 and passed the *First Reform Act* of 1832, Peel gave his party a new philosophy of more moderative Conservatism in the *Tamworth manifesto* of 1834. But the party was again split in 1846 with the *Repeal of the Corn Law* by Peel. The Conservative protectionists, led by *Derby* and *Disraeli*, acted as the spokesmen for the big landowners, while the *Peelites*, who supported *free trade*, represented the interests of the new manufacturing classes, and eventually allied with the Whigs, led by *Palmerston* and *Russell.*

This period of mid-century confusion was succeeded by a 20-year period when party lines appeared to be more finely drawn. By 1868, the *Liberal party*, with its policy of 'peace, retrenchment and reform' had been created by *Gladstone* out of 'Peelites' like himself; Whigs; and radicals like *John Bright.* Disraeli, on the other side of the House, had evolved a new Conservative philosophy of respect for property, the monarchy and constitution and the Empire, plus practical social reforms. But in 1886, the Liberal party was split over the first *Irish Home Rule Bill*, when *Liberal Unionists*, led by *Joseph Chamberlain*, left the party and eventually allied with the Conservatives to form the Conservative and Unionist party. Joseph Chamberlain split the Conservatives at the beginning of the present century over the issue of *tariff reform.*

Meanwhile with the extension of the franchise by the *Representation of the People Act, 1867* (the Second Reform Act), and the new theory of *socialism*, a third force had arisen in politics. The first working-class M.P.s, *Lib-Labs*, sat with the Liberals in the House of Commons, but an *Independent Labour party* was formed in 1893. In 1900 it combined with the trade unions and other socialist groups, the *Fabians* and the *Social Democratic Federation*, to form the Labour Representation Committee which became the *Labour party* in 1906. Some of the more extreme socialists left the Labour Representation Committee almost as soon as it was formed and others helped to found the *Communist party of Great Britain* in 1920.

Most party differences were temporarily forgotten during the First World War, when a *coalition government* was formed by *Asquith* in 1915, who was replaced as prime minister by another Liberal, *Lloyd George*, in 1916. After the *coupon election* at the end of the war, the coalition government stayed in office until 1922. The personal feud between Asquith and Lloyd George had so seriously weakened the Liberal party that it has never again held power, and the Labour party, which first formed a government in 1924, has become the alternative to the Conservatives. The Labour party was in power again in 1931, but was split when the prime minister, *Ramsay MacDonald*, agreed to form a *National government*, including members of all three parties. The National government, under different leaders, continued in power until 1940, though it was dominated by the Conservatives. It was then replaced by a wartime *coalition* government under Churchill.

Immediately after the end of the war there was a sharp divergence in the views of the Labour and the Conservative parties, but from the 1950s the policies of the leaders, at least, tended to converge in practice, as they sought to get support in the middle ground. This process of 'Butskellism' started in the early 1950s when similar financial policies were adopted by successive Labour and Conservative Chancellors—Hugh Gaitskell (1950–1) and *Lord Butler.*

Pollution. In the nineteenth century, *water supplies* from rivers were often polluted by sewage, and discharges from gasworks, bone mills, and tanneries. This pollution was one of the main causes of disease. The problem of pollution has grown in the twentieth century, with the discharge of poisonous chemical wastes into the rivers, oil slicks from *oil tankers* into the sea, and the fumes from the internal combustion engine into the atmosphere. A *Clean Air Act* was passed in 1956. A Royal Commisison on Environmental Pollution has been set up which issued its first report in 1971. It said that the danger of 'polluting air, water and land' was a 'matter of great concern', particularly as the discharge of industrial waste products might contaminate rivers or underground water supplies.

Poor Laws, passed in 1597 and 1601, which set up a nationwide system for helping the poor in times of need. They were not finally repealed until 1948. Local justices of the peace administered the scheme and appointed overseers to collect the poor rate from the residents of the parish. If a poor person was unemployed, sick, or too old to work, he could apply to the overseers for relief. They might give him a small sum of money or send him to a workhouse, part of which was sometimes used as a hospital for the poor. The system was unable to cope with the growing number of poor in the second half of the eighteenth century and in 1795 the *Speenhamland system* was introduced to supplement low wages by giving small cash allowances, based on the price of bread and the size of a man's family. But this led to such an increase in the poor rate that a *Poor Law Amendment Act* was introduced in 1834. (See next entry.)

Poor Law Amendment Act, 1834, tried to end all cash payments, or outdoor relief, to unemployed men who were fit to work and to force them to find a job, or to go into new, inhumane *workhouses* with their families. The workhouses were built by groups, or unions, of parishes and were run by *Boards of Guardians*, elected by local ratepayers. But many of the Boards, particularly in the north, continued to give cash allowances to men who were temporarily unemployed. By 1842, there were still 132 unions of parishes, out of 590, which were giving relief to the unemployed. *Edwin Chadwick* was largely responsible for the report on which the Act was based. He was appointed secretary to the new central body, the Poor Law Commission, which was meant to see that the Act was put into effect in all parts of the country. But after a scandal at Andover workhouse in 1847, where starving inmates had been forced to gnaw at old bones just to keep alive, the Commission was abolished and replaced by a Poor Law Board responsible to a Minister. The Poor Law was finally abolished by the *National Assistance Act, 1948*.

Popular Press. Newspapers designed to sell at a low price to millions of readers. Until the repeal of the *Taxes on Knowledge*, newspapers were too dear for most people to buy, but afterwards they could be produced to sell at ½*d.* The *Education Act, 1870*, created a new generation of people who could read, and in 1881 George Newnes (1851–1910) started publishing a magazine called 'Tit-bits' for this new mass market, and it soon reached a circulation of 1m. In 1896, *Viscount Northcliffe* published the first popular ½*d.* national daily—the 'Daily Mail'—which had an instant success. By 1937 there were six popular national dailies. The total sale of all national dailies in 1937 was about 10m. copies a day, which rose to a peak of nearly 17m. in 1950, and has since declined to its present level of about 14½m. copies.

POPULATION. It is thought that the population of England and Wales increased from about 6½m. in 1750 to about 9m. in 1801, though there is no certainty about the figures. The first *census* was not conducted until 1801, and even then it was not entirely accurate; *registration of births, marriages and deaths* did not begin until 1837. There was certainly a large increase in the number of people, which was sustained by the increase in food supplies brought about by improvements in *agriculture*, but we shall never know with complete accuracy how big it was. There is also a lively debate among historians, which is still continuing, over the cause of the increase—whether it was due to a rise in the *birth rate* or a fall in the *death rate.* The theories of *Thomas Robert Malthus*, which had a great influence at the time, are now largely discredited.

Historians are on somewhat firmer ground in the nineteenth century, though even then some of the statistics are inaccurate or incomplete. But there are certain broad trends which can be discerned. Foremost among them is the great growth in the population of the United Kingdom from under 16m. in 1801 to over 55m. in 1970. As a result, the *density of population* in Britain is one of the highest in the world, in spite of large-scale *emigration* in the nineteenth century.

This vast increase in population has been brought about by a number of different factors. There was a fall in the death rate from the middle of the nineteenth century, which continued at an increasing rate as *food* supplies improved, and better *sanitation*, *water supplies* and *public health* reduced the number of *epidemics* of Asiatic cholera, typhus and typhoid fevers. *Vaccination* against smallpox and improved *medicine* also played some part in reducing the death rate in the nineteenth century and improved medical facilities and the introduction of new drugs have played an even bigger part in the present century. From 1900 there was a dramatic reduction in the *infant mortality* rate. All of these factors have contributed towards the great increase in the *expectation of life.* The birth rate began to fall in the 1850s and declined sharply in the years between the two world wars, partly as a result of wider use of *birth control* methods. In recent years it has started to fall again, partly owing to the legalizing of *abortion.* Increased *immigration* from the Commonwealth since the end of the last war has been balanced by continued emigration at a high rate.

There has also been a great shift in the population. The industrial *towns* of the north started to develop at the end of the eighteenth century. By 1851 there were more people living in the towns than in the countryside for the first time. In the 1930s there was a drift of population away from the *depressed areas* to London and the more prosperous south-east of England which has continued ever since.

The population of the United Kingdom was:

1801	15,902,000	1891	37,802,000
1811	18,102,000	1901	41,538,000
1821	21,008,000	1911	45,268,000
1831	24,135,000	1921	47,168,000
1841	26,751,000	1931	46,074,000 (excluding Irish Free State)
1851	27,393,000	1941	48,216,000
1861	28,976,000	1951	50,225,000
1871	31,556,000	1961	52,709,000
1881	34,935,000	1970	55,711,000

Potato famine see **Irish famine**

Potwallopers, heads of households with their own fireplaces, who had the traditional right to vote in boroughs. The franchise was abolished by the First Reform Act, 1832, though existing potwallopers were allowed to vote for the rest of their lives.

Prefabs, or prefabricated houses, which are built in whole sections in factories so that they can be speedily erected on the site. They were put up to help solve the housing shortage after the Second World War. In all, 124,555 prefabs were built. They were designed to last a minimum of ten years, but 30,000 were still standing in 1971, because of the continuing housing shortage.

Press gang. The traditional method of recruiting seamen for the Royal Navy, under which merchant seamen and other men were taken off by force and made to serve in warships. The press gang of officers and men was one of the most dreaded sights in ports. The system died out following the Continuous Service Act, 1853, which allowed naval ratings to be given permanent engagements.

Pressure groups. Organizations representing a particular section of the community, like farmers, or a particular viewpoint, like the *temperance societies*, which try to influence the government to take a certain course of action by campaigns, propaganda, and 'lobbying' M.P.s and ministers. The *Anti-Corn-Law League* was one of the first major examples of a successful pressure group.

Prices and incomes freeze was introduced by the Labour government for six months in 1966 and by the Conservatives for three months initially in 1972, in an attempt to halt *inflation.* As in other countries, it has proved difficult to control prices and to stop them rising, even if legal powers to do so are available.

PRIME MINISTERS AND MONARCHS

(C)=Conservative (Co)=Coalition (L)=Liberal
(Lab)=Labour (Nat)=National (T)=Tory
(W)=Whig

George III (reigned 1760–1820)

1812 Liverpool (T)

George IV (1820–30)

1827 Canning (T)
1827 Goderich (T)
1828 Wellington (T)

William IV (1830–7)

1830 Grey (W)
1834 Melbourne W)
1834 Peel (C)
1835 Melbourne (W)

Victoria (1837–1901)

1841 Peel (C)
1846 Russell (W)
1852 Derby (C)
1852 Aberdeen (Co)
1855 Palmerston (W)
1858 Derby (C)
1859 Palmerston (W)
1865 Russell (W)
1866 Derby (C)
1868 Disraeli (C)
1868 Gladstone (L)
1874 Disraeli (C)
1880 Gladstone (L)
1885 Salisbury (C)
1886 Gladstone (L)
1886 Salisbury (C)
1892 Gladstone (L)
1894 Rosebery (L)
1895 Salisbury (C)

Edward VII (1901–10)

1902 Balfour (C)
1905 Campbell-Bannerman (L)
1908 Asquith (L)

George V (1910–36)

1915 Asquith (Co)
1916 Lloyd George (Co)
1922 Bonar Law (C)
1923 Baldwin (C)
1924 MacDonald (Lab)
1924 Baldwin (C)
1929 MacDonald (Lab)
1931 MacDonald (Nat)
1935 Baldwin (Nat)

Edward VIII (1936)

George VI (1936–52)

1937 Chamberlain (Nat)
1940 Churchill (Co)
1945 Attlee (Lab)
1951 Churchill (C)

Elizabeth II (1952–)

1955 Eden (C)
1957 Macmillan (C)
1963 Douglas-Home (C)
1964 Wilson (Lab)
1970 Heath (C)

(See also under individual entries.)

Probation. The first unpaid probation officer was appointed to the London magistrates' courts in 1876 by the Church of England Temperance Society to help drunkards. The number of 'police court missionaries', as they were then known, increased to eleven by 1880. By then they were then dealing with many other kinds of cases. In 1887, the Probation of First Offenders Act allowed young people to be put on probation for up to two years. In 1907 courts were allowed to appoint probation officers and a nation-wide, compulsory service of probation officers was started in 1925.

CRIMINAL JUSTICE ACT, 1948 →

Protection, the opposite of *free trade*, when tariffs or duties are charged on foreign goods to protect home manufacturers or farmers against competition. Protection for farmers was ended by the *Repeal of the Corn Law, 1846*, and for most manufactured goods in the following fifteen years. *Joseph Chamberlain* wanted to reintroduce tariffs again at the beginning of the twentieth century, but it was not until 1932 that this was done by the *Import Duties Act.*

PUBLIC HEALTH is concerned with trying to provide a better and healthier environment for people. In the early years of the nineteenth century deaths were caused by serious *epidemics* in London and other grossly overcrowded *towns.* The *Report on Sanitary Conditions* by *Edwin Chadwick* drew attention to the need for reform. A *General Board of Health* was set up under the first *Public Health Act, 1848*, and from that time on there were gradual improvements in *sanitation* and *water supplies* in the towns, which helped to reduce the number of deaths and the incidence of Asiatic cholera and typhoid fever. The appointment of *medical officers of health,* made compulsory under the *Public Health*

Act, 1872, was a great step forward in securing adequate inspection and control. But many people continued to live in extremely poor *housing* conditions and little real progress was made until the government gave councils subsidies to build homes under the *Housing and Town Planning Act, 1919*. In recent years there has been an increasing concentration on the problem of *pollution* in towns, caused partly by the growth of *road* traffic.

Public Health Act, 1848. The first attempt to deal nationally with the lack of *sanitation*. It created a *General Board of Health* with powers to set up local boards of health in towns where a tenth of the ratepayers wanted one, or compulsorily where the death rate was high. Only 183 local boards, covering about 3m. people, were ever set up. Edwin Chadwick and Lord Shaftesbury were members of the General Board which was abolished in 1858. (See next entry.)

Public Health Act, 1872, set up sanitary authorities in all parts of the country and made the appointment of a *medical officer of health* compulsory. (See next entry.)

Public Health Act, 1875. An important Act, passed by *Viscount Cross*, some parts of which are still in force to this day. It gave the local sanitary authorities powers to enforce better drainage, sanitation and water supplies. Section 91 gave them powers to prosecute landlords of 'any premises in such a state as to be injurious to health or a nuisance'.

Public libraries. Although many mechanics' institutes had libraries for their members and there were private subscription libraries for the middle classes, borough councils were not allowed to open public libraries until the Public Libraries Acts of 1845 and 1850. Many free libraries were set up in the big cities in the 1850s. At the beginning of the present century, *Andrew Carnegie*, the American millionaire provided many new buildings for public libraries. In 1970, there were well over 10,000 libraries (including mobile libraries); their book issues total over 500m. a year.

Public Order Act, 1936, made it an offence to wear political uniforms. It was directed mainly against the British Union of Fascists, or Blackshirts, formed in 1931.

Public Schools. Most of the older public schools, like Winchester, had fallen into a decline by the beginning of the nineteenth century, with an outdated classical education, harsh living conditions, and frequent riots by pupils, which were sometimes so violent that the troops had to be called in. The public schools were reformed in the nineteenth century by headmasters such as *George Butler* and *Thomas Arnold*, who emphasized Christianity, team games, character-building and the prefect system. 'The public school man bears a stamp moral, mental and physical which is easily recognized,' said one nineteenth-century author. They produced thousands of colonial officials and army officers to police and protect the Empire. Many new public schools, including Marlborough, Radley, Lancing and Wellington, were founded around the middle of the nineteenth century.

A Royal Commission—the Clarendon Commission—was set up in 1861 to investigate the nine main public schools—Eton, Harrow, Winchester, Shrewsbury, Charterhouse, Rugby, Westminster, St Paul's and Merchant Taylors'. Under the Public Schools Act, 1868, new governing bodies were established for the first seven of the schools. Fearing further government intervention in the affairs of public schools, Edward Thring, of Uppingham, formed a Headmasters' Conference in the following year to defend their freedom and independence.

The 200 schools, whose headmasters are members of the conference, constitute the public schools of today. Many of the pupils are boarders, and fees are high, ranging up to £900 a year or more. Since the end of the last war, the public schools have changed with the times and now concentrate far more on academic studies and examinations, and less on games and team spirit. Few people would deny that they provide an extremely good education, and some of the public school features, like the house system, have been incorporated into State schools. But many people are concerned that the schools should be reserved almost entirely for those who can afford to pay the high fees.

In 1944, the Fleming Committee recommended that a minimum of one-quarter of the places in public schools should be given to children from State schools, whose fees would be paid by local education authorities. But only a few authorities have sent children to public schools.

In December 1965, a Public Schools Commission was appointed under the chairmanship of Sir John Newsom (who produced the *Newsom report*) to advise how public schools could best be integrated with the State system. There are also public schools for girls: *Dorothea Beale* was headmistress of one of the first to be founded.

Pupil-teacher system, was introduced in 1846 to provide more teachers without too much expense. Children of thirteen or fourteen served a five-

year apprenticeship at an annual salary of £10 rising to £20, teaching children during the day and being instructed themselves by the schoolmaster or the schoolmistress in the evenings or during the dinner breaks. By the time of the *Education Act, 1870*, there was about one pupil-teacher to every teacher. The number started to decline after that with the expansion of training colleges for teachers.
← MONITORIAL SYSTEM

Purchase tax was introduced in 1940 during the Second World War to restrict spending on non-essential goods and to raise more money for the government. The rate varied, with a high rate on luxury goods; but essentials like food and children's clothing were exempt. The tax was added to the price of goods, and was, therefore, paid by the consumer. It ended in 1973.
VALUE ADDED TAX →

Q

Quadruple Alliance, 1815, between Britain, Austria, Prussia and Russia, who agreed to maintain the boundaries fixed by the *Treaty of Vienna, 1815*, for twenty years. They also agreed to meet 'at fixed intervals' to discuss measures 'for the maintenance of the peace of Europe', which led to the formation of the Congress system.
← TREATY OF VIENNA: CONGRESS SYSTEM →

Quadruple Alliance, 1834, between Britain, France, Spain and Portugal, by which the two major powers promised to help Spain and Portugal to expel their pretenders to the throne. This was done, but Palmerston was disappointed in his hope that Spain and Portugal would then become constitutional monarchies. He had hoped to create a bloc in the west to balance the despotic rulers in Russia, Prussia and Austria.

Quakers, or Society of Friends, a small sect of Christians who have been responsible for many reforms. The society was founded by George Fox (1624–91). Its members are opposed to war and to ceremony in religion. They have no paid ministers. They were persecuted after the Restoration in 1660, but were allowed to worship in their own way after the Toleration Act, 1689. But they were still banned from holding many public offices, and as a consequence many of them went into business where they prospered through their industry and their fair dealings with their customers. At the beginning of the nineteenth century, many of them still kept alive the customs of a vanished age, addressing each other as 'thee' and 'thou', and wearing plain, unadorned clothes. The men wore their hats indoors. But some members were in advance of their times by campaigning for prison reform and the abolition of slavery. The Quakers have taken a prominent part in relief work in wars and disasters, like the Irish Famine, 1845–9. There have been many notable Quaker reformers, like *Elizabeth Fry*, *William Tuke*, and *Sir Thomas Buxton*, and progressive employers, like Joseph Rowntree and Joseph Fry, the chocolate manufacturers. There were never more than about 50,000 Quakers in Britain and there are now 22,000. The name, Quaker, was first used in 1650 when George Fox advised men to 'quake and tremble at the word of the Lord'.

Queen Elizabeth. The world's largest liner of 82,998 tons, which made its maiden voyage secretly to New York in 1940 during the Second World War. During the war, it was used as a troopship, and with the *Queen Mary*, transported over one and a half million Servicemen. It was sold in 1968 for use as a floating hotel in the United States. Later, it was resold to a Hong Kong shipping magnate, who was going to convert it into a floating university, but it was destroyed by fire in 1972. The Queen Elizabeth II, of 65,863 tons, was launched as a luxury cruise liner in 1969. (See next entry.)

Queen Mary. A luxury liner of 81,237 tons, which went into service on the Atlantic route in 1936. Two years later, it set up a record by crossing the Atlantic at a speed of over 31 knots, which remained unbroken for fourteen years. In 1967, it was sold to the city of Long Beach, California, for use as a floating hotel and convention centre. (See previous entry.)

R

R 34. A British airship which was the first to cross the Atlantic in 1919. It took 108 hours.

← COUNT VON ZEPPELIN: R 101 →

R 101. A British airship which crashed into a hill and burst into flames on an experimental flight to India in October 1930, killing 46 of the 54 people on board. The building of airships was then abandoned in Britain, though if the airship had been filled with helium instead of inflammable hydrogen, the fire would probably not have occurred. (See previous entry.)

Race Relations Act, 1965, banned discrimination against any national or racial group in hotels and other public places and set up a Race Relations Board to investigate complaints. It also provided for people to be fined or imprisoned for inciting racial hatred by written or spoken words. It was designed mainly to protect blacks. (See next entry.)

Race Relations Act, 1968, made racial discrimination in housing, employment and insurance or credit facilities illegal. It established a new Community Relations Commission to try to help people of different races and cultures to live and work together. Although the Act has had some effect, there is still some 'hidden' discrimination against blacks in many firms and in other institutions. (See previous entry.)

Radar, short for radio detection and ranging. A device developed by *Sir Robert Watson-Watt*, which sends out a radio signal which is reflected back from any solid object as a blip on the screen of a cathode ray tube. It was used during the Second World War to track down German submarines and planes, and is now used extensively by aircraft and ships to avoid collisions.

Radicals, campaigners for reforms which are thought to be revolutionary at the time, but which are often accepted later as just and necessary. Throughout the first half of the nineteenth century radicals concentrated mainly on *parliamentary reform* in the hope that the reformed parliament would then introduce other necessary social and economic changes. The *Corresponding Societies* formed towards the end of the eighteenth century were succeeded by *Hampden clubs*, and the cause of parliamentary reform was later taken up by individual reformers like *William Cobbett* and *Henry Hunt*. When the *First Reform Act* failed to give the vote to the working classes, many radicals turned to *Chartism*, but this campaign collapsed in 1848.

The radical tradition then became represented by the *Manchester school* of *Richard Cobden* and *John Bright* and later in the century in the 'unauthorized' programme put forward by *Joseph Chamberlain*. He was succeeded by *Lloyd George*, whose '*People's Budget*' of 1909 proposed sweeping changes in the economic structure of society. After the Second World War, *Aneurin Bevan* represented the radical tradition with his demands for thorough-going socialist reforms. In recent years radicals outside parliament have tended to concentrate on social and racial issues, civil liberties, disarmament, and the plight of the Third World and they have increasingly used *direct action* to achieve their aims.

Radio and television. Radio broadcasting was started in November 1922, by the British Broadcasting Company. The first receivers were crystal sets with earphones, but radio sets with valves were on sale in the following year at prices of £10 to £50. By the time the company was taken over by a public authority—the British Broadcasting Corporation—on 1 January 1927, there were 2m. licence holders. Television broadcasts for the London area using *John L. Baird*'s system were started by the B.B.C. in 1929 from a transmitter on the roof of Selfridge's in Oxford Street, London. The world's first high-definition (405-line) regular TV service was started by the B.B.C. in November 1936, from Alexandra Palace in north London. Television broadcasts were stopped during the Second World War, but resumed again shortly afterwards and gradually extended to all parts of the country. The Independent Television Authority (I.T.A.) was set up in 1954 to supervise television broadcasts by commercial companies, which started in the following year. In 1949, there were about 150,000 television licences and in 1968, over 15m. There are local B.B.C. radio stations, and local commercial stations are being set up. Radio and television have become the main means of *mass communication* in place of the *popular press.*

Ragged schools provided education for homeless or destitute children. They were started by a crippled shoemaker, John Pounds (1766–1839) in Portsmouth in the 1820s. A Ragged School Union was founded by *Lord Shaftesbury* in 1844. By 1860, there were over 350 ragged schools with 43,000 pupils. Their importance declined after the Education Act, 1870.
← SUNDAY SCHOOLS

Raikes, Robert (1735–1811), newspaper owner and Sunday school organizer, born in Gloucester. With the Rev. Thomas Stock, he opened three *Sunday schools* for ninety children in Gloucester in 1780 to 'check the deplorable profanation of the Sabbath' by children playing in the streets. He then carried on a ceaseless campaign for more Sunday schools in his 'Gloucester Journal', which was then the most important newspaper in the West of England. As a result many other schools were started, where both adults and children could learn to read by studying the Bible. They were of great educational importance as they provided the first national opportunity for people to learn to read.

RAILWAYS. From about the middle of the nineteenth century to the First World War the railways were the dominant form of inland transport. They had an enormous impact on the rest of the economy and on society as a whole. They stimulated the demand for coal and iron; provided direct employment for thousands of navvies and for the men to run railways in all parts of the country; and indirect employment for thousands of men in the mechanical engineering and transport industries. The railways had other important effects in *communications*, particularly in the development of the *electric telegraph* and the *penny post* and in the introduction of a standard *time* throughout the country. They helped to bring remote regions into touch with the rest of the country; stimulated the growth of agriculture by making it possible for farmers to send their products to distant towns; and provided valuable exports of locomotives and other items. They made it cheaper for people to travel and allowed vast quantities of goods to be transported at high speeds. The railways were an essential part of the *industrial revolution*.

The first successful steam locomotive was built by *Richard Trevithick* in 1804. *George Stephenson* started making locomotives in 1814 and built the Stockton–Darlington line, which was opened in 1825. But the railway era really started with the opening of the Liverpool–Manchester line in 1830, which had been preceded by the *Rainhill trials* in the previous year. In 1835 *Isambard Kingdom Brunel* started to construct the broad gauge Great Western Railway; in the railway mania of the 1840s thousands of miles of other lines were built by contractors like *Thomas Brassey* and the 'Railway King' *George Hudson*. Attempts were made to increase passenger traffic by the *Railways Act, 1844*; the introduction of *excursion trains* which developed greatly during the *Great Exhibition, 1851*; and cheap *workmen's fares* particularly after 1883. Comfort was increased, too. The early trains had only open carriages for third-class passengers, but in 1875 the Midland Railway Company abolished the second class on its lines and turned over the closed carriages with their upholstered seats to third-class passengers without increasing their fares. Other companies soon followed this lead. The Midland also introduced luxury Pullman cars imported from the United States in 1874 which had a heating system, comfortable armchair seats and a lavatory. Improvements in locomotives and competition between railway companies, particularly on the route to Scotland, speeded up the trains. By 1845 trains were travelling from London to Exeter at an average speed of 45 m.p.h., and by the end of the century main line expresses were keeping up an average speed of 60 m.p.h. or more. Higher speeds were one of the causes of an increase in accidents, which were particularly frequent in the 1870s, and these were not reduced until companies started to introduce continuous braking systems, which operated on each wheel of the train, and the 'block' telegraph system, which allowed signalmen to keep trains at a safe distance from each other. Both were made compulsory by law in 1889.

During the First World War the railways came under government control. Owing to the war effort, repairs to rolling stock were neglected and old locomotives were not replaced. Much equipment was also shipped to the armies in France. As a result the railways were in a sorry state at the end of the war. In an attempt to restore some of their former vigour and prosperity, the *Railways Act, 1921*, amalgamated over 120 companies into four large concerns. But by then competition from *road* transport had increased so much that the railways never regained their former prosperity. The Southern railway started to introduce *electric trains* in the 1930s and there was a growth of commuter services as more people started to live in the country far away from their jobs in towns. *Underground railways*, which had first been opened in London in 1863 also expanded, but the general trend was downwards, with branch lines closing or becoming unprofitable and more and more goods traffic being taken over by road transport. The railways were nationalized by the *Transport Act, 1947*, and shortly afterwards the government gave them £1,200m. to modernize. More electric and *diesel* trains were introduced, but money continued to be lost. Following the *Beeching report* of 1963 many railway stations and lines were closed. The length of lines increased from 69 miles in 1830 to 8,054 in 1854, to 15,500 in 1870 and to over 18,000 miles in 1900. The length was reduced from 18,400 miles in 1960 to 11,800 in 1970, mainly because of losses caused by competition from road transport.

Railways Act, 1844, made it compulsory for railway companies to run at least one train every day on their lines at a fare of 1*d.* a mile, so that more people could afford to travel. They were known as 'parliamentary trains'. Companies often evaded the purpose of the Act by running the train during the night, with just a single carriage. They had to run at a minimum speed of 12 m.p.h., including stops.
← EXCURSION TRAINS: WORKMEN'S FARES →

Railways Act, 1921, amalgamated over 120 railway companies into four main companies—the London, Midland and Scottish; the Southern; the London and North-Eastern; and the Great Western railways—in an attempt to make them more profitable and better able to compete with road transport.
TRANSPORT ACT, 1947 →

Rainhill trials, 1829, were held to publicize the Liverpool–Manchester railway which was opened in the following year. The directors offered a prize of £500 for the fastest run by a locomotive along part of the track. It was won by *George Stephenson's* 'Rocket' at a speed of 29 m.p.h. Just before the trials, the locomotive had been fitted with a high-pressure steam jet, invented by Sir Goldsworthy Gurney (1793–1845), which more than doubled the speed of the 'Rocket'.

Read, Walter (1851–1902), American army surgeon, who helped to wipe out yellow fever by showing that it was transmitted by mosquitoes.
← SIR RONALD ROSS

READING increased enormously in the nineteenth century as the number of literate people in the population rose as a result of the work of *Sunday schools, voluntary schools* and *mechanics' institutes.* It increased yet again after the *Education Act* of 1870. The growth of the *public library* service provided more serious reading matter for ordinary people, while the repeal of the *Taxes on Knowledge* made it possible for the *popular press* to develop. The growth of *secondary* and *further education* in the present century has helped to stimulate the production of books for the education market, and the development of *paperbacks* from 1936 has made it possible for more people to buy books of their own. The number of book titles issued annually rose from 600 in 1800 to 6,000 in 1900 and to over 32,000 in 1971, of which 9,000 were reprints or new editions. Although *radio and television* have introduced new methods of *mass communications*, reading remains one of the most important means.

'Red Letter' election see **Zinoviev letter**

Redistribution of Seats Act, 1885, redistributed parliamentary seats more evenly throughout the country. The boundaries of constituencies were altered so that each one had the same number of inhabitants, as far as possible. Boroughs with fewer than 15,000 residents lost their M.P. Similar Acts have been passed later to keep up with shifts in population.
← REPRESENTATION OF THE PEOPLE ACT, 1884: REPRESENTATION OF THE PEOPLE ACT, 1918 →

Redmond, John (1856–1918), Irish politician who became leader of the Irish Nationalist party in 1900. He was the nominal leader of the

Irish Volunteers, but it was controlled by more extreme elements, including members of *Sinn Fein* which had become the dominant nationalist party in Ireland by the First World War.
← CHARLES STEWART PARNELL

Redundancy Payments Act, 1965, under which employees who have worked for a firm for more than a certain period must be given a lump-sum payment, which varies according to their length of service and wages, if they are made redundant.

Reformatories, were set up by charitable organizations from the end of the eighteenth century to help to reform young criminals. From 1854, courts were allowed to send juvenile delinquents to reformatories after a short prison sentence, mainly as a result of the campaign conducted by *Mary Carpenter*. Previously children and youths were transported, or served their sentence in an adult prison. Reformatories were replaced by approved schools in 1933.
BORSTALS →

Refrigeration. The first cargo of frozen meat arrived in Britain from Australia in 1880 in the steamship Strathleven of 2,436 tons—the first ship with a refrigerated hold. Large quantities of frozen beef, lamb and mutton soon started to arrive from Australia and New Zealand. It sold for about half the price of home-produced meat. Towards the end of the century chilled meat started to be imported from the Argentine. This cheap *food* allowed working-class people to have a more varied diet.

Domestic refrigerators started to appear in a few wealthier homes between the two world wars in place of the old ice-box, but it was not until after the Second World War that they became common. In 1970, two-thirds of all homes had a refrigerator.
← FOOD CANNING: FROZEN FOODS →

Registration of Births, Marriages and Deaths, including the cause of death, was made compulsory under an Act of 1836 and started in the following year. The information has contributed greatly to accurate knowledge of changes in the incidence of disease and has provided much other information about changes in population. It also made it somewhat less easy for factory owners to evade the regulations in the Factory Acts concerning the employment of young children.
← CENSUS

RELIGION had an equivalent impact on men's minds in the nineteenth century to that of *science* in the present century. The revival of religion as a great personal force in men's lives was brought about during the eighteenth century with the founding of *Methodism* by *John Wesley*. Towards the end of the century similar groups appeared in the *Church of England*, with the growth of the *Evangelicals* and the formation of the *Clapham sect*, who were dedicated to good works and pious habits. Their influence was very great in the movement for the abolition of *slavery*, the revival of *missionary* activity, the *Sunday observance* movement and the *temperance societies* in the nineteenth century. The *Quakers* took a far more individual, and perhaps more useful, line in social reform.

Apart from Scotland, the Church of England was the *established church* throughout the United Kingdom; it tried to get back into touch with the mass of people by starting *Sunday schools* and *voluntary schools*, which were also formed by many of the *nonconformist* churches. There was still some discrimination against both nonconformist and Catholics. The *Test and Corporation Acts*, which had excluded nonconformists from public office were still on the statute book even though they had not been used for many years, but they were finally repealed in 1828. The prejudice against Catholics, however, was much greater. The start of *Catholic emancipation* came with the passing of the *Roman Catholic Relief Act*, *1829*, though the *Oxford movement* of the 1830s and 1840s, led by *Henry Newman*, showed that anti-Catholic feelings still persisted.

Although religion played such a dominant part in the nineteenth century, it did not have an equal hold on all sections of the community, as the *religious census* of 1851 showed. Many of the poor never went near a church, except to get charity. The Church of England lost some of its authority with the *disestablishment* in Ireland in 1869. (It was disestablished in Wales in 1914.) But a much more serious blow to the whole basis of nineteenth-century religious belief came with the publication of *Charles Darwin*'s 'Origin of Species' in 1859. A new attempt to bring religion to the people was made by *William Booth* who founded the *Salvation Army* in 1878. But from about that time there was a gradual decline in religious belief, which has continued at an accelerating rate ever since. (The *abdication crisis* of 1936, however, showed that Church doctrine could still have an enormous impact on public life.) In an attempt to increase the strength of the Christian churches the *ecumenical movement* has brought about a number of mergers in modern times.

Religious census, 1851, the only official census of church-going ever made for the government. It was compiled by Horace Mann, who estimated that over $5\frac{1}{4}$m. people out of a total population of nearly 18m. people in England and Wales at that time deliberately stayed away from church or chapel on Sunday. The numbers who attended services on one Sunday in March 1851, were Church of England, 5,292,551; Nonconformist, 4,536,264; and Roman Catholic, 383,630.

Rennie, John, civil engineer, born at Phantassie, Scotland. In 1784 he was employed by *Boulton and Watt* to build the machinery for the Albion Flour Mills at Blackfriars Bridge, London, the first industrial plant to use a steam engine to drive machinery. It was burnt down a few years later. He also built many canals and bridges, including Southwark bridge and the old Waterloo bridge (now demolished) in London, and dockyards and harbours, including the breakwater at Plymouth.

Rent Act, 1957, introduced by the Conservatives, put up some rents by abolishing rent control on a number of the houses and flats owned by private landlords. There were then about 5m. houses with controlled rents and nearly 1m. dwellings with a rent of 5*s*. or less a week. Rent control was introduced in 1915 during the First World War as a temporary measure. (See next entry.)

Rent Act, 1965. Rent control was reintroduced by the Labour government over most privately-owned unfurnished accommodation.
← RENT ACT, 1957: HOUSING FINANCE ACT, 1972 →

Repeal of the Corn Law, 1846, abolished duties on foreign, imported wheat, apart from a small registration fee of 1*s*. a quarter, which was not abolished until 1869. It was put through by Peel, partly as a result of the *Irish famine, 1845–9*, the poor English harvest, which made imports of wheat essential; and the campaign by the Anti-Corn-Law League. Repeal of the *Corn Law, 1815*, was a victory for the new manufacturing classes, who wanted *free trade* and cheap food so that they could pay low wages to their workers. The Act split the Conservative party, with Disraeli leading the *protectionist* lobby of landowners in the House of Commons. The full effects were not felt until the 1870s, when the building of railways in the Mid West allowed huge quantities of cheap American wheat to be taken to Atlantic ports for shipment to Europe. The importing of cheap wheat was one of the main causes of the *agricultural depression*, which started in the 1870s.
← ANTI-CORN-LAW LEAGUE

Report on Sanitary Conditions, 1842, exposed the lack of adequate drainage and sewerage, water supplies and refuse collections in all parts of the country and stated that 'the annual loss of life from filth and bad ventilation is greater than the loss from death or wounds in any [modern] wars'. The report, whose full title was 'An Enquiry into the Sanitary Conditions of the Labouring Population of Great Britain', was written by *Edwin Chadwick*, secretary to the Poor Law Commissioners. As a result of the report and a new *epidemic* of cholera, the *Public Health Act, 1848*, was passed, and a start was made on improving the insanitary, unhygienic Victorian towns.

Representation of the People Act, 1867, gave the vote to working men in towns by enfranchising all male householders and lodgers who paid £10 a year rent in the boroughs, and to men who paid £12 a year rates in the counties. The number of voters increased by about 2m. The Act, which had been originally proposed by John Bright and Gladstone, was passed by Disraeli after he came to power 'to dish the Whigs'.
← FIRST REFORM ACT: BALLOT ACT, 1872 →

Representation of the People Act, 1884, gave the vote to farm workers by enfranchising all male householders and lodgers who paid £10 a year rent in the counties. It was supported by Joseph Chamberlain and passed by Gladstone.
← BALLOT ACT, 1872: REDISTRIBUTION OF SEATS ACT, 1885 →

Representation of the People Act, 1918, gave the vote to all men over twenty-one and to women over thirty if they were ratepayers or wives of ratepayers. (See next entry.)

Representation of the People (Equal Franchise) Act, 1928, gave the vote to all women over twenty-one. (See next entry.)

Representation of the People Act, 1948, abolished the right of some people to have two votes—one in the constituency where they lived and another in their place of business or in the university where they had been educated. (See next entry.)

Representation of the People Act, 1969, reduced the minimum age for voting from twenty-one to eighteen. Young people voted in a general election for the first time in June 1970, when the Conservatives were returned to power.

Retirement pensions see **Old age pensions**

Reuters, a leading news agency established by a German, Baron Julius Reuter, in London in 1851. It used the *electric telegraph* to send news from most parts of the continent to London. It still provides a world-wide news service and is now run jointly by British, Australian and New Zealand newspaper proprieters as a non-profit making concern.

Rhodes, Cecil John (1853–1902), multi-millionaire who believed that the English-speaking peoples had a divine right to rule, and who dreamed of a vast British empire stretching from Cape Town to Cairo. He was born in Bishop's Stortford and went out to join a brother in Natal, South Africa, for health reasons in 1870. As a young man, he made a fortune in the Kimberley diamond mines, founding the De Beers Mining Company in 1880. He also formed the Consolidated Goldfields Company in Johannesburg in 1887. He used his vast income from gold and diamonds to help build up an empire in southern Africa. His British South Africa Company, which was given a Royal charter in 1889, established itself in Salisbury, Rhodesia, in the following year and then began taking over the rest of the country which is named after him. In 1890, Rhodes had become prime minister of Cape Colony, South Africa, but he was discredited by the *Jameson raid, 1895*, and forced to resign in the following year. He left part of his £6m. fortune to provide Rhodes scholarships at Oxford for men from the colonies and the United States. (See next entry.)

Rhodesia, named after *Cecil Rhodes,* was founded when a small column of 200 men and 500 policemen from his British South Africa Company marched north and established a settlement in Salisbury in 1890. The company took over the rest of the country, including territories north of the Zambezi river, which became the British protectorate of Northern Rhodesia in 1911. The company continued to be responsible for Southern Rhodesia, however, until 1923, when it became a British colony with limited powers of self-government. In 1953, both territories were united with a neighbouring British protectorate to form the Federation of Rhodesia and Nyasaland, but this broke up in 1963. In the following year, the two black territories were given full independence: Northern Rhodesia became Zambia, while Nyasaland became Malawi. Southern Rhodesia (now Rhodesia), where a small white minority rules the blacks, was refused full independence, but in 1965, Ian Smith, the Rhodesian prime minister, made a unilateral declaration of independence (U.D.I.) of British rule. Neither *sanctions* nor talks had by 1972 brought about a settlement between Britain and Rhodesia, which remains an illegal regime in British eyes. (See previous entry).

Road Board, the first central authority for roads since Roman times. It was set up in 1910 to build new roads for the increasing amount of motor traffic. The roads were to be paid for from new taxes on cars and petrol, which were put into a Road Improvement Fund (later the Road Fund). But much of the money was used by other government departments. Of the £25m. collected between 1910 and 1920 less than £7m. went on roads. The Board was absorbed by the Ministry of Transport in 1919.
MINISTRY OF TRANSPORT →

Road safety. In 1969, 7,620 people were killed and over 350,000 were injured in road accidents. Because of improvements in the mechanical efficiency of vehicles, greater propaganda about road safety, and better medical services, the number of people killed in road accidents has not increased greatly in the last thirty-five years, in spite of a massive increase in traffic. In 1934, when there were about 1,300,000 cars against over 11m. in 1969, there were 7,353 fatal road accidents.
← BREATHALYZERS

Road Traffic Act, 1930, abolished the general speed limit of 20 m.p.h. which had long been ignored by most motorists, and also started the first police road patrols. Because of an increase in road accidents, a 30 m.p.h. speed limit in towns was introduced in 1934.
← MOTOR-CAR ACT, 1903

ROADS. In the eighteenth century many roads (the only means of communication apart from rivers, *canals* and the sea) were in a grossly neglected state, with ruts and holes four feet or more deep and a surface of loose stones of many different sizes. With the increased needs for better means of transport and communication in the early years of the *industrial revolution*, many new *turnpike roads* were built by *John Metcalf*, *Thomas Telford* and *John McAdam.* Faster and more reliable road services were started by mail coaches in 1784, and in 1802 *Richard Trevithick* invented a completely new form of road transport —the *steam carriage.* Although some steam-carriage services were opened in London and elsewhere in the 1830s, most were discontinued because of competition from *railways*, which dominated inland transport from about the middle of the nineteenth century to the First World War. As a consequence most of the main roads fell into disrepair again, though from about the middle of the century roads and streets in many cities were remade and resurfaced—often with wooden blocks— as much to improve *public health*, however, as transport.

County and county borough councils became responsible for building roads in 1888, in place of the old turnpike trusts, but not a great deal was done until the development of the motor car towards the end of the nineteenth century made it necessary to provide much better roads. The first internal combustion engines using petrol as fuel and the first motor vehicles were made by two Germans, *Gottlieb Daimler* and *Karl Benz. John Boyd Dunlop*'s pneumatic tyre, which was patented in 1888, was first used on *bicycles*, but was soon manufactured for motor cars, too. Early motor traffic was hampered not only by the poor state of roads, but also by the *speed limit* of 4 m.p.h., which had originally been introduced by the *Locomotive Act, 1865*, to control steam engines and carriages. The speed limit was raised to 12 m.p.h. by the *Locomotives on Highways Act, 1896*, and to 20 m.p.h. by the *Motor Car Act, 1903*. An attempt to provide better roads by the new *Road Board* of 1910 was not very successful and in 1919 it was absorbed by the *Ministry of Transport.* Before the First World War there was a great variety of traffic on the roads in towns, with motor cars and lorries, steam-powered vehicles, electric *trams*, horse-drawn and motor buses, and horse-drawn carts and carriages.

Most of the early motor cars and vehicles on British roads were of German or French manufacture, but *Frederick Lanchester* made the first successful English car in 1895. *Rolls-Royce* was founded in 1906. These cars were all expensive so that motoring remained a rich man's luxury; but in 1908 *Henry Ford* started to make cheap, mass produced cars in the United States. Cheap cars were made by the same methods in Britain after the First World War by *Viscount Nuffield* and *Lord Austin.*

Between the two world wars, the road accident rate was very high and in an attempt to increase *road safety*, *zebra crossings* and a 30 m.p.h. speed limit in towns were introduced in 1934. Britain, however, lagged behind many other European countries in the building of *motorways*, so that when the *mass motoring* age started in Britain in the 1950s there was no adequate road network for the vastly increased number of cars.

The motor car has given ordinary people opportunities for travel that they have never had before and has enabled many people to move away from overcrowded *towns* and live in new dormitory suburbs or the country. It has also provided employment for thousands of people. But as the Buchanan report of 1963 showed the adverse effects have also been considerable in *pollution*, particularly by Diesel engines, in a general increase in noise levels, and in the economic costs and psychological effects of traffic jams.

Rob Roy, the first steamship in the world to start a regular sea-going service, was built at Dumbarton, Scotland, in 1818. From 1819 to 1821 it was used on the Greenock–Belfast route and in 1821 it was transferred to the Dover–Calais route. It usually took two and a half hours to make the crossing of the English Channel. It was bought by the French government for their cross-Channel service in 1823.
← COMET: AARON MANBY →

Robbins Report, 1963, recommended that six new universities should be created immediately, existing universities should be expanded, and that some other higher education institutions should be made into universities. By 1980 it was recommended that there should be sixty universities and that 560,000 students should be receiving higher education. Following the report there was a great expansion of *further education* and by 1972 there were forty-five universities.

Roberts, Richard (1789–1864), Manchester engineer, who made a fully automatic spinning mule, with over 2,000 spindles, in 1825, which could be supervised by one skilled worker. He also invented a number of machine tools, including a punching machine for making rivet holes, and was one of the first engineers to use standard gauges to ensure accurate measurement. He was a pupil of *Henry Maudslay.*
← SAMUEL CROMPTON

Rochdale pioneers set up a shop in Rochdale, Lancs., in 1844, from which the modern *co-operative movement* has arisen.

Rolls, Charles Stewart (1877–1910), engineer, born in London, son of Lord Llangattock. He was the fourth person in Britain to own a car. After setting up a business to sell Continental cars, he met *Henry Royce* in 1904, and two years later they formed *Rolls-Royce Ltd.* Rolls was also a pioneer airman. He was one of the first men to fly across the English Channel, making a return flight in June, 1910, but he was killed the following month at a flying tournament in Bournemouth, becoming the first Englishman to die in an air crash. (See next entry.)

Rolls-Royce Ltd. A firm founded in 1906 by *Charles Stewart Rolls* and *Henry Royce* to make high-grade motor cars, which soon became a world-wide symbol of luxury and quality. From 1906 to 1925 the firm concentrated on producing just one kind of car—the 40 to 50 horse-power 'Silver Ghost'. During the First World War, Rolls-Royce started to make aero engines. Their engines are now used in many British and foreign military planes and in more passenger planes than those of any other manufacturer. When this side of the business got into financial difficulties in 1971, a government-owned company was formed to run it, because the engines were of such importance to so many Western air forces and airlines. The motor-car firm was put up for sale in 1973.

Roman Catholic Relief Act, 1829, allowed Catholics to become M.P.s and to hold all government posts, except for a few of the highest, such as Lord Chancellor. It was passed by the Duke of Wellington and Peel, who feared civil war in Ireland if *Daniel O'Connell* was not allowed to take his seat which he had won in the County Clare election of 1828. The Act, which was opposed by many right-wing Tories, divided the party, and the Whigs came into power in 1830 after nearly fifty years of Tory rule. To diminish the power of Catholics in Ireland, an Act was passed shortly after the Relief Act, which took away the vote from 40*s*. freeholders in Ireland—most of whom were Catholic—and raised the property qualification to £10 a year. Only eight Irish Catholic M.P.s were returned at the next general election.

Romilly, Sir Samuel (1757–1818), reformer, born in London. He was an M.P. from 1806 to 1812 and again in 1818. In 1808 he succeeded in persuading parliament to abolish the *death penalty* for picking pockets. He also supported the anti-slavery movement. Heartbroken by the death of his wife in 1818, he committed suicide four days later.

Röntgen, Wilhelm Konrad von (1845–1923), German scientist who discovered X-rays in 1895. While experimenting with a vacuum tube, he found that the shadow of the bones in his hand could be seen on a near-by screen. His discovery has many applications in medicine, science and industry.
MARIE AND PIERRE CURIE →

Roosevelt, Franklin Delano (1882–1945), President of the United States from 1933 to 1945. Before the Americans entered the Second World War, he provided Britain with war supplies under the *Lend-Lease* law of March 1941, and agreed on post-war aims with Churchill in the *Atlantic Charter* of August 1941. He was a great supporter of the idea of the *United Nations Organization*, which was founded shortly after his death.

Rosebery, Earl of (1847–1919), Liberal, who was more successful in winning the Derby than he was in politics. He was Foreign Secretary under Gladstone in 1886 and from 1892 to 1894, when he succeeded Gladstone as prime minister. His horses won the Derby in 1894 and 1895. He resigned in 1895 and moved increasingly to the right, supporting the second Boer War and opposing the *People's Budget* of 1909. He succeeded to his title in 1868.

← WILLIAM EWART GLADSTONE: HENRY CAMPBELL-BANNERMAN →

Ross, Sir Ronald (1857–1932), doctor, educated at St Bartholomew's Hospital, London. He helped to wipe out malaria—the most widespread and dangerous of all tropical diseases—by showing that it was transmitted to human beings by the bites of a particular kind of mosquito. While working in India in 1897 he identified the jet-black parasites, which cause the disease, in the stomach of a mosquito. The disease has gradually been controlled by destroying the breeding grounds of the insect; it was eliminated in Britain before his discovery by the draining of marshy land. Ross, who was also a distinguished poet, painter, and musician, was knighted in 1911.

WALTER REED →

Rothermere, Viscount (1868–1940), younger brother of *Viscount Northcliffe.* He helped to found the *Daily Mail* in 1896 and in 1914 started his own group of newspapers. He was made a viscount in 1919.

← VISCOUNT NORTHCLIFFE: LORD BEAVERBROOK →

'Rotten boroughs'. Some like Old Sarum, with its seven voters, were almost uninhabited, and others, like Dunwich, were half under water. But because they had once been sizeable little towns they still sent two M.P.s to Parliament. Most of them lost one or both of their M.P.s by the *First Reform Act, 1832.*

Royal Commission on the Housing of the Working Classes, 1885, exposed the shocking state of working-class houses in London and other great cities where the old houses were 'rotten from age and neglect' and the new ones were 'rotten from the first'. Many working-class people still lived in damp, unhealthy houses, without adequate *sanitation* or *water supplies.* The commission's main recommendations were that there should be more sanitary inspectors; that empty building sites should be charged rates; that the government should lend money cheaply to local authorities to build houses for the working classes; and that the prisons in London should be pulled down, and the sites used for building homes. Although there were so many prominent people on the Commission—including the Prince of Wales (later King Edward VII),

Cardinal Manning, and the *Marquis of Salisbury*—very little was done, because the money would have had to come out of the local rates.
← SELECT COMMITTEE ON THE HEALTH OF TOWNS

Royal Navy gave Britain mastery of the seas from 1815, which provided security, protection of the Empire, and a means of threatening smaller powers by a bombardment or by sending a gunboat as a warning. Steamships were introduced after the Napoleonic wars, but the last great battle fought under sail was at Navarino Bay, 1827, during the *Greek War of Independence.* Until 1853, when it was made possible to give naval ratings a 10-year engagement, the Royal Navy relied on volunteers in times of peace and on the *press gang* in times of war for its recruits. A uniform for ratings was introduced in 1857. The first iron-clad, the 'Warrior' was launched in 1861 : it had both an iron hull and armoured plating to protect the guns. In the 1880s, Britain adopted the 'two powers' standard, under which it tried to keep its navy at a strength which was equivalent to that of any other two major powers combined. This led to a naval arms race, which was increased after the launching of the British 'Dreadnought' in 1906. This 17,950-ton battleship had ten 12-inch guns and 16 anti-torpedo boat guns, and steam turbines which gave it a speed of 21 knots. It could outgun and outpace any other warship afloat. Other navies copied this example, building super dreadnoughts with nine 16-inch guns and speeds of 25 knots. By 1914, Britain was still in the lead with 19 Dreadnoughts against Germany's 13. Other powers had smaller numbers. The only major action in which they were ever engaged was the *Battle of Jutland, 1916.* After the First World War, attempts were made to limit the naval arms race by the *Washington Conference* of 1921 to 1922 and the *London Naval Conferences* of 1930 and 1936.

During the Second World War, the Royal Navy expanded greatly from 423 warships of all classes in 1939 to 3,470 in 1945. After the war, many warships were sold or scrapped. By 1972 the number of ships in the Royal Navy was down to 1 aircraft carrier, 2 cruisers, 4 assault ships, 6 guided missile destroyers, 25 general-purpose frigates and 23 submarines (including 4 *Polaris* submarines) and other smaller vessels. (See also *First World War* and *Second World War.*)

Royal Titles Act, 1876, made Queen Victoria Empress of India. It was passed by Disraeli against some opposition in parliament and in the country. She made Disraeli the Earl of Beaconsfield a few months later.

Royce, Sir Henry (1863–1933), engineer and motor-car manufacturer, born at Alwalton, near Peterborough. After his father died, he started work as a newspaper boy at the age of ten. At the age of twenty-one he and a partner set up a firm with a capital of £70 to make electrical equipment. In 1904 he made his first 10-horsepower car, which attracted the attention of a dealer in high-grade Continental cars, *Charles Stewart Rolls.* Two years later they formed *Rolls-Royce Ltd.*

← FREDERICK LANCASTER: HENRY FORD →

Russell, Lord John (1792–1878), son of the Duke of Bedford, who became a Whig M.P. in 1813. From 1819 he supported parliamentary reform. He piloted the First Reform Act through the House of Commons in 1830–2. As Home Secretary from 1835 to 1839 he was responsible for the *Municipal Corporations Reform Act, 1835*—the first reform in local government—and also reduced the number of offences punishable by death. He was prime minister from 1846 to 1852, when some reforms were made including the *Public Health Act, 1848.* But the ministry was dominated mainly by the foreign policies of *Palmerston* who was dismissed by Russell in 1851. Russell was Foreign Secretary under Palmerston from 1859 to 1865, when he succeeded him as prime minister. But he resigned in 1866 after his government had split over the question of introducing a Second Reform Bill. He was made Earl Russell in 1861.

← VISCOUNT MELBOURNE: VISCOUNT PALMERSTON →

Rutherford, Lord (1871–1937), nuclear physicist, whose team of scientists at Cambridge split the atom in 1932. He was born in New Zealand and worked at universities in Montreal, Canada and Manchester, before he became director of the Cavendish Laboratory at Cambridge in 1919. His nuclear theory established that an atom consists of a central, positively-charged nucleus—a proton—with negatively-charged electrons revolving around it. Under certain critical conditions, the atom of the heaviest element, uranium, could be split, releasing enormous power and energy. This discovery led eventually to the manufacture of the *atom bomb* and the production of *atomic energy*, or nuclear power. He received the Nobel prize in 1908 and was made a lord in 1931.

← SIR JOSEPH THOMSON

S

Sadler, Michael Thomas (1780–1835), Tory banker, who supported factory reform. He introduced a Ten Hours' Bill in parliament in 1831, which was taken up by *Lord Shaftesbury* after Sadler had lost his seat as an M.P.

JOHN FIELDEN →

Sale of Food and Drugs Act, 1875, banned the addition of injurious ingredients to food and allowed local authorities to appoint public analysts to test samples of food in their area. (See next entry.)

← ADULTERATION OF FOOD ACT, 1872

Sale of Food and Drugs Act, 1928, banned the use of any colouring, stain or powder, which might be injurious to health, in food. (See previous entry.)

Salisbury, Marquis of (1830–1903), Conservative prime minister for nearly fourteen years in all, longer than any other politician in the nineteenth century, except for Lord Liverpool. He was a member of one of the oldest aristocratic families—the Cecils—and was born at the family seat, Hatfield House, Hertfordshire. He was educated at Eton and Christ Church, Oxford. As a young man he visited South Africa, Australia and New Zealand and on his return was elected M.P. for Stamford in 1853. He was appointed Secretary for India under Derby in 1866, but, as a life-long opponent of parliamentary reform, he resigned in the following year when the Second Reform Bill (the *Representation of the People Act, 1867*) was introduced. Disraeli made him Secretary for India again in 1874. He became Foreign Secretary in 1878 and accompanied Disraeli to the *Congress of Berlin* in that year. On Disraeli's death in 1881, he became leader of the Conservative party.

He was prime minister for seven months in 1885–6 and again from 1886 to 1892 and from 1895 to 1902. Several domestic reforms were carried out, notably the Local Government Act of 1888, which set up county councils and the London County Council, and the abolition of *school fees* for most *elementary education* in 1891. But Salisbury's main interest was in foreign affairs and he acted as his own Foreign Secretary for much of his premierships. His foreign policy is sometimes mistakenly described as one of '*splendid isolation*'. This was a term he disliked and rarely used. He believed in constant involvement in foreign affairs, and was not opposed to some treaties, like the secret Mediterranean agreements of 1887, with Italy and Austria-Hungary, which were designed to preserve the existing situation in the Mediterranean and in the Aegean and Black Seas. But he carried on the traditional British foreign policy of avoiding any major alliances which might involve Britain in an unintended war. He was even opposed to diplomatic victories which might humiliate another great power and thus lead to further conflict. The major exception was when he firmly opposed the French occupation of *Fashoda* in the Sudan in 1898, during the *scramble for Africa.* But he did little to restrain the more aggressive policy of *Joseph Chamberlain,* his Colonial Secretary from 1895, which was one of the causes of the second *Boer War, 1899–1902.*

Salisbury held the courtesy title of Lord Robert Cecil as a young man, and succeeded his father as the third Marquis of Salisbury in 1868.

← BENJAMIN DISRAELI: ARTHUR JAMES BALFOUR →

Salvation Army was formed in 1878 by *William Booth* to fight a Christian war against evil in the poorest parts of cities, and to bring help and salvation to those who were most in need of it. It used brass bands, military-style uniforms and ranks, with women officers as well as men. It took religion on to the street corners and did much social work among ex-prisoners, tramps, prostitutes and drunkards from the 1880s. In 1878 there were 91 officers (41 of whom were women). The Salvation Army now has about 3,000 full-time officers in Britain and nearly 180,000 members. There are branches in 70 countries.

Sanctions. A method of trying to force a country to stop aggression, or some other action which has been condemned by the rest of the world, by restricting exports to it or by boycotting its goods. It has had little success. Sanctions were used by member-nations of the *League of Nations* against Italy following its attack on Abyssinia in 1935, but as the essential war material of oil was excluded they had little effect. Under two resolutions of the Security Council of the *United Nations* sanctions were applied against Rhodesia after its unilateral declaration of independence (*U.D.I.*) in 1965. But there have been many evasions and up to 1972 they have had little real success.

Sand River Convention, 1852, under which Britain recognized the independence of the Boers in the Transvaal. (For the background see *South Africa.*)

Sanitation. Lack of sanitation was responsible for many
the high *death rate* in nineteenth-century towns. In th
a number of families living in the same street often h
outside privy, containing a bucket which was emptied
council workmen. An improved water closet had be
Joseph Bramah in 1778, but it was not until about the middle
century that some richer people in towns started to install them. They usually drained into cesspools as most towns still had no sewers. The main campaigner for improved sanitation was *Edwin Chadwick*; Disraeli also made it one of the main points in his political programme in the 1870s. A *General Board of Health* was set up in 1848 to supervise the provision of better sanitation throughout the whole country, but it encountered local opposition and was abolished ten years later. Some of the larger cities started building their own sewerage systems; the first part of the main system in London was completed in 1865. But there was little general improvement in many other towns until the *Public Health Act, 1875*, had been passed when Disraeli was in power. Even then, many of the sewers which were built were defective and leaked; and in many towns, working-class areas were still not connected to them. Even in 1908, Nottingham, for example, had ten thousand more privies than water closets. It is only in the present century that the provision of sanitation in houses has become general.

School fees of a few pence a week were charged in most *voluntary schools* in the nineteenth century and also in the new Board schools set up by the *Education Act, 1870*, though poorer parents could be exempted from paying them. Fees for *elementary education* were abolished in 1891, except in a few voluntary schools which charged 1*s*. or more a week. These fees, too, were abolished in 1918. Fees continued to be charged for much *secondary education* until 1944, though there were an increasing number of free places at grammar and secondary schools after 1902. All primary and secondary education in State schools is now free, and there are grants for full-time further education, based on the parents' income. Public schools and independent schools continue to charge fees, which range up to £1,000 or more a year for boarders.

School leaving age. The minimum age for ending full-time education was made 10 by law in 1880; raised to 11 in 1893; to 12 in 1889; and to 14 in 1918. Children who had reached a certain educational standard were allowed to work in factories half-time and to go to school for the rest of the day. This half-time system was abolished in

1918, when all children were obliged to remain at school full-time until they were 14. The school leaving age was raised to 15 in 1944 and to 16 in 1972.

School meals for poor children were started by charitable organizations in some industrial towns towards the end of the nineteenth century. In 1906 local authorities were allowed to provide school meals, but only about half of them were doing so by 1939. The provision of school meals increased greatly during the Second World War, when many mothers were working in war factories. The school meal service continued after the war. In 1970 over 67 per cent of school children in England and Wales and 44 per cent in Scotland were having school dinners, but the proportion fell after the price of meals was increased in April, 1971.

Local authorities were allowed to provide a third of a pint of milk for children for $\frac{1}{2}$*d.* a day, or free if the parents could not afford to pay, in 1934. In 1946 free milk was provided for all children, but it was stopped in secondary schools in 1968, and for all children, except those under seven, in 1971. School meals and milk have been one of the main factors in improving the health of children.

School Medical Service. The first school doctor was appointed in London in 1890. In 1907 all local authorities were compelled by law to have the children in their schools medically examined three times a year, and school medical services were gradually set up in most parts of the country. The health of many children was then extremely poor. Some had serious diseases, such as tuberculosis and rickets, and many more had running ears, bad teeth, poor eyesight, or were infested with lice. School doctors played a major part in improving the health of children, which was also made better through the introduction of *school meals.* With the improved medical care provided under the *National Health Service Act* some local authorities have now stopped the routine medical examination of older children in their schools.

SCIENCE developed in the seventeenth century with the discoveries of the Italian astronomer, Galileo (1564–1642) and of three British scientists: Robert Boyle (1627–91), the founder of chemistry; William Harvey (1578–1657), who discovered the circulation of the blood; and Isaac Newton (1642–1727), who established the law of gravitation. During the nineteenth century there were notable advances in many different branches of science, but it is only in the present century that it has assumed such a dominant role. Modern life is inseparable from science and its application through technology. With the growth of research, education and organizational method, discoveries have come at an increasing pace in recent years. Attempts have been made to extend the scientific method into many other fields. Business management, for example, has attempted to apply the scientific method of collecting all known observable facts; making a theory or hypothesis based on them; and then testing the truth of the hypothesis by experiment.

Scientific research is basically international, but many notable contributions to pure science have been made by British and Commonwealth scientists working in Britain. *John Dalton* established the principle of atomic weight in the nineteenth century, and in the same field *Sir Joseph Thomson* discovered the electron in 1897, while *Lord Rutherford*, a New Zealander working in Cambridge, succeeded in splitting the atom in 1932. This new source of energy was used later in the development of the *atom bomb*, and nuclear power, or *atomic energy*.

Sir Humphry Davy and his assistant *Michael Faraday* made many important discoveries in chemistry and physics in the first half of the nineteenth century, which were applied by others in the second half of the century. The theory of evolution put forward by *Charles Darwin* in his 'Origin of Species' 1859, revolutionized views about the origins of man. Research in the field of nutrition by *Lord Boyd-Orr* between the two world wars had important influences on the foods that people eat. British doctors and researchers have also been responsible for many advances in *medicine*.

During the nineteenth century Britain led the world in the application of science in the *industrial revolution*, particularly in the development of the *steam engine*, *railways*, the *textile industry*, *mechanical engineering* and in the *iron and steel* industry. In modern times it has made big contributions to the development of *jet engines*, *atomic energy*, and the *hovercraft*.

Scot and lot voters, ratepayers in boroughs who were allowed to vote in parliamentary elections. The franchise was abolished by the *First Reform Act, 1832*, though existing voters were allowed to vote for the rest of their lives.

Scramble for Africa. At the beginning of the nineteenth century, British possessions in Africa were limited to trading settlements, forts on the coasts and Freetown, Sierra Leone, which was used to provide a home for former slaves. Nigeria was developed by chartered trading companies and came under British rule in 1900. The Gold Coast was taken over as a colony in 1874; the Ashanti territories to the north were added in 1901, and part of Togoland was added as a League of Nations *mandate* after the First World War. (The Gold Coast and the two other territories are now the independent country of Ghana.) On the east coast, British rule was extended to the island of Zanzibar (now part of Tanzania) in 1890, to Uganda in 1894 and to Kenya in 1895. Egypt was occupied by the British in 1882, becoming a British protectorate in 1914, and the Sudan was finally conquered in 1898 and ruled jointly by Britain and Egypt. All of these countries achieved independence in the 1950s and 1960s. In southern Africa, the British acquired the Cape of Good Hope from the Dutch in 1815, from which *South Africa* was gradually developed. The first British settlements were made in *Rhodesia* in 1890. Bechuanaland, now Botswana, became a British protectorate in 1885. Most of Africa was taken over in the last quarter of the nineteenth century by European powers, without much serious friction between them, the major exception being the *Fashoda incident, 1898*.

Second Reform Act (*Representation of the People Act, 1867*) was passed by Derby and Disraeli, and gave the vote to many urban workers.

SECOND WORLD WAR, 1939–45. Its main cause was aggression by Germany, Italy and Japan. The *League of Nations* failed to stop their aggression and so did the policy of *appeasement.* Hostility towards Communism was one of the factors preventing Britain and France from seeking an alliance with Russia, who signed a pact with Germany in August 1939. This left *Hitler* free to attack Poland, who had been given a guarantee by Britain and France in April 1939. Hitler started his *Blitzkrieg* (lightning war) against Poland on 1 September 1939, and Britain and France declared war against Germany on 3 September. Italy entered the war on Germany's side in June 1940. The Russians entered the war in June 1941, after being attacked by Germany, and the United States in December 1941, after the Japanese attack on Pearl Harbor, Hawaii, the main American naval base in the Far East. Before that, the Americans were already supplying Britain with war material under the *Lend-Lease* law of March 1941. The main events affecting Britain were:

War in Europe. During what the Americans called the 'phoney war', the British and French troops remained inactive behind the strongly-fortified *Maginot line.* In April 1940, the Germans occupied Denmark and captured Norway because its supplies of iron ore were important for German war production. On 10 May 1940, the Germans launched their Blitzkrieg against the Low Countries and France. The British and French forces were cut off and evacuated to safety from *Dunkirk.* Holland, Belgium and France had all fallen within five weeks, and Britain then stood alone until the Russians and the Americans came into the war in 1941. The *Dieppe raid* in 1942 was a failure. After the British victory in the North African campaign (see below), British forces invaded Sicily and Italy in 1943 under the command of *General Alexander.* After a fairly swift advance, they encountered stiff opposition. Following the successful landing at *Anzio* beach head they then fought their way slowly up the country. *General Eisenhower*, an American, was appointed Supreme Commander, Allied Forces in Europe, in 1944. On 6 June 1944, *D-day*, Allied forces landed in strength on the Normandy beaches in France. After fierce fighting the British and Canadians took Caen on 9 July. British troops liberated Brussels on 3 September, and took the Belgian port of Antwerp on the following day. An attempt to speed up the advance into Germany by dropping parachutists at *Arnhem,* to capture bridges over the Rhine, was unsuccessful. *General Montgomery* was the operational commander of all land forces until 1 September. In 1945, the Germans made their last counter-offensive in the Ardennes, which was defeated, and Germany surrended on 7 May 1945, after *Hitler* had committed suicide.

North African campaign. After Italy entered the war in June 1940, British military efforts were concentrated on the campaign in North Africa. The British soon defeated the Italians in the deserts of North Africa, but in February 1941, the German Afrika Korps, under Rommel, was sent there to stiffen resistance. Rommel advanced rapidly, crossing the Egyptian border and threatening the *Suez canal.* Tobruk, on the coast of Libya, was besieged, but was held by British and Australian troops. Later in the year, the *Eighth Army* was formed, and Tobruk was relieved. But Rommel counter-attacked and reached El Alamein in Egypt by July 1942. In October, the Eighth Army, now under General Montgomery, attacked at El Alamein and defeated the Germans—the first British major land victory in the war, and a great turning point in Allied fortunes. By May 1943, the Germans and Italians had surrendered in North Africa.

War in the Air. After *Dunkirk*, Hitler prepared to invade Britain, but failed to achieve the necessary mastery of the air in the *Battle of Britain*, July to September 1940. The Germans then tried to defeat Britain by air raids—*the Blitz*—but these were called off in May 1941. *Radar* played a major part in guiding night fighters against German bombers and also in guiding British bombers to their targets in later night air raids on Germany. The first 1,000-bomber British raid on Cologne took place in May 1942. It was followed by many other air raids on German cities. In 1944, Hitler launched his secret weapons, *V1*s and *V2*s against Britain, but they failed to halt his defeat.

War at Sea. In 1939, the Royal Navy cornered the pride of the German Navy, the 'pocket battleship' *Graf Spree* at the mouth of the River Plate, South America, when it sank itself. In July 1940, after the fall of France, the Royal Navy attacked the French fleet at Oran, North Africa, to prevent its coming under German control. In May 1941, the German battleship, the *Bismarck*, was sunk by British aircraft and warships in the Atlantic. During what became known as the *Battle of the Atlantic, 1940–3*, many British ships were sunk by German submarines. Britain and the Commonwealth lost over 1m. tons of shipping during the war.

The Far East. The Japanese entered the war in December 1941, by attacking Pearl Harbor, the United States naval base in Hawaii. By May 1942, they had occupied Malaya, captured Singapore, and taken Burma. The British fought back in Burma, at first with the 'Chindits' —a brigade of British and Gurkhas—under General Wingate, who penetrated deeply behind Japanese lines, and then in force with the Fourteenth Army under General Slim. Rangoon, capital of Burma, was captured in May 1945, and preparations were being made to invade Malaya, when the Japanese surrendered after the dropping of two *atom bombs* on Hiroshima and Nagasaki in August 1945. The war ended officially on 2 September 1945, VJ (Victory in Japan) day.

The Home Front. Just before the outbreak of the war, about 1m. schoolchildren were evacuated from cities which might be bombed, mainly into the countryside but some to North America. All lights had to be concealed at night by black curtains at the windows; cars had masked headlights; and trains had only faint blue lights in the compartments. Identity cards were introduced in 1939; *food rationing* and *purchase tax* in 1940; and clothes rationing in 1941. Railings were ripped up to provide materials for munitions, and few luxury goods were produced. After the day's work was done, many people did extra, unpaid work as air-raid wardens or fire-watchers during the *Blitz*, or as members of the *Home Guard. Churchill* replaced *Neville Chamberlain* as prime minister in May, 1940.

British casualities were much lower than in the First World War. A total of 373,372 British and Commonwealth Servicemen were killed; plus 624 female members of the Forces; over 30,000 merchant seamen, and over 60,000 civilians.

The estimated cost of the war to Britain was over £34,000m.

Secondary education was only provided, almost exclusively for the children of wealthy parents, at fee-paying *public schools* and *grammar schools* until the present century. After the *Education Act, 1902*, a number of brighter children were given free places at some grammar schools and the new secondary schools. The number of children receiving secondary education rose from an estimated 30,000 in 1901 to 200,000 in 1914 and to over 500,000 by 1939. Free secondary education was made available for all children by the *Education Act, 1944*.

Select Committee on the Health of Towns, 1840. A report which exposed the appalling living conditions in cities, with their back-to-back houses, lack of sanitation, and general squalor. It revealed that there were 39,000 people in Liverpool and 15,000 in Manchester living in underground cellars.
ROYAL COMMISSION ON HOUSING, 1885 →

Self service shops were introduced in Britain in 1950. The first one was opened in Detroit, U.S.A., in 1914.

Sex Disqualification (Removal) Act, 1919, allowed women to become solicitors, barristers and magistrates. As a consequence of the Act, women were also gradually admitted to other professions and, after a fight, to some top posts in the Civil Service from 1925.

Shaftesbury, Earl of (1801–1885), aristocratic reformer, who played a leading part in many of the main campaigns of the nineteenth century. He was born in London and known as Lord Ashley before he inherited his father's title in 1851. Educated at Harrow and Oxford, he became an M.P. in 1826. He campaigned for factory reform which resulted in the first effective *Factory Act* being passed in 1833. His *Mines Act* of 1842 prohibited the employment of women, girls and boys under ten underground in coal mines. He took a major part in the campaign for the *Lunacy Act, 1845*, which gave mental patients better treatment. He also played a part in the anti-slavery movement, the abolition of *agricultural gangs* of young children, and the campaign to stop the employment of *chimney sweep boys.* In 1844 he founded the Ragged School Union to provide education for destitute children, and remained chairman of it until his death. But he was no radical. He opposed the *First Reform Bill*, and, as an Evangelical Christian, was one of the main supporters of *Sunday observance.*

Sheffield outrages, 1866–7, when home-made bombs were exploded by strikers in the homes of some non-union workers. It led to the passing of the *Criminal Law Amendment Act, 1871*, by the Liberals.

Shipping companies. With the development of steam-powered *ships*, a number of companies were formed to introduce the new vessels on ocean routes. One of the first was the General Steam Navigation Company, formed in 1824, which started a steamship service to Portugal in 1826. The development of the companies was greatly stimulated when the government started giving them contracts to carry the overseas mail which had formerly been carried by naval frigates or by postal packets (sailing ships) based in Falmouth. Samuel Cunard (1787–1865), who was born in Halifax, Nova Scotia, was given the contract to carry the Atlantic mail in 1839, and the service was opened in the following year. In 1840 the Peninsular and Oriental line was given the contract for the Indian mails; in 1841 the Royal Mail Steam Packet Company was awarded the West Indian contract; and the Union line (later the Union-Castle line) was given the South African contract in 1853. These 'hidden' subsidies, which totalled £1m. a year by 1860, gave Britain a great lead in merchant shipping, which it was to hold for the rest of the century. But by the end of the century, Britain had to face an increasing challenge in passenger liners from the Germans, particularly by the Hamburg–America line, which by 1914 had over 200 vessels and was the biggest single shipping company in the world.

SHIPS. Britain led the world in merchant shipping and shipbuilding for most of the nineteenth century. It was the first country to use iron for building boats and the first to use *steam engines* to propel them. In 1787, *John Wilkinson* built the first iron barge and in 1802 *William Symington* demonstrated the first practical steamboat, the *Charlotte Dundas*, on the Forth and Clyde canal. The first iron steamboat, the *Aaron Manby*, entered service in 1822. Britain also pioneered the development of steamship services. The first regular passenger service in Europe was started by Henry Bell's *Comet* on the Clyde in 1812, and seven years later the *Rob Roy* started the first regular sea-going service on the Greenock–Belfast route. In the same year, 1819, an American steamship, the 'Savannah' of 350 tons crossed the Atlantic from Savannah, Georgia, U.S.A., to Liverpool, but it used sail for part of the journey. The first crossing by steamship unaided by sail was made by the *Sirius* in 1838, and twelve hours later it was followed into New York harbour by *I. K. Brunel*'s *Great Western*, the second steamship to make an Atlantic crossing.

Brunel went on to build two other steamships, the *Great Britain*, launched in 1843, and the *Great Eastern*, launched in 1858, both of which were far ahead of their times. Early steamships had been driven by paddle wheels; the 'Great Britain' was one of the first ships to be equipped with a more efficient screw propeller. The 'Great Eastern' was not surpassed in size for nearly forty years. The longer sea routes to China and India were still dominated by sailing ships—fast *clippers* which could reach a speed of 20 knots or more. But in 1854 *John Elder* produced a more efficient compound steam engine and ten years later *Alfred Holt* made an even more efficient engine. Ships with Holt engines could make the journey to China in sixty days instead of the clipper's ninety days or more. This spelt the end of the days of sail, though clippers continued to be used for taking emigrants out to Australia and New Zealand and for bringing back cargoes of wool to the end of the nineteenth century. It was not until the 1880s that the tonnage of British steamships exceeded that of sailing ships for the first time. Auxiliary sail, which had been carried by most steamships in case the propeller shaft broke, was also abandoned in the 1880s when more steamships started to be equipped with double screws.

The supremacy of the British merchant service owed much to the formation of new *shipping companies*, and the repeal of the main *Navigation Acts* in 1849, which forced British shipping companies to face competition from foreign companies. Partly as a result of this competition, many small shipowners neglected safety at sea. Masters and mates were often incompetent and untrained. Some ships were so badly built that they literally fell to pieces on their maiden voyage and essential repairs were badly done or neglected. Ships were grossly overloaded so that the owners could make a higher profit, and a minority of shipowners insured their vessels for more than they were worth so that even if they were lost at sea they would still gain. Attempts to improve safety at sea and conditions for crews were made by the *Mercantile Marine Act, 1850*, which introduced examinations for masters and mates of foreign-going vessels, while the *Merchant Shipping Act, 1854*, introduced improvements for crews. In 1876 the *Plimsoll mark*, or line, was introduced to show the level to which a merchant ship could be safely loaded, but it did not become effective until 1890, owing to a defect in the law.

A new and more efficient method of propulsion—the steam turbine invented by *Sir Charles Parsons*—was first used at sea in 1897, and this opened the way to the development of fast luxury liners, like the *Mauretania*, launched in 1907, and, later, the *Queen Mary* and the *Queen Elizabeth*. By 1900 the British merchant service had reached a peak with nearly 20,000 vessels with a total tonnage of 14m.—almost half the total in the world. Since then, however, Britain has gradually lost its predominant position in both shipbuilding and merchant shipping, because of increased competition from foreign countries, particularly the United States, Japan and Germany. In 1970, Britain had just under 14 per cent of the world's total tonnage.

Since the end of the Second World War, there have been enormous changes in merchant shipping. *Air travel* has replaced travel by sea bringing to an end the era of the luxury passenger liner after nearly eighty years. Cargo vessels have also changed, with the introduction of much bigger *oil tankers*, and a completely new kind of vessel—the *container ship*—in the 1950s. The first *nuclear-powered ship* for carrying cargo entered service in 1962. The *hovercraft* introduced a completely new method of sea transport which may have even bigger potentialities in the future. Changes have also been made in methods of shipbuilding, with a much bigger use of prefabrication. The latest cargo vessels now have completely straight sides, and are quick to build and easy to extend by welding in another section in dry dock. The first straightsided, prefabricated ship was launched at a shipyard in Hamburg, Germany, in 1968. (See also *Royal Navy*.)

Sidmouth, Viscount (1757–1844), incompetent Tory of the old school who, as Henry Addington, served as prime minister from 1801 to 1804, when he was made a viscount. He was Home Secretary from 1812 to 1822, and sent a letter of congratulation to the Manchester magistrates for their repressive actions in the *Peterloo* massacre of 1819. He was largely responsible for introducing the *Six Acts, 1819*, which greatly restricted civil liberties.

LORD LIVERPOOL →

Siemens, Sir William (1823–83), who patented in 1866 a new 'open hearth' process of making steel by passing hot air and gases over a molten mixture of pig (impure) iron and scrap steel in the bottom of the furnace. It was slower than the *Bessemer* process, but could be more easily controlled. The method was widely adopted in Britain and was being used to make over three-fifths of the total steel output by 1900. Siemens opened a steel-making plant at Landore near Swansea in 1867. He made many other inventions including the electric furnace in 1879. He was born in Germany, naturalized in 1859, and knighted in 1883.

← HENRY BESSEMER: GILCHRIST-THOMAS PROCESS →

Simpson, Sir James Young (1811–70), doctor, born Bathgate, Scotland, appointed professor at Edinburgh in 1840. In 1847 he discovered that chloroform could be used as an anaesthetic, and he started giving it to women to ease the pains of childbirth. It soon replaced ether as a general anaesthetic in operations, as it is about three times as strong, and allowed more complicated and longer operations to be performed. He was made a baronet in 1866.

← ROBERT LISTON: JOSEPH LISTER →

Sinn Fein ('Ourselves'), an Irish nationalist party formed in 1902 by Arthur Griffith (1872–1922). *Eamon de Valera* became president of the party in 1917. In the 1918 elections it won 73 out of the 105 Irish seats, but members refused to take their seats at Westminster and set up their own Dail (parliament) in Dublin, and proclaimed the Irish republic.

← EASTER RISING, 1916: IRISH REPUBLICAN ARMY →

Sirius, a British steamboat of 700 tons, which was the first in the world to cross the Atlantic using steam all the way. It arrived in New York from Cork several hours before the *Great Western* in 1838. The crossing had previously been made by three foreign ships, but they used sails for part of the journey.

← AARON MANBY: GREAT WESTERN →

Six Acts, 1819. After *Peterloo, Lord Sidmouth* rushed through a number of laws, the Six Acts, which greatly restricted the liberties of the individual and the freedom of the Press. The Acts, and their main effects, were:

1. Training Prevention Act, banning military training and drilling by civilians, an Act which has never been repealed.

2. Seizure of Arms Act, giving magistrates in 'disturbed' areas, the right to search people and private houses for arms.

3. Seditious Meetings Prevention Act, prohibiting the holding of meetings of more than fifty people, without the consent of a magistrate. Banners could not be carried and all the people at the meeting had to live locally. It was repealed after five years.

4. Misdemeanours Act to prevent delay in administering justice, which meant that some cases could be heard by a magistrate instead of by a judge and jury.

5. Blasphemous and Seditious Libels Act, which allowed magistrates to enter any premises, using force if necessary, to search for pamphlets.

6. Newspapers and Stamp Duties Act, which extended stamp duties to all periodicals 'containing observations on public events' which cost less than 6*d*. (The duty was reduced from 4*d*. to 1*d*. in 1836 and abolished in 1855.)

Many reformers were imprisoned and large quantities of radical periodicals were seized. It was one of the major attempts by the Tory old guard to wipe out all reform.
← PETERLOO: CATO STREET CONSPIRACY →

Slump, or **depression,** is a sudden fall in a country's profits and prices, usually associated with unemployment.
← BOOM

Slavery. The slave trade from Africa to America and the West Indies, in which Britain had taken a leading part, was abolished by Britain in 1807. The abolition of slavery within the British empire was achieved in 1833, when all slaves were freed. *William Wilberforce* was partly responsible for the abolition, but many others, like *Thomas Clarkson*, also played an important part.

Smuts, General Jan Christian (1870–1950), Boer general, who fought against Britain in the Boer War, 1899–1902, and then fought for Britain in the First World War. He was a member of the *Imperial War Cabinet*, from 1917 to 1919, and prime minister of South Africa from 1919 to 1929 and 1939 to 1948. He founded a moderate United party in 1934 which was opposed to racism and republicanism. He was made a British field marshal in 1941.

Soccer see **Association football**

Social Democratic Federation (S.D.F.), an extreme movement founded in 1881 by Henry Mayers Hyndman (1842–1921). *William Morris* was a member for a short time. The S.D.F. helped to found the Labour Representation Committee (later the Labour party) in 1900, but withdrew almost immediately because the Committee's policies were not socialistic enough. In 1911 it amalgamated with some *Independent Labour party* members to form the British Socialist party.
COMMUNIST PARTY →

SOCIAL SERVICES. From Elizabethan times the main help for poor people in times of need was provided under the *Poor Laws* of 1597 and 1601. In addition, small gifts of food, money or clothes, and almshouses, hospitals and schools were provided by individuals and charities in various parts of the country. During the seventeenth century and even more in the eighteenth century, groups of skilled workers started to band together to form *friendly societies* to provide benefits for members in sickness, unemployment and old age.

The official poor law system was unable to cope with the growing numbers of poor in the late eighteenth century and in 1795 the *Speenhamland system* was introduced to provide extra relief. This caused such a great increase in the poor rate that a *Poor Law Amendment Act* was passed in 1834 which tried to introduce a completely new approach. Instead of providing outdoor relief—cash payments to people living in their own homes—it tried to force all the unemployed men who were fit to work, and their families, into new *workhouses* run by *Boards of Guardians.* The workhouse soon became a source of terror and a symbol of shame for the working classes.

Throughout the nineteenth century there were many other attempts by organizations and individuals to relieve poverty. The new 'model' unions, like the *Amalgamated Society of Engineers,* formed in 1851, provided friendly society benefits for their members. Individuals, like *Dr Barnado* helped destitute children, while the Churches set up many charitable organizations. In 1878 the Salvation Army was formed: its members lived and worked among the poor they tried to help. But all of these efforts were unable to solve the problem of poverty in the overcrowded industrial towns. The beginnings of the modern national scheme of social services started with the Liberals' introduction of *old age pensions* in 1908 and the passing of the *National Insurance Act* in 1911. But the system of unemployment insurance introduced by the Act broke down in the *depression* between the two world wars, and a *means test* was introduced in 1931 to cut down on public assistance payments to the long-term unemployed.

The *welfare state*, as we know it today, was proposed in the *Beveridge report* published during the Second World War. Most of its recommendations were put into effect by the Labour government after the end of the war with the introduction of *family allowances* in 1945; and the passing of a comprehensive *National Insurance Act* in 1946 and the *National Health Service Act* in the same year. The *National Assistance Act* of 1948 finally ended the Poor Law after nearly 350 years. In 1970 government spending on social security benefits amounted to £3,908m. and on the National Health Service to £2,089m. In addition, the government also spent millions of pounds on *education* and *housing*, which most people now think of as social services. Local councils also provide many other smaller services out of the rates.

SOCIALISM. Under this system the means of production, distribution, and exchange would be owned and controlled by the whole people, so that the wealth could be distributed more fairly. A number of Socialist parties were formed in Britain in the late nineteenth century, including the *Social Democratic Federation* and the *Independent Labour party.* These combined with the trade unions in 1900 to form the Labour Representation Committee, which became the *Labour party* in 1906. The Labour party adopted a policy of *nationalization* in 1918, and many industries and bodies were nationalized by the *Attlee* government after the Second World War. A more extreme form of Marxist-Socialism was developed by *Karl Marx*, which was the basis for modern *Communist* parties.

← CAPITALISM

Society of Friends see **Quakers**

SOUTH AFRICA. The British gained the Cape of Good Hope, a settlement on the southern coast of South Africa, from the Dutch by the *Treaty of Vienna, 1815*. Becoming dissatisfied with British rule, the original Dutch settlers (Boers) decided to seek new lands of their own in the north. In 1836 they began the Great Trek, in which the Boers and their families set off in ox-drawn wagons to seek new lands in the interior of the country, which was peopled by fierce native tribes—the Matabele and Zulus. The Boers settled first in Natal on the east coast, but when the British annexed this as a colony in 1843, they trekked on across the Orange and Vaal rivers to new territories. Britain recognized the independence of the Boer state of the Transvaal by the Sand River Convention of 1852 and of the Orange River territory by the Convention of Bloemfontein, 1854. In 1877, in response to a new wave of British imperialism, Britain annexed the Transvaal, and two years later fought the *Zulu war* in its defence. But in 1881, the Boers in the Transvaal proclaimed their independence, defeated the British at the Battle of Majuba Hill, Natal, and *Gladstone*, who was then prime minister, granted them self-government under the Convention of Pretoria, 1881. They were given full independence three years later. But relations between the British and the Boers became steadily worse. In 1885, the British annexed Bechuanaland (now Botswana) to the west of the Transvaal. From 1890, *Cecil Rhodes*'s company started to establish settlements in Rhodesia to the north of the Transvaal, so that the Boers felt increasingly hemmed in. Meanwhile, the discovery of gold in the Transvaal, first near Pietersburg in 1871, and then further south around Johannesburg in 1886, brought in hundreds of 'Uitlanders' (foreigners). There was increasing trouble between the 'Uitlanders', who were mainly British, and the Boers. *Cecil Rhodes* made an unsuccessful attempt to overthrow the Boer government of the Transvaal, under President Paul Kruger, by the *Jameson raid* of 1895. The Boers started arming and the British sent reinforcements to South Africa. Negotiations went on between the Boers and the British but with few results and in 1899 the second *Boer War* broke out. It ended in 1902 with the Treaty of Vereeniging, under which the two Boer republics of the Transvaal and the Orange Free State became British colonies. They were granted self-government between 1906 and 1907.

In 1910, the Union of South Africa, a self-governing dominion, was formed out of these two colonies and Cape Colony and Natal. Votes were not given to the blacks, but only to the whites and to the Cape coloured (people of mixed blood), whose right to vote was specially safeguarded. After the Second World War, South Africa developed a policy of *apartheid*. The Cape coloured voters were put on a separate electoral roll in 1960. Because of protests from other members of the Commonwealth about apartheid, South Africa left the Commonwealth in 1961 and also became a republic. Nearly 4m. of the total population of 22m. was white in 1972.

Spa Fields Meetings, 1816. The first big radical demonstrations held in London after the Napoleonic wars to demand reforms. One meeting was held on 15 November and a second meeting on 2 December at Spa Fields in the City of London. Both meetings were addressed by *Henry Hunt*. After the second meeting, part of the crowd led by Arthur Thistlewood, who originated the *Cato Street conspiracy*, marched to the Tower of London and other parts of the City, breaking into gun-smith's shops on the way, and rioting for several hours before they were dispersed by troops. Following other disturbances, the government suspended the *Habeas Corpus Act* in 1817, so that people could be imprisoned without trial.

PETERLOO →

Space travel. The first space satellite, Sputnik I, which went into orbit around the earth, was launched by the Russians in October, 1957. It was unmanned. The Russians were also the first to send an astronaut into space, when Yuri Gagarin made one complete orbit of the earth in 1961. Two American astronauts, Neil Armstrong and Col. Edwin Aldrin from Apollo II, were the first men to set foot on the moon, on 20 July 1969.

← V2 ROCKETS: COMMUNICATION SATELLITES →

Spare part surgery consists of using organs from a dead person, or artificial units, to replace diseased organs, such as kidneys, livers and hearts. Much progress has been made in recent years, particularly in kidney transplants, which have been made successfully in Britain and in many other countries. Transplants of human livers have been carried out by Dr Starzl of Colorado, U.S.A. The first heart transplant was made in Cape Town, South Africa, by Dr C. Barnard in 1967, but the patient died shortly afterwards. Dr Philip Blaiberg, who also had a heart transplant in Cape Town in the following year, lived for 19½ months afterwards.

Speed limit on roads was set at 4 m.p.h. in 1865, raised to 12 m.p.h. in 1896, to 20 m.p.h. in 1903, and abolished altogether in 1930. Because of increased accidents, a new speed limit of 30 m.p.h. was imposed in towns in 1934. An experimental 70 m.p.h. speed limit was imposed on all unrestricted roads, including motorways, in 1965.

Speenhamland system. A method of helping lower-paid workers by giving them small cash grants from the poor rate, which were based on the price of bread—then the main item in the cost of living—and the size of a man's family. The system was introduced by the Berkshire justices of the peace (who were responsible for administering the *Poor Laws* in the county) at a meeting in the Pelican Inn, Speenhamland, near Newbury, on 6 May 1795. It was designed to cope with the growing problem of poverty and was soon afterwards copied by J.P.s in most other parts of the country, except the north and the west. When a loaf of bread, weighing just over 8½ lb. cost 1*s*., a married man with no children could have his wages made up out of the poor rates to 4*s*. 6*d*. a week, or to 15*s*. a week if he had 7 children. As the price of bread rose the cash allowances would increase. Although it was a genuine attempt to deal with the problem of poverty and low-paid workers, the scheme had a great number of drawbacks. It encouraged employers to pay low wages as they knew they would be made up from the rates; it took away the worker's self-respect by making him depend on charity; and it trebled the cost of the Poor Law by 1812. The system ended in 1834.
POOR LAW AMENDMENT ACT, 1834 →

Splendid isolation, a phrase often used inaccurately to describe the foreign policy of the *Marquis of Salisbury*, who was not opposed to treaties with other European powers for limited aims. But the phrase does have some truth in describing the general direction of all British foreign policy from the Crimean War to the end of the nineteenth century. Britain was able to shelter behind the protection of the *Royal Navy*, and was thus able to avoid major wars and commitments in Europe. The policy broke down after the second Boer War. An *Anglo-*

Japanese alliance was signed in 1902 and the *Triple Entente* was formed in 1907.

Stage coaches. Coaches, usually pulled by four horses, which were changed at stages along the route in coaching inns where passengers ate and stayed the night. They were introduced in the middle of the seventeenth century, but services developed greatly after better *turnpike roads* were built. The golden age lasted from about 1815 to 1840, when some coaches were travelling at an average speed of 14 m.p.h. *Railways* then took over and coaches had disappeared by 1850.
MAIL COACHES →

Stalin, Josef (1879–1953), Bolshevik revolutionary, who ruled Russia with a rod of iron. He became First Secretary of the Communist party in 1922 and got rid of all opposition by intrigues, trials, exiles and executions. He directed the Russian war effort against Germany from 1941 to 1945 and took over the Eastern European countries after the end of the war and set up 'puppet' Communist governments. His suspicions of the Western powers, which were partly justified, were one of the causes of the *cold war*.

Stanley, Sir Henry Morton (1841–1904), explorer and journalist, who 'found' David Livingstone. He was born in Denbigh, worked his way as a cabin boy to the United States in 1859, and became a journalist. He became a special correspondent for the *New York Herald*. In 1869 his editor ordered him to find Livingstone, which he did two years later. Stanley later explored and founded the Congo Free State for the King of the Belgians. He was knighted in 1899.
← DAVID LIVINGSTONE

Statute of Westminster, 1931, removed practically all of the remaining legal powers of Britain over the self-governing *dominions*, except for minor matters such as the right of appeal from law courts in the dominions to the Privy Council in London. The Act stated that British laws no longer applied to the dominions, except with their consent and that they had full rights to make their own laws.
← IMPERIAL CONFERENCE, 1926

Steam carriages. The first successful carriage powered by a steam engine was produced by *Richard Trevithick* in 1802. In August 1834, Walter Hancock (1799–1852) opened a regular passenger service between Moorfields and Paddington in London, which covered the five miles in half-an-hour. The owners of *turnpike roads* objected to steam carriages, because, so they claimed, their heavy weight damaged the surface of the roads. They made tolls so high that steam carriages were unable to compete successfully with *mail coaches.* Both forms of transport disappeared after the development of *railways.* Steam locomotives continued to be used for road-building and agricultural purposes, and towards the end of the nineteenth century some steam cars and lorries were made.

LOCOMOTIVE ACT, 1865 →

STEAM ENGINES, which gave man a greater source of power than he had ever had before, were primarily a British development. In 1706 *Thomas Newcomen* invented a primitive 'atmospheric' engine, but the first modern steam engine was patented by *James Watt* in 1769. His work was financed and developed as a commercial proposition by *Matthew Boulton.* These early engines were used mainly in coal mines and factories. *Richard Trevithick* introduced the high-pressure engine and was the first man to build a successful *railway* locomotive in 1804. *George Stephenson* made many improvements to the steam locomotive and other refinements were introduced by *Matthew Murray* and Sir Goldsworth Gurney (1793–1845), who invented a high-pressure steam jet successfully used by Stephenson in the *Rainhill trials, 1829.*

The steam engine was also used for propelling boats and ships. The first practical steamboat, the *Charlotte Dundas,* was built by *William Symington* in 1802. Further improvements to marine steam engines were made by *John Elder* who invented the compound engine in 1854 and by *Alfred Holt* who developed an even more efficient engine ten years later.

The steam engine was the essential source of power for the *industrial revolution.* It was used not only to drive machinery in factories but also for improving communications by rail and sea so that goods could be more easily transported. Watt's first steam engines developed no more than 50 horsepower, but by the end of the nineteenth century steam engines capable of developing 10,000 horsepower were in use. The steam engine was used in some early motor cars and lorries at the beginning of the present century. Steam engines were still being used in some factories as late as the 1930s. But they gradually went out of use in the present century as more efficient and greater sources of power were developed. These include *Sir Charles Parsons's* steam turbine, the internal combustion engine, *electricity,* and *atomic energy.*

Stephenson, George (1781–1848), pioneer of railways and locomotives,

born at Wylam, Northumberland. After working in various coal mines, he was made an enginewright at Killingworth Colliery in 1812 at a wage of £100 a year. He started experimenting with steam locomotives in 1814 and constructed an eight-mile-long railway line for Hetton Colliery, which was opened in 1822. In the following year, he started to build the 37-mile-long Stockton–Darlington line, which was opened in 1825. It was the first public railway for passengers and goods, though steam locomotives were not used along the whole length of the line. For 1½ miles at the western end, wagons were hauled up a hill and guided down again by ropes attached to a stationary steam engine. In 1826 Stephenson was asked to build the Liverpool–Manchester line. A year before the line opened, the *Rainhill trials* were held along part of the track, which Stephenson won in his 'Rocket'. The line was opened in September 1830. The opening ceremony was marred by the death of an M.P., *William Huskisson*, who was knocked down by the 'Rocket', but the line was a great success and led to many other railways being built in other parts of the country. Stephenson built many other locomotives and railways with a gauge of 4 feet 8½ inches, which became the standard gauge for England and Scotland in 1846. He also invented a safety lamp for miners at about the same time as *Sir Humphry Davy*. In 1847 he became the first president of the Institution of Mechanical Engineers.
← MATTHEW MURRAY

Sterling area. An arrangement which started between the two world wars by which many Commonwealth and some foreign countries kept their own currencies in a fixed relationship to the £. They also kept much of their reserves of money in £s in London. With the decline in Britain's international financial position after the end of the Second World War the importance of the sterling area has declined.

Stopes, Marie Carmichael (1880–1958), pioneer of *birth control*, born in Edinburgh. She was educated at North London Collegiate School and at University College, London. In 1904 she was appointed a lecturer in botany at Manchester University—the first woman to be appointed to the scientific staff there. In 1918 she published 'Married Love', the first outspoken general book on sexual relations, and in the same year 'Wise Parenthood' dealing with birth control. These two books brought her world-wide fame. She founded a Mother's Clinic for Birth Control in London in 1921—the first to make knowledge about contraception available to the public.

STRIKES. It was made much more difficult for workers to strike by the *Combination Acts* of 1799 and 1800. These Acts were repealed in 1824 and in the following year, owing to a wave of violent strikes, intimidation in strikes was made illegal. The *Criminal Law Amendment Act*, 1871, made picketing illegal, but the right of peaceful picketing in strikes was restored four years later. In 1888 there took place the first successful strike by unskilled workers—the *Match girls' strike*, which was followed in 1889 by the *London docks strike*. Just before the First World War, with increasing membership of *trade unions*, rising prices, and stationary wages, there was a wave of big strikes—by cotton workers and shipyard workers in 1910, railwaymen and dockers in 1911, and miners in 1912. The first *unofficial strike* was called by shop stewards in 1915 during the First World War.

Miners, who have always been among the most militant workers, called a big strike in 1921 and there were other strikes by engineers in 1922, boilermakers in 1923, and builders in 1924. The main causes were reductions in wages, increasing *unemployment* and the worsening economic situation. The *General Strike* of 1926 was followed by the passing of the *Trade Disputes Act* in 1927, which made general strikes illegal. It was repealed by the Labour government in 1946.

Contrary to popular belief the days lost by strikes in Britain in recent years has not been as high as in some other neighbouring countries. From 1958 to 1967, Britain lost on average 144 working days per thousand workers each year owing to industrial disputes, while France lost 151 days and Italy 891. During the same period the United States lost 486 days. The years since the beginning of the century in which the greatest number of days have been lost by strikes in Britain are as follows:

1908	10,785,000	1922	19,854,000
1911	10,155,000	1923	10,672,000
1912	40,890,000	1926	162,233,000
1919	34,969,000	1970	10,908,000
1920	26,568,000	1972	23,000,000
1921	85,872,000		

Subscriber Trunk Dialling (S.T.D.), which allows long-distance calls to be dialled direct, instead of being connected by an operator, was started in Britain in 1958.

← TELEPHONE

Suez Canal, in Egypt, linking the Mediterranean and the Red Sea, played a major part in British foreign policy as the vital link in the sea route to India. (Before the canal was opened in 1869, passengers sailed through the Mediterranean to Egypt, crossed the Suez isthmus by land, and then sailed in another steamer to India.) The canal was built and partly owned by the French. In 1875, the bankrupt Khedive (Viceroy) of Egypt put his shares up for sale. Hearing of this, *Disraeli*, who feared that the French might buy them, quickly stepped in and bought the shares for £4m., making Britain the largest shareholder. This purchase increased British interest in Egypt. In 1882, after a revolt in Egypt, British troops intervened to restore the Khedive and then remained in the country, which was made a British protectorate in 1914. The defence of the canal was one of the major strategic concerns of the British in the First and Second World Wars. Egypt became independent in 1922, but the British retained troops in the canal area. These were finally withdrawn in 1956 when the Egyptian government under Colonel Nasser nationalized the canal. Shortly afterwards Israeli forces, possibly acting in concert with Britain and France, invaded Egypt, and British and French forces attacked Egypt, claiming that they wished to separate the Israelis and Egyptians and restore peace. Threats of economic pressure by the United States caused Britain and France to stop their armed actions, illustrating the limits of independent military action by Britain, when these offended one of the super powers. The canal was blocked by sunken ships during the Six-Day war between Israel and Egypt in 1967, and was still closed in 1973. But it is no longer of vital concern to Britain since it has lost its empire and the building of much bigger *oil-tankers* has made it economic to transport oil by longer routes. Even if the canal were reopened, it would have to be widened or rebuilt before these new supertankers could use it.

Suffragette movement was started in 1903 when *Mrs Emmeline Pankhurst* and her daughter Christabel formed the Women's Social and Political Union to campaign for votes for women. Groups of women led by Millicent Fawcett (1847–1930) and others had been trying to obtain the vote for many years by quiet constitutional means, but without any success. In 1905 the suffragettes held their first big demonstration at an election meeting in Manchester, where they smuggled in a large 'Votes for Women' banner. During the next few years, they organized many demonstrations, broke up meetings, held protests inside and outside parliament, and 'invaded' No. 10 Downing Street, the home of the prime minister. Many of them were imprisoned and from 1909 started to go on hunger strike in prison. The authorities replied by forcibly feeding them—a painful, and even dangerous, process, in which a rubber tube is pushed up the nostrils or into the mouth. The Liberals introduced a number of Bills between 1910 and 1912, which would have given the vote to women householders and businesswomen, but they were all defeated. The suffragettes then turned to violence (though only to property and never to human life), smashing shop windows, cutting telephone wires, planting bombs, setting fire to the contents of letterboxes, and damaging pictures and statues in art galleries. In June 1913, Emily Wilding-Davison threw herself under the king's horse at the Derby as a protest and was killed. More and more suffragettes were arrested. The government, which had been much criticized for forcibly feeding them, passed the '*Cat and Mouse*' *Act, 1913*, in an attempt to avoid the need for forcible feeding. With the outbreak of the First World War, the suffragettes abandoned their campaign, though some individual members opposed the war as pacifists. But most of the leaders supported it. Women played a big part in the war effort by working in factories and some were given the vote for the first time by the *Representation of the People Act, 1918*.

Sunday observance. A campaign led by *Lord Shaftesbury* and other *Evangelicals* in the nineteenth century to stop all work—and entertainment—on Sundays, in accordance with God's command to keep the day 'holy'. They succeeded in having many shops, places of business and entertainment closed on Sundays, and respectable middle-class people avoided household tasks and stopped their children from playing games. A Lord's Day Observance Society was formed in 1831, which still exists.

Sunday schools were opened in a number of places, including Macclesfield, Cheshire, and High Wycombe, Bucks, in the second half of the eighteenth century to give poor children religious instruction and, incidentally, to teach them to read. Many parents were so keen to learn to read, too, that they attended with their children. The movement really got under way after *Robert Raikes* and the Rev. Thomas Stock opened three Sunday schools in Gloucester in 1780. By 1818 there were nearly 500,000 pupils, about 4 per cent of the population, in schools all over the county; and by 1851 nearly 2½m.—13 per cent of the population. Their importance declined with the passing of the *Education Act, 1870*, but they have continued to provide religious instruction for young children to the present day.
RAGGED SCHOOLS →

Swan, Sir Joseph (1828–1914), inventor of the modern electric light bulb, born in Sunderland. He produced his first bulb in 1848, but a successful version was not made until thirty years later. *Thomas Edison* also produced a light bulb in the same year and they formed the Edison and Swan United Electric Light Co. in 1883. Swan was knighted in 1904.

Sweated industries in which employees, many of them foreign, worked for very long hours in small, insanitary rooms—often in private houses—for very small wages. Tailoring was one of the worst of the sweated industries. The *Trade Boards Act, 1909*, set up boards to fix minimum wages.

'Swing' riots occurred in 1830 among farm workers all over southern England and in parts of the Midlands and East Anglia, against low wages and the high price of food. The riots were supposed to have been led by a mysterious character called Captain Swing. Some ricks were burnt; threshing machines destroyed; and bands of farm workers demanded higher wages from their employers. There were savage reprisals. Nineteen men and boys were hanged, all but three for burning ricks; 481 transported; and 644 imprisoned.
TOLPUDDLE MARTYRS →

Symington, William (1763–1831), steamboat pioneer, born at Leadhills, Lanarkshire. In 1788, he built his first steam engine for a boat, which was tried out on Dalswinton Lake, near Dumfries, with the poet, John Burns, as one of the five people on board. In 1802 he tried out the first practical steamboat in the world, the *Charlotte Dundas*, on the Forth and Clyde canal. But his plans to build a fleet of steamboats to tow barges on the canal, had to be abandoned, because the canal owners thought that the waves from the paddle wheels would damage the banks. He died in poverty in London.

T

Taff Vale judgment, 1901. A legal case which made unions responsible for paying damages to firms for losses they suffered in strikes. The Taff Vale Railway Company of South Wales was awarded £23,000 against the Amalgamated Society of Railway Servants for losses it sustained in an official 11-day strike in the previous year. The 'judgment' made it much more difficult for unions to strike, but the ruling was reversed by law five years later.
TRADE DISPUTES ACT, 1906 →

Tamworth manifesto, an address to his electors made by Peel in 1834 in which he explained his new philosophy of moderate Conservatism. He accepted the *First Reform Act, 1832*, which he had previously opposed. But he remained opposed, he wrote, to living in 'a perpetual vortex of agitation', though he would support 'the correction of proved abuses, and the redress of real grievances'. The statement had a long-lasting effect on the policy of the *Conservative party* in making it willing to accept moderate reform.

Tariff reform. From 1903 *Joseph Chamberlain* advocated that Britain should abandon its traditional *free trade* policy and charge duties, or tariffs, on imported goods, as many foreign countries were doing. His campaign split the Conservative party and contributed to its overwhelming defeat by the Liberals in 1906. Tariffs were introduced by his son, *Neville Chamberlain*, in 1932.

TAXATION. Taxes are of two main kinds. Direct taxes on income or capital, which include *income tax*, *estate duties* and *capital gains taxes.* These taxes are fairer, or progressive, as the rich pay more than the poor. If the rate of income tax is 30 per cent then a man with an income of £10,000 a year would pay £3,000 in tax, while the poor man with an income of £1,000 a year would pay only £300 (excluding all allowances). Furthermore, the allowances can be varied, so that the poor man pays no tax at all. This allows income to be redistributed, so that the heavy taxes paid by the rich help to pay for free State schools, for example.

The second kind of tax is an indirect or outlay tax, like *purchase tax* or *value added tax.* These impose a flat-rate of tax on goods or services and are therefore less fair than direct taxation. If the rate of tax is 10 per cent then the tax on a £1,000 car will be £100. This has to be paid by the man who buys the car, and it means much less to a rich man than it does to a poor man. (Subsidies have been used at various times to keep the price of essential goods, like food, low.)

The main purpose of taxation is to provide money for government spending on national services, such as defence, education, roads etc. Direct taxes can also be used to redistribute wealth. And all taxes can be used to influence the economy of the country. If, for example, the tax on motor cars is reduced, more people will be able to afford to buy one, and the motor-car industry will be able to expand.

Britain is one of the highest-taxed nations in the world, but not the highest. (Total taxation in France, Sweden, Norway and Holland is higher.) In 1969 taxes equalled nearly 42 per cent of the *gross national product*—over 20 per cent on expenditure, over 16 per cent on income and over $5\frac{1}{2}$ per cent on social security contributions.

Taxes on Knowledge. Taxes on newspapers introduced in 1712 deliberately to restrict the free flow of information. The taxes increased the prices of newspapers considerably, and as a result fewer people could afford to buy them and criticisms of the government were less widely read. In 1819, the taxes were also applied to some periodicals. The advertisement duty was abolished in 1853; the stamp duty in 1855; and the paper duty in 1861. Newspapers could then be sold at a lower price. Before the stamp duty was abolished, the total circulation of all daily newspapers was only 100,000, but circulations increased rapidly after 1855. The 'Daily Telegraph' and many provincial daily papers were founded in that year. By the end of the century with the development of the *popular press,* one newspaper had reached a circulation of 1m.

Teetotallers are people who do not touch alcoholic drink. The name originated in an American *temperance society* in 1827 when some members signed a T (Total) pledge to abstain from all alcohol.

Telephone was invented by *Alexander Graham Bell* in 1876. The first telephone exchange, with eight subscribers, was opened in London in 1879 and in the following year a United Telephone Company was formed to provide a telephone service in the capital and to license other companies to set up telephone exchanges in the provinces. In 1912 the Post Office took over all telephone services, with the exception of the one in Hull, which remains under independent control. In 1970, 35 per cent of households had a telephone. In 1972, the Post Office announced that it was going to spend £4,800m. in the course of the next few years, much of it on improving telephone services.
SUBSCRIBER TRUNK DIALLING →

Telford Thomas (1757–1834), one of the most remarkable engineers of the nineteenth century, born at Westerkirk, Dumfriesshire, the son of a shepherd. He was apprenticed to a stonemason at the age of fourteen. From the 1780s he started building roads by a new technique, using a hand-packed foundation of carefully-selected stones, which would not be washed away in rain and floods. He built about 1,000 miles of roads in Scotland, and specified that no main road should have a gradient of more than 1 in 30, to make it easier for horses to pull up coaches and carts. He also built many bridges, including the Menai bridge; constructed the *Caledonian canal*; and carried out improvements to many Scottish harbours. He became the first president of the Institute of Civil Engineers in 1818.

← JOHN METCALF: JOHN LOUDON MCADAM →

Temperance societies to persuade people to stop drinking alcohol were started in the 1820s. A Band of Hope for children was started in Leeds in 1847: they had to sign a pledge that they would become *teetotallers* and never touch an alcoholic drink. The movement soon spread to other parts of the country. *Nonconformists* were strong supporters of the temperance movement. As a result of their campaigns, a *Licensing Act* was passed by the Gladstone government in 1872, which restricted the hours at which public houses could open. Excessive drinking was certainly a grave social problem in Victorian times, with a public house on almost every street corner and huge gin palaces where a glass of gin could be bought for 2*d.* Convictions for drunkenness declined from 76 per 10,000 of the population in England and Wales in 1875 to 59 in 1900 and 20 in 1925. The decline was caused partly by the work of the temperance societies but also by the fact that higher wages gave people the choice of spending their money on the greater number of other goods that were then becoming available, instead of spending their few spare shillings on drink. Temperance workers were responsible for introducing other social reforms: the first *excursion train* was run to a temperance meeting and the first *probation* officer was appointed by a temperance society. Convictions for drunkenness started to rise rapidly again after the Second World War. In 1946 there were just over 20,500 and in 1970, over 86,000. One of the most serious effects was in the increase in road accidents caused by drunken drivers and in 1967 *breathalysers* were introduced in an attempt to diminish the number of accidents. More than £2,000m. was spent on alcoholic drink in Britain in 1970.

Ten hours' movement. The main demand of early factory workers in the *textile industry*, the first to be mechanized, was for a 10-hour working day. The men hoped to achieve this by limiting the working hours of women, young persons and children, without whose help the men could not do their work. A Ten Hours' Bill was introduced by *Michael Sadler* in 1831, but he lost his seat as an M.P. in the following year. *Lord Shaftesbury* then took up the Bill but it was defeated, though as a compensation the government put through the first effective *Factory Act* of 1833. In 1847 *John Fielden* successfully introduced a Ten Hours' Bill, which applied to women and young persons. But its intended effects were evaded by making women and young persons do shift work, so that men still had to work a 15- or 16-hour day. A 10½-hour day was obtained for all textile workers in 1853, but it was not until 1874 that women obtained the 10-hour day by law. As a result the hours of men were reduced, too.

Test and Corporation Acts prevented *nonconformists* from being an M.P., or becoming a government minister or a member of a town corporation. The Corporation Act was passed in 1661 and the Test Act in 1673. They were not applied from 1727 and were finally repealed in 1828.
UNIVERSITIES TESTS ACT, 1871 →

Test-ban Treaty, 1963, signed in Moscow, under which Britain, Russia, and the United States agreed not to test nuclear weapons in the atmosphere. Previous tests had produced much radiation, whose long-term effects are still not fully known. The treaty was one of the first results of the lessening of the *cold war.* But France and China refused to sign and have since carried out tests in the atmosphere, while Britain, Russia, and the United States have conducted many underground tests. The treaty failed to stop the nuclear arms race and the number of nuclear weapons, and their power, has increased enormously.

TEXTILE INDUSTRY was the first to be fully mechanized, mainly by British inventions. In about 1765 *James Hargreaves* invented the spinning jenny, which speeded up spinning by using a number of spindles instead of just one, and four years later *Sir Richard Arkwright* patented the spinning or water frame, which allowed an all-cotton cloth to be made. In 1779 *Samuel Crompton* invented a spinning mule which combined the advantages of both machines. An improved automatic version was made by *Richard Roberts* in 1825. The first machines were driven by horsepower or water power (hence the term 'cotton mill'), but in 1785 a *Boulton and Watt* steam engine was installed in a cotton mill for the first time—at Papplewick, Nottinghamshire.

Weaving was slower to be mechanized. *John Kay*'s patent of the flying shuttle in 1733 allowed one man to do the work of two, but it was not until 1787 that the *Rev. Edmund Cartwright* made a power loom. The first machines were not satisfactory, but, after improvements, they started to come into more general use in the 1820s. By the middle of the nineteenth century the cotton industry was highly mechanized with steam-powered spinning mules and looms. Machinery was introduced more slowly in the woollen industry, partly because of technical difficulties, and it was not until the second half of the nineteenth century that machines came into widespread use.

The textile industry had an enormous impact on social and economic affairs. The introduction of the *factory system* by Arkwright gradually brought the old *domestic system* of manufacture to an end, while the mechanization of weaving caused great unemployment among the handloom weavers, the former 'aristocrats' of the working classes, in the 1820s and 1830s. The early cotton mills were built outside towns near rivers, with a good flow of water, but the use of steam engines allowed them to be sited in *towns.* With their overcrowding, smokey chimneys, and lack of hygiene these fast-growing industrial towns soon disfigured the landscape of the north. Women and children were employed extensively in the early factories at starvation wages and the government was forced to intervene by passing a long series of *factory acts* which regulated conditions and hours of work. The textile industry was one of the mainstays of Britain's wealth in the first half of the nineteenth century. Between 1815 and 1850 it accounted for almost half the total value of British exports and even by 1914 it still produced about a quarter of all export earnings.

But by the end of the century Britain was already starting to lose its lead. It was slow to adopt the faster, ring-spinning frame developed in the United States in the 1830s. *Sir William Perkin* made the first artificial dye in 1856, but it was the Germans who took it up and developed a great industry. And Britain failed to equip its factories quickly enough with the automatic loom invented by J. H. Northrop of Massachusetts, U.S.A., in 1895. After the First World War there was increased competition from the Japanese, and a growth of textile industries in Britain's former export markets. As a result, there was a slump in the British textile industry between the two world wars. Since the Second World War, there has been a much greater use of man-made fibres. (Rayon was developed in the 1890s and nylon in 1935.) The textile industry employed just over 700,000 workers in 1970, about 3 per cent of the total labour force, against almost 13 per cent in 1841, when it was at its peak.

Third Reform Act see **Representation of the People Act, 1884**

Thomson, Sir Joseph John (1856–1940), physicist, born near Manchester. He was educated at Cambridge and was Cavendish Professor of Physics there from 1884 to 1918. His discovery of the electron in 1897 was a major contribution to atomic theory. He was awarded the Nobel prize for physics in 1906 and knighted in 1908.

← JOHN DALTON: LORD RUTHERFORD →

TIME. In the first half of the nineteenth century, there was no standard time throughout Britain. Clocks in London and Bristol, for example, were 20 minutes different. In the middle of the century, the *electric telegraph* was used to send a standard time to post offices and railway stations throughout the country from Greenwich Observatory. This was popularly known as 'railway time'. In 1880 Greenwich Mean Time (G.M.T.) was made the legal standard time throughout Britain. In 1916, during the First World War, summer time was introduced to economize on fuel, mainly as a result of a long campaign by a Chelsea builder, William Willett (1856–1915). During the Second World War, double summer time, in which the clocks are put forward two hours, was used from 1941 to 1945, and again during the *fuel crisis* in 1947.

Continental time is one hour ahead of G.M.T. throughout the whole year and in 1968 Britain adopted the same system for an experimental three-year period to bring us into line with our future partners in the *European Community.* But there were so many protests from farmers and from parents of young children about the darkness of the mornings that G.M.T. was restored in 1971, with summer time for half the year only.

Times, The. The most famous British newspaper, founded in 1785 as the 'Daily Universal Register', which adopted its present name three years later. It was founded by *John Walter* and had a succession of brilliant editors in the nineteenth century, including *John Delane*, which gave it a great political influence. It was owned by *Viscount Northcliffe* from 1908 to 1922.

Tithes, a tenth of the harvest or produce of the land payable to the local parson or tithe-holder. They were abolished in England by the Tithe Commutation Act of 1836, and in Ireland in 1838, when fixed rent charges were substituted. In 1936 an Act was passed to abolish rent charges over a 60-year period, under which the government compensated former tithe-holders.

Tolpuddle Martyrs. Six farm labourers (George and James Loveless, James Hammett, James Brine and Thomas and John Stanfield) of Tolpuddle, Dorset, who were prosecuted in 1834 for giving secret oaths when they formed a local branch of an agricultural labourers' union. The government intended the prosecution to serve as a warning to other members of the growing trade union movement who had joined the *Grand National Consolidated Trades Union* in their thousands. The six farm workers were sentenced to seven years' transportation, but owing to the pressure of public opinion were freed after two years. The National Union of Agricultural and Allied Workers still holds a national rally in the village every year.

← SWING RIOTS: JOSEPH ARCH →

Tory, a hostile name (from the Irish word meaning 'robber') sometimes used to describe a Conservative, particularly the more reactionary ones. The Tories were out of office for much of the eighteenth century, but they came back into favour under George III and were in power from 1783 to 1830. They supported the *established church* and the land-owning interests, and were opposed to *Catholic emancipation* and *parliamentary reform.* The Tories were held together after the Napoleonic wars by *Liverpool,* but a more progressive wing favouring some moderate reform developed under Canning and Peel. The Tories were split by the passing of the *Roman Catholic Relief Act* and the *Whigs* came into power in 1830.

CONSERVATIVE PARTY →

Town and Country Planning Act, 1947, was the first really major attempt to control the use and development of the land in the interests of the whole community. Under the Act county councils have to prepare plans, revised every five years, for the development of their area and were given powers to acquire land by compulsory purchase, paying compensation to existing owners. Property owners have to obtain planning permission from the local authorities to use their land or property for some other purpose and to make alterations to buildings. The aim of the Act was to provide a balance between the conflicting needs of agriculture, industry, housing, roads, and recreation by providing cleaner, healthier cities and dispersing some industry and people to *new towns,* preserving the 'green belt' around towns, providing improved road networks, and maintaining large areas of agricultural land. But the soaring value of land, particularly in cities, has made it impossible to achieve some of these aims. In the centre of cities, councils often cannot exercise their powers of compulsory purchase because they cannot afford to pay the huge compensation. As a result many city centres have been developed by private speculators for office or commercial uses, and the existing residents and small shopkeepers have been squeezed out. An earlier attempt at town planning was made under the *Housing and Town Planning Act, 1919.*

Towns. By 1851 there were more people living in towns—50.6 per cent—than in the countryside for the first time ever mainly as a result of the increase in industry and commerce. The trend has continued ever since, so that by 1970 about 80 per cent of people were living in towns in England and Wales. Since the 1920s there has been an increasing drift of population towards the more prosperous south-east, where about one in three of the entire population of England now live. In an attempt to reduce overcrowding in existing cities, many *new towns* have been built since the Second World War. The population (in thousands) of some selected cities in the modern period are as follows:

	1801	1851	1901	1970
Birmingham	71	233	523	1,084
Bradford	13	104	280	292
Coventry	16	36	70	335
Liverpool	82	376	704	667
London	1,117	2,685	6,586	7,612
Manchester	75	303	645	590
Oldham	12	53	137	108
Sheffield	46	135	381	525
Wolverhampton	13	50	94	264

Townshend, Viscount (1674–1738), known as 'Turnip' Townshend. After being dismissed from Walpole's government in 1730, he retired to his estates at Raynham, Norfolk, to devote himself to farming. He grew turnips to provide winter fodder for cattle, instead of leaving the field fallow or bare, and introduced a new four-course rotation of crops. His importance has been much exaggerated. He was not the first British farmer to grow turnips as a fodder crop and his four-course rotation could be used only in a small part of the country where the soil and the climate were suitable.

← JETHRO TULL: ROBERT BAKEWELL →

Tractors, with petrol-engines, were first made in the United States in 1889 and were produced on a large scale by *Henry Ford* from 1915. Tractors were used on some British farms during the First World War, but by 1939 there were still only 50,000 tractors and nearly 650,000 horses. The use of tractors increased enormously during the Second World War. By 1966 there were nearly ½m. tractors on British farms and only 21,000 farm horses.

← PATRICK BELL: COMBINE HARVESTERS →

Trade Boards Act, 1909, set up boards in a number of *sweated industries* to fix minimum wages. The industries were tailoring, paper box-making, chain and lace making. The Act was extended in 1918 to all

low-paid trades and industries, where there was no effective union organization. By 1945, there were fifty-two trade boards.
WAGES COUNCILS→

Trade Disputes Act, 1906, reversed the 'Taff Vale judgment' of 1901 by exempting trade unions from civil actions for damages by employers for strikes or other acts, unless the acts were in themselves illegal. Union members were also given greater protection for peaceful picketing. The Act was passed by the Liberals, partly as a result of pressure from the twenty-nine M.P.s from the Labour party, formed in that year.
← TAFF VALE JUDGMENT

Trade Disputes and Trade Unions Act, 1927, weakened both the Labour party and the unions, following the failure of the *General Strike* of 1926. Union members were obliged to state that they wanted to pay a levy to a political party ('contracting in'), instead of 'contracting out' if they did not want to pay the levy. As a result, the Labour party lost about a third of its union subscriptions. The Act also made general strikes and sympathetic strikes in other industries illegal, and civil servants were banned from joining unions affiliated to the Trades Union Congress. The Act was totally repealed by the Labour government in 1946, restoring 'contracting out' and the right to have sympathetic and general strikes.
← TRADES UNION ACT, 1913

Trade Union Act, 1871, gave full legal recognition to unions and protection for their funds by allowing them to register as a *friendly society.* The Act was passed by Gladstone's government after a court case in 1867, when the Society of Boilermakers tried to sue an official of their union for taking union funds. The judge ruled that the unions were not recognized by law and could not, therefore, sue in the courts. The government, however, was also very concerned about increasing violence in unions, manifested in the *Sheffield outrages,* and passed the Criminal Law Amendment Act in the same year to restrict the use of violence.
CRIMINAL LAW AMENDMENT ACT, 1871 →

Trade Union Act, 1913, restored some of the unions' rights to support political activities (i.e. the Labour party). It allowed them to make contributions to a political party if the majority of members wanted them to do so, but it allowed individual members to 'contract out' of paying the political levy, which was kept separate from other subscriptions.

It was passed by the Liberals, after the *Osborne judgment* had stopped unions subscribing to political parties.

← OSBORNE JUDGMENT, 1909: TRADE DISPUTES AND TRADE UNIONS ACT, 1927 →

Trade union amalgamations. Four large trade unions were formed by mergers of a number of smaller unions between the two world wars. The Amalgamated Engineering Union, the National Union of Distributive and Allied Workers (later renamed the Union of Shop, Distributive and Allied Workers) and the Transport and General Workers' Union in 1921; and the National Union of General and Muncipal Workers in 1924. The Miners' Federation of Great Britain was formed in 1889 and renamed the National Union of Mineworkers in 1945 and the National Union of Railwaymen was formed in 1913. Between them these six unions now account for almost half of the total trade union membership.

TRADE UNIONS. Low wages, unemployment, the introduction of the *factory system* and the influence of the French revolution caused great industrial unrest at the end of the eighteenth century. As a result *Pitt* passed two *Combination Acts* in 1799 and 1800 which made it far more difficult for workers to form unions. Workers in the declining industries turned to *direct action* instead and there were *Luddite* riots in many different areas from 1811 to 1817. The Combination Acts were repealed in 1824. Ten years later there was an attempt to form a nationwide union for all workers—the *Grand National Consolidated Trades Union*—but it was a dismal failure. In the 1830s there was great unrest not only in the towns but also in the country, as the '*Swing' riots* of 1830 showed. The prosecution of the *Tolpuddle Martyrs* in 1834 demonstrated the government's basic hostility to the new union movement. Many workers turned to *Chartism*, hoping to achieve their aims by first reforming parliament, but that movement also ended in failure in 1848.

In 1851 the first of the new 'model' unions, the *Amalgamated Society of Engineers*, was formed. It set a pattern for the rest of the century and many similar nationally-organized, moderate trade unions were formed for skilled workers only. A central organization, the *Trades Union Congress*, held its first meeting in 1868. But not all individual members of these new unions were so moderate, as was shown in the Sheffield outrages of 1866–7 when some trade unionists planted bombs in the homes of fellow workers who refused to join their union. This led to Gladstone's government passing the *Criminal Law Amendment Act*,

1871, which made intimidation and picketing illegal. Gladstone, however, was not opposed to unions themselves—only to violence—and in the same year passed the *Trade Union Act* which gave unions greater legal recognition. The right of peaceful picketing was restored by Disraeli in 1875.

Unions still existed primarily for skilled industrial workers, but in the 1870s *Joseph Arch* successfully organized a national union for farm workers and *Emma Paterson* campaigned for trade unions for women. After the successful *match girls' strike* of 1888 and the *London* dock strike in the following year more unions were formed for unskilled workers. Many of the younger union leaders, like *Tom Mann*, were dedicated socialists and in 1900 the trade unions combined with some Socialist groups and parties to form the Labour Representation Committee, which became the *Labour party* in 1906. There was still great opposition to trade unions among many members of the establishment and atttempts to curb their powers were made by two legal rulings before the First World War. The *Taff Vale judgment* of 1901 made unions pay damages to companies for losses caused by strikes, and the *Osborne judgment* of 1909 stopped unions from contributing to Labour party funds. These judgments were reversed by the *Trade Disputes Act, 1906*, and the *Trade Union Act, 1913*, respectively.

In spite of these attacks, membership of unions grew fairly steadily, increasing from 1,600,000 in 1892 to 4,100,000 in 1914. There was a wave of big *strikes* from 1910 to 1912. During the First World War many more workers joined unions and by 1920 the total membership was 8,300,000. *Trade union amalgamations* created much bigger and more powerful unions and gave their leaders, like *Ernest Bevin*, a new authority. But the failure of the *Triple Alliance* in the miners' strike of 1921 and of the *General Strike* in 1926 were both great blows to the union movement. These failures, combined with the great unemployment in the *depression*, reduced total membership to 4,400,000 by 1932.

During the Second World War, membership started to rise again and it has increased fairly steadily ever since so that by 1970 there were 11m. members. Although the powers of the T.U.C. leaders have increased as a result, they have had to face an increasing challenge from inside the movement from more militant shop stewards. Shop-floor leaders came to prominence in the First World War, calling the first *unofficial strike* in 1915. The T.U.C. has also had to face an increasing challenge from outside, and the *Industrial Relations Act, 1972*, caused conflict between the unions and the Conservative government.

The total number of unions declined from 1,279 in 1893 to 481 in 1970, mainly through amalgamations. The existence of so many smaller unions, rapid changes in technology, and increasing fears of *unemployment* have caused many demarcation disputes over which union has the right to do a particular job in recent times.

Trades Union Congress (T.U.C.), the central organization representing trade unions, which held its first meeting in Manchester in 1868, attended by 33 delegates. At the meeting in the following year in Birmingham, there were 40 delegates representing about 250,000 members. It was decided to form a parliamentary committee to make known members' views on proposed laws dealing with trade unions. This committee remained the only permanent central body until 1921, when a stronger General Council of 36 members was formed. The principal officer of the T.U.C. is the general secretary.

Trams. The first tramway, with trams pulled by horses, was opened in London in 1861 and by 1895 there were just over 1,000 miles of tramways in various cities carrying 650m. people a year. In 1895, the first electric tramway was opened in Bristol and by 1919, electric trams throughout the country were carrying nearly 5,000m. passengers a year. With their cheap fares, they enabled some workmen to live in new suburbs on the outskirts of the cities. Between the two world wars, many of them were replaced by motor buses. The last London tram was withdrawn in 1952.

Transport Act, 1947, passed by the Labour government, to nationalize railways, most canals, and road haulage. The latter was denationalized by the Conservatives in 1953.
← RAILWAYS ACT, 1921: BEECHING REPORT, 1963 →

Transportation of convicted men, women and children to New South Wales, Australia, started in 1788, when a former naval officer, Arthur Phillip, who had been appointed governor of the colony, landed at Port Jackson with 700 convicts. It was started to Tasmania in 1803. Convicts either worked for the government by building roads, barracks or ports, or were sent to work for free settlers on farms, where conditions varied greatly. Some were put in chain gangs to work on the roads, or sent to punishment camps. Many of them had been transported for what would now be considered trivial offences, such as stealing a few shillings. Others were transported for political reasons, like the *Tolpuddle Martyrs*, Irish agitators, like the leaders of the *Young Ireland* movement, and Chartists. The sentence was for 7 years, 14 years or for life. Very few ever returned home. Transportation to New South Wales

was stopped in 1840, to Tasmania in 1853, and to Western Australia in 1867, mainly because of protests from free emigrants in Australia. In all, 160,663 people were transported, including 23,500 women. Convicts had earlier been transported to America, but that stopped after the American Declaration of Independence, 1776.
NEWGATE PRISON →

Treaty of Nanking, 1842, ended the British *Opium War* against China and gave Hong Kong to Britain.

Treaty of Versailles, 1919, the main peace treaty at the end of the *First World War*. It declared that Germany was responsible for the war and ordered it to pay reparations or damages, to the Allies, later fixed at £6,600m., most of which was never paid. It limited the German army to 100,000 men, with no tanks or aircraft, and put its former colonies under the control of Allied powers as League of Nations *mandates.* Alsace-Lorraine, in north-eastern France, taken by Germany in 1871, was handed back to France; the Rhineland, a 30-mile-wide strip of territory on the right bank of the Rhine, was demilitarized; and East Prussia was separated from the rest of Germany by the Polish corridor, a strip of territory which gave Poland access to the Baltic. The port of Danzig at the mouth of the Vistula, which had formerly been Prussian, was put under international control. Other treaties dismantled the Austro-Hungarian and Ottoman (Turkish) empires. Austria and Hungary were made separate countries; Czechoslovakia and Jugoslavia were created; and the Turks lost most of their former colonies. The reversal of the treaty became one of the main aims of *Hitler* and the German people.
← FOURTEEN POINTS: LEAGUE OF NATIONS →

Treaty of Vienna, 1815, redrew the map of Europe after the defeat of Napoleon. One of its main aims was to prevent further French aggression by creating a stronger Kingdom of the Netherlands, consisting of Holland and Belgium, and a German confederation of thirty-nine loosely-linked states. Piedmont in northern Italy was also increased in size. Britain gained the Cape of Good Hope, South Africa; Mauritius in the Indian Ocean; Ceylon; Heligoland in the North Sea; Malta; and Trinidad, Saint Lucia and Tobago in the West Indies.
QUADRUPLE ALLIANCE, 1815 →

Trevithick, Richard (1771–1833), engineer and inventor, born at Illogan, Cornwall. He made a high-pressure steam engine, which could develop up to 100 horsepower and in 1802 exhibited the first successful *steam carriage* near Euston Square, London. Two years later, he built the first successful steam locomotive, which hauled five wagons from Penydarren to Abercynon, Wales, a distance of ten miles. He also built a steam threshing machine and tried, unsuccessfully, to build a tunnel under the Thames. He worked as a mining engineer in South America from 1816 to 1827.

JOHN BLENKINSOP →

Triple Alliance formed between three powerful unions—the miners', transport workers' and railwaymen's—in 1914 to 1915 to take joint action in support of each other in disputes. The First World War delayed its being put into operation. In 1921, the miners' demand for higher wages resulted in a lock-out by the owners. The other two unions agreed to start a sympathetic strike on Saturday, 16 April 1921, but on the previous day decided not to do so. The miners felt betrayed and 15 April became known as 'Black Friday'.

BLACK FRIDAY →

Triple Alliance, 1882. A secret treaty between Germany, Austria-Hungary and Italy, under which Germany and Austria-Hungary agreed to help Italy if it were attacked by France, and Italy to help Germany if it were attacked by France. But in 1914, Italy refused to help Germany, because France had not been the aggressor and came into the war on the Allied side in 1915.

TRIPLE ENTENTE →

Triple Entente, the informal collaboration between Britain, France and Russia in the seven years preceding the First World War. It was based on the Dual Alliance between France and Russia, of 1891, which was strengthened by a secret military agreement of 1893 to give military aid to each other if either were attacked by Germany; the *Anglo-French Entente, 1904*; and the *Anglo-Russian Entente, 1907*. The three powers did not make a military alliance until after the outbreak of the war, when they agreed on 3 September 1914, not to make a separate peace, though the Russians did so by the Treaty of Brest-Litovsk, 1918, after the Bolshevik revolution.

← TRIPLE ALLIANCE

Tuke, William (1732–1822), Quaker merchant, who founded the Retreat at York to treat the mentally ill with kindness instead of the brutality or neglect which was common at the time. Most mental patients were then kept in straitjackets day and night—like George III at the end of his life or chained up like beasts in dark, filthy cells.

Tull, Jethro (1674–1741), who invented a drill to sow seeds in rows, instead of scattering them by hand, so that fewer seeds were wasted. He also designed a horse-drawn hoe, which could go along the rows and keep the growing plants free from weeds. The drill and horse-drawn hoe were not widely used until the nineteenth century.
VISCOUNT TOWNSHEND →

Turnpike roads. Roads with a turnpike gate—or a bar—at each end, where vehicles and horsemen had to pay a small fee, or toll, every time they passed through. The roads were maintained and run by turnpike trusts, groups of local men who had obtained a special Act of Parliament to build the road. The first Act was passed in 1663, but the majority of Acts were passed in the eighteenth century, mainly because of the demand for better roads from commerce and industry. In 1837 there were 1,100 turnpike trusts with 22,000 miles of road, but the number gradually started to decline because of competition from the *railways.* Most of the main roads were neglected again until the twentieth century. Road tolls were abolished in London in 1871 and the last ended in Anglesey in 1895. Tolls are still charged on some bridges and ferries in Britain and also on some motorways abroad.

'Two nations'—the rich and the poor. A phrase used by *Benjamin Disraeli*, the Conservative, to describe early Victorian society. In his novel, 'Sybil', published in 1845, he wrote of: 'two nations: between whom there is no intercourse and no sympathy; who are ignorant of each other's habits, thoughts and feelings, as if they were dwellers in different zones, or inhabitants of different planets . . .' He blamed the industrial revolution for creating extremes of wealth and poverty.

U

U.D.I., unilateral declaration of independence made by Ian Smith, prime minister of *Rhodesia*, in 1965, after full independence had been refused by Britain.

Ulster, or Northern Ireland, consisting of six counties in the north-east of Ireland, was created in 1920, just before the *Irish Free State* was established in the south. It remained part of the United Kingdom and was given limited powers of self-government through its parliament at Stormont. It also has 12 M.P.s to represent it at Westminster. Ulster, with its shipbuilding and linen industries, had long been the most prosperous part of Ireland. It is dominated by the Protestants, but there is a large Catholic minority of about one-third of the population, who were discriminated against in many spheres. In the 1960s a Catholic civil rights movement started to practise *civil disobedience* to obtain equal rights in local elections, housing, employment etc. Violent clashes between Catholics and Protestants occurred in Londonderry and Belfast in August, 1969. Shortly afterwards, the *Irish Republican Army* renewed its operations in Ulster to bring about the final elimination of British rule in Ireland. Disturbances still continued in 1973, with bomb attacks and assassinations by both Protestants and Catholics. Many hundreds of people have been killed. Stormont was dissolved in 1972 and direct rule from London was instituted. (Ulster, before 1920, was composed of nine counties—Antrim, Armagh, Down, Fermanagh, Londonderry, Tyrone, Cavan, Donegal and Monaghan. Only the first six became part of Northern Ireland, and the last three became part of the Irish Free State, now the Republic of Ireland.)

Ulster Volunteer Force, a private army of Protestants in Northern Ireland formed in 1913 by *Edward Carson*, a Protestant lawyer, to resist *Irish Home Rule* by force if necessary. They were supported by some members of the Conservative and Unionist party in Britain and also attracted sympathy among some British army officers, which was demonstrated in the *Curragh incident*. The Catholics replied by forming the *Irish Volunteers*.

Unconditional surrender. The Allies' terms for ending the Second World War, announced by President Roosevelt during the Casablanca conference with Churchill in January 1943. The enemy countries had to surrender totally, without making any conditions. Critics claim that it helped to lengthen the war, by weakening moderates in the enemy countries who might have been willing to make a compromise peace; but there is not much evidence for this.

Underground railways. The first in the world was opened in 1863 between Paddington and Moorgate in London. It was built just below street level and steam trains were used. In 1890 the first deep-level Tube, using electric trains, was opened between King William Street and Stockwell in London. It is now part of the Northern line.

UNEMPLOYMENT is estimated to have varied between 2 and 10 per cent between the middle of the nineteenth century and the outbreak of the First World War. The worst period in modern times was during the inter-war *depression*. Between 1921 and 1938, unemployment never fell below 9.6 per cent. The worst year was 1932 when 2,843,000 people were without work—22 per cent of the total working population. There were still nearly 1m. unemployed in 1940, after the Second World War had started, but the total fell sharply after that. After the war, unemployment remained at a fairly low level, never exceeding 500,000, although it rose temporarily to over 2m. during the *fuel crisis* of March, 1947. In 1963, it reached 573,000 but fell sharply again, but it started to rise again from 1967 and by 1971 it had reached 1m. It started to fall again in 1972.

To help workers find new jobs *Labour exchanges* were opened in 1909, and government aid for *depressed areas* with particularly high rates of unemployment, were provided from the 1930s. The first workers were given State insurance against unemployment by the *National Insurance Act, 1911*, and *redundancy payments* were started in 1965.

United Nations Organization. An international organization, set up in October 1945, with the aims of avoiding war, preserving the fundamental rights of human beings, and promoting the economic and social advancement of all peoples. Its headquarters is in New York. The United Nations is open to all 'peace-loving nations'. It has a security council consisting of the Big Five—the United States, Russia, Britain, France and China—and a number of smaller powers elected for two years. A general assembly of all member-nations normally meets once a year. The chief official, the Secretary-General, serves for five years. The original hopes for the United Nations have not been fulfilled. The Security Council, which was designed to be the main body, was weakened from the start, because the Big Five each had a veto which enabled them to block any resolution which they disliked. This power was used increasingly by Russia as the *cold war* developed between the Eastern and Western powers after the end of the Second World War. Until 1971, Communist China was excluded from the United Nations and China's seat in the security council was held by the Nationalist government, based on Formosa, an island off the Chinese mainland. (The Nationalists had been defeated by the Chinese Communists under Mao Tse-tung in the civil war which ended in 1949.)

Unlike its predecessor, the League of Nations, the United Nations can call upon member-states to provide armed forces to help keep the peace or to restore it. (Originally, it was planned that the United Nations would have armed forces of its own, but this idea came to nothing because of disagreements between East and West.) The peace-keeping operations of the United Nations in the Congo, in Cyprus, and in the Middle East, have had only a limited success, and both Russia and France have refused to pay for some of these operations. *Sanctions* against Rhodesia had also not been very effective up to 1973.

The big powers have always tended to ignore United Nations resolutions when they have conflicted with their own interests, as Russia did in 1956 over the Hungarian uprising. More recently, smaller powers have started to do the same, too. To bypass the disagreements between the big powers in the security council, the general assembly was given more power. This worked for a time, but became less effective after so many new nations were admitted that they could dominate the general assembly if they were united. The United Nations has done some good work with refugees, education, and aid for developing countries, but it has been greatly hampered by a severe shortage of money and it still remains anything but united. (See also *Disarmament Commission*; *International Court of Justice*.)

← LEAGUE OF NATIONS

Universities. At the beginning of the nineteenth century, there were only two universities in England, Oxford and Cambridge. Only men who belonged to the Church of England were allowed to take degrees. The standards of scholarship were low; science was neglected; and many of the students were more interested in gambling and drinking than in study. The two universities started to improve from the middle of the nineteenth century. The government passed Acts to reform the finances of the universities. Reforms in teaching and a greater concentration on research and scholarship were introduced by such men as Benjamin Jowett (1817–93), Master of Balliol College, Oxford. But nonconformists and women were still not allowed to take degrees. In 1854 men of any religion were allowed to take lower degrees at Oxford; Cambridge followed suit in 1856. But it was not until the *Universities Tests Act* of 1871 that any man, regardless of his religion, was allowed to take higher degrees and to hold office in the universities. The first hall of residence for women students, which eventually became Newnham College, was opened at Cambridge by *Anne Jemima Clough* in 1871. Lady Margaret Hall was established for women at Oxford in 1879. But women were not allowed to take degrees at Oxford until 1920 and until 1921 at Cambridge, where, however, they were not admitted as full members of the university until 1948.

Meanwhile, a number of other universities had been opened in the provinces and in the capital. In 1828, Lord Brougham (1778–1868) and others founded University College, London, to provide higher education for men regardless of their religion. The Anglicans founded King's College, London, in the same year and the two colleges became part of London University, which was set up by Act of Parliament in 1836. It gave degrees to non-members of the Church of England from its foundation, and to women from 1878. The University of Durham was opened in 1833 and the Victoria University of Manchester in 1880. At the beginning of the present century a number of new universities were set up in industrial towns—Birmingham, Liverpool, Leeds, Sheffield and Bristol. By 1939, there were twelve universities and five university colleges in England and Wales. Many new universities have been created since the Second World War, particularly after the *Robbins report* of 1963.

Four universities were established in Scotland before the sixteenth century and the University of Wales was founded in 1893. Trinity College, Dublin, was founded in 1591 and Queen's University, Belfast in 1909.

Universities Tests Act, 1871, passed by Gladstone to please his *non-conformist* supporters. It allowed a man of any religion or of none to hold office in the universities of Oxford, Cambridge and Durham. The universities had to provide religious instruction for undergraduates who were members of the Church of England.

← TEST AND CORPORATION ACTS

University Extension Classes were started by Professor Stuart of Cambridge in 1873 to provide courses by university lecturers in industrial towns. The first courses were held at Derby, Leicester and Nottingham.

← MECHANICS' INSTITUTES: WORKERS' EDUCATIONAL ASSOCIATION →

Unofficial strikes are called, not by the official union leaders, but by shop stewards, who work with and represent the men and women on the factory floor. The number of unofficial strikes has increased considerably in recent years, mainly because *trade union amalgamations* have tended to make union leaders more remote from the men they represent, so that militant shop stewards have been able to exercise greater influence within the factory or plant. The first unofficial strike occurred in 1915 over a pay claim among workers on the Clyde after most official union leaders had co-operated with the government during the First World War, by agreeing to replace strikes by compulsory arbitration. (See also *Strikes.*)

Utilitarianism, the philsopohy of *Jeremy Bentham* which judged actions and institutions by their usefulness in providing the 'greatest good for the greatest number'. His philosophy had a great influence on many nineteenth-century reformers.

V

V1, or flying bomb. Pilotless, jet-propelled planes, loaded with about 1 ton of explosives, which were used to attack London and the south-east towards the end of the Second World War. About 10,000 were launched, the first one on 13 June 1944. It was one of Hitler's 'secret weapons', with which he hoped to win the war, but before the attacks ended in August 1944, about 70 per cent were being brought down by anti-aircraft guns and fighter planes. (See next entry.)

V2 rockets, were developed by the German scientist, Wernher von Braun (born 1912). More than 1,000 were sent against Britain, the first on 8 September 1944. They were a more serious threat than V1s as there was then no defence against them, except bombing the launching sites. After the war, von Braun went to the United States, where he helped to develop the American space programme.
← VI: SPACE TRAVEL →

Vaccination against smallpox, by inoculation with the similar disease of cowpox, was introduced by *Edward Jenner* in 1796–8. It was provided free from 1840 and was made compulsory for all babies in 1853. As vaccination very occasionally produced other diseases, parents were allowed to claim exemption from 1898, if they believed that their children's health might be affected. Compulsory vaccination ended in 1948. Smallpox, which used to kill thousands of people, has virtually disappeared from Europe, though it still occurs in many parts of the East. The last serious *epidemic* in Britain occurred in 1871–2.

Value Added Tax (V.A.T.) was introduced in Britain in 1973 to bring it into line with other members of the *European Community*. It was levied at a rate of 10 per cent at each stage of manufacture and distribution, according to the value that has been added to the goods (e.g. a wholesaler who bought goods from the manufacturer for £300 and sold them to a retailer for £400 would have to pay £10 tax—10 per cent of the difference between the selling and buying prices). It is also charged on services, like accountant's fees, meals in cafés and

restaurants etc. Some goods, like fresh foods, are exempt, and others are zero-rated, which is of benefit to exporters as they can claim back from the Customs and Excise the tax which has already been paid. V.A.T. replaced both purchase tax and selective employment tax, which had to be paid by the employer for each employee in many service industries such as shops.
← PURCHASE TAX

VE Day (Victory in Europe), 8 May 1945, on the day following Germany's unconditional surrender at *Eisenhower's* headquarters in Germany. It brought the Second World War to an end in Europe. *Hitler* had by then already committed suicide.
VJ DAY →

Velocipede, an early bicycle, with a front wheel slightly larger than the one at the back, which was used in the 1860s. The pedals were attached to the front wheel.
← DANDY HORSE: PENNY FARTHING →

Victoria, Queen (1819–1901). She succeeded her uncle, William IV, in 1837, and played an important part in both social life, where she set the pattern of Victorian respectability, and in political life. She was largely responsible for having Palmerston dismissed as Foreign Secretary in 1851, and made Rosebery prime minister without consulting the outgoing prime minister, Gladstone, when he resigned in 1894. Her favourite statesman was Disraeli, who flattered her and made her Empress of India in 1876. She married *Prince Albert* in 1840 and remained in mourning for the rest of her life, after he died in 1861.

Visible exports, the total amount of goods of all kinds sold to foreign countries. In 1970 they were worth over £8,000m.
INVISIBLE EXPORTS →

VJ Day (Victory in Japan), officially celebrated on 2 September, 1945, after the dropping of two *atom bombs* on Japan in August. It brought the Second World War to an end in the Far East.
← VE DAY

Voluntary schools were founded by religious bodies early in the nineteenth century to provide poor children with some elementary education in reading, writing and arithmetic. The National Society (for promoting the Education of the Poor in the Principles of the

Established Church) was founded by the *Rev. Andrew Bell* in 1811. Religious instruction, based on Church of England principles, played a prominent part. The Royal Lancasterian Society was established in 1808 and changed its name to the British and Foreign School Society in 1814. It was based on the work of a Quaker, *Joseph Lancaster*, and its religious instruction was non-denominational. There was rivalry between the two bodies, because of their different religious views, but both of them used a *monitorial system* of education, in which the older, brighter children taught the younger ones. In 1833, the government made a grant of money to education for the first time by giving the societies £20,000 to build 'school houses'. The importance of voluntary schools declined with the growth of State schools after the *Education Act, 1870*, but they have continued to receive grants from the government. There are now about 10,000 Church of England schools and about 2,000 Roman Catholic schools.
PAYMENT BY RESULTS →

W

Wages Councils were set up in 1945 to fix minimum rates of pay in all industries in which there were no strong trade unions. Over 3m. workers are now covered.
← TRADE BOARDS ACT, 1909

Wakefield, Edward Gibbon (1796–1862), advocate of planned emigration to the colonies. He believed that a balanced selection of all social classes should be encouraged to emigrate, not just the poor and adventurous; and that land prices in the colonies should be made high, so that the government could use some of the money from the sale of land to bring out more settlers. He first put forward his ideas in a pamphlet published in 1829, while he was serving a three-year prison sentence in Newgate for abducting an heiress. He formed the South Australian Association in 1834 and the New Zealand Association in 1837, which carried out a successful planned emigration to Canterbury province in the south island. Wakefield accompanied the Earl of Durham as an adviser on his trip to Canada and played some part in producing the important *Durham report*.

Wall Street crash, 1929, when a loss of business confidence led to a panic in Wall Street, the financial centre of New York. Share prices fell rapidly on the Stock Exchange; and many banks and firms went bankrupt. The crash had great financial effects in Britain and Europe and was one of the main causes of the depression of the 1930s.

Walter, John (1766–1847), chief proprietor of 'The Times' from 1812, and the son of the founder of the newspaper of the same name. He was joint editor of the paper with Thomas Barnes (1785–1841) from 1815 to 1841. The newspaper's independent opinions often brought it into conflict with the government and caused the paper to be known as the 'Thunderer' and Barnes as 'the most powerful man in the country'. John Walter was the first newspaper owner to appoint a war correspondent, Henry Crabb Robinson (1775–1867), who covered the Peninsular War in Portugal and Spain from 1808–9. His reports brought 'The Times' into conflict with the *Duke of Wellington*, who complained that they had given military information to the enemy. In 1814, Walter installed the first printing press, powered by steam, which could produce 1,100 sheets an hour, against 250 by the old manual methods.

JOHN DELANE →

Washington Conference, of 1921–2, called by President Harding of the United States in an attempt to halt the naval arms race between the great maritime powers. It was attended by representatives of Britain, France, Italy, Portugal, Belgium, Holland, Japan and China. It was agreed that the size of battleships should be limited to 35,000 tons; that no capital ships (battleships and cruisers) should be built for ten years; and that Britain, the United States, Japan and France should not strengthen the defences of their island possessions in the Pacific. As a result of the conference, the *Anglo-Japanese Alliance* was allowed to lapse.

LONDON NAVAL CONFERENCES →

Water supplies. Until the middle of the nineteenth century, water was in very short supply. Most people had to make do with water from a well or a standpipe, a brook or a river, or buy it in a bucket from a water carrier. Not all of the middle classes had a cold water tap in their home before 1840 and even where piped water supplies existed, they were often polluted. Of fifty towns inspected in 1842 only six had pure water supplies. Impure water helped to cause *epidemics* of cholera and typhoid, and made it difficult for people to keep themselves, and their homes, clean. In the 1840s some towns started to build public baths for the poor, who paid 1*d*. or 2*d*. for a bath, and for the rich, who paid a higher charge. In some cases the water from the rich man's bath drained off after he had used it into the poor man's bath. An Act was passed in 1846 which allowed towns to build baths and wash-houses, where people could wash their clothes. They were built in many towns. Baths and shower baths started to be installed in the homes of the rich from the 1850s. Drinking fountains to provide pure water for the poor were built in many towns from the 1860s. But it was not until much later that piped supplies of pure water became common in working-class homes and even in 1961 there were still almost a quarter of homes in Britain without a bath or a shower.

Watson-Watt, Sir Robert (born 1892), developer of *radar*, born at Brechin, Angus, and educated at Dundee and St Andrew's University. After working at the Department of Scientific and Industrial Research, he moved in 1933 to the National Physical Laboratory, where he developed radar. A chain of radar stations was built in the south of England before the Second World War. These were used to great effect in the *Blitz* to warn British fighters of the approach of German bombers. Radar was also used to guide fighter planes against German bombers at night, and later in the war to guide bombers to their targets in Germany. It was also used to direct anti-aircraft guns and fighter planes against flying bombs, or *V1*s, and by the Navy to track down submarines. Watson-Watt was knighted in 1942.

Watt, James (1736–1819), mathematical instrument maker, born Greenock, Scotland, who invented the first efficient *steam engine*, which played an essential part in the *industrial revolution.* In 1769, after several years of experiment with models of *Newcomen* engines, he took out his first patent. The main feature of Watt's steam engine was the separate condenser, in which the steam was cooled, so that the cylinder remained hot all the time and no heat was wasted. This made it more efficient than Newcomen's 'atmospheric' engine and more economical in the use of fuel. In 1775, Watt went into partnership with *Matthew Boulton* at Soho, Birmingham, and in the following year produced his first satisfactory steam engine. He was greatly assisted in doing so by *John Wilkinson*'s boring machine, invented in 1775, which allowed cylinders to be made with such great accuracy that no steam escaped. Watt made many further improvements to his steam engines, including a centrifugal governor for automatically regulating the speed. In 1784 he built a rotative engine, which could be used to drive machinery in factories and the first one was installed in the Albion Flour Mills, London, by *John Rennie.* He retired in 1800 when his original patent expired.

← THOMAS NEWCOMEN

Webb, Beatrice, (1858–1943) and **Sidney James** (1859–1947), Socialists, married in 1891, who were influential members of the *Fabian Society.* They wrote many books together on social, economic and historical subjects, and served on a number of Royal Commissions. Sidney Webb, who was also at various times a civil servant, a professor, Labour M.P. and minister, was made Lord Passfield in 1929.

Wedgwood, Josiah (1730–95), who developed the *factory system* in the pottery industry, born at Burslem, Staffordshire. He started work at the age of nine and opened his own works at Burslem in 1759. Ten years later he moved out to Etruria, a village he had built three miles away. He improved communications to and from the Potteries by having two *turnpike roads* built, and by helping to finance the *Grand Trunk Canal,* which ran past Etruria. Barges brought in clay and other materials and took away the finished pots. His cream-coloured pottery, with its attractive shapes, achieved great fame. He was appointed the Queen's potter in 1762. Wedgwood's is still one of the main pottery manufacturers.

'Weekly Political Register', or 'Twopenny Trash', an influential periodical written almost entirely by *William Cobbett* from 1802 to 1835. Its circulation among working men increased greatly after Cobbett reduced the price from 1*s.* to 2*d.* in 1816.

Welfare state. A system under which the State accepts responsibility for the welfare of its citizens in housing, education, health and social security and provides much of the money out of taxes for these services. The beginnings of the welfare state can be seen in the Liberal reforms of 1906–11, including the introduction of *old age pensions* in 1908 and the *National Insurance Act, 1911.* But it was really created by the Labour government after the Second World War with a massive extension of social services as recommended in the *Beveridge report* and the creation of a *National Health Service.* The *Education Act, 1944* and the *Town and Country Planning Act, 1947,* were other measures of 'welfare' reform. Since the welfare state was created, there have been increasing criticisms by some people that it is wasteful to give universal benefits to all, instead of more selective benefits to those who really need them.

Wellington, Duke of (1769–1852), one of the few great military commanders ever to become prime minister in Britain. Born Arthur Wellesley, he was educated at Eton and became an army officer in

1787, serving in India both as a soldier and an administrator. During the Napoleonic wars he won his great victories over the French in the Peninsular War of 1809 to 1814 in Spain and Portugal and was created the Duke of Wellington on his return to England. In June 1815, he helped to defeat Napoleon, who had returned from Elba, at the Battle of Waterloo and was granted £20,000 by parliament. He had been a Tory M.P. from 1806 to 1809 and resumed his political career, holding office under Liverpool from 1818 to 1827. He resigned when the more moderate Canning came into power in 1827, but was appointed prime minister himself in 1828. Through Peel's persuasion he passed the *Roman Catholic Relief Act, 1829*, even though he was basically opposed to Catholic emancipation. This offended Tories of the old school and they combined with the Whigs to vote him out of office in 1830, when Grey came into power. Wellington was a determined opponent of all parliamentary reform. His opposition to the First Reform Act, 1832, caused crowds of workers to stone his home in London. Wellington was Foreign Secretary in Peel's short-lived ministry of 1834 to 1835, and minister without portfolio during Peel's second ministry of 1841 to 1846. During the presentation of the last Chartist petition in 1848, he was put in charge of the defence of London to protect the capital from the expected riots, which, however, never took place.

← GEORGE CANNING: SIR ROBERT PEEL →

Wesley, John (1703–91), founder of *Methodism*, born at Epworth, Lincolnshire, the son of a parson. He was educated at Oxford and became a clergyman in 1725. Four years later he became a fellow of Lincoln College, Oxford, where he became the leader of a small club of undergraduates, formed by his younger brother Charles (1707–88), who was later to write over 6,000 hymns. The members of the club studied and prayed so strictly and methodically that they were soon called 'Methodists'. In 1736 he went out to Georgia as a missionary, and became acquainted with some members of a Protestant sect, called Moravians, who believed that a man could be saved in an instant from the misery of sin and converted to joy by trusting in Christ for salvation. On his return to England, Wesley experienced this conversion at a Moravian meeting in Aldersgate Street, London, on 24 May 1738. From this time on, he devoted his life to taking this good news to other people. Many clergymen refused to allow him to preach in their churches, so he often preached in the open air which attracted a new kind of audience. Before he died, he preached over 50,000 sermons in all parts of the country. Groups of a dozen people or so, called classes, were formed to collect donations, confess their sins, do good works, and pray together. At first, Wesley and his followers remained within the Church of England, but the *established church* became increasingly hostile, and refused to ordain Methodists. In 1784, Wesley started to ordain his own ministers, which marked the beginning of the final break with the Church of England. By the time he died there were over 130,000 Methodists.

Wheat Act, 1932, subsidized farmers by giving them a guaranteed price of 45*s.* a quarter for wheat, to protect them in the agricultural slump between the two world wars. One of the reasons for the fall in prices was the cheap food brought in from the Commonwealth by the *Ottawa agreement, 1932*; another reason was the 'dumping' of cheap food from the United States. Subsidies to farmers were later given for oats and barley.
← CORN PRODUCTION ACT, 1917: AGRICULTURE ACT, 1947 →

Wheatstone, Sir Charles (1802–75), who developed the first modern means of communications—the *electric telegraph.* With Sir William Fothergill Cooke (1806–79), he patented an electric telegraph in 1837, at about the same time as it was invented in some other countries. It allowed messages to be sent along a wire to a receiving instrument which had needles pointing to letters on a dial. It was first demonstrated at Euston Square station, London, in July 1837. Soon afterwards, it was adopted by the Great Western railway. Sir Charles, who started his working life as a maker of musical instruments, invented many other things, including the English concertina. He is also known for the Wheatstone bridge, an electrical circuit which tests the ratios of two resistances. He was appointed a professor at King's College, London, in 1834, and was knighted in 1868.
SAMUEL MORSE →

Whigs, the party which wanted to limit the powers of the monarch after the Revolution of 1688 and increase those of parliament. They were in power for much of the eighteenth century, but were replaced by the *Tories* from 1783 to 1830. When the Whigs got back into power in 1830, under *Grey*—who was prime minister until 1834—and *Melbourne*—prime minister from 1835 to 1841—they introduced a number of reforms. These included the *First Reform Act, 1832*; the abolition of *slavery* in the British empire, 1833; the first effective *Factory Act, 1833*; the *Municipal Corporations Reform Act, 1835*; and the *Registration of Births, Marriages and Deaths, 1836.* The *penny*

post was also introduced in 1840. The Whig nobility, such as Russell and Palmerston, continued to exercise great power into the second half of the nineteenth century.
LIBERAL PARTY →

Whittle, Sir Frank (born 1907), inventor, born at Leamington. He joined the R.A.F. as a boy apprentice and was educated at R.A.F. College, Cranwell, and Cambridge University. From 1928 to 1929, he served with a fighter squadron, and from 1931 to 1932 he was a test pilot. He started experimenting with jet engines, but did not receive much official encouragement until he was put on special duties to continue with his experiments in 1937. The first flight of a British jet plane, a Gloster, took place in May 1941. Whittle retired from the R.A.F. as an air commodore in 1948 and was knighted in the same year.
JET PLANES →

Whitworth, Sir Joseph (1803–87), engineer, born at Stockport, Cheshire, who revolutionized the engineering industry by making it common practice to have standard measures, accurate gauges, precision tools, and machine parts which were exactly alike, and therefore interchangeable. In 1833, he opened his own business in Manchester to make only machine tools, such as lathes, which are used to make other machines. Because of his high standards of accuracy, his planing, shaping, drilling and boring machines and lathes soon obtained a world-wide reputation. His micrometer, which was able to detect differences of one millionth of an inch, won a prize at the *Great Exhibition* of 1851. His standardized bolts and screw threads were adopted throughout Britain and helped to open the way to *mass production* methods of manufacture. He learnt many of his techniques from *Henry Maudslay*, but improved and developed them. From 1854 he turned increasingly to armaments manufacture. His rifle, invented in 1857, was adopted by the War Office in 1869. He was made a baronet in that year.
← JAMES NASMYTH

Wilberforce, William (1759–1833), anti-slavery campaigner, born in Hull, the son of a wealthy merchant. He was educated at Cambridge, where he came under the influence of *William Pitt*, who was a fellow student. As a young man he inherited a fortune. He was elected M.P. for Hull in 1780, and for Yorkshire in 1784. In that year he was converted to *Evangelical* Christianity and he became one of the leaders of the *Clapham sect*. With Pitt's encouragement he campaigned for the abolition of slave-trading. After many unsuccessful attempts a Bill to abolish slave-trading in the British colonies was passed in 1807. He then fought for the abolition of slavery itself. Eventually, in 1833, a Bill to free all slaves in the Empire was passed, eight years after Wilberforce had retired from parliament because of bad health. The slave owners were given £20m. compensation—about £37 per slave, which was then the current market price. Although Wilberforce gave away much of his fortune to various charities, and as a young man supported parliamentary and factory reform, he became increasingly conservative with age. He was the leader of the anti-slavery movement in parliament until he retired, but there were many others who were just as active in the campaign outside parliament, particularly *Thomas Clarkson.*

Wilkinson, John (1728–1808), inventor and ironmaster, who opened his first blast furnace for making iron at Bilston, Staffordshire in about 1748. His greatest invention was the boring machine, 1775, which was used by *James Watt* in making his steam engines and also for making cannons. In 1779, in association with *Abraham Darby III*, Wilkinson built the first cast-iron bridge over the Severn and in 1787 launched the first cast-iron boat on the Severn. He patented a method of making lead pipes in 1790, which were used for water pipes.

Wilson, James Harold (born 1916), President of the Board of Trade, 1947–51, and Labour prime minister, 1964–70, when a considerable number of reforms were passed, including the *Race Relations Acts* and the *Rent Act, 1965*. The *devaluation* of the £ in 1967 helped to restore Britain's *balance of payments*, but the long-standing economic problems of Britain were not solved.
← CLEMENT ATTLEE

Window tax was introduced at the end of the seventeenth century and reached its highest level in 1808, when the tax on houses with six, or fewer, windows was 8*s.* a year and proportionately more for houses with a larger number. As a result, the windows of many houses were bricked up and workers' houses were built with as few windows as possible, which made them dark and unhealthy because of the lack of ventilation. The tax was abolished in 1851.

Wollstonecraft, Mary (1759–97), one of the first women to advocate equal rights and opportunities for women. She was born near London and started work at the age of nineteen as a schoolmistress and then worked as a translator for a publisher. She published her most famous book, 'A Vindication of the Rights of Women' in 1792 and then went to Paris to write a book about the French revolution. While she was there she had an illegitimate daughter by an American, Captain Gilbert Imlay. On her return to England she lived with the writer William Godwin (1756–1836) and married him five months before the birth of their daughter, Mary. She died shortly after the child was born. Her daughter later became the second wife of the poet, Shelley.

WOMEN'S EMANCIPATION. The struggle by women to achieve equal rights in all spheres of life has a long history and still continues to this day. It has been one of the major features of the nineteenth and twentieth centuries. One of the first women to campaign for equal opportunities was *Mary Wollstonecraft* at the end of the eighteenth century. The first sphere in which women made some progress was in education when Frances Mary Buss founded the North London Collegiate School in 1850 and two clergymen founded Cheltenham Ladies' College in 1853, of which *Dorothea Beale* became principal five years later. The first hall of residence for girls was opened at Cambridge by *Anne Jemima Clough* in 1871, though girls were not allowed to take degrees there or at Oxford until the 1920s. The newer *universities*, like London, allowed women to take degrees from the start. (There is still not full equality in educational opportunity, however, as in 1970 there were 162,700 male students at universities and only 64,300 female.)

The work of *Florence Nightingale* raised the status of nurses, though nursing became one of the notoriously low paid professions. Women were admitted to the medical profession from 1858 when *Elizabeth Blackwell* registered under the *Medical Act* of that year. Throughout the nineteenth century there were a number of women who conducted individual campaigns for reforms, including *Elizabeth Fry* (women prisoners and home nursing); *Mary Carpenter* (juvenile delinquents); *Emma Paterson* (women's trade unions); and *Josephine Butler* (the white slave trade). The *Match Girls' Strike* of 1888 was one of the first examples of collective action by unskilled women workers. During the nineteenth century women were given greater legal equality, including the right to obtain a *divorce* for the first time in 1857, though it was many more years before it was as easy for them to do so as it was for men. The *Married Women*'s *Property Acts* of 1870 and 1882 gave them the right to keep their own wages and wealth.

But women's rights really became a major national issue for the first time when *Mrs Emmeline Pankhurst* and her daughter Christabel started the *suffragette movement* in 1903. Their flair for publicity and the increasing violence of the campaign attracted enormous public attention to their causes of votes for women. Some women were given the vote by the *Representation of the People Act, 1918*. The first woman to be elected an M.P. was *Countess Markievicz* in 1918; the first woman to take her seat as an M.P. was *Nancy Astor* in 1919; and the first woman to be appointed a Cabinet minister was *Margaret Bondfield* in 1929. Women were admitted to the House of Lords for the first time under the *Life Peerages Act, 1958*.

Between the two world wars, the opening of the first *birth control* clinic by *Marie Stopes* started to give women greater sexual freedom. The *Sex Disqualification (Removal) Act* gave women greater opportunities in the law and the professions. And the record-breaking flights by *Amy Johnson* attracted a new kind of respect for women. After the Second World War attention tended to be concentrated on greater opportunities in *women's employment*. An *Equal Pay Act* of 1970 was due to come into operation by 1975, but it gives no guarantees that women will obtain equal opportunities, responsibilities, or chances of promotion. In the 1960s women made increasing demands for much greater equality in status, sex, and employment—symbolized by the term, women's lib(eration).

Women's employment. In the eighteenth century, the main jobs for women were on farms, in coal mines, and in their own homes under the *domestic system* of manufacture, as spinners, hat-makers, glove-makers etc. Many other women worked as *domestic servants*. Some middle-class women worked as teachers and governesses. With the start of the industrial revolution, women and girls were employed as cheap labour in textile factories, and from the 1840s a number of *Factory Acts* were passed to improve their conditions of employment. From the 1860s the range of jobs for women started to increase and they were increasingly employed as nurses, shop assistants, telegraphists and hairdressers. The invention of the modern typewriter in the 1870s opened a new career for women as typewriters (as they were first called), or typists. During the First World War, they took over many of the jobs that had previously been performed only by men, such as crane-driving, carpentry, and concrete-mixing, and also did many different kinds of jobs in factories. After the First World War, women started to become increasingly common in some professions, but there are some careers from which they are still excluded, and many more in which women have never held the top appointments.

The proportion of working women has not changed greatly in the last hundred years. In 1861, women accounted for nearly 31 per cent of the total labour force and in 1966 it was just under 36 per cent. The main change has been in the kind of work they do, and the increase in the number of middle-class women who go out to work.

Women's Social and Political Union founded in 1903 by *Mrs Emmeline Pankhurst* and her daughter, Christabel, to campaign for votes for women.

Work-in, the modern answer to large-scale redundancies, closure of a factory, or a lock-out, when workers take over a factory or a plant and run it themselves. In 1971 shop stewards at the Upper Clyde Shipbuilders organized a work-in, when the shipyards were threatened with closure.

Workers' Educational Association (W.E.A.) was founded in 1903 by Albert Mansbridge (1876–1952) to provide courses, mainly in politics and economics and similar subjects for working men and women. It attracted some lecturers and teachers of high quality and played an extremely important part in educating trade union leaders, particularly in the early days. The historian, Richard Henry Tawney (1880–1962) was the president of the W.E.A. from 1928 to 1944, and a member from 1905.
← UNIVERSITY EXTENSION CLASSES: OPEN UNIVERSITY →

Workhouses. Huge, prison-like buildings, many of which were built after the *Poor Law Amendment Act, 1834.* The conditions were deliberately made harsh and unattractive, so that inmates had a worse life than the poorest labourer outside. This was based on the false theory that most unemployed men who were fit to work were just too idle to do so, and that they could find a job if they wanted one. Man and wife were kept apart in the workhouse, so that they could not breed any more children who might become a burden on the poor rate. Able-bodied men were given hard labour, such as breaking stones. Food was kept to a minimum, with bread and watery porridge, soup, and cheese on most days, and meat only twice a week. And the inmates were subjected to all kinds of minor and major insults and humiliations. The new workhouses soon became known as '*Bastilles*' and *Edwin Chadwick*, who was largely responsible for them, became one of the most hated men among the British workers. It had never been intended to stop outdoor relief to the old or infirm, who were given a few shillings a week from the Poor Law to live on. And it had been proposed that separate workhouses should be built for different kinds of inmates. But, in practice, old people were refused outdoor relief in some areas, and the old, the sick, the insane, the unemployed, and orphans were all herded into the same workhouse. There were some slight improvements in workhouses later in the century. From 1885 old couples were given the right to live together and in the 1890s better food was given to the 'deserving poor', but not to those who were considered to be just too lazy to find a job. The introduction of *old age pensions* in 1908 and the *National Insurance Act, 1911*, helped to keep many people out of the workhouse. Many workhouses were closed after they were taken over by county and county borough councils in 1929, and others were converted into municipal hospitals. But in 1946, there were still 22,000 old people living in workhouses, which had then been renamed public assistance institutions. After the *Poor Law* was finally abolished by the *National Assistance Act, 1948*, some workhouses were painted up and converted into old people's homes.

Workmen's Compensation Acts. The first Act of 1897 made employers liable to pay compensation for accidents in certain dangerous occupations, even if the worker concerned could not prove that his employer had been careless or negligent. An Act passed in 1906 extended this protection to practically all workers and also covered certain industrial diseases. A State insurance scheme was set up under the National Insurance (Industrial Injuries) Act, 1946.

Workmen's fares. Cheap fares were introduced on many railway lines after the Cheap Trains Act, 1883, to encourage workers to live outside the overcrowded cities. The fares were very cheap. The workmen's fare, for example, for the eight-mile journey from Glasgow to Clydebank in 1900 was only 1*s.* a week. The fares resulted in the building of many working-class suburbs on the fringes of great cities. The workmen's fares scheme, under which passengers had to arrive at their destination before 8 a.m., was abolished in 1952.
← RAILWAYS ACT, 1844

World Wars see **First World War** and **Second World War**

Wright Brothers, Wilbur (1867–1912) and **Orville** (1871–1948), born in Dayton, Ohio. After constructing a number of gliders, they built a biplane which was driven by a small petrol engine. On 17 December 1903, they made the first controlled flights in an aeroplane at Kitty Hawk, North Carolina. The first of the four flights they made that day

lasted 12 seconds. They continued to develop their planes, and two years later they were making flights of 20 miles.
← SIR GEORGE CAYLEY: LOUIS BLERIOT →

Wyndham's Land Act see **Irish Land Purchase Act, 1903**

X

X-rays, which make it possible to see inside things without taking them apart, were discovered by the German scientist, Wilhelm Konrad von Röntgen, in 1895. They have many uses in medicine; in radiotherapy, for treating some skin diseases and cancer; in industry, for example, in detecting hidden fractures in metals; and in science generally.

Y

Yalta conference held at a town in the Crimea, Russia, in February 1945 by the Allied leaders, Churchill, Roosevelt and Stalin. It was agreed that when the war ended Germany should be split up into separate zones to be occupied by the three Allied powers and France; Nazis in Germany were to be deprived of all positions of power; and German war criminals were to be tried. (The biggest trial was held at *Nuremberg.*) It was also decided to set up the *United Nations.*

Young, Arthur (1741–1820), influential writer on agriculture, born in London, who travelled all over Britain and to many parts of the continent (20,000 miles in all) to investigate farming conditions. He was one of the main critics of the old *open field* system of farming. His work encouraged big landowners to sponsor *Enclosure Acts* and to invest more money and time in their farms. He wrote many books and edited the forty-seven volumes of the 'Annals of Agriculture', 1784–1809. He was appointed first secretary of the *Board of Agriculture,* which was formed in 1793 to make a county-by-county report on farming. In 1808 his eyesight started to fail and shortly afterwards he became blind. Although he had a number of farms himself, all of them failed, but his importance in changing the structure of land ownership and improving agriculture was considerable.
THOMAS COKE →

Young Ireland. A group of young, revolutionary Irish nationalists, both

Protestants and Catholic, who were opposed to O'Connell's more moderate policy. In 1848, they tried to promote a revolution in Ireland, but got little support from the Irish peasants who had been decimated by the *Irish famine*. Many of the leaders were arrested and transported to Tasmania, including John Mitchel (1815–75), who escaped to the United States in 1853, and William Smith O'Brien (1803–64), who was pardoned in 1854.

← DANIEL O'CONNELL: FENIANS →

Z

Zebra crossings, or Belisha crossings, with a flashing yellow beacon, introduced in 1934 when Leslie Hore-Belisha was Minister of Transport. London had introduced road crossings in 1927, with a sign marked 'Please cross here'.

BREATHALYZERS →

Zeppelin, Count von (1838–1917), German Army officer who pioneered the development of airships. His first airship, powered by two engines and built with an aluminium frame, made its maiden flight in 1900. In 1909 he formed the first air travel company for passengers in the world. Zeppelins, as his airships were popularly called, were used in *air raids* on Britain during the First World War.

R 34 →

Zinoviev letter was published in British newspapers a few days before the 1924 election and was partly responsible for the Labour party losing 42 seats at the election. The letter was allegedly written by Gregori Zinoviev (1883–1936), then Russian chairman of the Communist International, to the Communist Party of Great Britain, though it has never been proved that it was authentic. It advised Communists how to promote revolution in Britain. The minority Labour government, led by Ramsay MacDonald, which was then in power, had recognized Communist Russia earlier in the year and was trying to arrange a trade treaty with it. Some voters believed that the Labour party, therefore, must contain many fellow travellers who secretly sympathized with Communist Russia and its plans for a British revolution. The Conservatives got into power and Baldwin became prime minister.

Zulu War, 1879. Britain fought this war against the Zulu tribes under their king, Cetewayo, to protect the Boers in the Transvaal, South

Africa, which had been annexed by Britain in 1877. The Zulus massacred the British at Isandhlwana, but were prevented from invading Natal by the heroic defence of Rorke's Drift on the River Tulega by a small force of British troops. British reinforcements defeated the Zulus at Ulundi and captured Cetewayo, who was deposed, but who was restored as king in 1883.